THE STORY OF PARSONS CORPORATION

THE STORY OF PARSONS CORPORATION

JEFFREY L. RODENGEN

Edited by Mickey Murphy
Design and layout by Sandy Cruz and Rachelle Donley

Write Stuff Enterprises, Inc.
1001 South Andrews Avenue
Fort Lauderdale, FL 33316
1-800-900-Book (1-800-900-2665)
(954) 462-6657
www.writestuffbooks.com

Publisher's Cataloging in Publication Data
(Prepared by The Donohue Group, Inc.)

Rodengen, Jeffrey L.
The story of Parsons Corporation / Jeffrey L. Rodengen ; edited by Mickey Murphy ; design and layout by Sandy Cruz and Rachelle Donley ; [foreword by Daniel K. Inouye].

p. : ill. ; cm.

Includes bibliographical references and index.
ISBN: 1-932022-04-X

1. Parsons, Ralph M. 2. Parsons Corporation. 3. Engineering—Management—United States—History. 4. Structural engineering—United States—History. 5. Civil engineering—United States—History. 6. Building—United States—History. I. Cruz, Sandy. II. Donley, Rachelle. III. Inouye, Daniel K., 1924- IV. Title. V. Title: Parsons Corporation.

TA23 .R63 2005
620.00973 2003108361

Completely produced in the
United States of America
10 9 8 7 6 5 4 3 2 1

Also by Jeffrey L. Rodengen

The Legend of Chris-Craft

IRON FIST: The Lives of Carl Kiekhaefer

Evinrude-Johnson and The Legend of OMC

Serving the Silent Service: The Legend of Electric Boat

The Legend of Dr Pepper/Seven-Up

The Legend of Honeywell

The Legend of Briggs & Stratton

The Legend of Ingersoll-Rand

The Legend of Stanley: 150 Years of The Stanley Works

The MicroAge Way

The Legend of Halliburton

The Legend of York International

The Legend of Nucor Corporation

The Legend of Goodyear: The First 100 Years

The Legend of AMP

The Legend of Cessna

The Legend of VF Corporation

The Spirit of AMD

The Legend of Rowan

New Horizons: The Story of Ashland Inc.

The History of American Standard

The Legend of Mercury Marine

The Legend of Federal-Mogul

Against the Odds: Inter-Tel—The First 30 Years

The Legend of Pfizer

State of the Heart: The Practical Guide to Your Heart and Heart Surgery with Larry W. Stephenson, M.D.

The Legend of Worthington Industries

The Legend of IBP

The Legend of Trinity Industries, Inc.

The Legend of Cornelius Vanderbilt Whitney

The Legend of Amdahl

The Legend of Litton Industries

The Legend of Gulfstream

The Legend of Bertram with David A. Patten

The Legend of Ritchie Bros. Auctioneers

The Legend of ALLTEL with David A. Patten

The Yes, you can of Invacare Corporation with Anthony L. Wall

The Ship in the Balloon: The Story of Boston Scientific and the Development of Less-Invasive Medicine

The Legend of Day & Zimmermann

The Legend of Noble Drilling

Fifty Years of Innovation: Kulicke & Soffa

Biomet—From Warsaw to the World with Richard F. Hubbard

NRA: An American Legend

The Heritage and Values of RPM, Inc.

The Marmon Group: The First Fifty Years

The Legend of Grainger

The Legend of The Titan Corporation with Richard F. Hubbard

The Legend of Discount Tire Co. with Richard F. Hubbard

The Legend of Polaris with Richard F. Hubbard

The Legend of La-Z-Boy with Richard F. Hubbard

The Legend of McCarthy with Richard F. Hubbard

InterVoice: Twenty Years of Innovation with Richard F. Hubbard

Jefferson-Pilot Financial: A Century of Excellence with Richard F. Hubbard

The Legend of HCA

The Legend of Werner Enterprises with Richard F. Hubbard

The History of J. F. Shea Co. with Richard F. Hubbard

True to Our Vision with Richard F. Hubbard

The Legend of Albert Trostel & Sons with Richard F. Hubbard

The Legend of Sovereign Bancorp with Richard F. Hubbard

Innovation is the Best Medicine: The extraordinary story of Datascope with Richard F. Hubbard

The Legend of Guardian Industries

The Legend of Universal Forest Products, Inc.

Changing the World: Polytechnic University—The First 150 Years

Nothing is Impossible: The Legend of Joe Hardy and 84 Lumber

In It For The Long Haul: The Story of CRST

New Horizons: The Story of Federated Investors

Table of Contents

FOREWORD

BY

DANIEL K. INOUYE

UNITED STATES SENATOR

THE STORY OF PARSONS Corporation is a story of the American Dream—the resilience of the American spirit, the supremacy of American ingenuity, and simply, old-fashioned hard work. It provides an insight into American entrepreneurship post-World War II, as Parsons Corporation developed a national reputation as a premier engineering and construction company, synonymous with quality and the latest in technology.

America has benefited from Parsons Corporation's skillful good work, including the building of our airports, mass transit systems, highways, byways, freeways, and bridges to allow us to move safely and swiftly throughout our country. I would venture to say that Parsons Corporation's legacy can be seen in just about every state, including my home state of Hawaii.

In more recent times, and to meet the ever-changing business climate and fluctuating markets, Parsons Corporation has taken its expertise abroad. It has quietly reinforced some of our nation's diplomatic ties in strategic areas—"developer diplomats" who have helped to improve the quality of life of our international allies and friends.

From rags to riches, the story of the Parsons Corporation, of founder Ralph Monroe Parsons, the son of a fisherman, is the embodiment of such core American values as integrity, respect, innovation, and competency. He lived his life by this code and challenged all who would follow him to meet his standards. Through it all, Parsons Corporation has met each challenge with tenacity and integrity, propelling itself to a level of national and international prominence many dream of, but few are able to achieve and sustain.

The Parsons Corporation—living the American Dream, inspiring excellence and leadership in action.

—*Senator Daniel K. Inouye*
Honolulu, Hawaii

INTRODUCTION

NOW PAST ITS 60TH YEAR of operations, Parsons Corporation (Parsons) was founded in 1944 by a man who loved engineering and solving challenging problems. The story of this man—and the growth of the corporation he founded—offers insight into American entrepreneurship during post-World War II and a company's evolution over the past six decades as it met the challenges of ever-changing business climates and fluctuating service markets.

Parsons' legacy is seen in the design, engineering, and construction of some of the world's most complex infrastructure and industrial facilities. However, its intrinsic worth is perhaps even more important in today's business community. Parsons' founder bequeathed to his staff the core values of safety, integrity, respect, innovation, diversity, and competency that carried his company into the 21st century. Parsons' story is a testament to the thousands of employees who embraced these values—the engineers, managers, technical specialists, and skilled support staff who made the corporation the success that it has become.

One does not have to look very hard to see first evidence of Parsons' accomplishments and contributions to the world's infrastructure. When traveling by airplane, you are more than likely to pass through one of the 400 airports whose construction or expansion was managed by Parsons. If you cross a bridge and marvel at its beauty, capacity, stability, or shear strength, know that Parsons has designed and engineered most of the world's long-span suspension bridges and has retrofitted some of the most heavily traveled, historically significant bridges in the United States.

When riding on a city's mass transit system—think of Parsons—which has engineered light rail and subway systems for every major transit system in North America and many overseas.

While driving an automobile, be aware that Parsons has also designed and/or managed the construction of over 10,000 miles of highways in 40 countries through crowded cities and empty deserts, across rivers and mountains, and over frozen tundra. Parsons operates and manages vehicle safety and environmental inspection stations in many states and Canada.

As you fill up your car with gas or buy a petroleum-based product, it is likely Parsons' engineering and construction achievements made possible the refining and processing of crude oil, natural gas, and their byproducts.

When you flick a switch to turn on an electrical appliance, know that Parsons designed a new generation of coal-fired power plants that burn fuel more effectively and reduce pollution. Parsons has been instrumental in supplying more than 35,000 megawatts of coal-fired generating capacity worldwide and has completed designs for over 150 coal-fired units. Parsons also has put into operation 16 nuclear generating units, totaling over 11,100 megawatts of electrical output, in both the United States and abroad.

While using a telephone or cell phone, be aware that Parsons designs, builds, and maintains highly reliable "24/7" critical facilities, including telecommunications, Internet data, and secure command/control centers around the world. In wireless and wireline communication, Parsons' engineering and facility management staff has provided the largest telecommunications companies and their customer bases with the highest quality in signal distribution and operating systems that have also reduced connection time and costs.

When you or someone in your family requires medicine to fight off disease or maintain your health and well-being, know that Parsons is designing and building pharmaceutical and biotechnology manufacturing plants for the world's largest drug companies. Parsons is retained to design and construct one-of-a-kind, first-of-a-kind research and development laboratories, as well as active pharmaceutical ingredient and secondary pharmaceutical pilot plants and manufacturing plants. Plants designed by Parsons are up and operational in Ireland, Puerto Rico, and the United States and are presently formulating or producing life-saving medications.

As you follow the news of an unfolding international crisis, understand that Parsons has helped in all recent post-conflict recovery programs by rebuilding schools, security systems, and justice facilities; destroying unexploded ordnance; and refurbishing power grids, water conveyance systems, and oil fields in places such as Bosnia-Herzegovina, Kosovo, and Iraq.

When recalling the Cold War decades, know that Parsons designed and is helping to construct chemical agent and nerve gas neutralization plants in the United States. Parsons is currently assisting the Russians design and construct their own chemical demilitarization plants and is monitoring the destruction of the former Soviet Union's sea-launched ballistic missiles.

When you drink a glass of water, think of Parsons' early international ventures into water well development for crop irrigation or major domestic programs that increase water capacity and systems reliability in the largest and fastest-growing metropolitan areas in the United States today.

In addition to all of these vital projects, Parsons is a leader in urban planning and has designed and built an entire city in Saudi Arabia. It engineers and operates facilities for the National Aeronautics and Space Administration (NASA) and the aerospace and electronic industries. Parsons' design of the missile silos for the Minuteman and the Titan II and III programs gave confidence to the citizens of the United States that the country was secure. The skills of Parsons have been retained by every technologically based industry in most countries and at all levels of local, state, and federal governments, in both peace and in war, during the past 60 years.

As of this publication, Parsons is again evolving to meet a new era of global change. But even as it changes, it is still relying on its core values in engineering, constructing, and managing infrastructure development to better the standards of living for the citizens of the world.

As to how Parsons came to be one of the world's most prominent engineering, construction, and technical services firms, the story begins with Ralph Monroe Parsons, a quiet man, the son of a fisherman, who founded The Ralph M. Parsons Company. The story then progresses through more than 60 years of technical and managerial excellence.

ACKNOWLEDGMENTS

NUMEROUS INDIVIDUALS ASSISTED IN THE planning, research, development, and publication of *The Story of Parsons Corporation*. Vital to this effort was the time and cooperation extended by Parsons' Chief Executive Officer (CEO), Jim McNulty, and Erin Kuhlman, Parsons' vice president of corporate relations. They provided access to the interviewees as well as the corporation's archives and historical photographs. Holly Klotz of Parsons was instrumental in the editing and research of the manuscript, and her project management skills were fabulous.

Numerous Parsons executives provided their valuable time and expertise, not only with their own insights regarding Parsons through historical interviews, but also in other astute and expert commentary concerning the development of the book, and its individual chapters, prior to publication. In addition to Mr. McNulty, these executives include Jack Scott, Curt Bower, Gary Stone, David Goodrich, Jim Thrash, Jim Shappell, Chuck Harrington, Dave Backus, Tom Roell, and Andy Albrecht.

Lesley Santo and Amy Pieper, corporate relations, were a tremendous help compiling photographs, records, and footnote sourcing. Judith Herman, Parsons' managing editor, significantly contributed to editing the entire manuscript, as did Jerry O'Rourke, a Parsons precontracts specialist, who reviewed the early chapters. Tom Schweiner, manager of Parsons' technical publications, afforded access to his talented staff. Paul Zamora and Sharon Quiero scanned many of the photographs, and Alisha Parker helped design the book's timelines.

Claire Hammond, Parsons' librarian, provided expert guidance regarding the company's corporate archives and also provided an original 1917 *National Geographic* magazine for essential reference. Marie Darr, corporate human relations executive assistant, and Sharon Miller, human resource records service manager, searched databases for employees' titles, their length of employment with Parsons, and contact information.

A debt of gratitude also is extended to several organizations that provided photographs for

This is part of Parsons' staff who contributed to *The Story of Parsons Corporation*. First row (left to right): Sharen Clark-Keck, Claire Hammond, Gladys Porter, Marie Darr, Susan Cole, Erin Kuhlman; Second row: Judith Herman, Sally Iott, Amy Pieper, Cathy Olson, Ann Hicks; Third row: Holly Klotz, Lesley Santo, Virginia Baca, Jerry O'Rourke, Vic Tavlian, Mel Weingart; Fourth row: Cathy Meindl, Jim Ridings, Dave Backus.

the book, including Bechtel Corporation; the Evansville Museum of Arts, History, and Science, in Evansville, Indiana; and Kasha Bali, assistant property manager, at MAS Asset Management Company in Los Angeles, California.

Many Parsons executives, along with numerous employees, retirees, and associates and friends of the firm, enriched the book by discussing their experiences and Parsons' more than six decades of corporate activities. The author extends particular gratitude to these men and women for their candid recollections and guidance.

In alphabetical order they are: Larry Alvarez, Virginia Baca, Marty Badaracco, Tom Barron, Kevin Barry, Philip Bates, Bob Bax, Marty Blachman, Dante Boccalero, Mike Brady, Mary Brown, Melvyn Brown, Rob Brueck, Bill Buchholz, Larry Burns, Dave Burstein, Jim Callahan, Jane Charalambous, Sharen Clark-Keck, Frank Collins, Susan Cole, Ed Cramsie, Mike D'Antuono, Bob Davidson, Ray DeClue, Frank DeMartino, Larry Dondanville, Knisely (K) Dreher, Karl Drobny, Alan Duncan, Charles Dutton, Cliff Eby, Les Engle, Marty Fabrick, Paul Farmanian, Fred Felberg, Ralph Fernandez, Roger Fetterolf, Anita Freeman, Lee Freeman, Dan Frost, Roy Gaunt, Bill Glade, Stan Goldhaber, Roy Goodwin, Graham Gosling, Bill Haas, William Hall, Jess Harmon, Andy Hauge, Brent Harvey, Jeff Hermann, Ann Hicks, George Hull, Dwight Hunt, Sally Iott, Peter Jahn, Tom Johanson, Harvey Joyner, Ray Judson, Dave Kays, Jake Kostyzak, Don Lassus, Claude Le Feuvre, Tim Lindquist, Greg McBain, Tom McCabe, Marvin McClain, Billy McGinnis, Brynna McNulty, Cathy (Gribbin) Meindl, Roland (Hap) Meissner, Bill Millhone, Trudy Mysliwy, Tom Neria, Bob Nugent, Cathy Olson, Bob O'Neil, William Opel, Otha (Charlie) Roddey, Joe O'Rourke, Craig Pearson, Greg Perry, Leonard Pieroni III, Gladys Porter, Nick Presecan, Steve Quinn, Gene Randich, Doug Reehl, Earnest Robbins, Karsten Rothenberg, Walter Rowse, Ron Russell, Keith Sabol, Robert Salvadore, Fred Schweiger, Bob Sheh, Bruce Shelton, Tom Spoth, Manny Stein, John Stewart, Joe Szlamka, Charles Terhune III, Graydon Thayer, Chuck Thomas, Keith Timlin, Larry Tollenaere, Richard Trembath, Ray Van Horn, Mel Weingart, Ken Whitman, Bill Whooley, Rick Wilkinson, Earle Williams, Sam Wright, and Jess Yoder.

These individuals offered priceless insights on their coworkers' and managers' contributions along with Parsons' technical accomplishments that have vastly improved the world's infrastructure. Each person interviewed is quoted in the book. Several individuals allowed us to borrow personal mementos illustrating their time with Parsons, which provided valuable context to their stories. In addition, staff members who verified specific facts are referenced within the footnotes.

While each and every person interviewed provided their unique stories, in particular, we would like to recognize the contributions of Dr. James Holwerda, Stan Goldhaber, and John Small, each of whom provided additional information above and beyond their initial interviews. We also give special thanks to Bill Leonhard, former Parsons CEO, for his valued historical perspective and insights.

We enjoyed all of the conversations and came away with the very real sense that Parsons is indeed a family devoted to providing quality services and loyalty, both to their customers and to one another.

In addition to the Parsons executives and employees, past and present, listed above who played a vital role in book development, some other individuals also made substantial contributions. The principal research and assembly of the narrative time line was accomplished by research assistant Bob Wisehart. He also coordinated with Parsons to secure many photos, illustrations, and other graphical items. Senior Editor Mickey Murphy was responsible for text editing and photo placement, as well as overall book project coordination. The graphic design of Creative Director Sandy Cruz brought the story to compelling visual life.

Special thanks is also extended to the staff and associates at Write Stuff Enterprises: Mary Aaron, transcriptionist; Stanimira "Sam" Stefanova, executive editor; Amy Blakely, Jill Gambill, and Ann Gossy, senior editors; Rachelle Donley and Dennis Shockley, art directors; Dianne Cormier, Dawn LaVoir, Bill Laznovsky, and Susan Monseur, proofreaders; Connie Angelo, indexer; Amy Major, executive assistant to Jeffrey L. Rodengen; Marianne Roberts, executive vice president of publishing and chief financial officer; Steven Stahl, director of marketing; and Sherry Hasso, bookkeeper. Richard F. Hubbard conducted additional interviews.

A formal studio portrait of Ralph M. Parsons in his mid-30s. Ralph would soon alter the landscape of global business.

CHAPTER ONE

The Early Years

1896–1937

What we need is knowledge of our operations, guts, and confidence.

—Ralph M. Parsons, in a memo to his employees

In a pose typical of the day, seven-year-old Ralph Parsons, bedecked in a sailor suit, poses for the camera in 1903.

RALPH MONROE PARSONS POSsessed knowledge, guts, and confidence—three of the traits he communicated to his employees that he thought were necessary to succeed. He also loved his work. Ralph exhibited these characteristics as a young man before he founded The Ralph M. Parsons Company, and he built a lasting legacy based on these valuable attributes.

Ralph was small in stature and frequently described as shy by those who did not know him well. Yet, his enthusiasm for engineering, his integrity, his energy, and his drive attracted customers and the talented people who wanted to work for him.

One of Ralph's first employees, James E. Halferty, an engineer who was instrumental in the company's initial success in foreign ventures, is quoted as saying that Ralph "was the most unforgettable character I was ever privileged to know well. He was a man of great integrity, singleness of purpose, and essentially fearless. Working for him was mostly a pleasure. The drive we all had was to help him succeed."[1]

An American Heritage

Ralph Parsons was born on June 22, 1896, in the community of Springs on Long Island, not far from what is now the upscale town of East Hampton, New York. Early on, Springs was a rough-and-tumble place where the sea met the land and toughened the people who made a living there.

An early ancestor, Seth Parsons, was born in East Hampton in 1664, according to *East Hampton History and Genealogies*, and Ralph's family may have been the first of the Parsons to settle in Springs,[2] although other branches of the family lived in nearby areas. Over the years, Ralph's forefathers raised sheep, cattle, and poultry, or caught and sold anything that could be gleaned from the ocean. When Ralph was born, the Parsons family had lived in the area for hundreds of years and was intimately familiar with both the surrounding land and the sea.[3]

At the time of Ralph's birth, his parents were both 31 years old. His father, Frank, was a fisherman, and his mother, Sara, stayed at home with the children. Ralph's middle name, Monroe, was Sara's maiden name. He had three siblings but was closest to his elder brother, Vivian.

Growing up as a fisherman's son, young Ralph was no stranger to hard work. His first job as a young boy was as a lobsterman. In an interview

The Parsons' homestead on Long Island in 1875. Ralph's father, Frank, is one of the three boys perched on the fence in the background.

later in life, Ralph remembered, "I steered the boat and my brother [Vivian] lifted the [lobster] pots."[4]

Vivian remembered those early days too. In a letter to his brother, he recalled:

> *It seems like only yesterday that we were going after lobster in that old 18- or 19-foot boat we had when we were kids. The old engine had to be cranked by hand and I well remember the time (I think you were eight or nine then) when you were cranking away and it "kicked" you and broke your arm. The nearest doctor was some 16 miles away and the only means of transportation was by horse and carriage. I finally came up with the idea of rowing you out in the boat to the SS* New York *(or was it the SS* Brooklyn*?) that had sailed into Fort Pond Bay that morning so that the doctor on board could set your arm.*[5]

The family moved twice during Ralph's childhood but never strayed far from Long Island. They moved from Springs to Montauk Point and finally to Amagansett, thanks to a major change in Frank Parsons' life. Opting for stability over the unforgiving up-and-down life of a fisherman, in 1905 he bought a lumberyard in Amagansett, and the family moved there to stay.[6]

Natural Tinkerers

Both Vivian and Ralph enjoyed tinkering with machinery of all kinds. They were influenced by their uncle, Charles Parsons, who was described as "a man who could make just about anything," from engines to wagons. Charles, who had no children, was close to his nephews and employed the teenage Vivian in his blacksmith shop in Amagansett.[7]

At age 18, Vivian opened a garage and machine shop in Amagansett. In his first sign of business savvy, 13-year-old Ralph worked with Vivian and over the course of several years managed to save $2,000 that he reinvested when he became a partner in Vivian's shop.[8]

By his own account, Ralph was not much of a student: "Somehow I barely managed to get through the best part of the first year of high school" before dropping out to work full time. He enjoyed working with his brother and tinkering with machinery more than going to school. When he was 17, Ralph broke the same arm he had broken years earlier on the lobster boat in an accident at the garage. As painful as it must have

This rare photograph shows a young Ralph (holding a hammer with both hands) at the family machine shop. The young man working at the anvil with Ralph presumably is his older brother, Vivian.

been, the injury gave Ralph some time to pursue another all-consuming interest.

Ralph was smitten by a young lady named Ruth Halsey Bennett, whose family lived across the road from the Parsons' home in Amagansett.[9] As Vivian recalled:

During the time you were recuperating, you spent most of your time driving around town in your car with your girl, Ruth Bennett, whom you later married. I can still see you, reaching over with your left arm to shift that old Chalmers car, which had the gear shift in the middle.[10]

As he recovered from his broken arm and spent time with Ruth, Ralph was also contemplating his future. One thing was certain: this ambitious young man did not intend to repair automobiles the rest of his life. In 1914, despite not finishing even the first year of high school, Ralph enrolled in the Pratt Institute in Brooklyn, New York, for a two-year course in machine design. He was 18. About his time at Pratt, Ralph said, "I didn't graduate with honors, but I learned a very valuable lesson. Don't try to memorize everything. Just remember where the information can be found when you need it."[11]

Another of Ralph's favorite sayings expressed the same idea: "The man who knows 'how' will always have a job, but the man who knows 'why' will be his boss."[12] Ralph Parsons fully intended to know why.

Although he did not graduate at the top of his class, Ralph did well enough at Pratt that he was asked to stay on as an instructor, which he did for a year. In 1916, The *East Hampton Star* proudly reported, "Our young mechanical genius, Ralph Parsons, has been appointed instructor at Pratt where he has classes of 50 Navy men each day, giving instructions in steam and gasoline engines."[13]

Ralph returned to Pratt 41 years later on June 7, 1957, to receive an honorary doctorate of engineering, only the sixth such award in the institute's history.[14] He also served as a Pratt trustee for many years.

When he completed his service in the Navy at 25, Ralph Parsons looked much younger than his age in 1921.

The War to End All Wars

Ralph's life changed dramatically in 1917 as it did for thousands of other young men. It was the beginning of World War I, "the war to end all wars." Ralph joined the U.S. Navy and married his sweetheart, Ruth, on October 21 that same year. However, his naval experience did not start quite the way he thought it would when he joined.

"Some fellow came to my town with a lot of braid on his arm and said, 'Sign here and be an admiral.' " Ralph joked, "I thought it was a swell idea. Since then I've learned to read the fine print, because I turned out to be landsman for machinist's mate—the lowest rating in the Navy."[15]

In addition to his disappointment at not being given a higher rank, the 21-year-old Ralph never left the country during the war. First, he was sent to the newly created Aviation Offices Material School at Columbia University, where he graduated with its first class. He was then transferred to the Navy's Great Lakes Training School, where he was assigned to teach aviation mechanics. Ralph wanted more hands-on duty and was eventually assigned to the engine section of the Bureau of Aeronautics at Anacostia Air Station near Washington, D.C. This restless young man complained to the brass that everyone else in his Columbia University class graduated as an ensign, while he was only made warrant officer. "I asked why," he said, "and they told me I looked too young to be an ensign."[16]

The Navy had a point. Ralph looked very young for his years. But by age 25, Ralph had made lieutenant, junior grade. It is hard to imagine how young he must have looked four years earlier.

After being discharged from the Navy in 1921, Ralph joined another kind of service, the U.S. Civil Service, working as a naval aeronautical engineer at the aeronautical engine testing laboratory at the naval aircraft factory in Philadelphia. He stayed with the U.S. Civil Service until the end of 1924.[17]

Hanging on for Dear Life

A few months before he left the U.S. Civil Service, a close call nearly ended his life on a test flight 800 miles off the coast of Massachusetts while serving on the USS *Shenandoah*, the first American-built dirigible. Ralph accidentally stepped off the eight-inch, narrow catwalk that ran beneath the airship for its full football-field length and fell through the fabric of the airship. Clawing desperately to save himself, he managed to catch the edge of the catwalk as he fell and struggled back up to safety. Without mentioning Ralph's name, this hair-raising event found its way into an article that was published in the January 1925 issue of *National Geographic*:

> *The thin cotton covering 12 inches below the catwalk gives a false sense of security, but the ground, usually 3,000 feet below, is only two steps removed.*

Ralph Parsons' hair-raising misstep on the catwalk of the USS *Shenandoah*, America's first dirigible, is recounted in *National Geographic*. This graphic from the magazine shows the dirigible in detail. *(Charles Riddiford/National Geographic Image Collection.)*

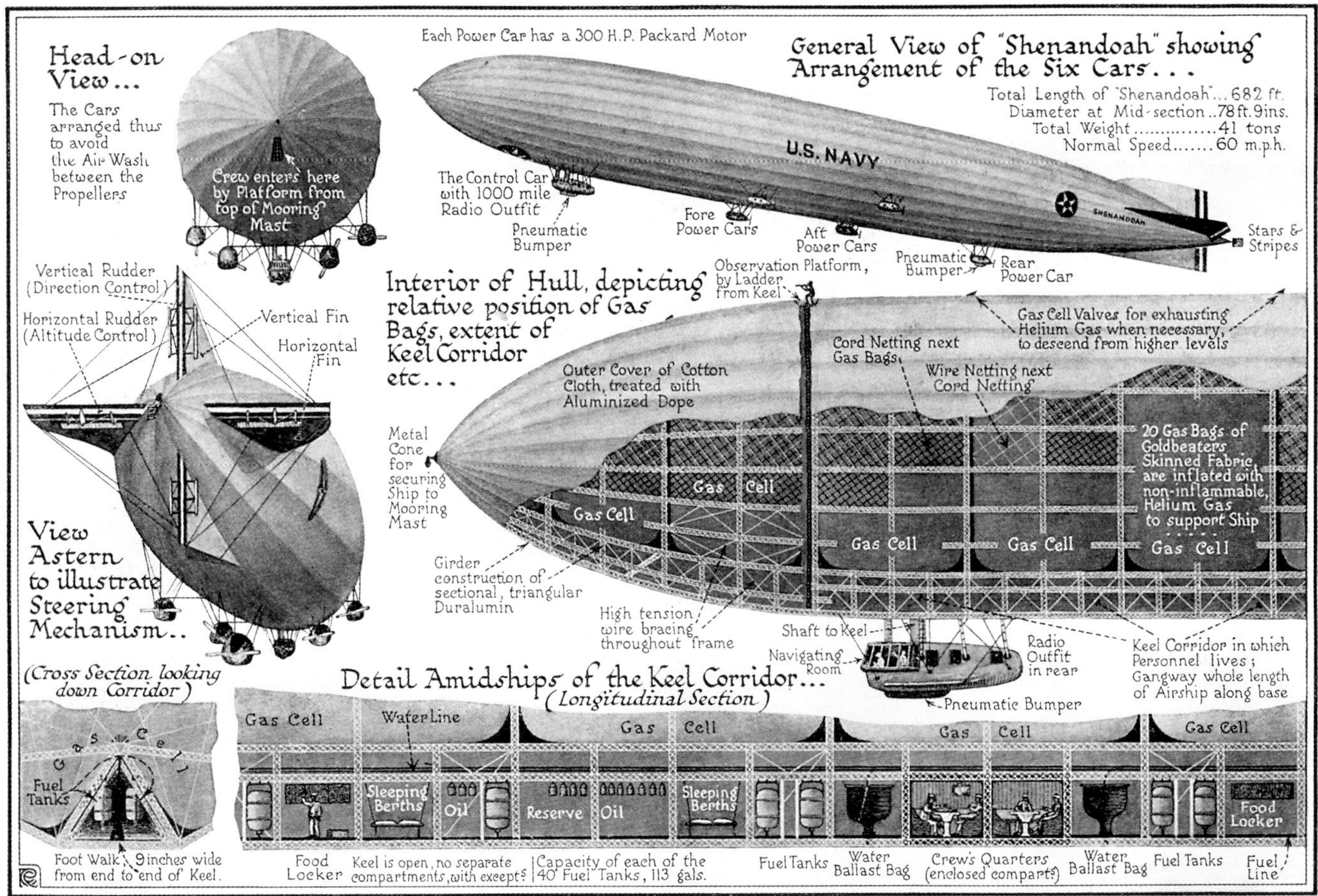

© National Geographic Society

Drawn by Charles E. Riddiford

A PICTORIAL DIAGRAM OF THE SHIP THAT MADE THE HISTORIC FLIGHT

A roughly stitched rent in the bottom shows where one man made the first step, and with true sailor tenacity the marks of his fingers are shown where he gripped the steel-hardened duralumin to save himself.[18]

The Petroleum Business

The year after Ralph left the U.S. Civil Service, 1925, he worked at the Interocean Oil Company before joining the Leamon Process Company where, as chief engineer, he was responsible for designing and constructing catalytic cracking units for the production of high-octane gasoline. ("Cracking units" or "cracking plants" break down crude oil to basic molecular components, the primary function of a refinery.) Field assignments took him to Couts in Alberta, Canada; Bakersfield, California; and Spokane, Washington.[19]

For a young man whose experience was in the aeronautical engineering field, getting into the oil business meant dealing with a steep and formidable learning curve. During his time in the oil fields, Ralph discovered he had an affinity for designing and engineering oil refineries and petroleum and chemical facilities. He enjoyed the technical challenges associated with this industry and would later pursue it as his core business.

"I discovered that I'd been talked into something and had to really work hard while learning about the oil business," he said.[20]

Always trying to improve himself, he took correspondence business courses from the Alexander Hamilton Institute in 1927, which were "pre-MBA" in nature and covered topics such as banking, insurance, personnel, enterprise management, marketing, and the social perspective of business. Ralph was furnished with a set of study books and assignments that he mailed back to the institute on a scheduled basis.

In 1929, Ralph struck out on his own as a consulting petroleum engineer, based in New York City.[21] He later joked that a person with the title of "consulting engineer" was really an engineer who was out of a job.[22] The following year, he designed a small cracking plant that Universal Oil Products approved for license under the Dubbs process, referencing the improbably named Carbon Petroleum Dubbs, president of Universal Oil Products Company. (Dubbs' father Jesse, a research chemist, named his son "Carbon" because of the element's importance in science and "Petroleum" because of the chemist's interest in the mineral.) This cracking plant was so successful that many similar ones were built throughout the country.

The Ralph M. Parsons Company

A few years later, Ralph summoned the courage to form his own company. The Ralph M. Parsons Company was incorporated in Delaware in 1934 with headquarters in Mount Vernon, Ohio. The company's announced business was the design and construction of oil refineries and chemical plants.

Being on his own did not mean getting work was easy. Although Ralph was now in his mid-30s and had a great deal of experience in various engineering disciplines, he started his business at the lowest point of the worst depression the United States had ever experienced. He soon discovered that it was virtually impossible to attract clients without a proven track record.

The Ralph M. Parsons Co.
a Delaware Corporation

announces it has acquired and will carry on the engineering business formerly conducted by Ralph M. Parsons individually.

THE RALPH M. PARSONS CO.
Consulting and Contracting Engineers
Mt. Vernon, Ohio

A Valuable Endorsement

"When I wanted to get into business, I could not convince others that I could do a good job," he said. Faced with competition that was well established, better financed, larger, and more experienced, Ralph needed help.[23] He got a major break when he was befriended by Carbon, who wrote a letter stating that his company would stand behind any work Ralph performed. Ralph commented on both the importance of this endorsement and the limitations he faced in expanding further into this market:

> *We spent the summer preparing plans for a thermal cracking plant, and then I went to the Universal Oil Products Company and talked them into backing the design with their guarantee. We built eight plants, and they all worked beautifully. The problems of building an organization and getting financing were what kept us from selling more plants.*[24]

In The Ralph M. Parsons Company's first advertisement, Universal's supporting role and the importance of the Dubbs process is clear. In the sixth and next-to-last paragraph, the advertisement declares, "Parsons-built Dubbs units are legitimate, they are profitable, and they are safe—guaranteed by Universal as well as by Parsons."[25]

Milton Lewis: The Right-Hand Man

In 1934, Ralph hired the person who would be his right-hand man over much of the next 40 years. The introduction came via a telegram sent to Ralph at his office by that individual—Milt Lewis, himself. Ralph recalled, "This fellow said that he had 85 percent of the independent refiners in the palm of his hand. We could do big things

Opposite: Ralph Parsons ran this ad when he formed his company. It informed that he was now working as a company and not as a private individual.

Right: This 1934 ad for The Ralph M. Parsons Company promoted Parsons-built cracking units.

It must fit

the small refinery

You don't have to crack on a large scale to make money. Cracking can earn profits for the small refiner as well as for the big one—if he has the right operation.

In size, the right cracking unit matches the refiner's crude supply, in design it fits in with his other refinery equipment to save labor and other operating costs, in action it must produce high yields of good products.

In cost it *must* fit his pocketbook.

Investment and operating cost must be held down to insure profit on the small throughput.

Parsons designs and builds such cracking units.

Parsons-built Dubbs units are legitimate, they are profitable and they are safe—guaranteed by Universal as well as by Parsons.

It will cost you nothing to find out what we can do for you.

THE RALPH M. PARSONS CO.

MT. VERNON, OHIO

Ralph Parsons' earliest customers included Standard Oil of California and Shell Oil. This photograph shows one of his first engineering design projects at a chemical facility owned by Shell Oil.

together."[26] Ralph ignored the telegram. But like any good salesman, Milt was persistent. Milt followed up with several more telegrams—so many, in fact, that he became an irritation. Ralph still did not respond.

According to Milt, who was eight years Ralph's junior, "I tried to tell Ralph what a salesman I was; tried to impress Ralph, in fact, that I was the best in the country. Ralph ignored the wires, and Ruth [Ralph's wife] told him to go to Los Angeles and get rid of 'that guy.'"[27] But instead, Ralph hired "that guy" perhaps because he was ultimately impressed by the flamboyant reception Milt put together in Los Angeles.

"Talk about a dramatic entrance," Ralph said. "He had arranged for me to enter the city in a block-long limousine escorted by police cars with sirens screaming and all that goes with it."[28] According to Ralph, his decision was simple. "I decided that the only way I could shut him up was to hire him."[29]

Except for a nine-year period between 1940 and 1949 when Milt went to work for the Fluor Corporation, Ralph and Milt worked together until Ralph's death in 1974. Ralph said hiring Milt "was one of the best decisions I ever made. He's been my right hand ever since."[30]

Milt understood Ralph's way of doing business. After Milt joined the company, Ralph moved his operations to Chicago. In those early days, the firm's payroll consisted of only two men: Ralph Parsons and Milt Lewis.

Hallmarks of Progress

At first, Ralph and Milt experienced more rejection than success. They spent many hours traveling and sitting in potential clients' waiting rooms because the person they wanted to see was "too busy," only to later find out they were simply being rebuffed. Milt recalled an incident that occurred after a long and frustrating wait. "We inadvertently had an opportunity to look in one man's office on our way to the men's room, and saw him with his feet on the desk reading the *Wall Street Journal*," Milt said.[31]

However, one business trip to Artesia, New Mexico, became especially meaningful to Milt personally, thanks to a "cute" airline stewardess he met during the flight. Her name was Lolly, and she later became Mrs. Milton Lewis.[32]

Persistence Pays Off

Ralph's and Milt's persistence led to refinery design contracts with several oil companies, and the success of those projects established the company's reputation as an innovative and reliable engineering consulting firm. Within a very short span of time, the company was able to support a core group of engineers who would become longtime associates of Ralph.

Among the original staff who worked in The Ralph M. Parsons Company's Chicago office were Elwood Layfield, Glenn B. Taylor, Winchell Parsons, Paul C. McGibney, Charles W. Nelson, E. J. Beers, and H. O. Balzer.

These men either joined Ralph in his next business venture, Bechtel-McCone-Parsons (BMP), which existed between 1937 and 1944, or rejoined Ralph when he reincorporated The Ralph M. Parsons Company (RMP—the predecessor to Parsons Corporation) in 1944. Elwood went on to become a vice president and managed Parsons' London operations. Glenn also was promoted to vice president and managed the Los Angeles headquarters. Winchell, Ralph's nephew, became a vice president and director after managing multiple sulfur plant projects. Paul was Parsons' proposal manager. Charles rose to be a respected project manager, and E. J. and H. O. were key men in executing construction projects.[33]

"Over the years a following had developed," Ralph said. "A good man from here, another from there, each interested in his job, and in progress. Without them, [the work] could not have been accomplished."[34]

Formula for Success

Ralph Parsons had a simple formula for success. He put it this way: "What we need is knowledge of our operations, guts, and confidence."[35] And that formula worked. In only three years, the engineering skills of The Ralph M. Parsons Company and its founder had risen to such prominence that in 1937, the firm caught the eye of construction industry leader Steve Bechtel. This attention led to the next phase of Ralph's professional career, as a partner in one of the most comprehensive engineering/construction corporations the world had ever seen—BMP.

An aviation fuel refinery in Richmond, California, built by BMP in 1942. *(Photo credit: Bechtel Corporation; copyright © Bechtel Corporation.)*

CHAPTER TWO

AN INTERIM PARTNERSHIP

1937–1944

One or all six—business analysis, engineering, design, procurement, construction, and management of operations—your needs determine the services we render.

—Corporation advertisement by Bechtel-McCone-Parsons in *Fortune* magazine, March 1942 edition

bmp

WITHIN THREE YEARS OF founding The Ralph M. Parsons Company, Ralph met Stephen Bechtel Sr. Steve was the president of the company bearing his family's name, Bechtel, a San Francisco–based construction firm that helped build many famous structures, including Hoover Dam and the San Francisco–Oakland Bay Bridge.[1] Like the rest of the engineering world, Ralph was impressed with Bechtel's abilities to complete such large undertakings. For his part, Steve was impressed with Ralph's personal engineering track record and with The Ralph M. Parsons Company's accomplishments in designing and engineering oil, petroleum, and chemical facilities.

The Formation of Bechtel-McCone-Parsons (BMP)

While at work on Hoover Dam, Bechtel purchased steel from Consolidated Steel of Los Angeles. John McCone, who later became assistant secretary of the Navy, chairman of the Atomic Energy Commission (AEC), and head of the Central Intelligence Agency during the John F. Kennedy and Lyndon Johnson administrations, represented Consolidated Steel during the sale. He had already earned a strong reputation as a brilliant, hard-driving businessman. John knew Steve from when they had both attended the University of California at Berkeley in the early 1930s.

Although Steve and John knew each other, they were not close. Steve had learned the construction business from his father, Warren A. Bechtel, who founded the firm. The company was a huge success, and the Bechtel family was financially secure. However, John's path was more difficult. His father died when John was a junior at Berkeley. He and his mother and sisters had little money. When he graduated from college in 1922, jobs were scarce, so John went to work as a riveter for the Llewelyn Ironworks, in California, and worked his way up to becoming a superintendent in that company. He went to work for Consolidated Steel, where he held various executive positions, and then formed his own company, McCone Engineering.[2] John was an intense person, and his character differed from Ralph's, who was more quiet and reserved.

Separately, each of the three men sensed that the construction industry, along with infrastructure development, particularly in the western United States, was poised for significant growth. They

The partnership of Bechtel-McCone-Parsons (BMP) became synonymous with the "turnkey" concept of providing all of the necessary disciplines to design, engineer, construct, and operate petroleum and chemical, shipbuilding, and manufacturing facilities.

were able to look beyond their differences in backgrounds and personal characteristics and form a company that made substantial contributions in building the infrastructure to support the petroleum, shipbuilding, and manufacturing industries during World War II. Steve's idea was to "turnkey" construction projects by creating a single firm that could do it all—analyze, engineer, design, procure, construct, and operate.[3] He asked John and Ralph to join him in a partnership, and in 1937, they established BMP with $75,000 and set up operations in an office suite in Los Angeles. Ralph dissolved The Ralph M. Parsons Company and put its assets into BMP. With one or two exceptions, Ralph's staff followed him to BMP.[4]

As chairman, Steve, at 36, held controlling interest in BMP. John, at 35, was president, and Ralph, at 43, was vice president and director of engineering. The responsibilities of the three partners would shift from project to project, but generally Steve ran construction, John largely concentrated on administration and shipbuilding, and Ralph handled much of the engineering, especially for petroleum projects. Steve also continued to operate Bechtel as a separate entity with BMP sometimes functioning as a virtual affiliate.[5]

Above: The partners of BMP—Steve Bechtel (right), John McCone (center), and Ralph Parsons (left). *(Photo credit: Bechtel Corporation; copyright © Bechtel Corporation.)*

Below: A wide-angle view of the Port of Los Angeles, California, prior to World War II shows the leisure crafts in the harbor that would soon be replaced by warships.

A Singular Concept

BMP brought something new to the table. As a completely self-contained company, it could analyze a client's plans for a new facility, then design, engineer, procure needed equipment and material, construct, and, upon completion, manage its entire operation. Such a firm would spare clients the expense and headaches of dealing with dozens of subcontractors because it delivered facilities that only required the client to turn the front door key—thus the term "turnkey"—to begin operations.[6]

Realizing that they had something unique to offer, the firm's partners stressed their all-inclusive services in their various promotional and marketing activities. Typical was the wording for one advertisement run by BMP in the March 1942 edition of *Fortune* magazine:

> *One or all six—business analysis, engineering, design, procurement, construction, and management of operations—your needs determine the services we render.*[7]

Within the same year it was founded, BMP successfully designed and also built a petroleum hydrogenation plant in Richmond, California, for Standard Oil of California (later to become Chevron and now known as ChevronTexaco). Within four years of startup, BMP had either completed or was in the process of finishing 11 more refineries.

By any business standard, BMP immediately prospered. Within three years it was building pipelines, refineries, and chemical plants from "Alaska to Cape Horn," as detailed in its July 1942 *Fortune* magazine advertisement.[8] In addition to establishing itself as a major player in the petroleum industry, BMP also became instrumental in the massive shipbuilding effort that took place at the beginning of World War II. During the war, BMP built and operated the aircraft modification center, in Birmingham, Alabama, that restored battle-fatigued aircraft.

FORTUNE

MARCH 1942

BUSINESS ANALYSIS

ENGINEERING

DESIGN
PROCESS • MECHANICAL • STRUCTURAL

PROCUREMENT

CONSTRUCTION

MANAGEMENT OF OPERATION

One *or all six*

Your needs determine the services we render. You may assign every detail, or any phase of your engineering, planning and construction problems to us.

We are prepared to analyze your business; plan and engineer extensions to it; build a new plant, or modernize an old one; perform all process, mechanical and structural designing, purchase and expedite delivery of materials and equipment; perform the construction, and consult with you regarding management.

Any one or all of these services are available to you. We have the experience, organization and resources to undertake a project of any size, any place—to do the job the way you want it done.

Our staff of investigators, engineers, purchasers, expediters, constructors and operators are qualified to perform any assignment.

1941 PRIVATE PROJECTS... Petroleum refining units, including distillation, cracking, solvent treating and special by-products plants, chemical processing and power plants.

1941 DEFENSE PROJECTS... Shipyards; power and heating plants; harbor and terminal facilities; magnesium, smokeless powder, ammonia, and chemical by-products plants.

BECHTEL-McCONE-PARSONS CORPORATION

Engineers—Constructors bmp Los Angeles

This ad in *Fortune* showcased BMP's all-inclusive services—establishing the word "turnkey" in the construction vernacular.

Wartime Growth and Development

By 1939, Europe was at war. Nazi Germany seemed unstoppable as it blitzed through country after country. By the summer of 1940, most of Europe had fallen to the Germans, and Great Britain was preparing to defend itself from imminent invasion. At the same time that British Prime Minister Winston Churchill had become the embodiment of his nation's defiance of Adolf Hitler, he was also imploring the United States and President Franklin Roosevelt to provide vital equipment and materials to fight the Nazis. "Give us the tools," the prime minister said, "and we will finish the fight."[9]

Most important for Great Britain, the "tools" included ships. With German submarine "wolf packs" prowling the North Atlantic, the British were losing essential supply vessels at an alarming rate. In early 1940, Admiral Howard L. Vickery, the No. 2 man at the U.S. Maritime Commission, received a request from the British Purchasing Commission to arrange for the construction of 60 tankers to replace convoy ships that the British had lost to German submarines.[10]

Every shipbuilder on the East Coast, where most of the nation's shipyards were located, was already producing to capacity, which meant that the admiral had to look to the West Coast and, perhaps, even to someone new to the business. Alden G. Roach, the president of Consolidated Steel, was an old friend of the admiral. Alden was John McCone's former boss and had also supplied steel to the Bechtel consortium for the Hoover Dam, among other projects. Alden made the connections between the admiral and BMP.[11]

Introductions were made, strategy sessions were held, and an agreement was reached that the shipbuilding operation required a fast turnaround, which meant relying on a standardized design, along with production line techniques used in automobile manufacturing. BMP entered into a joint venture, named Calship, with Todd Shipyards, located in the port of Los Angeles, and began building the 60 tankers for the British. One month after the Japanese attack on Pearl Harbor, Calship received its first shipbuilding contract and began building Liberty and Victory cargo ships and troop transports for the United States. Within a year, Calship was employing 42,000 workers and building as many as three dozen Liberty Ships simultaneously in its prefabrication and subassembly lines.[12]

One-and-a-Half Times the Size of a Football Field

To get a sense of the size of the undertaking at Calship, consider that a Liberty Ship, approximately one-and-a-half times the size of a football field, required more than 2,000 tons of steel plate and almost 7,000 individual components ranging from stair railings to boilers. The ship's three-cylinder, reciprocating steam engine, fed by two oil-burning boilers, produced 2,500 horsepower and a speed of 11 knots. The ship's five holds could carry over 9,000 tons of cargo, plus airplanes, tanks, and locomotives lashed to its deck.[13] In total, Calship built 366 Liberty Ships and tankers, the last one christened on October 27, 1945.[14]

Barely three months after the attack on Pearl Harbor, Steve received an urgent request from the U.S. Maritime Commission requesting a new shipyard be mobilized to support the war effort. Within days a shipyard named Marinship, located at the former Northwestern Railroad terminal outside Sausalito, California, in the port of Richmond, was building tankers, Liberty Ships, and oilers for the war.[15]

BMP was also involved in a five-member alliance to build a shipyard as far away as possible from any potential enemy attack on either coast. The site selected was on the Ohio River in Evansville, Indiana, roughly 700 miles from the Atlantic Ocean and about 2,000 miles from the Pacific Ocean. After getting the go-ahead from the government on February 16, 1942, the alliance (BMP, Missouri Valley Bridge & Iron Company, Winston Brothers Company, C. F. Haglen & Sons Inc., and Sollit Construction Company) began designing the proposed 45-acre shipyard. Construction was under way by March, with 2,000 employees onsite. This number would swell to 19,200 by the time the shipyard was in full operation.[16]

In an amazing feat of engineering and construction, the first keel was laid down on June 25, 1942, as the shipyard was being built. Only four months and six days later, on October 31, 1942, the first ship was launched, an LST 157 (landing craft).[17] Decades later, The Ralph M. Parsons Company would be involved in another massive "Shipyard of the Future"—Litton Industries' immense Ingalls Shipyard in Pascagoula, Mississippi, which it would design in 1968 and later begin refurbishing in 2003 for Northrop Grumman, the current owner.[18]

Above: BMP was one of five companies in a joint venture that designed and built a fully operational shipyard in Evansville, Indiana, between March and October of 1942. *(Photo courtesy of The Evansville Museum of Arts, History and Science.)*

Below left: At Marinship in the port of Richmond, California, BMP expanded its shipyard to support the building of Liberty Ships.

North to Alaska

Until the Japanese attacked Pearl Harbor, Alaska was far from the minds of the U.S. military and the nation at large. It was perceived as distant, cold, and barren—and, in fact, it was. However, the importance of Alaska changed after the Japanese attack on Pearl Harbor when it seemed entirely possible that the "Empire of the Rising Sun" might invade this future state and sweep south through Canada and perhaps even into the United States.

A few U.S. troops were already in Alaska, and there were plans to build more bases there from which American bombers and ships could refuel on their way to the Pacific theater or to the Soviet Union, an American ally during the war. It was known that Alaska possessed large oil reserves, enough to supply the war effort, and this meant a pipeline would need to be built to transport the oil from Alaska across Canada to the United States. One possible route for the fuel was the Alaska Highway that was already under construction. But due to severe weather conditions, it was acknowledged that the highway would be closed most of the year.

A Well-Kept Secret

Because of the urgent wartime circumstances, the United States and Canadian governments decided to construct a major refinery at the Norman Wells oilfields in Canada's Northwest Territory and run a pipeline 1,200 miles through the Yukon Territory into Alaska. The project was known as "Canol," short for Canadian Oil. Several thousand troops from the Army Corps of Engineers were committed to the project, but the bulk of the work would fall to civilian contractors.

The Army worked with several oil companies to develop the plan. Standard Oil of New Jersey (later known as ExxonMobil) was the parent of Imperial Oil of Canada, to whom the drilling work was assigned. Standard Oil of California got the refining work. With that, Army Corps of Engineers

THIS IS NO PICNIC!

WORKING AND LIVING CONDITIONS ON THIS JOB ARE AS DIFFICULT AS THOSE ENCOUNTERED ON ANY CONSTRUCTION JOB EVER DONE IN THE UNITED STATES OR FOREIGN TERRITORY. MEN HIRED FOR THIS JOB WILL BE REQUIRED TO WORK AND LIVE UNDER THE MOST EXTREME CONDITIONS IMAGINABLE. TEMPERATURES WILL RANGE FROM 90 DEGREES ABOVE ZERO TO 70 DEGREES BELOW ZERO. MEN WILL HAVE TO FIGHT SWAMPS, RIVERS, ICE AND COLD. MOSQUITOES, FLIES AND GNATS WILL NOT ONLY BE ANNOYING BUT WILL CAUSE BODILY HARM.

IF YOU ARE NOT PREPARED TO WORK UNDER THESE AND SIMILAR CONDITIONS DO NOT APPLY.

JUNE 15, 1942

Above and below: Recruitment efforts for the Canol project made sure to inform all applicants in no uncertain terms that working conditions in Alaska would be extremely harsh and challenging.

General Brehon Somervell began his search for a contractor with the resources and ability to put the pipeline in place. The general's search led him to Steve Bechtel, who signed up to construct the pipeline.[19]

Steve committed his family's company, Bechtel, as a key participant in a joint venture with the H. C. Price Company and the W. E. Callahan Construction Company (Bechtel-Price-Callahan) to build the top-secret Canol project that would secure the availability of an oil supply necessary in defending Alaska against a possible Japanese invasion.[20] Although the exact percentage of the work completed by Bechtel-Price-Callahan is not known, it is historically referred to as the entity that built the lion's share of the project. While BMP was not part of the joint venture, Steve asked Ralph to serve as director of engineering. Ralph supported this endeavor and provided his valuable oil field and refinery engineering expertise.[21]

Canol was a forbidding project, being undertaken over some of the most rugged landscape on the planet where temperatures dropped to as low as 70 degrees below zero. Aside from the isolated location and miserable conditions, the job itself was remarkably ambitious. It involved building a crude oil pipeline, pumping stations, refinery, and petroleum facilities, as well as roads, airfields, a railroad, seaport facilities, and housing for 2,500 workers.[22]

According to an internal Parsons newsletter article, "Parsons and Alaska," preserved by Dwight Hunt, who held planning, engineering support, project management, business development, and program director positions within Parsons for 20 years, the plan called for the development of the most northerly producing oil field in North America. Simultaneously, a pipeline would be built to a point on the Alaska Highway, which was also under construction. There, a refinery would be constructed to turn the crude into gasoline for plants, trucks, and other wartime uses.[23]

Final approval for the Canol project came in April 1942, and notices began appearing in employment offices throughout the United States and Canada. Because Canol was top secret, the solicitation did not mention the project or the location. It was considered so vital that deferment from military service was offered during the war.

Originally budgeted at $30 million, the costs of Canol skyrocketed to $134 million due to the remote location, rapid schedule, and severe weather conditions.[24] Winter blizzards often halted construction. But conditions were no better in the spring when "the subsoil began to thaw [and] it swallowed up men and machinery like quicksand."[25]

Despite the brutal environment, within six months many of the facilities were online and supporting the war effort. Within 24 months, the entire project was complete, and a local fuel supply was now guaranteed for the balance of the war. Some were calling Canol "the greatest project since the Panama Canal."[26]

In retrospect, the project's assistance to the war effort was not as strategic as originally planned. By the time Canol was completed at the end of 1944, the United States had regained control of the Pacific, and the end of the war was only months away.[27] However, Canol gave the engineering world a hint of things to come. In the early 1970s, Parsons would be heavily involved in the development of Alaska's famed North Slope oil fields.

Aircraft Assembly in Alabama

Midway through 1942, the U.S. Army decided on a new strategy to increase the rate at which critically needed military airplanes were produced. The country's industrial might had already turned almost entirely to the war effort, but the aircraft industry, which was still relatively new in terms of mass production, was struggling.

The production of aircraft engines was developing well enough. Automobile manufacturers such as General Motors and Ford had joined forces with aircraft engine firms like Pratt and Whitney.

Despite these productive alliances, the airframe problems remained unsolved. Most of the work was still being done by a small number of firms that had been around for many years, and the existing processes did not lend themselves to mass production. The U.S. Army Air Corps and BMP found that "making airplanes was not only a more demanding process than making cars, it was a slower one, too."[28]

Changes in aircraft design occurred so frequently and were so disruptive that efforts to increase production were becoming progressively more frustrating. The war saw an explosion of aeronautical technology that often rendered certain design details obsolete by the time the aircraft came

A Consolidated B-24 Liberator heavy bomber from the four-engine pilot school at Maxwell Field, Alabama, glistens in the sun as it makes a turn at high altitude. *(U.S. Air Force photo.)*

off the assembly line. Battle planners sometimes demanded changes based on newly recognized enemy combat techniques or technological advances. Complicating these already complex challenges were the vast expanses of terrain over which the global war advanced. For instance, innovations that worked in Europe with shorter flight distances and colder climates might not be reliable for the longer expanses and hot and humid weather of the Pacific.

In response, the U.S. Army adopted a system that the British had used for years. The British took American aircraft and altered them to suit their own needs after they were delivered to England. The changes were made simultaneously by separate crews at multiple locations, which resulted in a dramatic increase in the rate at which aircraft were put into combat. Following this example, the U.S. Army Air Corps decided to defer any physical changes or modifications to an aircraft until after its basic manufacture and then send the aircraft to specialized facilities that were equipped to make the necessary modifications.

The strategy of building a network of aircraft modification centers around the nation required finding firms that were capable of quickly designing and building the facilities and that could operate them with a high degree of efficiency.

The initial program called for constructing 10 of these centers, but that goal was soon increased to 30. All but two were designed, built, and operated by firms that sprouted up from either the aircraft manufacturers themselves or from the maintenance shops of the fledgling commercial airlines. Of those two remaining centers, BMP was awarded one, the Birmingham, Alabama, aircraft modification center,[29] which required that two million square feet of manufacturing space be designed quickly and built on 285 acres of boggy ground, adjacent to the city's airport.[30]

Although BMP had never designed an aircraft plant, it had completed an impressive array of other engineering work. Another compelling reason to award BMP the Birmingham facility was Ralph's background in aeronautical engineering. It was agreed that BMP would design and build the $15 million facility under one contract—ensuring that all of its design and construction costs, including overhead and management salaries, would be fully reimbursed, but to which it would add no profit. BMP would also manage the plant operations for a fixed fee of about four percent of the cost to staff and operate the plant.[31]

With Steve Bechtel focused on Canol, John McCone handled the administration of the Birmingham plant and Ralph managed its engineering. Construction got under way by mid-January 1943. The project was segmented into three parts: the swampy site had to be filled and graded for runways and buildings, temporary wooden structures had to be built to provide shelter for the aircraft and for the workers, and permanent steel frame buildings had to be erected.

The speed at which the project progressed was extraordinary—even by wartime standards. By late February, only five weeks after work began, the first B-24 bombers began to arrive from a Ford plant in Michigan. By March 18, 1943, modification work was finished on the first bombers, and they were on their way to Europe. Fast did not mean easy. The largest problem was recruiting and training the 8,000-person workforce. Most of the region's qualified workers had either gone off to war or were working elsewhere in equally critical positions. As happened often during World War II, an expert workforce was created from the ground up. It is estimated that 86 percent of the workers brought into the training program had never done similar work.[32]

Robert Salvadore was one of the first 25 people BMP hired. He was a flight engineer, and part of his responsibilities was performing the ground-check for the pilots prior to their test flights. He recalled his experience in Birmingham:

> *We had about 18 pilots at the plant. Jim Parwick was the chief pilot. We started modifying B-24s and then B-29s. I was also assigned to a program called "5F5" that retrofitted planes with aerial photography equipment. In one plane, the P-38, we placed five cameras in its nose.*[33]

After his time with BMP, Robert stayed in the aerospace industry for the remainder of his professional career. He stated, "Looking back, I really enjoyed working there. We had a lot of talented people."[34]

With intense on-the-job training the workers rapidly increased productivity and efficiently modified the airplanes. However, completing and managing the plant took its toll on John and Ralph's professional working relationship and prompted Ralph's decision to leave BMP in 1944.

The Legacy of the Bechtel-McCone-Parsons Partnership

The intense efforts the partners of BMP made to help win World War II led to each man, starting with Ralph, concluding that it was time to go in different directions. Ralph was well paid for his shares in the company; according to one source, he received $250,000.[35]

In the seven years that BMP existed, from 1937 to 1944, the partnership would hone the business interests of all three men and further their individual careers in extraordinary ways. The shipbuilding expertise John acquired during World War II helped him rise to important positions within the government. Similarly, the partnership allowed Steve to expand his already successful family business from heavy construction into the areas of energy and power, which led to Bechtel's becoming the world's largest design and construction firm. Ralph and Steve remained in contact over the years and, today, Parsons and Bechtel are joint venture partners on several large, complex projects.

When Ralph Parsons entered the BMP partnership, he was a small refinery designer. When he left seven years later in 1944, his horizons had broadened far beyond any pre–World War II possibilities. In returning to Los Angeles from Birmingham, Ralph began a new chapter in his life and founded his second company, now a global corporation that is a major contributor to the world's economic and governmental infrastructure—Parsons.

Below left: BMP's airplane modification plant in Birmingham, Alabama, required workers to have extensive training sessions during World War II. Shown third from left in the front row is Robert Salvadore and the BMP test flight engineering team in one such meeting. *(Photo courtesy of Robert Salvadore.)*

Below right: BMP employed pilots to test the modified airplanes. Jim Parwick (front row on the far left) was the chief pilot who tested the most unique aircraft modifications, including the P-38. *(Photo courtesy of Robert Salvadore.)*

Incorporation Milestones, Acquisitions, and Divestitures

1934–2005

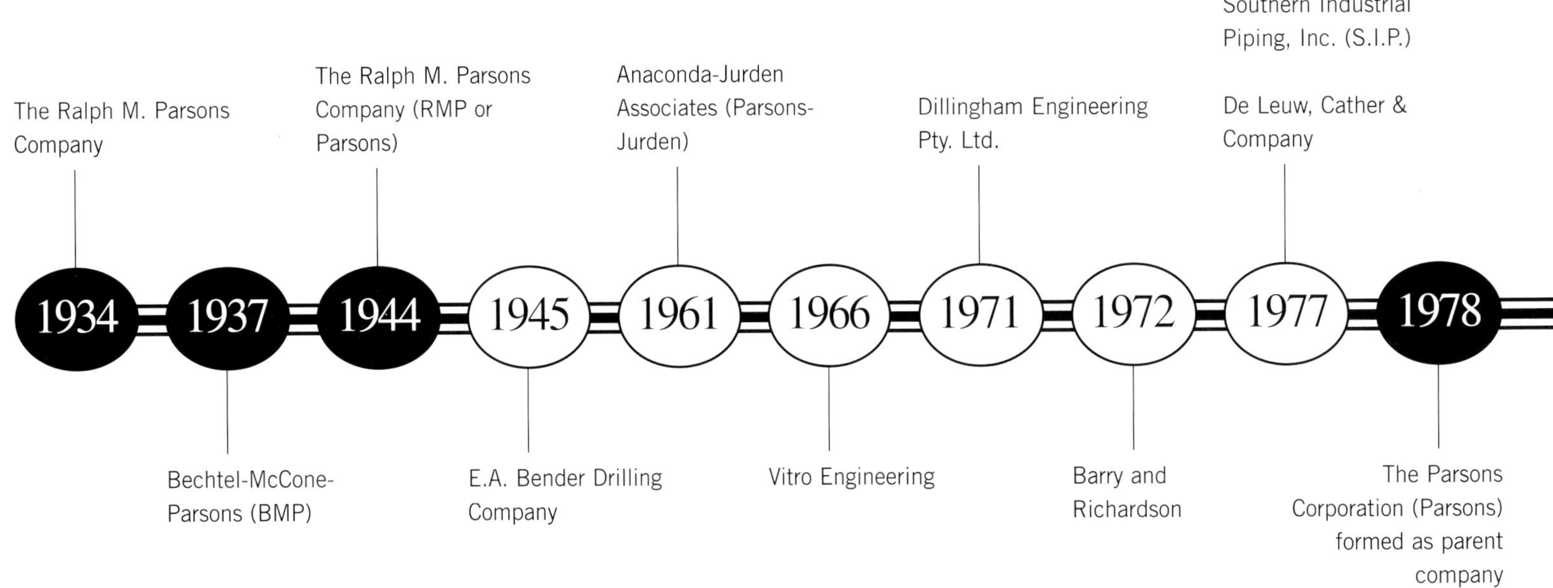

LEGEND

Incorporation Milestone

Acquisition

Divesture

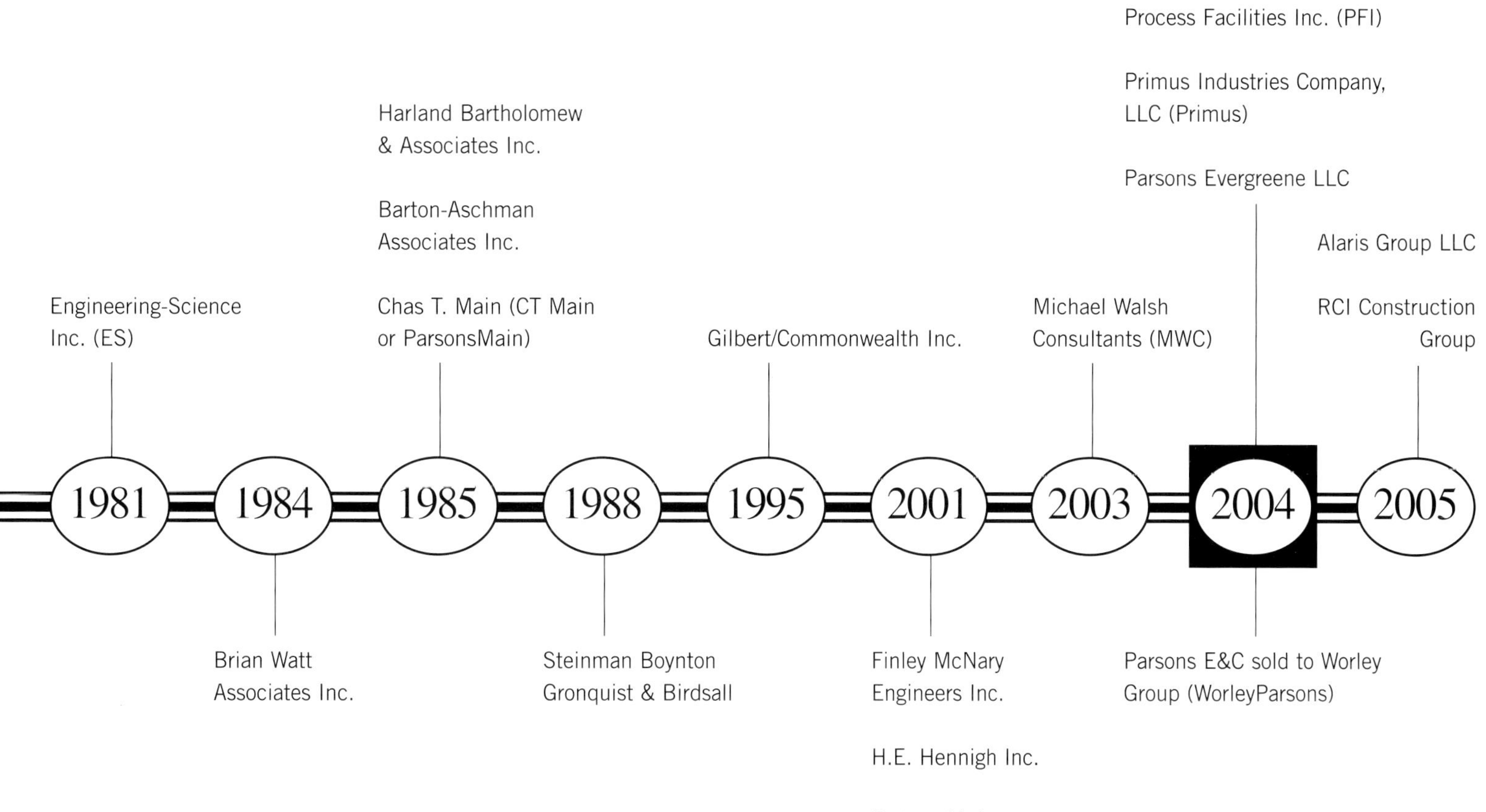
Engineering-Science Inc. (ES)
1981
1984
Brian Watt Associates Inc.
Harland Bartholomew & Associates Inc.
Barton-Aschman Associates Inc.
Chas T. Main (CT Main or ParsonsMain)
1985
1988
Steinman Boynton Gronquist & Birdsall
Gilbert/Commonwealth Inc.
1995
2001
Finley McNary Engineers Inc.
H.E. Hennigh Inc.
Protect Air Inc.
Michael Walsh Consultants (MWC)
2003
Process Facilities Inc. (PFI)
Primus Industries Company, LLC (Primus)
Parsons Evergreene LLC
2004
Parsons E&C sold to Worley Group (WorleyParsons)
Alaris Group LLC
RCI Construction Group
2005

After long and intense negotiations with the Turkish government's oil company, Turkiye Petrolleri A.O., The Ralph M. Parsons Company was contracted to build the country's first oil refinery. Work began in 1952.

CHAPTER THREE

A Brand-New Start

1944–1954

I formed The Ralph M. Parsons Company with the intention of operating a small business. However, the reputation we had established over the years stuck with us, and the next thing I knew we were doing the same things [as BMP]—oil refineries, chemical plants, government facilities.

—Ralph M. Parsons

In 1944, Ralph left BMP and formed a new venture. It was incorporated on June 12, 1944, in Nevada under the same name of Ralph's first company, The Ralph M. Parsons Company (RMP). He capitalized the firm with $100,000—a substantial portion of the $250,000 he had received when exiting BMP. He was eager to start over again.

After being discharged from the U.S. Navy, James E. Halferty joined RMP in 1946 as an engineer and became its first foreign operations manager. He remembered:

Ralph conveyed the impression of a man who could already see the mansion and the rose garden at the end of the road. He exuded self-confidence—not by word—but just by the way he was. Hard to describe, but impossible not to feel.[1]

A Savvy and Seasoned Veteran

Ralph celebrated his 48th birthday just 10 days after the incorporation of his new company. At an age when many men are at the height of their careers, he was rolling the dice all over again. However, he was a savvy and seasoned veteran of the business world, having already succeeded in designing, engineering, and building infrastructure on a scale that would have been virtually impossible before World War II. More important, he had earned a reputation for reliability and for saying what he meant and meaning what he said. His strong experience quickly paid off for the new firm, as Ralph explained:

I formed The Ralph M. Parsons Company with the intention of operating a small business. However, the reputation we had established over the years stuck with us, and the next thing I knew we were doing the same things [as BMP]—oil refineries, chemical plants, government facilities.[2]

RMP opened its doors at suite 230 in the Edison building at 601 West Fifth Street in Los Angeles with eight employees—six engineers, one secretary, and Ralph. This art deco building constructed in 1931 reflected the modern age by being the first in the western United States to be heated and cooled by electricity. Murals in the building's lobby represented the architectural and technological themes that complemented Ralph's business interests: light, power, and hydroelectric energy. The business grew so successfully that, only four

Ralph Parsons (right) turns the valve initiating oil flow to the Batman, Turkey, refinery pipeline with the Republic of Turkey's president, Celal Bayer (center).

months later, Ralph had to move his company to larger quarters. He rented 1,790 square feet in the Oviatt building at 617 South Olive Street in Los Angeles.[3] This building also incorporated a splendrous art deco architectural styling, even down to its decorative glass elements designed by René Lalique.

In the beginning, the company won many contracts simply because of Ralph's reputation for being reliable in performing a contract successfully. To many clients, the name "RMP" was synonymous with "project management." Ralph's reputation led to RMP's becoming one of a few select firms that could be counted on to be successful in completing massive and complex engineering and construction projects.

The timing was right for Ralph's new company. Domestic modernization programs that had been delayed by World War II kicked into high gear in the postwar years. These programs offered a rich array of opportunities and the chance to use the skills Ralph had developed as an independent engineering consultant and as a vice president of engineering at BMP.

Focusing on Petroleum Clients

Ralph began his new venture by focusing on petroleum clients while setting his sights on expanding into new lines of work. In one of its first advertisements, RMP proudly announced its abilities to provide "complete oil property services, in addition to designing, building, and operating pipelines, refineries, and natural gas plants."[4]

On August 1, 1944, less than two months after incorporation, the company signed a contract to provide engineering, management, and oil well drilling services on The Great Divide Project, in Colorado.[5]

Top: The Edison building murals depicted the business interests on which Ralph Parsons would base his company. He later commissioned murals for Parsons' headquarters building. *(Photo courtesy of MAS Asset Management Corporation.)*

Below: The art deco-inspired Oviatt building in downtown Los Angeles became company headquarters shortly after the formation of RMP.

To complete RMP's portion of the Canol project, Ralph purchased a fleet of trucks for his engineers to transport their equipment and supplies and traverse the length of the pipeline over the rough Alaskan terrain.

Other projects that immediately came in the door included providing appraisal and engineering services on a refinery in Husky, Nebraska, for Peter Kiewit Sons Inc., a construction firm that Parsons would work closely with in the future; an engineering study for Portland Gas and Coke, in Portland, Oregon; and an engineering study for Richfield Oil Corporation (which became Atlantic Richfield and is now a part of BP) for its midway crude pipeline, in Los Angeles.

During that same year, RMP was retained to finish engineering work on Canol due to Ralph's former involvement on the project while at BMP. RMP also won key design contracts for oil refineries and petroleum and chemical plants from Koppers, Standard Oil of California (now ChevronTexaco), Shell Chemical, and Union Oil of California (now Unocal).

By the end of 1944, RMP grew from a staff of eight to 35 people.[6] In 1945, Ralph made his initial foray into acquisitions by purchasing the assets of the E.A. Bender Drilling Company of Bakersfield, California. The acquisition added to Ralph's project portfolio with Standard Oil of California, which began contracting with RMP to drill oil wells, in addition to providing engineering services.[7]

Diversification into Defense

On March 5, 1946, almost a year to the day that the Allies declared a victory in Europe, Winston Churchill delivered his famous speech warning of an "Iron Curtain" descending over Eastern Europe. The Soviet Union, the world's most powerful Communist regime—and an atomic power—had become a political enemy of the United States rather than its ally. The Cold War had begun.

Although Ralph's primary business interest was designing and constructing petroleum and chemical plants, he knew that diversification was critical for his company to survive and thrive. He understood that the Cold War would cause a huge defense buildup, especially with the advent of atomic energy and missile defense systems. Ralph adeptly positioned his company to enter into those two markets.

The year 1948 saw the inception of RMP's role as a significant defense contractor and engineering consultant. The company signed a joint venture contract with Aerojet (now part of GenCorp, the former General Tire and Rubber Company) to design a medium-range missile launch site for the U.S. Navy at Point Mugu, on the southern California coast.[8]

Constructing infrastructure at oil fields was rough and rugged as depicted in this photograph of work being conducted by the company's first acquisition, an oil well drilling company in Bakersfield, California.

This site was instrumental in developing various missile configurations, including the Sparrow, Polaris, Trident, Harpoon, Tomahawk, SLAM, and Sidewinder.[9] This project launched RMP's long and distinguished service to the Department of Defense, a relationship that remains a cornerstone of its present-day operations.

After the Point Mugu project was completed, RMP went on to design similar facilities in Huntsville, Alabama, and Banana River, Florida (now known as Cape Canaveral and before that, Cape Kennedy). The company then went on to help validate the feasibility of firing missiles from underground silos by designing and building a test facility at Vandenberg Air Force Base in California. These projects led to RMP's securing complex design contracts that would span the course of the Cold War: the Minuteman and Titan II silos, the Titan III test facility, and test facilities for Nike-Zeus, Nike-X, the Peacekeeper, and the Sentinel antiballistic missile systems.[10]

Develop Expertise and Then Build on It

The Point Mugu project reflected RMP's growth strategy. Ralph and his staff began to take on the challenge of new or difficult technology development, engineering, design, and/or construction management projects. They would collaborate with clients, peers, and subcontractors to develop workable solutions, produce results by doing whatever it took to execute the tasks successfully, and then secure other opportunities based on the skills, technology, and relationships they had established.

Stan Goldhaber, who joined the company in 1948 as senior project manager and retired from the firm as a senior vice president and corporate officer, described how the company created its niche in the high-profile area of missile defense:

We focused hard and fast on the missile development program. I traveled around the country and the world selling the concept of missiles to the military units stationed in various parts of the world, along with other military components of the government. There is no question that our work in this area became a very important contributor to the growth of the company.[11]

Atomic and Nuclear

With both the United States and the Soviet Union having the ability to launch an atomic strike, the Atomic Energy Commission (AEC), the precursor to the Department of Energy, retained RMP in 1948

This page: RMP, in a joint venture with Aerojet, designed a medium-range missile launch site at Point Mugu, in California, that presaged future defense projects.

to design a research facility that would conduct advanced nuclear experiments at the Idaho National Engineering Laboratory (INEL), originally named the National Reactor Testing Station. INEL was established as a remote site to work with experimental civilian and military reactors. The AEC and the U.S. Air Force hoped the experiments would result in a nuclear-powered airplane. Turbojet engines were to be connected to a reactor and powered via nuclear energy.

RMP designed all of the facilities to conduct the tests and related operations. These included an airplane hangar, an earth-covered control room for the "initial test," a huge assembly and maintenance building that contained the world's largest "hot shop," a shielded room into which the engine/reactor assembly was moved after nuclear operations, and several other reactor buildings. The airplane hangar would be used to manage the airplane remotely as it returned from a flight mission after becoming radioactively contaminated. Special elevators, coupling stations, shielded passageways for the crew to leave the aircraft, and other features made this airplane hangar a one-of-a-kind facility. General Electric was the contractor for the AEC.

At the time of construction, RMP's design of the INEL facility required the largest cast-in-place concrete arch ever poured, a span of 3,000 feet.[12] Ray DeClue, who joined RMP in 1956 and worked predominantly on the Minuteman and space program projects before retiring in 1989, was a structural engineer on INEL as it was nearing completion. He said:

> *A memorable thing about the facilities in Idaho was the hangar we [designed]. It was equal to the largest clearspan hangar that was ever built.*[13]

Appraisal of Government Facilities

Another defense-related diversification that grew into a series of financially lucrative projects involved the appraisal of various types of federally owned facilities that had been built during World War II. These facilities were designed, built, and often operated by private industry during the war. They had been paid for and were owned by the federal government, which now wanted to sell them as quickly as possible at fair market prices. Company records show that the first contract was signed with

In the late 1940s and early 1950s, RMP designed the initial nuclear research facilities at INEL that included the longest clearspan concrete structure built to date.

the War Assets Administration on October 24, 1945, a "cost and process appraisal" for facilities operated in Richmond, California, by Standard Oil Company of California. By final contract closeout on February 9, 1949, RMP had completed 43 appraisals in 17 states and the District of Columbia on gasoline refineries, synthetic rubber plants, shipyards, and steel plants.[14]

Keith Timlin, who joined Ralph's new company in 1946, was its 65th employee. He recalled these assessments:

> *This was right after the war. There were a lot of war asset companies or factories, and Parsons got a lot of those jobs to make an appraisal to determine the value of these facilities, set a sale price, and come up with some ideas [as to] what they could be used for as an alternate in peacetime.*[15]

Keith had served in the U.S. Navy in World War II and held his master's degree in mechanical engineering from the University of Pittsburgh. He later became the project director on the company's engineering and construction program in Alaska that was responsible for oil processing facilities. He retired in 1985 and frequently attends a popular retiree luncheon held every other month at the Beckham Grill restaurant in Pasadena, California, for former Parsons employees.[16]

A Lesson Learned

While his company was growing, Ralph soon learned that not every strategy worked out as planned. The GI Bill put through college tens of thousands of young men who would not have even considered seeking higher education before the war. These ex-servicemen were also eligible for low-cost home loans subsidized by the government, which soon led to the greatest demand for housing in the history of the country and the growth of America's middle class.

Until the postwar era, home builders were generally small-time operators. The typical prewar contractor put up fewer than five houses a year. But by applying the same mass production techniques used to build America's jeeps, ships, and supplies during the war, home builders could now provide inexpensive single-unit housing for ordinary families in short time periods.[17]

Ralph saw the housing boom as a golden opportunity and entered into the market eagerly. His idea was to mass-produce prefabricated and preassembled homes that would be reassembled at the construction site. The houses could be completed quickly and at low costs, which would benefit both the builder and the buyer.

SIGNIFICANT PROJECTS

1934–1953

1934

Universal Oil Products Company, Cracking Units Engineering/ Construction, Various Locations

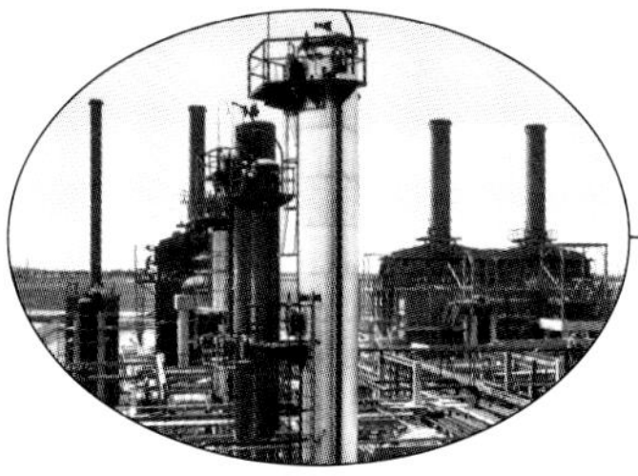

1937

Standard Oil of California (now ChevronTexaco), Turnkey Refinery, Richmond, California

1940

U.S. Maritime Commission, World War II Liberty Ship Construction, California

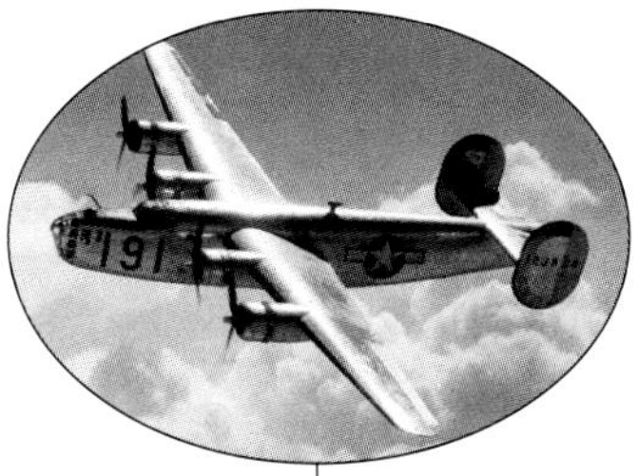

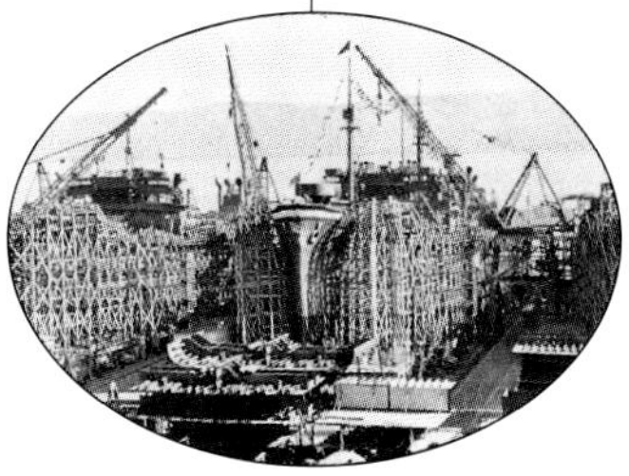

1943

U.S. Army, Design-Build-Operate World War II Aircraft and Jeep Modification Center, Birmingham, Alabama

1944

Army Corps of Engineers, "Top Secret" Canol Pipeline Engineering Support, Alaska

The Great Divide Project, Engineering, Management, and Oil Well-Drilling Services, Colorado

LEGEND

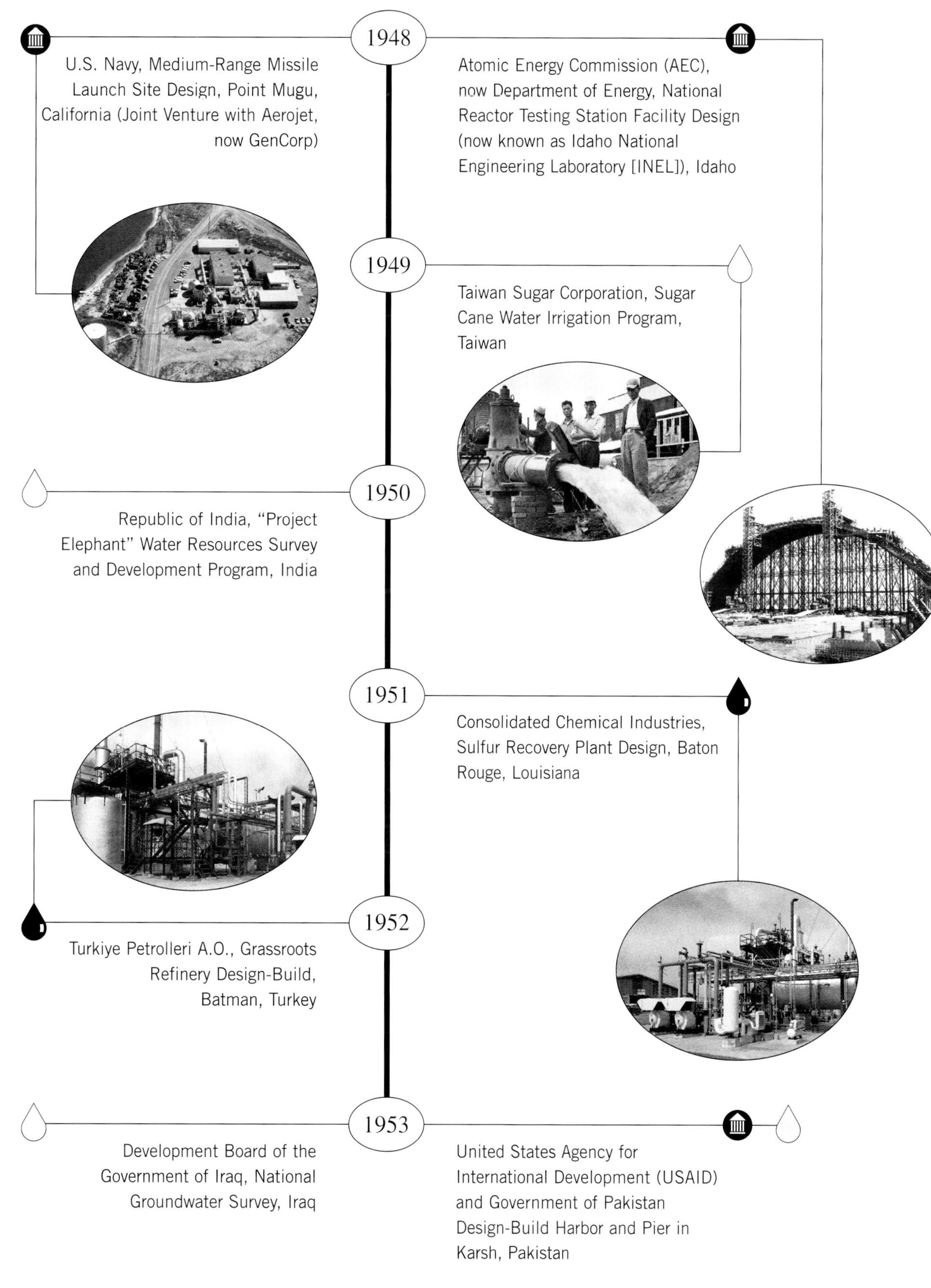
1948
U.S. Navy, Medium-Range Missile Launch Site Design, Point Mugu, California (Joint Venture with Aerojet, now GenCorp)
Atomic Energy Commission (AEC), now Department of Energy, National Reactor Testing Station Facility Design (now known as Idaho National Engineering Laboratory [INEL]), Idaho
1949
Taiwan Sugar Corporation, Sugar Cane Water Irrigation Program, Taiwan
1950
Republic of India, "Project Elephant" Water Resources Survey and Development Program, India
1951
Consolidated Chemical Industries, Sulfur Recovery Plant Design, Baton Rouge, Louisiana
1952
Turkiye Petrolleri A.O., Grassroots Refinery Design-Build, Batman, Turkey
1953
Development Board of the Government of Iraq, National Groundwater Survey, Iraq
United States Agency for International Development (USAID) and Government of Pakistan Design-Build Harbor and Pier in Karsh, Pakistan

An RMP document entitled, "Highlights of the 1940s," refers to an Eastern Group that was created within the company in 1946 to handle investments, equipment rentals, real estate, and housing for veterans. The Eastern Group was a precursor to RMP opening a Washington, D.C., office in 1948.[18]

Ralph's instincts to pursue the veterans' housing market were correct, but where he went wrong was in buying plots that did not border each other. Each housing unit had to be hauled, one by one, to its own lot, thus entirely missing out on the efficiency of building hundreds of thousands of homes in one location or "tract."

The Tract Housing Concept

William Levitt created the tract housing concept at Levittown, New York, a futuristic community on Long Island that was the largest housing project in American history. The basic Levitt Cape Cod house sold for $7,990. The sales office opened in March 1949, and 1,400 contracts were signed in a single day.[19] By the time Levittown was finished, more than 17,000 houses had been built, 82,000 people lived there, and William Levitt had invented the suburban bedroom community.[20]

Unfortunately, Ralph had not foreseen the necessity of a centralized location on which to build his homes. By the time he realized his mistake, he had lost at least $100,000.[21] As a result, he quickly got out of the single-home construction business. This important lesson is one that many entrepreneurs never learn: Take the risk, but if the market does not support your concept, cut your losses and quickly move on.

Honed Instincts

Ralph's ability to learn from his mistakes served him well for the rest of his life. Dr. Bill Opel, the executive director of the Huntington Medical Research Institutes, in Pasadena, knew Ralph well through his charitable work and socialized with him often. He characterized Ralph as a down-to-earth individual who was able to quickly learn from experience:

Ralph claimed he didn't do very well in school. I don't know if that's true or not. But he told me he always found that if he could get the contracts, he could then hire the "smart guys" to work for him. He was a very practical guy who didn't judge himself to be very smart. But there was no question that he had an excellent business model regarding how you handle large projects and keep them going. Also, he wasn't afraid to take risks. And he knew how to put together a team. Always, his talent was absolutely outstanding and I think that clearly was a function of him.

He talked about how he often tried and failed, and how he always learned from these experiences. It reminds me of that old adage, "What do you learn from success? Not much. What do you learn from failure? Hopefully, a great deal." And Ralph Parsons clearly could learn from his failures. In so doing, I think he's left a great legacy for the country and the things that can be built today.[22]

As the years unfolded, they honed Ralph's instincts to validate opportunities in new markets. His willingness to reinvest in his company, acquire others, and divest unprofitable ventures allowed the company to sustain revenues and grow during the up-and-down business cycles.

Renewal of an Old Business Friendship and the Beginning of a New Professional Relationship

In addition to his instincts and business savvy, Ralph Parsons was able to guide his firm because he was a practical man who recognized good talent and moved quickly to hire, as he put it, the "smart guys" who would handle his projects, and thus advance his business.

One important hire or, more accurately, "rehire" was Milt Lewis, who rejoined Ralph in October 1949 after a nine-year stint with Fluor Corporation. Milt's sales efforts contributed heavily to the success of Ralph's first company and would do so again. Together, Ralph and Milt spent the next 25 years securing major projects that made RMP a leader in the rapidly evolving world of engineering and construction.

Milt joined the company as an executive vice president and assumed the responsibilities of RMP's top salesman. "Milt Lewis became one of [Ralph's] top rainmakers," said outside counsel and former board member Dan Frost.[23] Milt became president in 1965 and remained with the company after Ralph's death in 1974 as its chairman and CEO until retiring in 1978.

Another person critical to Ralph's success would join Parsons in 1952. Her name was Barbara (Stokes) Dewey, and she became Ralph's corporate administrative manager. She was Ralph's second assistant. Vi (Wamsley) Leslie, who joined the firm in 1944, was his first.[24]

In addition to directly supporting Ralph, Barbara developed RMP's office procedures and trained the administrative staff to meet his high-quality standards of professionalism and accuracy.

After Ralph died, she served as The Ralph M. Parsons Foundation's first executive director and helped frame its culture and grant-making guidelines for the charities it funds.[25] Barbara died in 1986, but the long-time staff remember her as being a woman of character, intelligence, and wisdom.

Water and Oil *Do* Mix

The E.A. Bender Drilling Company that RMP bought in 1945 was never a particularly profitable oil drilling endeavor; however, in retrospect, it was an excellent acquisition because it led to RMP's first overseas project. On September 17, 1949, contracts were signed by RMP with the Taiwan Sugar Corporation for a sugar cane irrigation water well program that required the construction of 139 wells—including locating, drilling, casing, developing, testing, and installing permanent pumps—at various locations in central and southern Taiwan. By the end of the project, a number of Taiwanese engineers and drillers were trained to carry on the program after RMP's team of 32 personnel departed.[26]

E.A. Bender had drilled oil wells for Thomas W. Simmons, owner of the Bolsa Chica Oil Company. Thomas also owned the Johnston Pump Company, of Pasadena, which made vertical turbine pumps. One of Thomas' salesmen, Hany Edell, was friendly with a man named Bob Ely, who had been hired by the Taiwan Sugar Corporation to help get Taiwan's sugar industry running again after the war.[27]

With nine months of dry weather each year and only three months of rain, Bob calculated that Taiwan's sugar output could increase by 100 percent if the crops were irrigated during the dry season. The solution: construct an extensive well and irrigation system. This strategy fit nicely with the Johnston Pump Company's ability to supply the vertical turbine pumps for the water wells.

The vast majority of RMP's groundwater and mineral surveys around the world were performed by a core group of geologists, such as the professionals shown here in India, who were trained and educated in southern California.

WATER RESOURCES

TWO-THIRDS OF THE EARTH IS COVERED by water, and 80 percent of the world's population lives within 30 miles of open water. Nevertheless, finding and accessing sources of clean, potable water has been a major challenge in sustaining most of the world's population.

RMP's first overseas water development project, in Taiwan in 1949, was the cornerstone for its future water resource services. The project team located groundwater and developed 139 water wells for a sugar cane field irrigation system. Sugar became the major export of Taiwan and helped restore Taiwan's economic health after World War II by facilitating trade. This project ultimately led to RMP's improving water quality, distribution, and reuse in more than 20 countries by 1969—which equates to one new country per year for 20 years.[1]

From the 1950s through the 1970s, RMP proceeded to perform groundwater surveys for the countries of India, Iraq, Iran, Pakistan, Thailand, Lebanon, Kuwait, the United Arab Emirates, Algeria, Saudi Arabia, Egypt, and Vietnam. RMP went on to design, engineer, and construct water treatment and process plants; pipelines, dams, and reservoirs; cogeneration and hydroelectric facilities; and watershed management programs in these and other countries over the decades.

Iraq's groundwater survey is vividly remembered by those who engaged in the project. "We covered all 14 provinces and wrote a report on each of the areas," said Dr. James G. Holwerda, who joined RMP in 1950 as a geologist and was instrumental in executing many of RMP's international projects. "I had no problem whatsoever with any of the Iraqis anywhere, anytime. I had to live out with the Bedouins on occasion."[2]

The groundwater survey and well development program enhanced the lives of the Iraqi people. Today, Parsons is part of the U.S. reconstruction engineering, procurement, and construction team that is building a series of new infrastructure projects, including municipal water and sewage systems in Iraq.

In 1953, RMP was first retained by the U.S. Agency for International Development (USAID) and also by the government of Pakistan to develop a modern fish harbor as the commercial and private fishing center in Karachi, which serviced Pakistan's large fishing fleet. The company designed and supervised the harbor's modernization. The scope included dredging channels and a mooring basin and managing the construction of a breakwater, a pier with market facilities, a fish processing plant, and cold storage warehouses; plus roads and other appurtenances for accessing the harbor.[3]

In addition, RMP assisted in solving a recurring health threat in East Pakistan (later Bangladesh) by engineering and providing construction oversight of water storage and sanitation systems that were instrumental in containing cholera epidemics. The company had active water-related projects in this country for 27 years. For 20 of those years, RMP's project manager, Hank White, survived numerous riots, strikes, and, in 1971, the revolution that ousted the West Pakistan government and created the country of Bangladesh in former East Pakistan. Because of Hank's dedicated efforts on the project, he became "a legend in his own time," according to James Halferty's memoirs.[4] Other international ventures that followed were water, sewage, and marine outfall projects in Brazil, Uruguay, Colombia, Haiti, and Ghana.

RMP's most ambitious—and indeed, visionary—water resource endeavor, the North American Water and Power Alliance (NAWAPA), never became a reality. NAWAPA was conceived by Ralph to do nothing less than provide a solution to North America's water resource problems by diverting water from Alaska and northern Canada into southern Canadian provinces, the western United States, and three states in Mexico. NAWAPA's remarkable scope and the story of its inception are told on pages 78–79 in Chapter Four.

Parsons' Water Expertise: Solving a Worldwide Problem

As the global population continues to rise, the distribution and use of potable water is becoming more critical with each passing year. Water resource capabilities are so important that, in 2003, Parsons Corporation formed a separate global business unit solely focused on solving water-related problems. Parsons provides a fourfold solution to the problems of global water quality, distribution, and reuse:

1. Increase the availability of fresh water supplies for human consumption and agricultural use.
2. Extract substances or material generated by industrial wastewater and public sanitation systems that could be harmful to human health or the environment.
3. Remove contaminants from groundwater to protect potable sources of water.
4. Provide flood control to prevent damage and destruction of communities along the rivers and oceans.

"We were always very prominent in the water business," said Parsons' retired president and chief operating officer (COO), Frank DeMartino. "In fact, that was one of Ralph's initial areas when he formed the firm."[5]

Municipal, military, and industrial clients all over the world are using water and wastewater treatment systems designed, engineered, and constructed by Parsons. The size of these systems ranges from massive water treatment plants capable of handling 550 million gallons per day (mgd), to those as small as 0.5 mgd serving rural communities.[6]

Parsons also has extensive expertise in developing water and sewerage systems for public works projects that feature various components, including treatment plants, pipelines, reservoirs, storm drainage, and flood-control structures.

Parsons' professional services include water supply and wastewater system planning; feasibility studies; preliminary engineering; preparation of drawings and specifications; and necessary bidding documents for design and construction. It also provides program management planning, construction management, turnkey construction, startup, operation, and maintenance.

Examples of recent megaprojects (presented in later chapters) are the Eastside Reservoir for The Metropolitan Water District of Southern California and The Southern Nevada Water Authority (SNWA). For Metropolitan, Parsons designed and built a 4.5-mile-long reservoir that covers 4,500 acres. As of this printing, Parsons is completing for SNWA a $2 billion water distribution system for the Las Vegas Valley that, in its first phase, includes 105 miles of pipeline, 12 pumping stations, and 16 reservoirs and forebays; a large new intake in Lake Mead; three large hard rock tunnels; a new ozone/direct filtration plant; the addition of ozone treatment to the existing water treatment plant; and turnouts or distribution points to the various water retailers. All of this is being supported by a greatly enlarged power system, including 13 substations. The second phase of the project is being planned.[7]

With its unmatched resources, vast project experience, and superior expertise, Parsons has proved itself entirely able to meet the challenges of supplying water to a thirsty planet. Indeed, as many local, state, and national governments and public authorities will attest, if the problem is water, the solution is Parsons.

The 300-foot inlet/outlet tower at Diamond Valley Lake has completely filled the 61.2-billion-gallon reservoir and doubled the surface storage capacity in southern California.

But Thomas Simmons' expertise did not include managing and coordinating a complex drilling and pumping project, so he turned to Ralph for help. RMP's role was to execute and manage the project from beginning to end, including procurement and shipping of all equipment and supplies, completion of reconnaissance studies for adequate groundwater of high quality, and supply of all pertinent technical data.[28]

An Innovative Solution

With all parties ready and willing, the only remaining question was how to finance the Taiwan deal. Thomas came up with an innovative triangular arrangement that satisfied the mutual goals of three nations. The way it worked proved ingenious. Since the Taiwan wells would now produce a much larger sugar crop, most of the surplus could be exported for sale. Postwar Greece had a critical need for sugar. Greece had come dangerously close to falling under communist influence. Under the guidelines of the Truman Doctrine, the U.S. Economic Development Commission, carrying out its duties to administer foreign aid, appropriated money to help boost the Greek economy. Greece purchased Taiwanese sugar with American dollars, which then funded the irrigation system contract.

The money was placed in the joint venture account, and the work was completed on a cost-plus fee basis—in effect, a prefinanced contract.[29] This $2 million contract was a significant win for RMP. The money the client invested in the project was well spent. The size of the sugar crop that was exported paid for the entire cost of the project within an astonishing 28 months.

Upon receiving the financing, RMP conducted the hydrogeology and engineering studies, bought and shipped the equipment to Taiwan, and drilled and developed the water irrigation wells. By installing the wells and irrigating the fields during Taiwan's nine-month dry season, the Taiwan Sugar Corporation's sugar production doubled in size to approximately one million tons per year. Sugar became a major export of Taiwan, and this project was instrumental in restoring Taiwan's economic health after World War II by facilitating trade.[30]

RMP's success in locating underground sources of water and well development in Taiwan and in other parts of the world was based primarily on the skills of geologists who gained their professional experience in finding water in the arid southwestern states, particularly southern California. The project manager was Milton Rote, who worked for Ralph at BMP and was one of the original six engineers Ralph employed to begin RMP. Milt Rote went on to manage the construction division, and one of his most notable accomplishments was the completion of the Honolulu Airport over an eight-year period, for which he was nominated as man of the year by *Engineering News-Record* in the 1970s. Milt Rote and his wife, Mildred, relocated 43 times in the

Left and opposite: Photos on this and next page show RMP's Taiwanese and international team members at one of the groundwater wells developed for the sugar cane irrigation system.

course of their 73-year marriage, the majority of these moves to design and construct oil refineries and airports for RMP clients throughout the world.[31]

The reconnaissance field studies were completed by Dr. William I. Gardener, geologist, and David Stoner, civil engineer, both of whom temporarily left the U.S. Bureau of Reclamation to join the project team. Groundwater geologist Jim Holwerda was employed by RMP for this project straight out of graduate school at the University of Southern California and took classmate Richard S. Davis with him to Taiwan. Together, they determined the location of each well and then monitored the drilling, development, and water quality testing. Jim later became Dr. Holwerda, after receiving his doctorate in groundwater geology from the University of Southern California, and spent 28 years overseas on assignments with the company. Richard joined Jim on an assignment in Iraq to survey groundwater, after which Richard went to work for the Government of Saudi Arabia in its irrigation department.[32]

The Taiwan project was deemed a success for all parties involved and served as the cornerstone for RMP's remarkable future in water projects overseas. In 1950, the same year that its workforce reached 300, the company began a water resources survey and development program for the Government of India. The project was among the pioneering regional programs conducted by the company around the world. Designated "Project Elephant" by Ralph, the project involved the drilling and pump installation of 410 potable water wells throughout India. RMP would be active in India for more than 20 years, working on such projects as groundwater development and irrigation, mineral exploration, and oil refinery work near Bombay.[33]

SULFUR RECOVERY

SULFUR, ALSO CALLED BRIMSTONE, played a significant role in the evolution of science, medicine, and agriculture. Pre-Roman civilizations used it as a medicine, fumigant, bleaching agent, and even as incense in religious ceremonies. With the advent of the industrial revolution, sulfur became a major component in the manufacturing of thousands of products. It proved especially important to agriculture as a major ingredient of fertilizer. In fact, sulfur and its sister chemical, sulfuric acid, are so vital in numerous manufacturing processes that their output serves as a reliable indicator of the demand for products from U.S. businesses, and their production helps gauge the standard of living of societies around the world.

Although sulfur enjoys various highly profitable applications, it is not welcome in oil refining. Sulfur resides naturally in many "sour" natural gas fields. It occurs in the form of hydrogen sulfide, a highly corrosive and poisonous gas with an overpowering odor—a smell likened to that of rotten eggs. It can kill almost immediately. As a result, the oil and natural gas industries long searched for a way to recover the sulfur from hydrogen sulfide to protect its workers, minimize corrosion, reduce the odor, and, if possible, turn a profit.

Claus Kiln Process

The Claus Kiln process, invented in Germany, was found to be effective in recovering sulfur from hydrogen sulfide. The process involved reducing "sour" gas via incineration in a reduced atmosphere and then sending the reduced gas countercurrent through a converter, which extracted elemental sulfur. The final step was condensing the

Below and opposite: For many years, Ralph Parsons displayed a bright yellow free-form sulfur formation in a handsome glass case directly outside his office. The sulfur mound came from Hancock Oil's Los Angeles oil refinery and commemorated RMP as the world leader in gas processing and sulfur recovery.

elemental sulfur in sulfur condensers. Hancock Chemical Company, whose parent company was Hancock Oil, significantly improved the Claus Kiln process in the early 1950s.

To test the enhancements to the process, Hancock Oil retained RMP to design a plant using the improved technology for its Los Angeles refinery. "During the course of our work with Hancock, Milt Lewis cut a deal with the company whereby RMP acquired the rights to Hancock's Claus process," said Roland E. "Hap" Meissner, who worked for the company for 30 years in process engineering, project management, and business development.[1] This deal proved to be a stroke of brilliant contract negotiations. Milt understood that large profits could be realized from sulfur recovery, and now RMP owned the singular Claus process that could produce a constant source of valuable income for the company in years to come.

According to Hap, RMP proved adroit in promoting its rights to the Claus Kiln process in order to secure new refinery and "sour" natural gas business worldwide, and it patented many of its process and mechanical design components. In the heyday of sulfur recovery, RMP would sometimes design 15 sulfur recovery plants at once. The sulfur recovery process plants were designed by a team of engineers and six project managers who were responsible for the success of this market sector, which was critical to RMP's financial health.[2] Charles (Chuck) H. Terhune III, who initially worked in RMP's petroleum and chemical division and later became a Parsons senior vice president, was instrumental in the design specifications for several major components of the sulfur recovery process.

Chuck's father, Charles H. Terhune II, was a member of RMP's board and the deputy director of the Jet Propulsion Laboratory in association with the California Institute of Technology.[3]

Chuck described his company experience:

> *When I started at [the company], I specified the heat transfer equipment, fired furnaces, and filters. I was working on 15 fixed-priced projects at one time. RMP had a tight-knit group that designed all of these plants. The design, procurement, and field construction operations were fast paced and involved a significant amount of professional collaboration. Ralph had about six project managers that ran this work. I had a great time engineering these plants as a young man and had a lot of responsibility.*[4]

Two-Foot Yellow Sulfur Cube

In total, RMP designed and engineered more than 300 sulfur recovery plants using its patented processes. To commemorate the importance of the original patent, a two-foot cube of sulfur produced from the Hancock Oil sulfur recovery plant was displayed for many years in a glass case on the executive floor of the company's downtown Los Angeles headquarters and then in its Pasadena headquarters, which opened in 1974. It was a striking impression—a bright yellow cube of sulfur displayed against the background of the Pasadena headquarters' vivid red carpeting. All visitors to the executive floor, including future clients, would see this impressive display.[5]

RMP's geologists all had a strong sense of adventure and enthusiasm for their work. Their efforts ultimately helped countries such as India, Pakistan, Iran, Iraq, and Kuwait locate and develop previously undiscovered sources of life-sustaining, potable water and mineral deposits. Their legacy is the foundation upon which Parsons has built its global contributions to water resource infrastructure development.

Searching for Water in the Mideast

In 1951, RMP was selected to perform a groundwater study in various areas of Iran, which began with the siting of 200 exploratory wells. RMP's project manager was geologist Fred K. Houston, who joined RMP on July 10, 1944, less than one month after it was incorporated.[34] Fred was so highly regarded by his peers that a geological formation was named in his honor: the Houston Formation in the Danakil Depression in Ethiopia.[35] When he retired in 1960, he was a vice president with the company. Fred and his team started siting the exploratory wells during the first uprising against the Shah of Iran. After the study was completed, Fred returned to RMP's headquarters in downtown Los Angeles to write the groundwater report while out of harm's way.

The political unrest did not subside, and seven years passed before RMP was instructed to send the groundwater reports to Iran. These reports were then used to help develop groundwater in areas that were in critical need of water. This project eventually led to a collaboration with the C. Brewer Company of Hawaii; to a contract to design, engineer, and construct a large sugar refinery in Khuzestan, in southwestern Iran; and a series of contracts for the design and construction oversight of gas-processing plants for the Iranian National Oil Company.

In 1953, RMP was retained by the development board of the Government of Iraq under the only contract granted by Iraqi authorities to conduct groundwater surveys of all 14 *liwas* (provinces) in the country. A contract for the development of 50 wells in the Sinjar area of northwestern Iraq had been previously awarded to an American company named Resources Development Corporation.

Two other drilling outfits were also involved in the project. Harold T. Smith, an American company, was responsible for drilling 150 wells. Nashat Al Sinawi, an Iraqi company, was to install 10 wells east of Baghdad. RMP's agreement with the Iraqis included preparing contract documents and supervising the well drilling contractors. RMP sent over Jim Holwerda, as project geologist, and Richard Davis, both of whom had completed the Taiwan irrigation project. Charles Bettinger, another talented groundwater geologist; Stanley Butler, from the University of Southern California; other technical personnel; and a number of Iraqi trainees formed the team. Al Braithwaite, who always introduced himself as hailing from Enid, Oklahoma, was the initial project manager. Charles later became a noted Middle East groundwater expert.[36] Jim described the project activities:

> *I was sent over to Iraq as the project geologist and became the project manager after Al Braithwaite returned to the U.S. I was there for almost five years. We put in several hundred potable water supply wells and trained 20 or so Iraqis, who accompanied us on our field trips. Members of the RMP team traveled over 750,000 kilometers in Iraq and covered every* liwa *in the country.*[37]

While Jim was in Iraq, he met his future wife, Sandol (Bunny) Ortiz, the daughter of Paul and Anne Ortiz. Paul was the vice president of the Harold T. Smith Company that was drilling 150 water wells on the project. The Holwerdas were married in Baghdad in 1955. They returned to the United States in 1958, where Jim completed his doctorate with a thesis entitled "Groundwater Geology of Iraq." He went on to work in Ethiopia for 10 years, Australia for six, Singapore for three, and then he was assigned to RMP's London office and was responsible for business development. Jim felt comfortable at RMP because, as he put it, the company permitted him a wide degree of latitude to follow up on potential new projects:[38]

> *Ralph always treated me like a prince. Both he and Bill Leonhard [who became president and CEO after Ralph and Milt] always allowed me to pursue the opportunities I thought had merit.*[39]

The Iraqis continued the groundwater project for a total of nine years, even through the revolution of 1958. The company's involvement in the project led to Iraq's development board awarding RMP a contract for a large gas-processing and sulfur recovery plant in the city of Kirkuk. After delays exceeding a year, RMP formed a joint venture with Powergas, a British company that eventually completed the project.

Water: Key to the Growth of RMP

With these projects, the firm established its remarkable future in water projects overseas. Ralph realized water development was becoming very important to the growth of his company and was quick to seize all opportunities in this burgeoning area.

"Ralph Parsons really had one love and that was refining. That's where it all started for him—but then he made his money on USAID jobs overseas, primarily in water," said Bill Hall, president of WorleyParsons USA, a wholly owned subsidiary of the Worley Group.[40]

During the next several decades, the RMP groundwater team performed surveys in many countries, including Pakistan, Thailand, Lebanon, Kuwait, the United Arab Emirates, Algeria, Saudi Arabia, Egypt, and Vietnam.[41]

"Sour" Natural Gas Processing and Sulfur Recovery

In 1951, RMP built its first sulfur recovery plant for Consolidated Chemical Industries Inc., Baton Rouge, Louisiana. Sulfur recovery was an important byproduct of the oil and natural gas industry. In "sour" natural gas, the sulfur occurs as hydrogen sulfide, a highly poisonous substance. Because the oil and natural gas industries were producing so much hydrogen sulfide, developing a means to convert it

Batman Refinery

BATMAN, ALSO KNOWN AS ILUH, IS THE capital of the Batman province located in southeastern Turkey. It is situated in the Mesopotamian lowlands, just north of the Tigris River, in a region inhabited largely by the Kurds. The area surrounding Batman is Turkey's major oil-producing region. The refinery that RMP built in 1952 for Turkiye Petrolleri A.O. was the first one that started oil production as the area's chief economic activity. RMP designed, engineered, and provided construction oversight, as the refinery was built by mostly unskilled workers—a mammoth undertaking in what was then a largely underdeveloped part of the country.[1]

This project also required the construction of an oil collection system and pipeline from the fields to the refinery. A railroad adjacent to the refinery provided the only access. Therefore, the design of the facility and the dimensions for the vessels of the various processing units were constrained by the dimensions of the preexisting tunnels and bridges along the route from the jobsite to the seacoast.

To accomplish these tasks, more than 800 Turkish nationals were enrolled in an RMP training program and became electricians, welders, pipefitters, and other craftsmen. Eventually, Turkiye Petrolleri A.O. was able to take over and run its own facility. The Batman job established the precedent for managing many other RMP refineries in countries where there was a shortage of skilled craftsmen.[2]

Above: James E. Halferty was RMP's first foreign operations manager. In 1990, he wrote a memoir based on his career for his children entitled "Foreign Operations or Life without Father," which was a valuable resource for this book.

Left: The finished oil refinery in Batman, Turkey, was the country's first. Negotiating the contract was a learning experience for Parsons.

Negotiation Difficulties, Including a Word-by-Word Contract Review in Two Languages

It would be an understatement to say that negotiating the Batman refinery contract was a steep learning curve for a company that had fewer than a handful of international projects under its belt. The difficult process illustrates just how green RMP really was to global business. To RMP and the Turkiye Petrolleri A.O. representatives' credit, they saw the negotiations through to the end so the refinery could be built.

Armed with a draft of the proposed contract, RMP representatives went through the document page by page and word by word with their counterparts. Each sentence was translated into Turkish and carefully explained, so the task took several long and exhausting weeks. Despite this snail's pace, RMP thought the process seemed to be going well. According to one participant, after each page the Turkiye Petrolleri A.O. representatives would say, in effect, "okay."[3]

After the painstaking line-by-line review ended, the Turkiye Petrolleri A.O. representatives left for a few days to analyze the material on their own. As RMP's chief negotiator James Halferty recalled, "I thought that as soon as they came back, we would probably have a few points to discuss and clarify, and then we could sign the document and get on with the job."[4]

The "Okay" Conundrum

Instead, the Turkiye Petrolleri A.O. representatives returned to announce they did not agree with anything in the contract. Asked what all the "okays" meant, they explained that "okays" meant only that they had heard the words, not that Turkiye Petrolleri A.O. agreed with or even understood them.[5]

"We then commenced a terribly tedious and nerve-racking six-day week, working all day and many evenings, that lasted almost two months," said Halferty. "It was necessary to go over every word and phrase, translating everything as best we could and then try to explain the meaning."[6]

The RMP team discovered that their Turkiye Petrolleri A.O. counterparts had never heard of a cost-plus-fixed-fee agreement and that they suspected it might be some kind of trick. RMP was adamant, however, that it was the only kind of contract possible under the circumstances.

Moreover, Turkiye Petrolleri A.O. wanted the contract translated into Turkish with that language controlling the agreement. RMP officials explained that no one in the company spoke or read Turkish, and, because RMP was responsible for the work, the project had to be governed by an English contract. When Turkiye Petrolleri A.O. realized that certain technical appendixes such as design specifications could not be adequately translated into Turkish, it was conceded that at least the appendixes could be in English. After long negotiations, the two sides finally agreed that the contract would be written and signed in both languages and that each language would have equal weight.[7]

A Preview of Things to Come

The Batman project, while one of RMP's earliest international projects, nevertheless exhibited some key characteristics that would eventually become strongly associated with the firm: the ability to manage a project in what was geographically, and sometimes technically, uncharted territory; diplomatically forge a solution tailored to the client; and establish viable working arrangements with the project stakeholders. Indeed, these characteristics would stand RMP in good stead into the 21st century.

The Batman refinery was the harbinger of RMP's growth in the Middle East. Its ability to work with the intricacies of Middle Eastern business, politics, and religion became a key element in the company's rise to global preeminence.

The project also set a pattern for RMP's work on refineries, sulfur recovery, and natural gas processing plants in other countries and the United States. Over the next few decades, as new sources of oil were discovered and oil fields were developed, RMP constructed several major oil refineries and cornered the market on designing and building sulfur recovery and natural gas processing plants.

into elemental sulfur and then sell it to those who could benefit from its use would prove very lucrative. RMP had obtained the rights to the Claus Kiln process that recovered sulfur from hydrogen sulfide.

Within a few years, the company had become the world leader in "sour" gas processing combined with sulfur recovery, with 20 plants operating in the United States and Canada. Indeed, the Claus Kiln process became an important path leading to new refinery work for RMP. Typically, after the company designed a sulfur recovery plant, the same client would ask RMP to design or retrofit equipment or process units connecting to the recovery plant, and then to the units that feed those units and so on.[42]

In many instances, RMP was retained to work on all aspects of the refinery. Ralph and his staff further developed this core group of petroleum clients by providing proven and reliable engineering involved in operating a refinery.

Opposite: The Consolidated Chemical sulfur recovery plant in Baton Rouge, Louisiana, was the first of its kind designed by RMP. The completion of this plant, followed shortly thereafter with the company's obtaining the rights to the Claus Kiln process from Hancock Oil, resulted in RMP's world-wide preeminence in sulfur recovery design and engineering. When tallied, RMP completed over 300 projects involving sulfur recovery.

The First Overseas Refinery

In 1952, RMP designed and built its first grassroots refinery in the Republic of Turkey for Turkiye Petrolleri A.O. Located in the city of Batman in remote eastern Turkey, the refinery was to process crude oil from two newly discovered oil fields.

Ralph Parsons knew how much was riding on this refinery, and Dante Boccalero, who spent 45 years with the company, the last 16 as logistics manager supervising material shipping, travel coordination, and procurement of project supplies, recalled how Ralph worked 16 to 18 hours a day just to land the job and then make it all come together:[43]

> *He concentrated so hard on that job because it was [the company's first] grassroots refinery and we had to get experience. He was determined to get that job, and he did. From there, we went on and started building many, many refineries.*[44]

RMP's initial projects in the petroleum, defense, and international markets affirmed Ralph's already established reputation for reliability and performance, despite often seemingly insurmountable challenges. The legacy of these projects formed the basis of RMP's roots in offering exceptional project management. His company would be noted for this same skill in later years during the execution of massive and complex projects around the globe.

The drafting room of RMP's downtown Los Angeles headquarters was a hub of work productivity. The draftsmen were the key to RMP's reputation for producing quality design documents. Inset: An early RMP photo showing women employees at their desks.

CHAPTER FOUR

THE POSTWAR EXPANSION

1955–1964

The success of the company depends on its project managers. If a project manager's jobs go well, the company will prosper.

—Ralph Parsons, in an early memo to his project managers, as reported in *Parsons News & Views*, 1969, No. 19, p. 7

IN ITS FIRST 10 YEARS OF operation, RMP grew rapidly, built petroleum plants for major oil companies, acquired a drilling company, designed the first of many facilities for the AEC, engineered a missile launch site, entered into the international water resources market, designed and constructed its first overseas refinery, and ventured into sulfur recovery process design.

Ralph expanded the company into these diverse areas, partly because of his own interests and experience and partly because of his skill in hiring—and retaining—dedicated and talented people. By combining his business acumen with the drive and strengths of his staff, RMP would win contracts to design, engineer, build, and/or manage every type of infrastructure needed during the post–World War II expansion.

By the 1950s, RMP had built its core business and cornered the market on designing sulfur recovery and natural gas processing plants that, at its apex, produced 80 percent of the world's recovered sulfur. RMP broke into airport design and engineering in 1958 with the award-winning Dhahran Air Terminal in Saudi Arabia. In 1960, it began a groundwater survey for Kuwait and then designed a demonstration saline water conversion plant at Point Loma, California. RMP was also involved with the beginning of the space race by designing the Apollo test program facilities for the National Aeronautics and Space Administration (NASA).[1]

Global Expansion

Ralph was always eager for expansion, and the international conditions after World War II opened new markets to pursue. The growth of the company during this decade reflects his enthusiasm and confidence that RMP could complete complex engineering and construction projects anywhere in the world.

Whenever an opportunity presented itself, Ralph, Milt Lewis, or a member of RMP's key executive team was there to promote RMP's successful track record and enthusiasm to take on new challenges. In pursuing these global opportunities, RMP's engineers learned valuable lessons in diplomacy, along with a respect for and insight into diverse economic, political, and religious beliefs.

David Goodrich, who began his professional career with the firm in Saudi Arabia in human resource management and is now vice president of human resources for the entire corporation, said:

> *One of the main reasons RMP got so involved internationally back [then] was partly because that's*

The globe in the photograph with Ralph Parsons and Milt Lewis was featured in many of the company's trade show exhibits to exemplify RMP's worldwide capabilities.

where the money was being spent in the developing world. Typically, those countries would want us to come in and they would say, build us a refinery, give us the operating manuals. But there was always a transfer of technology component in it, and this allowed a lot of these countries to build up engineering companies in these areas of the world. So it's a strong tradition of passing on wisdom to other people.[2]

Self-Reliance and Autonomy Reflect Staff Characteristics

Ralph Parsons put great stock in the ability of the people he hired to manage projects without a lot of direction from him. He emphasized self-reliance, and it is not surprising that his company attracted self-motivated, independent people who were willing to bet on themselves and their abilities to succeed, regardless of—and often because of—the challenges they faced. They welcomed the opportunity to succeed—or fail—on their own merits.

In his memos and correspondence to key executives, division heads, and project managers, Ralph would encourage them to maintain their belief in themselves and in their "strength, capacity, responsibility, and authority." Furthermore, he would insist that each manager "must find

A Guide for Project Managers

RMP FURNISHED ITS PROJECT MANAgers with a three-ring binder that contained a manual of useful company information and guidelines.[1] The manual included a list of qualifications the company required of its project managers. Although some of the phrasing is outdated, the basic principles are as timely today as when they were written:

Characteristics of a Parsons Project Manager

The project manager represents The Ralph M. Parsons Company to his client. Within the guidelines established in this manual, he has the responsibility to serve both the company and the client. The successful project manager is one who instills within his team a strong sense of TEAMWORK, URGENCY, and ENTHUSIASM.

Qualifications

In selecting project managers and measuring their performance, we look for characteristics and high-level skills in the following areas:

1. Leadership—Can he give independent and consistent direction? Does he set a "follow me" example? Can he lead by quiet persuasion? Can he distinguish between the leader and the driver?
2. Strength—Does he have the qualifications to lead his project team's moral fiber as well as technical experience? A leader looks and acts like a leader, on and off the job.
3. Ability to Recognize Basic Objectives—The first move on a job is to identify clearly what is to be done. Can he distinguish the essential from the minutiae?

some way to accomplish [the] mission." He counseled them to be "resourceful, skillful, self-reliant, and determined."[3]

Ed Cramsie, who joined the company's civil engineering group in 1959, stated, "I was really impressed with the people. At the time, the company was really just beginning to take off. So it was a pretty exciting place to work. It was in the early days of the buildup of the missile program, and RMP was getting a lot of that work, and I just saw a great future with that company."[4]

Ed's first assignment was working on the access roads to the first Minuteman base. He worked on many prominent international projects in the Middle East, Southeast Asia, and the Dominican Republic. Ed then went on to manage the company's computer department in the early 1970s, held positions in operations, and was RMP's engineering manager before he retired in 1996.[5]

Salary: Not Always Everything

This strong focus on self-reliance and autonomy that the company offered to its prospective employees became a key selling point during the hiring process. In addition to seeking out these unusual "business" traits, RMP maintained a hiring policy of

4. Ability to Plan—Successful work generally doesn't just happen. It is caused to happen by diligent execution of a carefully prepared plan.
5. Ability to Organize the Project Staff—A successful team can be much stronger than the sum of its individual stars. Can the project manager organize his staff to get the most out of his assigned resources?
6. Ability to Delegate Properly—How does the successful project manager free himself of routine activities and still maintain effective control of his project?
7. Toughness and Resiliency—Few projects proceed without problems. The project manager must be correct in his management judgments and stick by them. No one can win them all, and he must rebound from adversity and resume control.
8. Accept Responsibility—The buck stops at the desk of the project manager. He must think through problems and state his position without hedging. Accept upper-level management decisions and support them.
9. Client Relations—The client is why we are in business. Never criticize openly. Work closely to understand his position and to ensure that he understands yours.
10. Be Flexible and Resourceful—There is more than one way to skin a cat. Be imaginative in solving problems when ordinary methods fail.
11. Attitude—Few problems totally defy solution. The first essential step is to adopt a "can-do" attitude.
12. Candor—Does he place his cards on the table? Most problems can be solved if caught in their incipient stage. He must first recognize that a problem threatens and be willing to talk about it.
13. Sense of Perspective—Can he keep his eye on the target—to design and build a plant, and avoid peripheral distractions?
14. Special Foreign Jobs—Particularly those of huge size in remote locations involving unusual client relationships, a hostile climate, foreign language and culture, untrained third-world country or indigenous labor forces, long logistics chains, and exasperating government red tape on visas, customs, taxes, and insurance matters, call for project managers with unique skills and attitudes, who must be carefully groomed for the particular job in hand.

paying its new employees the same salaries they had earned at their previous jobs instead of offering a raise for coming to work at RMP.

Company records described the rationale behind this policy: "If a man really believed in the company and its future, he was willing to forego a salary increase to start with. He knew that as the company prospered, so would he."[6]

This policy also reflected Ralph's entrepreneurial character. He had invested his own money in starting the firm and believed that his staff should exhibit a willingness to take a minimal risk to join his company.

As RMP grew, most employees certainly did prosper. Other engineering or construction firms may have paid higher starting salaries, but Ralph offered his staff unparalleled independence. Of course, along with this freedom came significant responsibility. For many, the technical challenges and professional future presented by RMP proved more attractive than the initial paycheck.

Project Management Approach

In the early years of the company, Ralph was known for his attention to detail in the guidance and instructions he gave his staff.

Jim Holwerda, who worked very closely with Ralph on many of the company's initial international groundwater and mining projects, recalled, "I soon learned that Ralph was a perfectionist and insisted upon accuracy, neatness, and correct spelling. He would instruct on the proper folding of a letter so that it would be creased properly to fit into its envelope. Ralph told us everything we did reflected on the company's image."[7]

But with the hundreds of employees joining the firm, Ralph's management style evolved out of necessity. He began to entrust key management positions with greater authority. He created an organization that would continue to promote the autonomous behavior so cherished at RMP along with ensuring personal accountability. In doing so, he relied on his core beliefs in developing his managerial structure: know the inner workings of the operations, follow your gut instincts, and exhibit confidence. Ralph's own memos (quoted earlier in this chapter)[8] and the stories told by his staff reflect the freedom of his division and project managers to develop their own approaches to solving problems. In short, he delegated responsibility.

Knisely Dreher, simply known as K, described how Ralph encouraged project managers to assume responsibility and call their own shots. K started out as an estimator, then a project engineer, became a registered architect, and managed Middle East business development. Highlights of K's career include the Minuteman and Titan II missile programs, pool reactor projects, and building the Yanbu Industrial City in Saudi Arabia.[9] He said:

> *I think the secret to the company's success goes right back to Ralph Parsons and his philosophy, his techniques of management, and the type of people he brought in. What made it so unique was the fact that you were allowed to assume as much responsibility as you felt you could handle. This was unlike a lot of companies where you were restricted and directed. What this did was encourage people to act on their own.*[10]

It is evident by the firm's accomplishments that this autonomy produced results. What is also notable about Ralph's management style is that he had little use for long-range corporate planning. In one memo to his management team, Ralph expressed his great displeasure with the overly complicated organization charts and graphs that crossed his desk.[11]

What he did mandate was management continuity to ensure the success of the company's projects. Ralph and Milt Lewis made sure that for every undertaking they committed to, anywhere in the world, the designated management staff was assigned to that project for its duration. It was each division manager's responsibility to hire staff and then solve the operational problems to comply with this mandate. Ralph outlined his expectations to the division managers in brusque terms:

> *You are on your own. You have no one to lean on. You are responsible for the successful operation of your division. It is your responsibility to smooth the troubled waters. If company policy is established which you think interferes with successful operation of your division, you can find no comfort in hiding behind it. Making divisional decisions is your responsibility.*[12]

As the division managers grappled with operational issues, the project managers oversaw the technical, cost, and scheduling aspects of the individual projects. They were trusted to "deliver a reasonable profit to the company" and to establish a relationship with the client "that will ensure favorable consideration for follow-on work."[13] Ralph and Milt developed this breakdown of responsibilities for a "Project Management Team" to ensure speedy decisions and avoid costly field delays.

In addition to encouraging the division and project managers to take on operational issues, Ralph was equally emphatic with the precontracts staff to develop quality proposals and marketing material. Greg Pearson, former precontracts manager, described the history of the department and the dedication of its staff:

Ralph Parsons was a real entrepreneurial, [and an] interesting guy. The company had been marketing itself more or less successfully during its entire existence—[it] had a lot of successful growth without major acquisitions—[and had entered] into new markets. [Precontracts is] what most engineering companies call the marketing department. In other words, the materials to help the company acquire new business—statements of qualifications, brochures, proposals, presentation materials. When you work on proposals, sometimes it's an all-day, all-night, weekend affair. They had good people in that department.[14]

Greg started at RMP as a technical editor and then worked on long-term assignments in Saudi Arabia and Louisiana prior to managing precontracts. He left the company in 1999 and said, "I have a lot of good memories. I worked with some great people. I think I have lifelong friendships."[15]

Ralph was also very adept at personally acknowledging his staff by giving motivational plaques on special occasions. Alan Duncan fondly remembered this aspect of Ralph's personality:

He would send birthday [plaques]. They were little, framed with glass. I have one, which I still treasure. It's about business development, and the theme is "Keep up a full head of steam and whistle at all the curves." His plaques were themes to live by. [They] killed two birds with one stone. It was a nice gift, but it was also words of wisdom.[16]

In 1955, RMP was hired to engineer the largest "sour" gas and sulfur recovery plant in the world in Lacq, France. Five phases of construction were involved, with the first commencing in 1955.

SIGNIFICANT PROJECTS

1955–1964

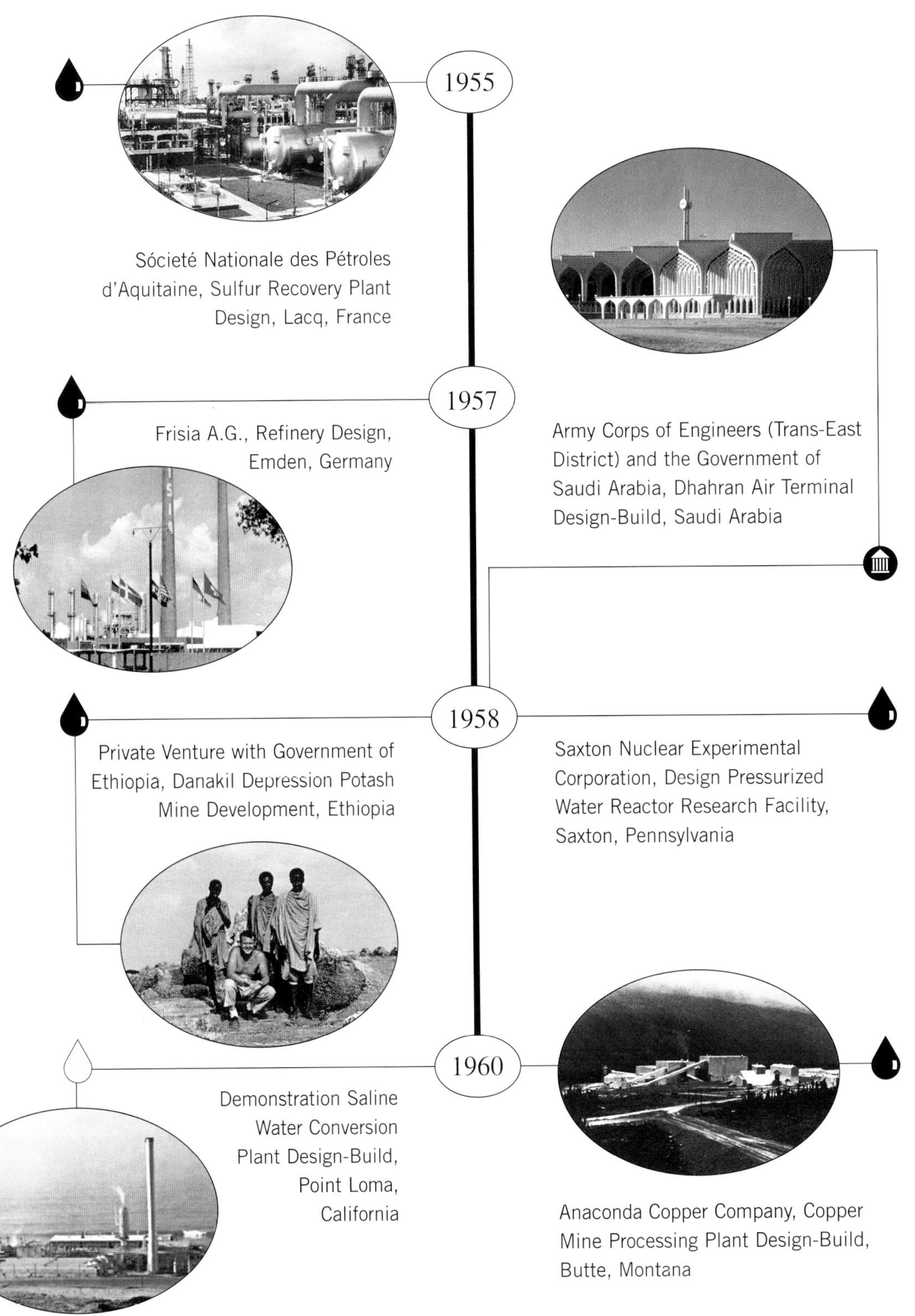

1955

Sóciete Nationale des Pétroles d'Aquitaine, Sulfur Recovery Plant Design, Lacq, France

1957

Frisia A.G., Refinery Design, Emden, Germany

Army Corps of Engineers (Trans-East District) and the Government of Saudi Arabia, Dhahran Air Terminal Design-Build, Saudi Arabia

1958

Private Venture with Government of Ethiopia, Danakil Depression Potash Mine Development, Ethiopia

Saxton Nuclear Experimental Corporation, Design Pressurized Water Reactor Research Facility, Saxton, Pennsylvania

1960

Demonstration Saline Water Conversion Plant Design-Build, Point Loma, California

Anaconda Copper Company, Copper Mine Processing Plant Design-Build, Butte, Montana

LEGEND

Commercial — Energy/Petroleum and Chemical — Government — Transportation — Water

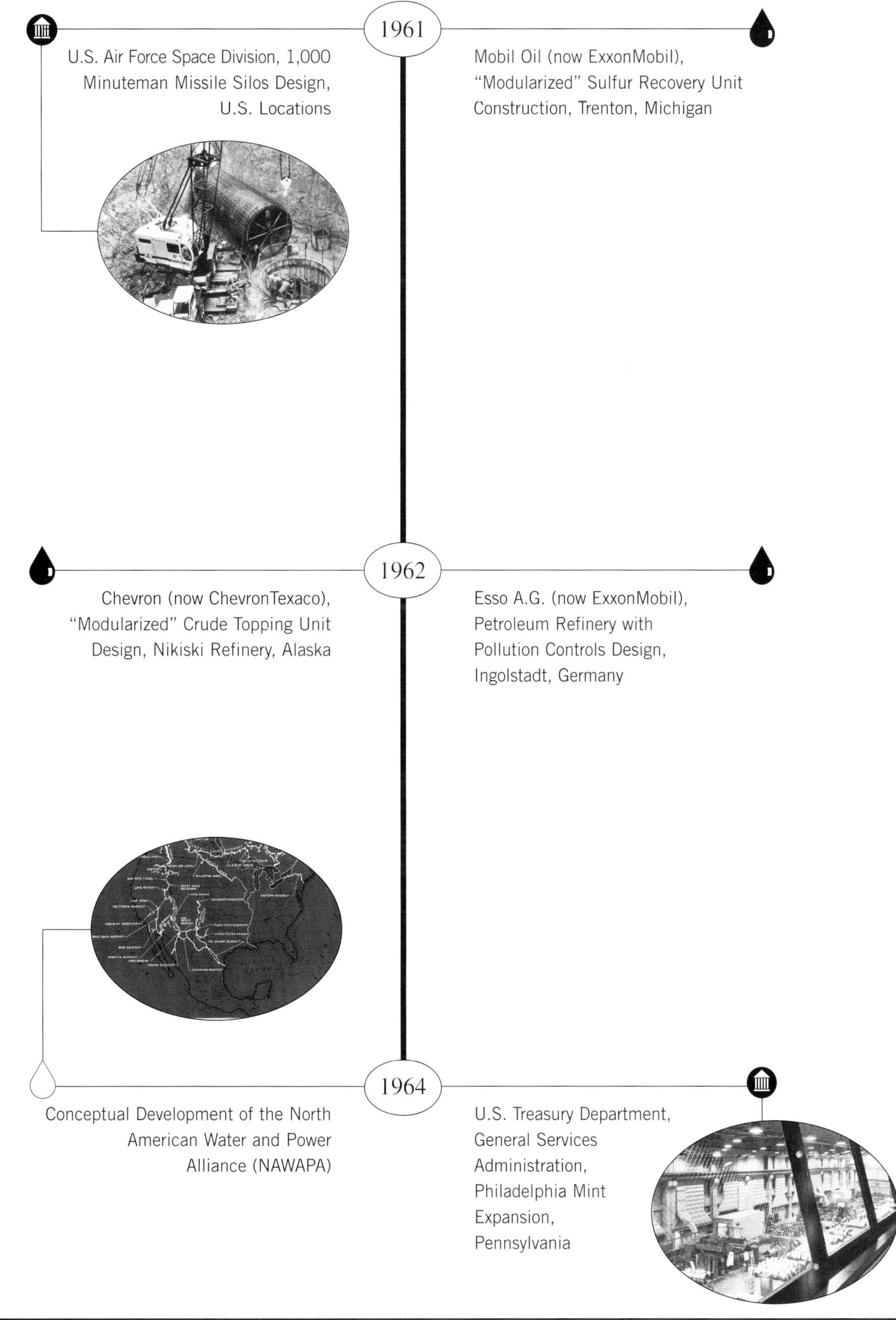
1961
U.S. Air Force Space Division, 1,000 Minuteman Missile Silos Design, U.S. Locations
Mobil Oil (now ExxonMobil), "Modularized" Sulfur Recovery Unit Construction, Trenton, Michigan
1962
Chevron (now ChevronTexaco), "Modularized" Crude Topping Unit Design, Nikiski Refinery, Alaska
Esso A.G. (now ExxonMobil), Petroleum Refinery with Pollution Controls Design, Ingolstadt, Germany
1964
Conceptual Development of the North American Water and Power Alliance (NAWAPA)
U.S. Treasury Department, General Services Administration, Philadelphia Mint Expansion, Pennsylvania

Alan joined the company in 1964 and was a former business development manager for RMP's Systems Division. Until he retired in 1986, he was a key member of the sales and marketing teams that developed the strategies to win landmark projects such as the Northeast Corridor and U.S. Postal Service (USPS) Program. Alan also fostered relationships with the Department of Transportation, the U.S. Navy, the Army Corps of Engineers, and the Department of Energy, all of which are important customers of Parsons.[17]

Ralph's management style worked. RMP continued its rapid expansion and built up the strength of its core businesses. By the end of 20 years in operations, RMP had completed major projects in water resources, airport design, national defense, energy systems, and oil production including the extraordinarily successful sulfur recovery plants.

The design of the Frisia A.G. petroleum refinery in Emden, Germany, was one of eight European refinery projects undertaken by RMP in 1958.

France's Mega Sulfur-Recovery Plant: A True Megaproject

A notable project that began in 1955 was the design of the sulfur-recovery plant for Sóciété Nationale des Pétroles d'Aquitaine, a company organized to explore for, and develop, fuel sources in France. The same year RMP built its first sulfur-recovery plant in Louisiana, 1951, the Societe Nationale des Petroles d'Aquitaine discovered a huge gas deposit near the village of Lacq, some 370 miles south of Paris, France. After seven test wells were drilled, the gas reserves were estimated at an astonishing 8.8 trillion cubic feet, but with a hydrogen sulfide content of 15 percent and carbon dioxide at 10 percent, the gas was extremely "sour."[18]

Based on its unsurpassed expertise in the field, RMP was hired in 1955 to develop a plant that would process the "sour" gas, recover the sulfur, and separate the fluids. In accordance with RMP's master plan, the Lacq plant was developed in five phases to process 750 million cubic feet of raw gas and recover 4,000 long tons of sulfur each day, making it the largest plant of its kind in the world.

By the mid-1960s, Lacq increased its efficiency, producing one billion cubic feet of gas per day (a 5,000-ton-per-day sulfur capacity) while providing natural gas to Paris and other major cities throughout Europe. The resulting gas generated as much energy as six million tons of coal annually.[19] Natural gas from this deposit is still being processed today.

The Beginning of Modularization

Sulfur recovery also led to RMP's adapting the concept of modularization; that is, designing and building portions of a facility or operating unit in sections or "modules." In 1961, RMP applied modularization on a sulfur recovery unit fabricated in Norwalk, California, that was shipped for installation to the Mobil Oil refinery in Trenton, Michigan.

The next year, RMP designed a 22,000-barrel-per-day crude topping unit in two modules for Chevron's Nikiski refinery on Alaska's Kenai Peninsula. The two skid-mounted modules were preassembled in two months on a converted naval vessel at Tacoma, Washington. The 130- and 280-ton modules were welded to the deck of a barge that was then towed 1,600 miles from Tacoma to Nikiski. When the modules arrived, they were skidded 4,000 feet to a previously prepared site and installed.[20] This construction technique became vitally important in the company's future two decades later on Alaska's North Slope.

Oil Production

Given Ralph's primary interest and credentials in the petroleum and chemical industry and sulfur-recovery process, the company continued with designing and building oil production facilities. In 1957, RMP won a contract to design a petroleum refinery for Frisia A.G. in the port town of Emden, Germany. It was one of eight European refineries being engineered or that had been built by RMP.[21]

This refinery was followed in 1962 by the design of a petroleum refinery in Ingolstadt, Germany, for Esso A.G. (now ExxonMobil) that was ahead of its time in its emphasis on pollution control and plant beautification. By this time, the company was also involved in refinery projects in Canada and in 18 Latin American countries. The capabilities not only to design and engineer, but to build refineries required that RMP hire skilled labor to construct these facilities. This growth greatly expanded the number of people the company employed. By 1964, RMP employed 7,000 worldwide.[22]

This decade also brought a key manager to the Petroleum and Chemical Division, who made great contributions to the company. Otha C. (Charlie) Roddey joined RMP in 1961 as a business development engineer. In 1965, he was promoted to vice president of process engineering and then senior vice president and manager of the Petroleum and Chemical Division, which, at that time, was responsible for over 50 percent of RMP's revenue. Charlie became president of RMP and was elected to its board of directors in 1977. Later he served as a member of Parsons' board of directors.[23] He recalled his experience joining RMP:

> *I was recruited by Bob Peaslee, vice president, to be RMP's sales engineer based in New York City to call on major oil clients. We had about 30 engineers in sales. Ralph Parsons and Milt Lewis called us "peddlers." They personally referred to themselves as such, and to be called a peddler was considered a great compliment—you were in the same league as them.*[24]

The Danakil Potash Project, Ethiopia

Like sulfur, potash is used primarily as an agricultural fertilizer because it is a good source of soluble potassium, a key plant nutrient. Potash mining plays a relatively obscure but important role in RMP's history. Ralph needed to find a market that could augment any "down cycles" in refinery construction and would reduce the dramatic fluctuations in overhead and RMP's ability to maintain a significant worldwide staff.

The sizable engineering and construction endeavors undertaken by RMP required a great amount of labor in order to bring a facility "on line." Ralph could not afford to lose or lay off a large number of staff at the end of a large project and then hope to rehire them when the next "big one" hit. Jim Holwerda, the geologist who had been instrumental

Like Ralph, many of RMP's project managers were amateur photographers. This picture was supervised by the late Charlie Bettinger, one of Parsons' core group of geologists who would travel the globe, while surveying Ethiopia. He is with three Danakils (Afars) in the fumerole/hot spring area of Dallol Mountain, about one-quarter mile from the Parsons camp in the Danakil depression, the bottom of which is 410 feet below sea level. All of the natural surroundings in the picture are solid salt.

THE *ARGO*

NO STORY OF RMP WOULD BE COMplete without mentioning the *Argo*, the company yacht that played an important role in entertaining clients. Purchasing the *Argo* dovetailed with Ralph's love of boats. Being a son of a fisherman, Ralph grew up on the water. His first job as a pre-teenager was as a lobsterman off the coast of Long Island. Ralph chose to serve in the U.S. Navy in World War I and in World War II, as a partner in BMP, built shipyards that produced hundreds of Liberty Ships.

The *Argo*'s Predecessor

Almost 14 years after Ralph founded RMP, the company purchased the *Dangin*, a 190-foot, steel-hulled motor yacht built in 1950. Its previous owner, shipping magnate Daniel K. Ludwig and his wife, Ginny, named the yacht using a combination of their first names, Dan and Ginny (Dangin). Daniel was one of RMP's financial backers in its potash mining endeavors, and the Dangin was one of the three largest yachts built post–World War II. Ralph renamed it the *Argo*, after the ship in Greek mythology in which Jason and his Argonauts pursued the Golden Fleece.[1] As the company yacht, the *Argo* served as an unusual venue to host clients ranging from heads of state to captains of industry. The *Argo* was also for Ralph's personal use, and occasionally he allowed key staff access to the yacht as a "perk."

The *Argo*, one of the world's largest yachts built after World War II, was a unique setting for RMP to host and entertain clients.

Spacious Accommodations

The *Argo*'s large salon provided seating for 20, and the teak quarterdeck could seat 20 more. It could accommodate 40 additional guests by using the sun and boat decks. The formal dining room seated 16, and the den seated eight. There were five spacious air-conditioned staterooms with baths.[2] It was powered by two 950-horsepower diesel engines, carried 78 tons of fresh water, and had the capability to distill seawater into fresh water at the rate of up to seven tons per day.[3]

Ralph loved being on the ocean and envisioned designing yachts to support the creation of a viable marine division within RMP. While this idea never came to fruition, he had meticulous models made to test their design. Several of these models, such as the one photographed, are carefully stored at Parsons' headquarters.

Ralph may not have been completely satisfied with the *Argo*, which might account for his interest in building a better boat. Ralph decided to employ a yacht designer to design, and then build, models of yachts. Jake Kostyzak began his career with RMP in 1962 on the Titan II program as a mechanical engineer. He worked on the Ingalls shipyard design project and was integral to the Chemical Stockpile Disposal Program (CSDP) for almost 18 years. Jake was CSDP's director when he retired in 2004. He described how intent Ralph was on perfecting a design:

> *I'd go over once a week to visit Mario Caldi [the yacht designer], and Ralph would pop in occasionally to say hello. All of these yachts that were designed, models were built of them, actual working models. They had electric engines in them and radio-controlled guidance systems and all kinds of things. They were working models—beautiful, beautiful ships. The last one that was designed, I guess Ralph finally decided he was going to build that [one]. Then just before they signed the contract, I guess Ralph decided to hold up for some reason or other, and it never got started.*[4]

Graham Gosling, business manager of WorleyParsons USA, tells how latter day executives at Parsons inadvertently rediscovered the yacht models years after Ralph's death:

> *Back in the 1980s, the firm had the idea of refurbishing cruise ships, thinking this could be a real potential market for us. We hired a guy who was an architect. His whole thing was to go out and look at cruise ships that were maybe 10–15 years old and come up with a design refurbishment. In doing that, he found that there was some sort of [storage area] on the roof of Parsons' world headquarters that contained various boat models that Mr. Parsons had commissioned. The architect also found photographs of various swimming pools in Los Angeles [that] had giant fans to create various ripple patterns. He was doing elementary research, like wind panel testing for cars.*[5]

Pegasus II

Instead of building a yacht, Ralph decided to buy the *Pegasus II*, which was a smaller vessel than the *Argo*. He purchased the *Pegasus II* with his personal funds, and it was solely for his use. The company sold the *Argo* after Ralph's death in 1974. The *Pegasus II* was eventually sold by Parsons' estate.

on the Taiwan and Iraq groundwater surveys, brought to Ralph a potential solution that involved developing a potash mine in Ethiopia.[25]

In 1954, while working on the Iraqi groundwater project, Jim was asked to accompany Thomas J. Smith, an RMP engineer in Beirut, on a trip that included Ethiopia to investigate the occurrence of sulfur in the Danakil Depression, considered to be one of the largest single geologic features on earth. It was immediately apparent to Jim that the sulfur was of little economic interest; however, there were immense deposits of saline and potash minerals. After documenting his findings, Jim returned to the groundwater project in Iraq for three years and then returned to RMP headquarters in 1957.[26]

Upon Jim's return, Ralph mentioned his concerns over the company's fluctuating overhead. Ralph asked Jim if he had some thoughts on how to address this problem.

He said, "Ralph, remember that you are asking a geologist. I believe that one way to protect the company would be to obtain a significant ownership position in an essential natural resource from which income would flow, regardless of the company workload or overhead."[27]

Ralph asked for an example of such a natural resource, and Jim recounted his findings at the Danakil Depression and suggested potassium—one of the three major elements needed to grow plants and fertilize crops. Potassium is found in potash, which was abundant in the Danakil Depression. If additional investors could be found, a consistent source of income could be secured for RMP. Jim was tasked by Ralph to find a way to promote this project.

Through his personal business contacts, Jim arranged for a meeting with shipping magnate and financier Daniel K. Ludwig, who was at that time one of the wealthiest persons in the world. He owned the largest private shipping fleet and was father of the bulk cargo carriers common today.[28]

In the course of the first meeting with Daniel and Ralph, Jim presented the information on the Danakil Depression and sold Daniel on the idea of investing in the development of the potash mine.

Daniel and Ralph met privately after the meeting and worked out a deal whereby Daniel would

Above left: Jess Burks was one of RMP's earliest executives. He had astute organizational skills and could be considered a forerunner of a corporate project controls director or operations vice president. His advice was highly sought after by program and project managers, particularly when pursuing or implementing projects that required a significant amount of the company's resources.

Below: RMP wrote the specifications for the Curtiss-Wright Corporation's research reactor and laboratory that was used to develop nuclear technologies.

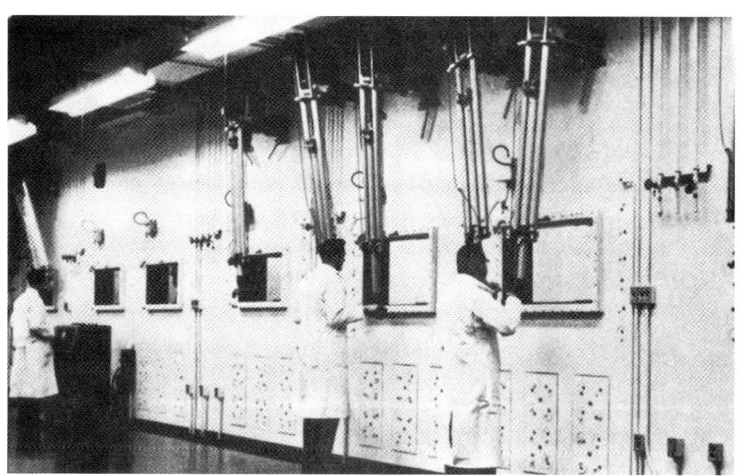

RMP's equipment was used in the survey of sunken ships in the Suez Canal after the 1956 hostilities.

have exclusive shipping rights and RMP would carry out the exploration work, plant design, construction, and mining operations. RMP and Daniel's subsidiary, Seatankers, would each own 50 percent of the venture. While working out the particulars of the potash project, Ralph concurrently made an offer to purchase Daniel's yacht, the *Dangin*, which Ralph later renamed the *Argo*.[29]

After negotiating the rights to develop the mine with the Ethiopian government, field work began in 1958. Jim managed the project with support from Jess C. Burks, who was a highly regarded senior executive of RMP's technical staff.[30]

Jess was a chemical engineer and joined RMP in 1948. He served as RMP's engineering and construction manager and its executive vice president before retiring in 1968.[31] Charlie Bettinger, who had been instrumental in the 1953 Iraqi groundwater project, was the lead geologist. The project team consisted of 10 Americans, 10 Europeans (Italians, Greeks, and Armenians), and 15 Eritreans from Asmara, 10 support staff in Asmara, and approximately 300 Danakils or Afars.[32]

Word spread of the magnitude of the deposit and generated considerable interest from mining, oil, and fertilizer companies, which enhanced both RMP's and Seatankers' reputations. However, because of the safety concerns regarding the flooding in the mine, the production of potash never reached fruition.[33]

Both Daniel and Ralph decided to withdraw from the potash venture in 1967. This venture did lead to other mining projects, the purchase of the *Argo*, and—should the political situation between Ethiopia and Eritrea stabilize—perhaps a future opportunity.

Expansion of Nuclear Experience and Commercial and Aerospace Projects

In this decade, RMP designed and engineered 25 nuclear-related projects, primarily in the United States, but also in India and Italy. RMP continued its top-secret work for Idaho National Engineering Laboratory (INEL) and began designing projects for Lockheed's (now Lockheed Martin) nuclear aircraft development center in Georgia.[34]

In 1958, RMP was selected as the design engineer for the Saxton Nuclear Experimental Corporation's developmental pressurized water reactor. Located midway between Pittsburgh and Harrisburg, Pennsylvania, this was the second commercial nuclear facility built in the United States. Between 1962 and 1972, it was primarily used for research and training.[35]

Curtiss-Wright Corporation, the legacy company of the legendary aviation pioneers the Wright brothers and Glenn Curtiss, retained RMP in 1956 to develop detailed specifications for the research reactor and radioactive materials laboratory building in Quehanna, Pennsylvania, which would develop nuclear jet engines and conduct research in nucleonics, metallurgy, electronics, chemicals, and plastics.[36]

Between 1958 and 1965, the company designed a test building and laboratory for Atomics International, a division of Rockwell (now a part of Boeing), and the Atomic Energy Commission (AEC) in Santa Susana, California.[37]

Another key individual who joined RMP in 1960 was Joe Volpe Jr., who came to the company from the AEC where he had been its first general counsel.

Joe had a sterling reputation and had previously been involved in the Manhattan Project's complicated and highly secret negotiations to secure uranium and other raw materials for the United States' first atomic bombs.

Joe, who was personally recruited by Ralph Parsons, expanded the Washington, D.C., office and went on to hold a number of key senior management positions within the company. He was a trusted advisor to every CEO, working for $1 a year, until his death in 2001 at the age of 88.[38]

Water Resource Experience Continues to Grow

Internationally, RMP was gaining a strong reputation for its groundwater surveys and ability to perform esoteric projects. For example, Egypt first retained RMP in 1957 to survey the damaged ships that had been sunk in the Suez Canal during the 1956 hostilities among Egypt, Israel, Great Britain, and France.[39] Egypt needed this critical survey to be performed so that it could determine whether the sunken ships were a hazard to navigation through the canal, and RMP provided recommendations for mitigating the potential hazards.

In 1959, water brought RMP to Indochina (Laos, Cambodia, and Vietnam). The firm developed a master plan for harnessing the region's vast hydrological resources in a time of great political upheaval. The military conflagration that roared throughout Vietnam for over a decade did little to diminish RMP's presence. Its projects included the design of water supply systems for 32 towns and villages, as well as a feasibility study to design the port of Cam Ranh Bay.[40]

The Government of Kuwait retained RMP in 1960 to conduct a groundwater survey. Kuwait was, and still is, one of the richest oil countries in the world but had not discovered any significant sources of potable water. The Kuwaiti government

Ralph Parsons was hungry for international projects. The Kuwait hydrogeologic project was one of many new initiatives in the Middle East.

was moving forward with a seawater desalination program but, in the course of building a highway near Kuwait City, came across a source of fresh water that looked promising. Charlie Bettinger, who had been in Ethiopia working on the Dankil mining project, led RMP's team sent to Kuwait. John Foster, a groundwater engineer and geologist, joined the team, which discovered "perched" water tables—zones of unpressurized water held above the water tables by impermeable rock strata.[41]

After the survey was completed, RMP was awarded follow-up work to design and supervise the construction of a large-diameter water pipeline, gathering systems, and pump stations to supply fresh well water to Kuwait City. To show the country's appreciation for John's efforts in finding water, the Minister of Kuwait presented both John and his wife with "gifts of state" that were deeply cherished by the couple, including a museum-quality necklace.[42]

Right: This certificate recognized RMP's "patriotic civilian service" for its valuable Department of Defense work, including its involvement with the nation's Nike–Zeus program.

Below: RMP designed 1,000 underground silos for the Minuteman program during the Cold War. The missiles now have all been decommissioned, and some silos have actually been converted to private residences.

THE DEPARTMENT OF THE ARMY
CERTIFICATE OF APPRECIATION FOR
PATRIOTIC CIVILIAN SERVICE
IS AWARDED TO

Ralph M. Parsons Company

FOR OUTSTANDING SERVICE TO THE UNITED STATES ARMY CORPS OF ENGINEERS IN CONNECTION WITH ITS MILITARY CONSTRUCTION ACTIVITIES FOR THE ARMY MISSILE PROGRAMS FROM MARCH 1956 TO JULY 1960. BY A HIGHLY PROFESSIONAL APPROACH, OUTSTANDING INITIATIVE, SUPERIOR OVERALL CAPABILITY, EXCEPTIONAL COORDINATION, AND EXCELLENT MANAGEMENT AND THROUGH COOPERATIVE AND ENERGETIC EFFORTS IN THE PERFORMANCE OF A LARGE VARIETY OF DESIGN WORK, INCLUDING HIGHLY TECHNICAL FACILITIES FOR THE UNITED STATES ARMY BALLISTIC MISSILE AGENCY AND IN SUPPORT OF THE NIKE-ZEUS PROGRAM, THE RALPH M. PARSONS COMPANY CONTRIBUTED MATERIALLY TO THE CRITICAL UNITED STATES ARMY MISSILE PROGRAM. THIS REPRESENTS A PATRIOTIC CIVILIAN SERVICE TO THE ACCOMPLISHMENT OF THE CORPS OF ENGINEERS' MILITARY MISSION IN THE NATIONAL DEFENSE.

13 MARCH 1961

E. C. Itschner
E. C. ITSCHNER
Lieutenant General, USA
Chief of Engineers

Also in 1960, RMP designed an experimental saline water conversion plant at Point Loma, near San Diego, California. This project was important in terms of advancing RMP's knowledge of desalination technology, which over the years has merited further research for producing a cost-effective source of drinking water from saltwater.[43]

Defense Projects

Cold War hostilities led to the American people electing the former World War II general, Dwight D. Eisenhower, as the nation's 34th president. President Eisenhower declared in his first State of the Union address that "American freedom is threatened so long as the Communist conspiracy exists in its present scope, power, and hostility."[44]

He went on to outline the strategy for America's defense during the Cold War era. "We will not be aggressors," he said, "but we have and will maintain a massive capability to strike back."[45]

Memorable Affairs, Notable Guests

Sally Iott, who manages Parsons' internal travel center that coordinates all airplane, hotel, and other transportation for the company, has fond memories of her visit to the *Argo*, Ralph Parsons' beloved yacht. She joined RMP in 1972 and early in her career transferred to California from the Midwest to work on a Monsanto project. As part of RMP's project team, she was invited to attend a party on the *Argo* in honor of Monsanto's management. She described this event:

> *That was probably the highlight of my 21st year. I can tell you I remember exactly what I wore. The service was excellent. There was a piano on board. The fixtures in the restrooms were all in gold [actually brass plate]. It was pretty fantastic.*[1]

Full-Time German Crew of 22

To maintain and operate the excellent condition of the yacht and ensure that its guests completely enjoyed their visit, the *Argo* had a full-time German crew of 22. Karl Drobny, who started with RMP as the purser on the *Argo*, went on to manage projects for clients such as Southern California Edison (SCE) and is now serving as the construction manager on a chemical weapons neutralization plant design-build program, describes the crew:

> *We had a captain, first mate, second mate, third mate. We had a machinist, first officer, second, and third officers. One of the officers was always a medic to take care of any medical emergencies that were aboard. I, myself, had [a] crew of seven responsible for serving the guests.*[2]

Karl has many memories of Ralph and the *Argo*. Ralph did not often attend the client parties on the *Argo* but would check in with Karl to see how everyone on his staff hosting the event behaved and if clients had a good time. Karl said:

> *When the [RMP] people came aboard, he expected everybody to behave properly. There were obviously no wild parties.*[3]

His Imperial Majesty Haile Selassie I

One memorable event that Ralph did host and attend was on April 25, 1967, when the *Argo* entertained His Imperial Majesty Haile Selassie I, Emperor of Ethiopia, on a port of Los Angeles cruise, complete with a carved-ice lion of the Tribe of Judah.[4]

A young Karl Drobny (in tuxedo), when he was the purser on the *Argo*. He is still working for the company as a construction manager.

The Emperor of Ethiopia, Haile Selassie, and Ralph Parsons relax on the deck of the *Argo* prior to setting sail on a cruise around the port of Los Angeles.

A frequent client visitor to the *Argo* was Clyde Weed, the CEO of Anaconda Copper from whom RMP acquired Anaconda-Jurden Associates and started the Mining and Metallurgy Division, Parsons-Jurden.[5]

Karl also recalled that Harry Broom, who joined RMP from Anaconda and played a significant role in Parsons-Jurden's success as its president, frequently entertained on the *Argo*. Harry was good friends with Garry Moore, the late comedian, and often Garry and Harry would be on the yacht together.

Go Sail a Kite

The *Argo* was on the East Coast from June until the end of the year. Then it passed through the Panama Canal to be docked at the port of Los Angeles. Karl remembers the parties and guests who stayed aboard the yacht, but he also remembers the quieter times with Ralph. While back East, Ralph would take the *Argo* up the coast and duck hunt. When it was docked in San Pedro, Ralph would sometimes go out with just the crew. Karl recalled, "Ralph would take the *Argo* out, and he would sail a kite off the back of the boat to unwind."[6]

Whether he was entertaining or not, Ralph always slept in the smallest cabin, which also happened to be the noisiest due to location of the engines. Karl said, "He didn't want his guest[s] to have the noisy room. He would take it himself."[7]

The American Institute of Architects
1963 Honor Award Program
First Honor Award
To Dhahran International Air Terminal
Dhahran, Saudi Arabia
United States Government, Corps of Engineers
Owner
Ralph M. Parsons Company
Architects and Engineers
Minoru Yamasaki, FAIA
Consulting Design Architect
The Octagon
Washington, D.C.
President
Secretary

Left: Shown is the American Institute of Architects' (AIA) First Honor Award for RMP's engineering accomplishments on the Dhahran Air Terminal and its incorporation of well-known Arabic designs into its architecture. This was a prestigious acknowledgment of the company's first major endeavor within this field.

Above right: RMP ventured into major airport design and engineering with the world-renowned Minoru Yamasaki as its consulting architect on the Dhahran Air Terminal in Saudi Arabia. The company received professional accolades for this effort and has built a portfolio of over 400 related airport projects worldwide.

Two years after President Eisenhower's election, 1955, saw America develop a strong and responsive missile defense system. The backbone of this system was called the "Minuteman," the name given to a member of an elite military force that was highly mobile and could quickly assemble in the early days of American history.[46]

The Minuteman was preceded by the Titan I and Atlas programs. They were America's first intercontinental ballistic missiles (ICBMs) that had begun on parallel tracks. The major difference between the Minuteman and the Titan I and Atlas programs was the fuel. The Minuteman used solid propellants, and the Titan I and Atlas relied on liquid fuels. The solid fuel was less volatile, which made launching a Minuteman missile an almost instantaneous event. Unlike the Titan I and Atlas liquid fuel, which required their missiles to be raised up from their underground locations by elevators prior to ignition, the Minuteman could safely be deployed from its underground silo.[47]

Based on scientific advances in missile fuel technology, the U.S. Congress appropriated $140 million for the Minuteman program in 1958. The following year, it allocated $2 billion for the next five years. In 1961, the U.S. Air Force began the construction of 1,000 underground Minuteman silos throughout the United States.[48]

These sites were classified "top secret" because the missiles were fitted with nuclear warheads. The only aboveground signs of the missiles below were antennas and security fencing that could easily be explained as equipment for radar or radio stations.

After the sites were selected, RMP prepared the installation plans for each of the 1,000 locations. Peter Kiewit Sons Company of Omaha (now Kiewit Construction) was awarded the construction contract whose estimate of $56,220,274 was nearly $10 million below government projections. To this day, Parsons and Kiewit still work together on infrastructure programs.[49]

The U.S. Air Force retained RMP on the Titan II missile program to design the launch sites and write the maintenance procedure manuals. RMP went on to design and engineer the Titan III facility at Cape Kennedy and test bases for Nike–Zeus, Nike–X, the Peacekeeper, and the Sentinel antiballistic missile systems.[50]

Come Fly Away

In 1958, RMP began its first major airport project as the architect-engineer for the Dhahran Air Terminal in Saudi Arabia. RMP was retained by the Saudi government to produce an evaluation report, definitive drawings, renderings, and an architectural scale model of the air terminal and support facilities to be located on the shores of the Persian Gulf.

RMP also provided the preliminary and final design documents, including drawings, specifications, cost estimates, design analyses, and construction supervision. RMP worked with consulting architect Minoru Yamasaki, who incorporated sophisticated themes of well-known Arabian designs throughout the interiors and exteriors of the air terminal.

A new power plant supplied air-conditioning for the facility and for separate immigration and cargo storage areas. The terminal was mostly precast concrete, separated into two areas for domestic and international travel, with a courtyard, similar to an oasis providing an area to greet travelers. The American Institute of Architects (AIA) presented its 1963 First Honor Award to RMP and Minoru for the appropriateness and creativity of the design.

The Dhahran Air Terminal represented the beginning of RMP's involvement in the design, engineering, and construction management of airports worldwide.[51]

Expanding the U.S. Mint in Philadelphia

When the framers of the United States Constitution created the newly formed republic, they realized the critical need for a respected monetary system. On April 2, 1792, Congress authorized construction of the United States Mint in Philadelphia, the nation's first capital. Alexander Hamilton, Secretary of the Treasury, personally prepared the plans for the Mint, and it was the first federal building erected by the government.[52]

As the United States' economy grew, it required more coins and larger Mint facilities. The Mint expanded accordingly and moved three times within Philadelphia. The last move was to a five-acre site that incorporated portions of the preexisting Mint buildings. The development study for the new facility was awarded to RMP by the U.S. Treasury Department, General Services Administration, in 1964.[53]

RMP analyzed the various phases of the United States' coin manufacturing process. The company conducted field studies to investigate the latest methods of manufacturing coins and to determine a plant layout based on maximum production efficiency. RMP designed the Mint, prepared all construction plans (including equipment specifications), oversaw construction, and prepared the operation and maintenance manuals for the facility.[54]

The Mint was completed in 1969. It is an amazing production operation. For example, between January and September 2004, the Mint produced coins in the following quantities: 5,521,200,000 pennies; 1,259,520,000 nickels; 2,028,000,000 dimes; and 1,937,400,000 quarters. Few know that Paul Revere's metals company once supplied the Mint with rolled copper for the production of early cents, or that the Mint once considered producing doughnut-shaped coins.[55]

Mining Acquisition

With RMP's sulfur and potash processing experience, the company was making a name for itself in the mining industry. These projects were so successful that Ralph decided to invest in expanding RMP's mining and metallurgy capabilities.

In 1961, RMP acquired Anaconda-Jurden Associates from Anaconda Copper, a large mining conglomerate. Anaconda-Jurden became a wholly owned subsidiary, Parsons-Jurden, which was a very lucrative component of the company for the next two decades. Parsons-Jurden designed mining

RMP designed the fourth U.S. Mint facility in Philadelphia and also performed the construction management. It also prepared the highly specialized equipment specifications and developed detailed operations manuals to ensure the Mint would be properly maintained.

THE NAWAPA STORY

BY THE MID-1960s, A WATER CRISIS gripped much of the United States. After four years of subnormal rainfall, New Yorkers were rationing water. Hydrologists warned that the water level in the Great Lakes was falling to a dangerously low level. And, in the West, especially the Southwest, the land was parched. Conversely, some areas of North America faced routine flooding or were receiving more water than they needed—or wanted. It was widely acknowledged that the situation would not improve, especially in the western United States where rainfall, groundwater, and runoff could not maintain pace with the rapidly growing population, agriculture, and industry.

A viable solution to the problem was outlined in the 1950s by Donald McCord Baker, a planning engineer for the Los Angeles Department of Water and Power. He suggested that a water distribution system could be built that would even out the drought and flood conditions across the continent. Donald died before the water crisis reared its head in the mid-1960s, but Ralph Parsons knew of his idea, undertook the development of his broad concept, and turned it into a specific plan.

Using more than $1 million of the company's money, Ralph unveiled a plan he entitled "The North American Water and Power Alliance" (NAWAPA) on March 17, 1964. It presented an integrated system of dams, channels, tunnels, reservoirs, hydroelectric plants, and pumping stations. This system would tap into the vast, unused waters of Alaska and northern Canada and divert these vital resources south throughout southern Canada, the United States, and into northern Mexico. Without a doubt, NAWAPA was the most ambitious engineering concept the world had ever seen. Even today, more than 40 years after its inception, the sheer numbers for the plan are dazzling. NAWAPA would create a source of water for agricultural, industrial, and municipal use that would equal more than 17 Colorado Rivers.[1] It would also accomplish these other important tasks:

- Divert 36 trillion gallons of water annually from Alaska and northern Canada south to various Canadian provinces, 33 U.S. states, and three Mexican states.
- Irrigate 40 million acres of land.
- Yield 100 million kilowatts of electricity, the equivalent of 75 Hoover Dams.
- Return the Great Lakes to their normal levels and increase the electrical output of Niagara Falls.[2]

NAWAPA's specifics called for constructing a series of dams to block the northern rivers. Water from the resulting lakes would be pumped uphill through pipes running more than 1,000 feet. The water would then flow down into the Rocky Mountain Trench, a 500-mile-long natural gorge feeding the Columbia, Fraser, and Kootenay Rivers into the reach of northern Montana. There, several dams would hold the water. The Rocky Mountain Trench would also capture water from smaller rivers that would also be diverted to flow into it. From that point, the water would feed into existing riverbeds—the Colorado and Snake Rivers, for example—through a network of tunnels and canals, and then flow on into the Southwest, generating electricity as it ran.

A separate branch of NAWAPA would extend eastward, across Canada, toward the Great Lakes. This branch would supply water to the Great Plains states and others as far east as New York. In effect, this branch would become a transcontinental canal. An article in the February 22, 1965, edition of *Newsweek* called NAWAPA "the greatest, the most titanic, colossal, stupendous, supersplendificent public-works

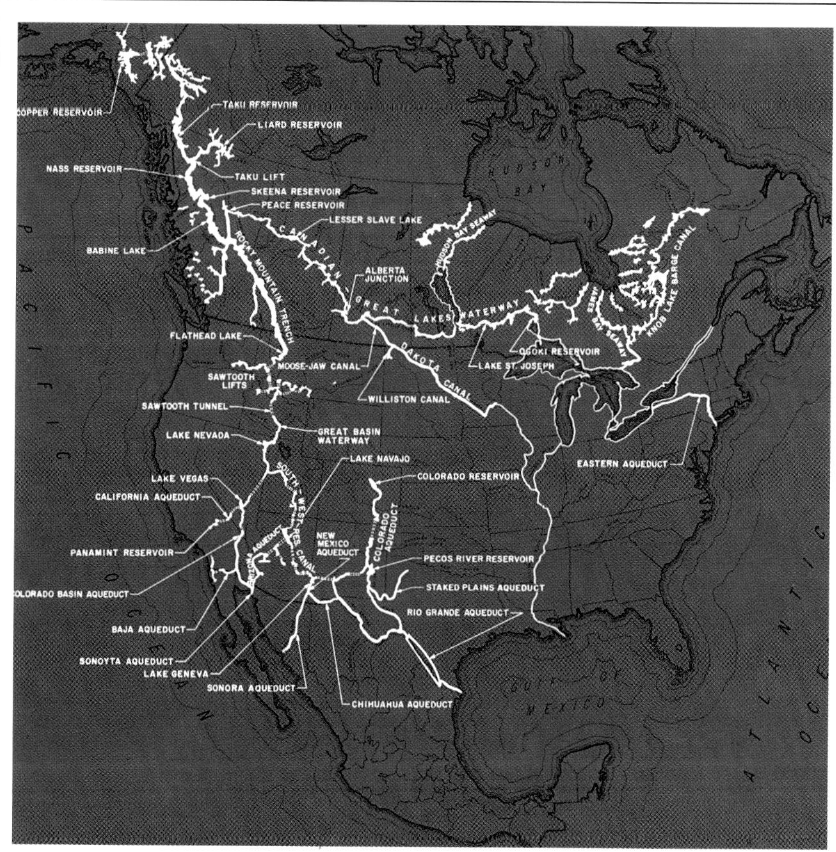

This map outlines the extensive geographical expanse, features, and infrastructure that NAWAPA would require. The three-dimensional model of NAWAPA displayed at Parsons' headquarters has been lent to museums for public exhibitions on the history of water rights and conservation awareness.

project in history. For years, planners have been looking longingly at the rivers of the far north, such as the Yukon, Tanana, Copper, and Susitna rivers of Alaska and Canada," reported *Newsweek*. "These rivers pour 663 million acre feet—an acre foot equals 325,851 gallons, the amount that would flood an acre to the depth of one foot of clean, pure water—unused into the Pacific Ocean each year. NAWAPA would take about 20 percent."[3]

The ambitious plan was greeted with a great deal of official enthusiasm. The supporters included then-Secretary of the Interior Stewart L. Udall and Utah Senator Frank Church. "We must not be deterred by its size," expressed Senator Church. Another supporter, Colonel Frank W. Reiner of the Army Corps of Engineers, said, "If you don't think big, you don't accomplish big things." NAWAPA would not be cheap. The cost was estimated at anywhere from $80 billion to $200 billion in mid-1960s dollars.[4]

But since that time, not one drop of NAWAPA water has gone anywhere. Why not? The Canadian response was tepid at best. President Lyndon Johnson never fully supported the project, which lacked the glamour of the space program and was not as urgent as the Vietnam Conflict. The rising environmental movement did not gravitate to offer its support for NAWAPA, despite the fact that it would reduce water pollution, raise the continental water table, encourage the growth of wildlife, and repair damaged soil. And, finally, for all its benefits, it would still cost a stupendous amount of money.

There have been occasional outbursts of wistful enthusiasm for NAWAPA over the years, but rare today is the person who remembers that the plan exists. However, a three-dimensional scale model for NAWAPA is still on display at Parsons' headquarters. This solitary monument greets those who visit Parsons' water group as a symbol of what might have been—and could still be.

complexes for all the leading companies in the mining sector, including Anaconda Copper, Andes Copper Mining Company, Chile Exploration, Duval, Erie Mining, Freeport Minerals, Kennecott, Phelps Dodge, Texas Gulf, and U.S. Borax.[56]

Les Engle, a retired senior vice president and division manager of RMP, remembered Wilbur Jurden, founder of Anaconda-Jurden Associates, who became chairman of the board of Parsons-Jurden, and recounted some of the projects that put RMP on the map in this market:

> *Mining and metallurgical work was Wilbur Jurden's birthright, so to speak, after having been chief engineer of the Anaconda [Copper] Company for many, many years. Wilbur was very famous around the world. When you count up what he had accomplished with Anaconda, plus what Parsons-Jurden and RMP did later over the years, you could say that we, or our antecedents, designed and built more copper production facilities than probably anyone else in the world.*[57]

One of Parsons-Jurden's first projects was a copper concentrator at Butte, Montana, that featured a completely centralized and automated control system to support the 42,000-ton-per-day ore production facility. The rich veins of ore in the area had already been mined to such a depth that further exploration was thought not to be economically feasible. The new copper concentrator revitalized Butte and prevented it from becoming a ghost town.[58]

Other key projects were the Kidd Creek Mine in Timmons, Ontario; the Rio Blanco underground copper mine complex, located 12,000 feet high in the Chilean Andes; and a lead-zinc concentrator for the Anvil Mining Corporation in the Yukon Territory.[59] Les Engle described additional mining projects:

Above: RMP purchased Anaconda-Jurden from Anaconda Copper to form Parsons-Jurden, its Mining and Metallurgy Division. One of Parsons-Jurden's first and most notable accomplishments was to completely automate the control systems of Anaconda Copper's 42,000-ton-per-day ore production concentrator in Butte, Montana.

Below left: The Anaconda-Jurden acquisition was valuable to Parsons' expansion. From left: Ralph Parsons, Milton Lewis, and Wilber Jurden shake on the deal.

> *Key projects included [the copper/zinc Kidd Creek Mine owned by] Texas Gulf in Timmons, Ontario. This was a discovery that shook the world in many respects. It was almost accidental, one of the proverbial stories about a geologist, kicking the ground and hitting the mother lode. The [copper/zinc processing] plant we built for them earned a great reputation for the company. It also led to a major electrolytic zinc plant for Texas Gulf. Another accomplishment was the Greenvale Nickel plant in Australia. It was built for Freeport Minerals. It was at the time of construction (1970s) the largest nickel/cobalt plant engineered and built in Australia. It was a technical challenge and a wonderful project for the company.*
>
> *There is even an RMP mining and metallurgical project that is a true, honest superlative. It's called the Red Dog Mine project, and it is the world's*

richest zinc mine. It's 100 miles north of the Arctic Circle in the foothills of the Brooks Range.[60]

Location, Location, Location

Successful on all fronts, RMP opened up branches to serve its clients more quickly and effectively. It had already opened branches in Washington, D.C. (1948), in New York City (1952), and Tulsa, Oklahoma (1953). Offices followed in Houston (1958), Paris (1958), London (1960), Tokyo (1961), and Frankfurt (1961).

In addition to these new offices, the number of staff in Los Angeles had grown so quickly that its corporate headquarters in the Oviatt building could no longer house them. Over the years, RMP had leased extra office space throughout downtown Los Angeles, and in 1958, these offices were consolidated into one headquarters building at 617 West Seventh Street.[61]

The Waldorf Towers was RMP's executive office in New York City between 1957 and 1974.

Settling into the Role of a Figurehead

As his company grew, Ralph settled into a comfortable role as his company's figurehead. His professional and personal interests reflected a man who had reached an extraordinary position in life. His personal style is indicated by his choice of a New York office location and his purchase of the *Argo*—a luxury yacht that played a prominent role in adding to Ralph's mystique.

His professional vision is evident by the creation and promotion of NAWAPA.

New York City—The Waldorf

By the late 1950s, the well-traveled Ralph Parsons could be found in New York City just as often as he was in his Los Angeles headquarters.[62] Needing an appropriate address to receive politicians, dignitaries, and business executives from all over the world, Ralph began looking for a combination office/residential space that would project a stately image for the company but would also serve as a home away from home.

He eventually found it at New York City's elegant Waldorf Towers, apartment 37A, where he had once spent several days in meetings with a group of British businessmen. The largest apartment in the Waldorf complex at the time was 37A, and it featured a living room with a spectacular view of Manhattan, plus a dining room, kitchen, and six bedrooms.

When the apartment had originally become available, Ralph reluctantly concluded that it was too expensive and settled for the smaller, but still impressive, Waldorf apartment 30A, which he leased in 1957.

In the meantime, General Douglas MacArthur moved into 37A. When the general died in 1964, the apartment then became available again. Ralph immediately leased the majestic apartment and refurbished it. Any RMP manager who was in New York City on business could stay there and entertain clients or visiting dignitaries. The company leased apartment 37A until Ralph's death in 1974.[63]

Parsons is a world leader for airport construction. All told, Parsons has been involved in airport capital programs valued in excess of $135 billion. Honolulu Airport, where RMP was responsible for airport design, engineering, development, and construction, was begun in 1968. The artist conception depicting the Honolulu Airport is from the cover of *Parsons News & Views*, No. 18, April 1969. The photo inset shows the completed Honolulu control tower at dusk.

CHAPTER FIVE

CORPORATE EVOLUTION

1965–1974

Nothing happens until somebody sells something.

—Ralph Parsons

THIS CHAPTER HERALDS A period of singular transition for the company. As Ralph's final decade, it is a sad period. However, it is also the story of important, indeed, vital, new leadership and direction. Between 1965 and the end of 1974, the focus of the company's management shifted from that of Ralph's one-man entrepreneurial brio to corporate management and hard-headed financial controls that would anchor RMP during a period of astounding growth while it executed numerous new megaprojects around the world.

This period marked the contributions of several key leaders in the company's history: Milt Lewis, William (Bill) E. Leonhard, Stan Goldhaber, and Charlie Roddey. Under their guidance, and supported by the contributions of many others, RMP transitioned through what could have been a difficult period for any business: transforming a company from its entrepreneurial stages into a sophisticated organization with strategic, long-term financial and operational plans.

RMP was executing contracts worth almost $1 billion a year in engineering and construction services. It had three major operating divisions: the Systems Division handled the military work, missiles, launch complexes, and test facilities; the Petroleum and Chemical Division focused on refining and oil/gas processing; and Parsons-Jurden specialized in mining and metallurgy. It later added a Construction Division.[1]

The company was at the point where it needed someone to take over the daily operations, bring in greater efficiency and economic planning, and take it to its full potential. For the first 20 years, Ralph and Milt focused a significant portion of their energies on selling RMP's capabilities wherever and whenever the opportunity arose. Ralph was often quoted as saying, "Nothing happens until somebody sells something."[2] But, both men knew that the size and complexity of the projects they were selling could start to overwhelm the company. In 1965, they decided that managerial changes were necessary. Ralph became chairman of the board and CEO with Milt as the president—and this was when Bill Leonhard entered the picture.

Bill Leonhard

When Bill arrived at RMP in 1966, he came with a client's perspective of the organization, having worked closely with RMP on the Titan II and

A staff photographer at the 1974 opening of Parsons' headquarters building in Pasadena, California, captured a personal moment between Ralph and Kathryn Parsons.

Minuteman missile programs. Bill was a career military man with 28 years of experience. He began his service in the Army and retired as a one-star general in the Air Force. Bill was involved in developing, testing, and deploying ballistic missile programs, starting out with the liquid fuel Atlas and Titan programs, followed by solid fuel Minuteman missiles. When Bill retired from the Air Force in 1964, he joined United Technologies, directing its solid booster rocket development on the Titan III missile program.[3]

Two years after Bill joined United Technologies, Stan Goldhaber, who was RMP's Systems Division manager and had worked with Bill on both the Titan II and Minuteman programs, mentioned Bill's skills to Ralph and Milt as a potential hire. Ralph and Milt were so impressed with the former Air Force one-star general that they hired him immediately as senior vice president and assistant general manager.[4]

Stan joined RMP in 1948 as a soil mechanics engineer, and his first project was the initial missile launch site designed at Point Mugu, California. After managing the Systems Division, he became a senior vice president and corporate officer. He had the respect of his staff and every president and chairman he worked with up until his retirement in 1987.[5] Stan described how Bill came to RMP:

I brought him into the company. He retired [from the Air Force] and was [with] one of the companies associated with the missile program. I had him come in and interview with Ralph Parsons and Milton Lewis. [Bill] sat down in my office, we talked, and I told him what

Above: Stan Goldhaber, a retired RMP senior vice president and corporate officer, was actively involved in numerous high-profile projects for the company, including missile defense work.

Below: The period from 1965 to 1974 was marked by great diversification for Parsons, as reflected by its missile defense work, including the Titan programs.

STAN GOLDHABER

STAN GOLDHABER PERSONIFIES THE leadership qualities, integrity, and technical abilities found in RMP's key management staff. He began his career with the company in 1948 on the Point Mugu project, RMP's initial foray into designing and engineering facilities for the U.S. missile program. Stan was an astute civil engineer who went on to become the manager of the Systems Division, where he helped win many landmark projects.[1]

Stan always understood the organization's strengths and the areas in which it needed to improve. He is credited with arranging the initial meeting with Ralph Parsons, Milt Lewis, and Bill Leonhard, which led to Bill's being hired and ultimately becoming Ralph and Milt's successor as CEO. He was promoted to senior vice president and a corporate officer and served in both capacities until his retirement in 1987.[2] Stan recalled the importance of the missile programs and how they formed the basis of the Systems Division:

> *I started with The Ralph M. Parsons Company in 1948 as a member of what was then a joint venture between Aerojet and The Ralph M. Parsons Company at Point Mugu, California. From this initial venture the company handled all of the Titan missile protection programs and all of the Minuteman programs.*
>
> *The Titan program concept was originally developed by Martin [now Lockheed Martin]. We had a contract to do the architectural engineering for the [Titan] facilities, the grounds, the underground silos, and everything else. The program represented a remarkable organizational set-up. It was a combined activity of the government's people, Martin's people, Parsons' people, and all of the other ground support people who were working on the project at the same time. Everything was handled as a total missile systems program. I traveled around the country and the world selling this concept. [The Systems Division] became a very important contributor to the growth of the company to the point where, parenthetically, the Systems Division is now The Parsons Corporation with divisions all over the world.*[3]

Stan also recounted his initial efforts on Yanbu Industrial City in Saudi Arabia:

> *When I was heading up the Systems Division they called me over to review this concept [of building] a city in Saudi Arabia. I developed the first concept of the master plan ... I made some very good friends there ... and as a matter of fact, when we first opened the first industrial plant at Yanbu, I was, of course, invited over.*[4]

Ray Judson, former CEO and member of the board who joined the company in 1966 as a project manager on refineries and gas plants in Europe and Iran, described Stan this way:

> *I was a petroleum and a chemical guy, and he was building missile sites and other things. He was very nice to me and [would] explain his part of the business. I could come over and talk to him and absorb from him.*[5]

Jim McNulty, CEO and chairman, concurred with Ray:

> *When I moved to Pasadena in 1992 to take over as the manager of the Systems Division, one of the first things I did was get in touch with Stan. I invited him to lunch and asked him to share his experiences, strategies, and leadership philosophy with me. We spoke for over three hours. His advice and observations proved invaluable to me as I assumed my new responsibilities.*[6]

Larry Burns, who managed the construction of several RMP projects on Alaska's North Slope and became a senior vice president with the company, summed up Stan by saying, "He's a good guy. First class."[7]

this was all about. He asked me a lot of questions about how to answer certain things. Then about two or three hours later, he came back down and said, "they hired me." So in one fell swoop, he became my boss again.[6]

Bill recalled his impressions of Ralph during the interview and the opportunities presented at RMP:

I liked Ralph. He was very cordial, and he really was interested in his company, but he was in his 70s. He gave me a wonderful opportunity. He made me the senior vice president of the company, so I had all the opportunity that I needed to get to learn the business and be ready for the next step.[7]

Going Public at 25

Bill arrived at RMP just as new operational challenges were beginning to unfold within the company. This was the first time since RMP's founding in 1944 that the global economy and political unrest were causing a decline in infrastructure expansion. While still a strong market, core clients such as international governments and the petroleum and chemical industries were not building at the same rapid pace they had been doing immediately after World War II.

Up until this point, Ralph owned the company lock, stock, and barrel, and he spent all profits according to his personal decisions, both professionally and personally. By 1969, this mature and expanded company was in greatly diverse markets. It needed capital from investors to expand and to remain effective in competing against other international engineering and design firms such as Fluor (where Milt Lewis had once worked during the 1940s) and Bechtel (the construction giant that comprised one-third of the BMP partnership that Ralph left in 1944).

The company's executives realized that RMP needed to sell stock to the public in order to generate capital for future endeavors and to create name-brand recognition throughout the business community. On December 2, 1969, the year that marked the company's 25th anniversary, the American Stock Exchange traded its first shares of common stock in The Ralph M. Parsons Company under the ticker "RMP."[8]

A series of small strokes prevented Ralph from traveling to New York City for the opening trade ceremonies. However, he played an active role in the legalities of taking the company public and retained 65 percent of the company's stock. Milt Lewis had the honor of purchasing the first share, customary when Wall Street admits a new company to its exchange. The initial offer was $16 per share. RMP's senior vice president and treasurer Harry Burton, Parsons-Jurden's president Harry P. Broom, and RMP's senior vice president Bob Peaslee attended this momentous event with Milt.[9]

Below, left to right: Harry Burton, treasurer; Harry Broom, Parsons-Jurden president; and Bob Peaslee, senior vice president. These three RMP executives attended the opening ceremony admitting the firm to the American Stock Exchange. Milt Lewis purchased RMP's first public share. As Ralph's senior executives, each man was instrumental in the firm's early success in managing finances, operations, and sales. They helped transition RMP from a private company to a publicly traded entity.

MILTON LEWIS: DYNAMIC SALESMAN

MILTON LEWIS WAS RMP'S CONSUMmate salesman, whom Ralph Parsons described as his "right-hand man."[1] He was the first person Ralph hired into the original Ralph M. Parsons Company in 1934.[2] They formed a dynamic sales team that established the company's reputation for innovation and reliability. When Ralph entered into the BMP partnership, Milt was a part of that organization until 1940 when he decided to join Fluor Corporation as vice president and assistant general manager. After a nine-year hiatus in their business relationship, Milt rejoined Ralph in 1949, as RMP's executive vice president.[3] They worked tirelessly together and built a multimillion-dollar project base while cultivating the core values that are still integral to Parsons today.

In 1965, Milton Lewis became president of RMP when Ralph Parsons assumed the title of chairman and CEO. Milt saw the company through 29 years of growth, and, under his presidency, RMP transitioned from a privately held company—solely owned by Ralph—to a public company that was structured to be accountable to its shareholders.[4]

Consummate Salesman and Business Development Expert

When Ralph's health started to fail in 1969, he entrusted Milt and Bill Leonhard with the day-to-day operations of the company. In 1974, Milt was elected chairman of the board and was at the helm of RMP upon Ralph's death later that year. Milt had the professional insight to help Bill Leonhard assume the responsibilities of the company's operations.[5]

"It was Leonhard and Lewis," recalled Walter Rowse, the company's former assistant general counsel. "Milt was the salesperson. He kept the contacts and knew the people. Bill could follow through on things that were left to him to do, to take more of the daily administrative work of the company with help from Harry Burton [treasurer] and a few others."[6]

Dan Frost, RMP's outside counsel and former board member, summed up Milt in one word: "Rainmaker."[7]

Milt continued on as chairman until his retirement in 1978. As *Parsons News & Views* stated: "Throughout his career at Parsons, he exercised a strong influence in formulating the company's policies." His contributions and dedication were deeply appreciated by the management team and the staff members who worked with him.[8]

The three men who joined Milt during the ceremony all had illustrious careers with RMP. Harry Burton was a certified public accountant and started his career with RMP in 1956. Within six short years he was made vice president. In 1963, he became RMP's treasurer and was elected to the board of directors. Harry was then promoted to senior vice president in 1968 and executive vice president in 1971.[10]

Harry Broom joined the company in 1952 and worked closely with Ralph and Wilbur Jurden as vice president and manager of the New York City office. After Wilbur retired, Harry became president of Parsons-Jurden during the apex of RMP's growth in mining and metallurgy. He later became executive vice president and director of advance planning for the company.[11]

Like Harry Broom, Bob Peaslee was based in New York City and was heavily involved in the success of Parsons-Jurden. In addition to his role as senior vice president, Bob became director of advance planning upon Harry Broom's retirement.[12] Harry Burton, Harry Broom, and Milt Lewis all retired in 1978.[13] Collectively, these executives typified RMP's senior management—autonomous and accountable, yet willing to take on the new challenges of operating the company as a public entity.

A Major Milestone for RMP

Becoming a publicly traded company marked a major turning point in RMP's corporate history; however, the independent thinking and creativity of the firm's project managers and engineers remained the cornerstone of RMP's operations. A *Parsons News & Views* article commemorated the company's 25th anniversary and described the well-known freedom of RMP's engineers and other professionals to call their own shots:

> *Its size and growth are not the only reasons we are satisfied at Parsons. The modus operandi breeds a sense of loyalty in a most unusual manner. While precedent is referred to, it is not always followed. You don't have to do it the same way again and again. Engineers and other technical people are encouraged to come up with new ideas, creating a freedom of thought and action in a world generally regulated*

"CLANCY" AND THE "OLD GRAY MARE"

MANY EMPLOYEES REMEMBER Ralph Parsons' fondness for Cadillacs, and he was famous for his candy-apple red limousine. He named several automobiles in his colorful Cadillac collection. "The green one was 'Clancy' and the gray one was the 'Old Gray Mare,'" recalled Dante Boccalero, who joined Parsons in 1951.[1] He first worked in the mailroom, then in procurement, in public relations, and later as logistics manager responsible for all material shipping, travel coordination, and procurement of project supplies.[2]

The mailroom position often required long hours; many times it would be Ralph, Vi (Wamsley) Leslie, his personal assistant, and Dante working late into the night. Ralph relied on Dante to run errands and often gave him permission to drive his beloved Cadillacs.

"Hello ... This is Ralph"

Ed Cramsie, who enjoyed a long career with Parsons, retiring in 1996 as the head of engineering, recalled his first encounter as a young engineer with Ralph:

I was working on a proposal for a groundwater survey in Zambia, Africa. The problem was getting our people around the country, which had a substandard transportation system. We started investigating the use of helicopters to get around, and I was given the assignment of finding which helicopter at which cost and capabilities would be most suitable for the project. I was collecting all this research on helicopters and working furiously to get this proposal out, and the phone rang. This guy said, "Hi, Ed. It's Ralph. I understand you're working on a proposal in Zambia that involves helicopters."

I said that I was.

He said, "Well, I'm very interested in it. Would you mind collecting whatever material you have and bringing it up?"

Well, I didn't know who the hell this guy was, and I said, "Well, who is this?"

And he said, "Ralph."

I said, "Ralph who?"

He said, "Ralph Parsons. Come up to my office."

Oh, brother! So I went up there and I spent about an hour with him. He was a little guy but a fascinating man. When you first met him, he almost appeared to be a meek person. He was very quiet and very soft-spoken, and very reflective in the way that he spoke.[1]

by blueprint and slide rule. You so often hear the question: "Isn't there a better way to do this?"[14]

Responding to Economic Changes

By 1971, fluctuating construction costs translated into flat earnings. These factors, coupled with a low demand for engineering and construction services, created a noticeable decline in the company's backlog of work. New business had tapered off due to a lack of specific legislative direction on combating air pollution associated with the petroleum and chemical industries.[15] The annual report for 1971 stated:

We believe this low level of demand was, and is, due to the relatively unsettled condition of the economy. The results of governmental constraint upon it are still unpredictable. In addition, a continuing lack of firm guidelines for environmental protection has resulted in continued delay of new orders from refiners and other process industries for new facilities.[16]

The next few years were not much better in terms of operating a company in a tumultuous business and social climate. The federal government showed instability due to numerous dramatic factors, including the increasingly unpopular conflict in Vietnam, the 1973 resignation of Vice President Spiro Agnew, and the Nixon administration's involvement in the Watergate scandal. However, RMP's senior management remained optimistic that the world economy, particularly the petroleum industry and Middle Eastern governments, contained a pent-up demand for infrastructure. But the management team understood that RMP needed to focus on continuing its expansion into other markets until these clients were ready to build.

Gary Stone, Parsons' general counsel, has reviewed legal documents, proposals, and memos from this era and believes RMP's management responded to the economic downturn by broadening its scope of services:

They were able to react quickly to things. They had good sensitivities. They understood the business. They were in the process of building capabilities and strengths that we lacked. Plus, they were trying to develop a broader base in our industry, in engineering construction, program management, and project management.

EDUCATIONAL AND PHILANTHROPIC INTERESTS

RALPH PARSONS WAS IN many ways a self-taught and self-made man. He nevertheless enjoys a robust legacy regarding collegiate education, and any discussion of his life must include his private philanthropic activities. He quietly supported many local charities and made significant contributions to such educational institutions as Pratt Institute and the Massachusetts Institute of Technology (MIT). In 1957, he received an honorary doctorate of engineering from the Pratt Institute, which had been founded by Charles Pratt, the owner of Astral Oil that was merged into Standard Oil.[1] Ralph had attended a two-year machine design course at Pratt between 1914 and 1915 and accepted the school's invitation to stay on as an instructor, a position he held until joining the U.S. Navy in 1917 to serve in World War I.[2]

On bestowing this honorary doctorate, the Pratt Institute acknowledged Ralph's achievements "in recognition of his many practical applications of scientific theory and research in industry and the consequent economic, social, and political development of his own and other nations, and of his contributions to the field of management."[3] In 1963, the Pratt Institute followed up this honor by electing Ralph as a trustee to its board of directors.[4]

Ralph also was associated with MIT and, in 1964, became a visiting committee civil engineering member.[5] In the late 1960s, Dr. James R.

[RMP] would represent and sell services to different segments of the business. So if one segment was off or down, the others hopefully might counteract that. By then we had the oil services, the petroleum/chemical side, transportation, mining and metallurgy, various planning groups, government programs, and environmental work. We tried to fill things in like that with the environment, transportation, and other kinds of business, so that we would have a broader scope of services and clients that we would support.[17]

Staying with Petroleum and Chemicals

The petroleum and chemical industries were on the cusp of change. The environmental movement took hold in the mid-1960s, and two of its primary positions focused on exposing the long-term effects of air and water pollution and on the growing exploitation of natural resources by all types of corporations throughout the world and various levels of government. The petroleum industry's oil extraction and refining processes were highly contentious issues of the movement.

Ultimately, the public's increased awareness of the environment, regulatory mandates, and technical innovations placed sufficient pressure on the oil industry to alter its practices markedly by minimizing waste, pollution, intrusive exploration, and well-field development activities. However, the magnitude of the movement and the required changes took the petroleum and chemical companies some time to accept and implement.

Slowdown in Construction

By the late 1960s, petroleum and chemical construction was slowing down because of the increased strength of the environmental movement and growing inflation. The federal government was drafting its first set of environmental regulations to respond to public concerns. The oil companies did

Killian, president of MIT, approached Ralph and asked for a gift of money to double the size of MIT's hydrodynamics laboratory. Dr. Killian came to Ralph because of RMP's recently unveiled concept of NAWAPA, a plan to ensure the water supply for the western portion of the North American continent.[6]

Dr. Killian hoped that Ralph would view the laboratory expansion as an important investment in developing the science that could make NAWAPA feasible. Ralph agreed and made a significant contribution. As a result, the Ralph M. Parsons Laboratory for Aquatic Sciences and Environmental Engineering was dedicated in 1970.[7]

In the early 1990s, MIT upgraded and refurbished the laboratory with funds from the National Science Foundation, alumni, and friends. Given Ralph's love of the ocean and yachting, he would have been delighted that this facility still maintains its focus on aquatic research.

In 1961, Ralph established The Ralph M. Parsons Foundation as the vehicle for the company's charitable contributions to the fields of engineering, education, and medicine. In 1976, The Ralph M. Parsons Foundation became a completely autonomous entity, capitalized by the transfer of nearly 600,000 shares of Parsons' stock and $4 million in cash. It focuses on providing grants to human services, health care, education, and cultural organizations.[8]

In 1968, Ralph was elected a trustee of the Harvey Mudd College, and in 1971, the college granted Ralph its first honorary engineering degree.[9] Harvey Mudd served as a director of Texas Gulf Sulfur, the company that had retained RMP to design copper/zinc and electrolytic zinc plants. Harvey became the chairman of the board of fellows of Claremont College in Southern California, now The Claremont Graduate University, and helped plan the undergraduate college of science and engineering. Shortly after Harvey's death, the university received its charter in 1955 and named the school in his honor.[10]

To honor Ralph, the company funds the Ralph M. Parsons Memorial Scholarship for the benefit of children of Parsons' employees attending the Independent Colleges of Southern California, which includes Harvey Mudd College.[11]

not want to design or construct facilities that would then require significant and costly changes in order to meet the new state and federal environmental pollution guidelines that had not yet been accepted. And, they also knew it would be less expensive to build facilities after inflation was in check. Thus, while the federal government debated environmental policy and how to whip inflation, the oil industry was far more cautious about its infrastructure investments and concentrated on exploration.

The investment in exploration led to a discovery in 1968 that would become the impetus for transforming oil production capabilities within U.S. borders and establishing RMP's reputation as the preeminent engineering construction company for Arctic conditions. The discovery was Prudhoe Bay on the North Slope of Alaska, the largest oil field in North America. The major oil companies involved in the North Slope exploration were euphoric about the sheer size and significance of the discovery; however, incredible technical and logistical challenges

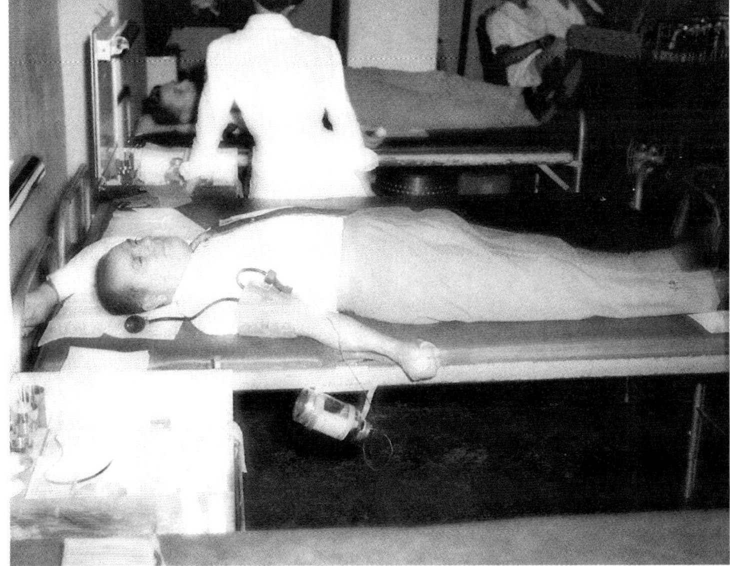

Throughout his life, Ralph was generous in his support of humanitarian and charitable work. Sponsoring and participating in employee blood drives was one example.

Above and right: RMP designed and constructed a $100 million grassroots refinery for Atlantic Richfield in Cherry Point, Washington. The facility incorporated cutting-edge air and water pollution control systems to protect the surrounding area from environmental hazards common to petroleum refining.

needed to be overcome before Arctic oil production could become a reality.[18]

In 1970, Atlantic Richfield (later known as Arco, which was acquired by BP) and Exxon (now ExxonMobil) retained RMP to provide an engineering study on the North Slope. By 1974, the company was appointed managing contractor for all oil and gas facilities for Arco and Exxon's portion of Prudhoe Bay.[19] Chapter Six discusses two oil and gas megaprojects—the North Slope and Yanbu Industrial City in Saudi Arabia—in greater depth.

While taking into account the costs associated with retrofitting facilities for environmental compliance during a period of global inflation and the capital needed for developing the North Slope, the petroleum and chemical companies continued to design and build refineries, but at a slower pace.

The search for new sources of oil was global. In 1967, the Government of India and USAID selected RMP to survey the central portion of the country for petroleum and minerals. This program lasted several years and became known as "Operation Hardrock," the sister of "Project Elephant," the groundwater survey RMP completed in India two decades earlier. Conrad Heikes, one of RMP's internationally renowned geologists, managed Operation Hardrock and used aerial photography to assist in assessing promising geologic anomalies that could indicate oil or mineral deposits.[20]

Prior to 1970, RMP had completed 93 petroleum and chemical plants in 14 countries, including numerous grassroot refineries similar to its first in Batman, Turkey.[21] The tide began to turn in favor of domestic petroleum and chemical expansion in the early 1970s due to the rising costs of oil from the Middle East. In addition, the federal

government began mandating pollution control measures. The oil companies complied by retrofitting existing and designing new refineries to meet regulatory requirements.

Petroleum and chemical project highlights of this period include the design of a steam cracker for Esso's (now ExxonMobil) petroleum refinery at Point Jerome, France. RMP also designed pollution control equipment and constructed the refinery expansion for the Lago Oil and Transport Company (a subsidiary of Esso) on the island of Aruba in the Netherlands Antilles. For Mobil Oil (now ExxonMobil) in Woerth, Germany, RMP designed, engineered, and constructed an ultramodern facility with extensive pollution controls that processed 3.5 million tons per year of crude oil. For Texaco (now ChevronTexaco), RMP engineered a $15 million hydrocracker at its refinery in Port Arthur, Texas. Also in Texas, Dow Chemical U.S.A. awarded RMP the engineering and construction contract for a crude oil processing unit that produced 200,000 barrels per day.[22]

Two major grassroots refineries, designed and constructed by RMP in the late 1960s and early 1970s, were the $45 million refinery for Gulf Oil Canada Limited (a subsidiary of Gulf Oil, later bought by Chevron, now ChevronTexaco) in Point Tupper, Nova Scotia, and the $100 million refinery in Cherry Point, Washington, for Atlantic Richfield.[23]

The Cherry Point refinery was an exciting opportunity for RMP and for Bill Glade. Bill's father, George W. Glade, was with the company for 30 years and became president of the Construction Division.[24] Bill worked for RMP on summer jobs during high school on many refinery projects in the Los Angeles Basin. However, after Bill had graduated from college, George was hesitant to hire his son, concerned that fathers and sons should not work together. George's thinking did not reflect RMP's employment policies.[25] In fact, RMP encouraged the hiring of the children and family members of its employees because they would have experienced first-hand RMP's work ethics.

Bill joined a different engineering company but maintained his interest in a career at RMP. Vi Leslie, Ralph's personal assistant, intervened. Ralph had hired Vi within three months of forming the company in 1944. She worked many long hours to manage Ralph's schedule and was an important link between Ralph and his staff.[26] Vi interviewed Bill for the Cherry Point area supervisor and field engineer position, offered him the job, and gave him three minutes to accept it. He did. Bill Glade joined the company in 1969 and was assigned to the project. Typical of many RMP's employees, Bill relocated his family to live in the Cherry Point area during this full-time assignment:[27]

> *That first job was my first time really out of southern California as an adult and with a new family, and it was quite a challenge.*[28]

Cherry Point would produce 100,000 barrels per day and incorporate the most technically advanced air and water pollution control systems available.[29] Bill Glade is still with Parsons as the construction manager on an ExxonMobil project in Beaumont, Texas.

Remembering Ralph Parsons

A FLATTERING 1966 *LOS ANGELES Times* article entitled, "Ralph Parsons: An Engineer Who Made A Mountain Out of A Molehill," described the 70-year-old Ralph as looking "not more than 55. He works about 15 hours a day, starting fairly late in the morning and working often well into the night. Any day he might be found in his Los Angeles headquarters in the Parsons building on W. 7th St., in his New York City office, in his offices in Washington, D.C., London, Paris, or Frankfurt, or at job sites, which at the moment could take him to any of 32 foreign countries."[1]

At the time of this article, the company had been in existence for only 22 years. In this relatively short time, Ralph's small firm had grown from a staff of eight into a $935 million engineering conglomerate, employing 5,000 engineers and 10,000 construction workers worldwide.[2]

Honors, Awards, and Professional Memberships

During his career, Ralph earned numerous accolades and participated in many industry organizations. In 1963, he received the prestigious Golden Beaver Award from The Beavers, a social and honorary organization formed in 1955 by construction companies and individuals who are or have been engaged in heavy engineering construction. Ralph's skill in managing some of the world's most impressive engineering construction projects earned him this honor for his lifetime achievements.[3]

In 1966, Ralph was appointed a trustee for the Webb Institute of Naval Architecture, Glen Cove, New York, and an associate of the Woods Hole Oceanographic Institute, Woods Hole, Massachusetts. Ralph also belonged to the American Institute of Mining, Metallurgical, and Petroleum Engineers and the National Council of Foreign Policy Association.[4]

Staff Recollections

The impressions of Ralph Parsons as the founder and head of an international corporation—and his own management style—are described throughout this book and in the following recollections that show how Ralph's professional ethics and personal demeanor were one and the same.

Trudy Mysliwy joined the company in 1948 working in document control and, before her retirement in 2003, was responsible for all specifications and correspondence on the Chemical Stockpile Disposal Program (CSDP). She remembered that Ralph always took the time to acknowledge his staff on a personal basis during the work day:

> *When I first came to the company, he used to come around and shake your hand or say hello or just pop his head in the office. He was down-to-earth and a really sweet guy.*[5]

Dan Frost, Ralph's personal attorney and outside corporate counsel, served for 25 years as a member of the board of directors and then as a director of the Ralph M. Parsons Foundation. He described Ralph this way:

> *He was a rather short man. Plus, he was a shy man, I felt, but he was a paradox in the sense that even though he was a shy man, he was a terrific salesman, a dynamic leader, and a great speaker. I heard him give many rousing talks to the employees.*[6]

Ralph did his best to stay healthy and trim, occasionally dieting to maintain his weight. But he sometimes strayed, according to Gladys Porter, who started with RMP in 1968 and is now the administrative assistant to the chief financial officer:[7]

> *I remember one time I was up there [in the executive offices], and he was coming out. He wasn't supposed to have candy, but he went to my friend Jeannie, the receptionist, and he says, "Come on, give me some of that candy," because she kept candy in her desk.*
>
> *Now, I never would have dreamed of doing this, but Jeannie, who was a young girl, too, at the time, pinched his cheek, and she goes, "Now come on, puddin', you know you can't have any candy." He was a real person, you know.*[8]

A High Energy Level

Until the end of the 1960s, Ralph exhibited a level of stamina usually found only in much younger men. He was actively involved in the management of many high-visibility projects, including the engineering designs for the U.S. Mint in Philadelphia, Minuteman missile installations, and various water resource and oil refinery construction endeavors.[9]

These projects, and the staff associated with them, all flourished under Ralph's tutelage, which always involved the inculcation and practical application of his singular and robust project management principles.

A Driven and Devoted Leader

Ralph was exceptionally driven and devoted a great many hours to his company. But when his wife Ruth died in 1960 after 43 years of marriage, her passing left a palpable void in his life. After some time alone he decided to move from their home in Hancock Park, a well-to-do section of Los Angeles, to the affluent and "old money" town of San Marino, just a few miles from downtown Los Angeles, near Pasadena. He hired interior decorator Kathryn Crawford to help him furnish his new home and to redecorate the *Argo* and the Waldorf apartment in New York City. Their relationship blossomed into romance, and they married in 1971.[10]

In 1969, Ralph experienced a series of strokes, and his health began to decline. As a result, he slowly began to withdraw from the company that he had founded in 1944.[11] In 1971, Bill Leonhard, who was now an executive vice president, and Milt Lewis, the president and general manager of Parsons, began making most of the important decisions within the company, with input from Ralph when his health permitted.[12]

Company Reorganization

On April 17, 1974, a reorganization of the company's top management officially announced what had been the reality for some time. The board of directors elected Ralph M. Parsons, who had been chairman of the board, to the newly created position of founding chairman. Milt Lewis was designated as chairman of the board and CEO, and Bill Leonhard, as president and general manager.[13] Ralph passed away eight months and three days later. He had ensured his company would continue under the leadership of his "right-hand" man and his protégé, respectively, Milt and Bill.

Above: Another facility engineered by RMP, Chevron's gas processing and sulfur recovery plant in Alberta, Canada, was technically advanced in its application of extensive environmental protection equipment and its use of two parallel sulfur recovery trains.

Sulfur Removal Process Patents

RMP continued to enhance its stature as an innovative leader in sulfur recovery. Its engineers further refined the Claus Kiln process and expanded the company's market share in the oil and "sour" natural gas industries. David Beavon, RMP's director of process operations, held 21 patents on petroleum processing and, in 1971, developed the Beavon sulfur removal process that increased the effectiveness of sulfur recovery in crude oil refineries and "sour" gas plants around the world.[30] Hap Meissner recounted the importance of the Beavon process:

> *As environmental regulations became more and more stringent, it became necessary to remove even more of the sulfur compounds from the tail gas, which would go up the stack. A Parsons' engineer named Dave Beavon developed a process to remove these residual sulfur compounds from the tail gas.*[31]

To broaden its technical capabilities, in 1972, RMP acquired the Canadian engineering design firm of Barry and Richardson in order to support its sulfur recovery, mining, and petroleum and chemical projects. This included Chevron's gas processing and sulfur recovery plant at Kaybob in Alberta, the largest facility of its kind in Canada, for which RMP engineered extensive environmental

Below: Dave Beavon received numerous honors throughout his career for his groundbreaking work in sulfur removal and related areas. In this photo, Dave received a Personal Achievement Award from the highly respected *Chemical Engineering* magazine. Dave (left) is shown with Calvin S. Cronan, *Chemical Engineering's* editor-in-chief (center), and Charlie Roddey, of Parsons (right). Dave also was the recipient of the Chemical Engineering Practice Award, presented by the American Institute of Chemical Engineers.

protection and reliability safety controls into the plant's two parallel sulfur recovery trains.[32]

RMP's proprietary technology, the double-contact/double-absorption (DC/DA) process, significantly reduced air pollution. The DC/DA process was incorporated into the largest sulfuric acid plant in Japan and the Agrico Chemical Company's sulfuric acid complex in Louisiana. By 1974, RMP had designed and constructed 235 sulfur recovery units and sulfuric acid plants with dozens more under contract.[33]

Expansion of Power Generation and Nuclear Expertise

Another important acquisition came in 1966, when RMP purchased the Vitro Engineering Division from a subsidiary of the Vitro Corporation (of New York and Bombay). Their experience helped RMP become the leader in nuclear fuel reprocessing—the "back end" of the nuclear fuel cycle—and expand services to government clients, such as the Atomic Energy Commission (AEC) and its successor, the Department of Energy, which contributed significantly to the company's earnings in the late 1970s and 1980s.[34]

An article in the trade newspaper, *Chemical Age of India*, on RMP's acquisition of Vitro Engineering offers an interesting look at how the company's philosophy of providing autonomy to its project managers was being recognized as a valuable asset in producing engineering solutions. The article pictured RMP's senior vice president Harry Broom and vice president Hank White—who had been project manager on water resource projects in Pakistan and Bangladesh—signing the agreement:[35]

> *At [RMP], the responsibility for a project always rests with one person—the project manager—irrespective of the complexity of the project. Over the years, the company has acquired a reputation for imaginative and brilliant engineering. [RMP's] experience in the engineering and construction field is widely diversified, embracing as it does virtually every facet of modern technology.*[36]

General Atomic, Kerr-McGee Chemical Corporation, Detroit Edison, and SCE were all very important power clients in this decade. In nuclear energy, General Atomic awarded RMP the engineering design work for its high-temperature, gas-cooled reactor power plants. The Detroit Edison Company retained RMP as its general contractor to provide engineering and quality assurance for the 1,150-megawatt Enrico Fermi-2 boiling water reactor nuclear power plant on the shores of Lake Michigan.[37] RMP also engineered and performed construction management on all three Kenneth C. Coleman coal-fired power plant units located on the Ohio River to serve 500,000 people in Kentucky.[38]

In 1973, SCE selected RMP to engineer and construct a 472-megawatt, combined-cycle generating plant in Daggett, California. RMP was already modifying SCE's existing fossil fuels units' pollution control equipment in the Los Angeles area. The company won a contract from the San Diego Gas and Electric Company (now Sempra Energy) to provide extensive testing of its geothermal facility in Niland, California. And, for the City of Chicago,

RMP was actively involved with engineering and constructing power-generation facilities. The photograph was taken shortly after construction was completed on Southern California Edison's 472-megawatt, combined-cycle generating plant in Daggett, California, that was engineered and built under RMP's supervision.

Significant Projects

1966–1974

1966

Washington Metropolitan Area Transit Authority (WMATA), General Engineering, Washington, D.C.

1967

Litton Industries (now Northrop Grumman), Ingalls Shipyard Design, Pascagoula, Mississippi

Government of India and USAID, Operation "Hardrock" National Mineral Exploration Program, India

1967

Mobil (now ExxonMobil), Grassroots Refinery Design-Build, Woerth, Germany

1968

State of Hawaii, Engineering and Construction Consultant, Honolulu Airport

1969

Dallas-Fort Worth Regional Airport, Construction Management, Texas

Atlantic Richfield (now BP), Refinery Design-Build, Cherry Point, Washington

LEGEND

Commercial · Energy/Petroleum and Chemical ·  · Transportation · 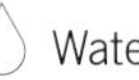

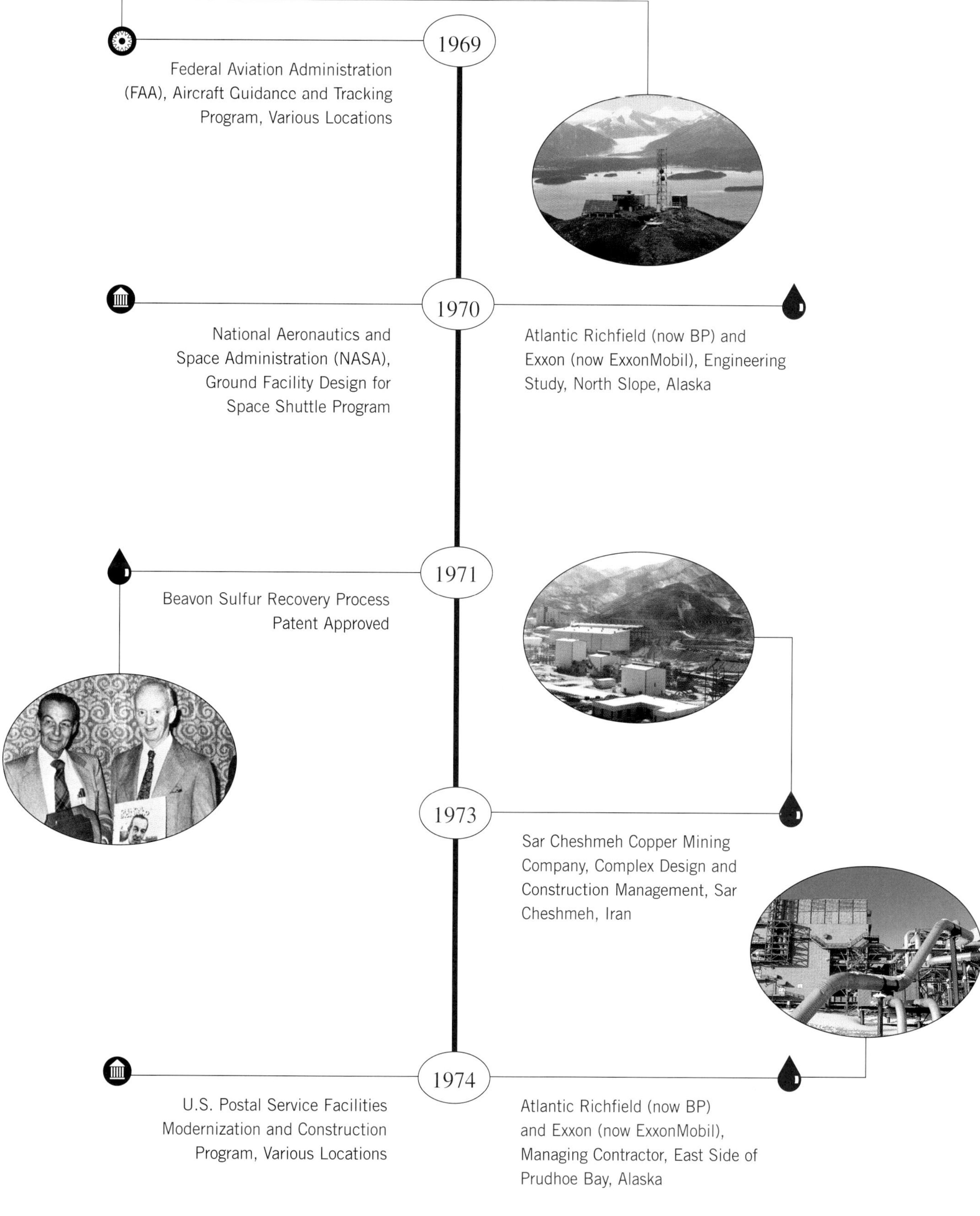
1969
Federal Aviation Administration (FAA), Aircraft Guidance and Tracking Program, Various Locations
1970
National Aeronautics and Space Administration (NASA), Ground Facility Design for Space Shuttle Program
Atlantic Richfield (now BP) and Exxon (now ExxonMobil), Engineering Study, North Slope, Alaska
1971
Beavon Sulfur Recovery Process Patent Approved
1973
Sar Cheshmeh Copper Mining Company, Complex Design and Construction Management, Sar Cheshmeh, Iran
1974
U.S. Postal Service Facilities Modernization and Construction Program, Various Locations
Atlantic Richfield (now BP) and Exxon (now ExxonMobil), Managing Contractor, East Side of Prudhoe Bay, Alaska

RMP designed a solid waste energy-recovery system that converted 2,000 tons per day of raw residential refuse into 9.2 million kilowatt hours per week to provide electricity to more than 50,000 homes.[39]

Kerr-McGee Chemical Corporation retained RMP to engineer and construct a first-of-its-kind soda ash power plant in Trona, California. A combination of coal and coke powered this 200-megawatt plant, engineered to exacting environmental standards that included an extremely stringent flue gas cleaning requirement.[40]

RMP was also involved with several new ideas for advancing power and fuel technology. The U.S. Office of Coal Research, Department of Interior, awarded a contract to RMP to develop an economically viable commercial process that would produce clean synthetic fuels from coal. In South Carolina, Westinghouse awarded RMP a contract to study and design the first commercial nuclear recycling facility. Distrigas Corporation on Staten Island in New York City hired RMP to design the largest liquid natural gas (LNG) bulk-receiving terminal in the United States. As of this publication, LNG technology is just now beginning to be accepted in the United States, and nuclear recycling is still being considered.[41]

Airport Design and Construction

With the petroleum and chemical industry slowing down in the mid to late 1960s, RMP's engineering design and construction capabilities took center stage in airport, aerospace, and transportation projects. Two major domestic airport projects that

Parsons is a major innovator in the design of airports around the world, including the spectacular Honolulu Reef Runway.

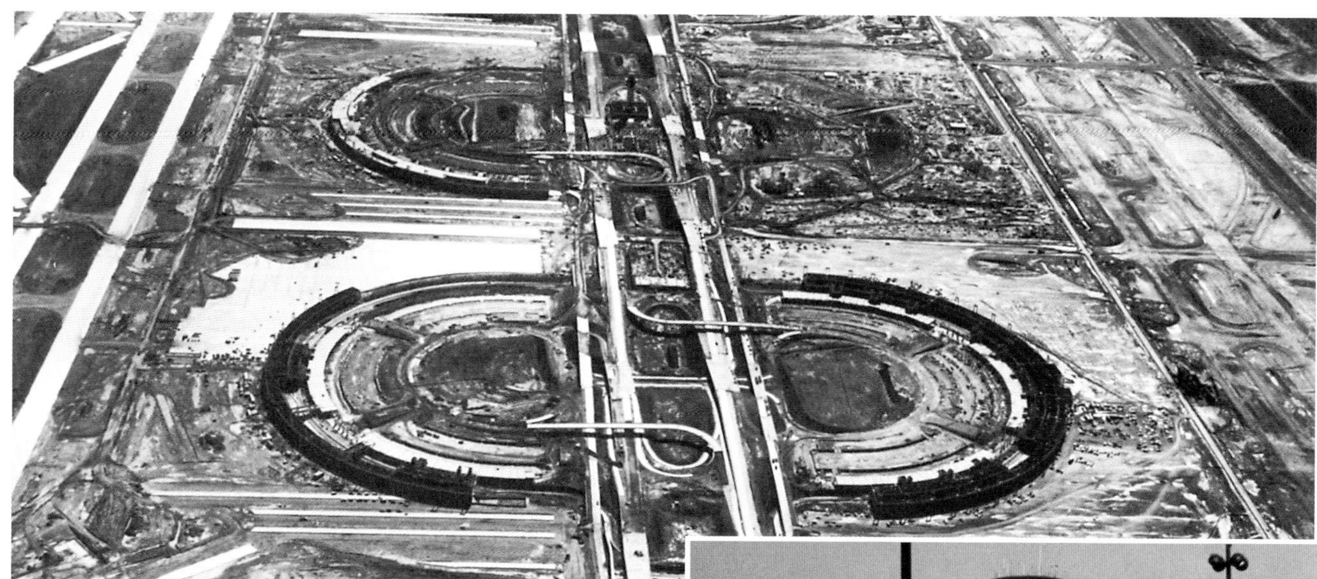

This early photo shows the immensity of construction that was involved in the Dallas-Fort Worth (DFW) Airport project, which sprawls over 17,600 acres of land, midway between the two cities. The passenger terminal complex itself is 3.5 miles long.

were important to the company, and were technically innovative, were the three-phased expansion and modernization program for the Honolulu Airport in Hawaii and the Dallas-Fort Worth (DFW) Regional Airport in Texas.

In 1968, the State of Hawaii engaged RMP as its engineering and construction consultant, the first time a single consulting firm won a contract from a government agency to design and construct an entire airport. RMP was responsible for all aspects of the work, including 18 major subprojects that were completed without interrupting passenger and aircraft services. Stan Goldhaber, who was managing the Systems Division at that time, was instrumental in contract negotiations. Milton Rote, one of Ralph's most trusted engineers and one of the original eight employees of RMP, was assigned to manage the project.[42]

One particularly innovative design was the 12,000-foot runway engineered on a reef off the shores of Honolulu. Its location minimized noise in downtown Honolulu while providing a spectacular view to passengers landing on the island. The runway is still in use today.[43]

The Honolulu Airport project, however, was dwarfed by the mammoth DFW Regional Airport, which RMP won in 1969. DFW construction was estimated at $110 million, and the complex was so large that it could contain the combined airports of New York City's John F. Kennedy, Chicago's O'Hare, and Los Angeles' International. In an approach that was unusual for the time, RMP constructed a full-scale mockup of a typical terminal segment, permitting the builders to test the design. This model not only let the subcontractors bid the work more accurately, but airlines and other airport tenants could "pre-decorate" their terminals at a savings conservatively estimated up to $5 million.[44]

With 234 passenger gates and 11 runways, DFW's design required a sophisticated mobile link to connect all the parts, and the Airtrans "people mover" system became the first of its kind in the country. In a joint venture with a Dallas-based contractor, Robert E. McKee Inc., RMP provided construction management for the terminal buildings, Airtrans guideways, and access roads. Once again, RMP was able to showcase its strong project management capabilities and expertise through this high-profile project.[45]

Between 1975 and 1984, RMP also received contracts for airport master planning and engineering projects on the Pacific Islands of Saipan and Truk. It developed the first airport system plan for the Illinois Department of Aeronautics, and in Tunisia, built the Tunis/Carthage International Airport.[46]

The company also began working for the Federal Aviation Administration (FAA) in 1969 on a $950,000 contract to provide plans, specifications, and standards for aircraft guidance and tracking that would expand and modernize 19 air traffic control centers.[47] The FAA remains an important client, and Parsons is currently under contract to provide "24/7" technical support services, 365 days a year, in each of the FAA's nine regions.

Shipyards and Ports

For three centuries, ships have been built at Pascagoula, Mississippi, where the Pascagoula River

Below and inset: Litton Industries retained RMP to design the "Shipyard of the Future" in Pascagoula, Mississippi, in 1967. This was the first shipyard built in the United States since World War II. Thirty-six years later, Parsons was retained to modernize and expand the shipyard for Northrop Grumman, its current owner.

empties into the Gulf of Mexico. In the early 1700s, the French government instructed its settlers "to breed the buffalo, to seek for pearls, to examine the wild mulberry for silk, and to fell timber for shipbuilding."[48] The piney woods of southern Mississippi furnished timber, turpentine, tar, pitch, and resin for the growing number of shipbuilders. By the time wooden ships gave way to heavier vessels of iron and steel, the Pascagoula area had become a major shipbuilding center.

In the 1930s, the Ingalls Iron Works Company, a builder of commercial ships, constructed a shipbuilding facility in Pascagoula on a 160-acre tract on the eastern bank of the Pascagoula River, which had a deep water channel, rail access, and room to grow. In 1961, Litton Industries purchased Ingalls as a vehicle to apply its broad technological capabilities to marine defense and commercial shipbuilding. The timing was right. The U.S. Navy was getting ready to award contracts to replace its aging World War II fleet of merchant ships by updating and commissioning many commercial vessels.[49]

In the summer of 1967, Litton announced its plans to build a totally new ship manufacturing facility on the western bank of the Pascagoula River. Litton's innovative idea was to apply modular techniques in building ships. This facility would be the first shipyard constructed in the United States since World War II, and the project harkened back directly to Ralph's BMP experience. Litton retained RMP to design its $130 million "Shipyard of the Future." On a 611-acre tract directly across the river from the old Ingalls facilities, ground was broken on January 11, 1968, for the new design and production facility.[50]

Several decades later, Northrop Grumman, the world's largest naval shipbuilder, purchased Litton. In May 2003, Parsons won a master services agreement to be the engineer, designer, construction manager, and program manager for a five-year, $400 million facilities modernization and expansion program at three of Northrop Grumman's shipyards—and one was in Pascagoula.[51]

Other water-based infrastructure projects included the design, master plan, and engineering for a new port and dock facilities in Algeria to accommodate the huge tankers exporting LNG to the United States and Europe.[52]

Government Contracts Continue

The U.S. government continued to expand its own programs at the same time the petroleum industry explored new sources of oil and the power industry focused on advancing technology. The Energy and Research Development Administration selected RMP to provide architectural and engineering services for a $160 million, high-temperature gas reactor (HTGR) fuel-reprocessing facility in Idaho that would recover uranium by processing irradiated commercial HTGR.[53] In 1970, NASA awarded a key contract to develop a ground facility for the space shuttle program to RMP, which was still heavily involved in the ballistic missile programs.[54]

The year 1972 saw Parsons branch out from the design and engineering services it historically offered NASA by performing the agency's first studies to comply with the National Environmental Policy Act of 1969.[55] Marty Fabrick, executive vice president, was on the team that conducted the site analysis for the new space shuttle program at Cape Canaveral (then Cape Kennedy). He discussed this activity:

> *We studied the wetlands and waterways surrounding the cape as part of the preliminary engineering reports developed to modify the Apollo-era vehicle assembly building and construct the new runway for the space shuttle. Our team came to realize that if a shuttle spilled a significant amount of fuel, it could affect endangered marine species, such as the manatee. We suggested NASA build a system of gates in the waterways that could be closed in such an event.*[56]

Marty also prepared the environmental assessment report that allowed NASA to tow the first space shuttle from its Palmdale, California, assembly plant to Edwards Air Force Base. Marty has over 30 years of experience with Parsons in business operations, project management, and systems/environmental engineering with defense, energy, aerospace, environmental restoration, and ordnance and explosive cleanup projects. In his current role, Marty is responsible for all water infrastructure sales activities. Previously, he managed the company's federal business development, the defense and aerospace business sector, and demilitarization projects, as well as Department of Defense, NASA, and FAA programs.[57]

In 1974, RMP began a three-year contract with the U.S. Postal Service (USPS) to furnish management and technical support on a $3 billion facilities modernization and construction program. RMP provided nationwide services on the new construction of over 100 major postal installations. In addition, RMP refurbished and upgraded local post offices and large mail-handling facilities. Based on the work completed under this contract, the USPS became a long-term client of the company, and Parsons continues to provide architect and engineering services to this day.[58]

Mass Transit

A key transportation project that began in 1966 is the world-renowned Washington, D.C., rapid transit system. Since its inception, the company has served as general engineering consultant to the Washington Metropolitan Area Transit Authority (WMATA) for the 103-mile, $11 billion rapid transit rail system that connects Washington, D.C., to its suburbs.

Parsons has designed and engineered 84 stations and intermodal transfer terminals, commuter car parks for 30,000 vehicles, and 48 miles of subways (22 miles of cut-and-cover tunnels, 11 miles of earth tunnels, and 15 miles of rock tunnels). The awards this project has received are laudable:

WMATA is one of Parsons' landmark transportation projects. The corporation has been its engineering consultant since WMATA's inception in 1966. The 103-mile, $11 billion rapid transit rail system has received numerous engineering and design awards and is vital in transporting commuters and visitors safely and efficiently in and around Washington, D.C.

1997 Washington Building Congress Craftsmanship Award in recognition of outstanding work for traction power equipment installation

1996 Washington Building Congress Craftsmanship Award in recognition of outstanding work in connection with the Greenbelt service and inspection shop

1991 Engineering Achievement Award presented by the American Society of Civil Engineers for the Metrorail Green Line waterfront to Anacostia

1988 American Public Transit Association Outstanding Achievement Award presented for excellence in planning, construction, safety, operation, and maintenance; and recognition of WMATA as "America's Number One Transit System"

1988 Excellence in Concrete Award for the creative use of concrete by the Maryland Chapter of the American Concrete Institute

1979 The American Society of Civil Engineers' "Outstanding Civil Engineering Achievement" Award

1977 Award for Excellence in Design Using Precast by the Concrete Prestressed Concrete Institute (PCI) for the Dupont Circle Metro Station

1975 Award for Superior Design Achievement by PCI for the Rhode Island Avenue Station canopy[59]

Above: Joe O'Rourke set up RMP's office in Saigon and helped organize and administer a program to train South Vietnamese Army engineers.

Left: Jerry O'Rourke, Joe O'Rourke's son, was in Vietnam at the same time as his father, serving with the U.S. Army in Qhi Nhon. He eventually joined Parsons and is currently responsible for government bids and proposals.

Vietnam—A Story of Father and Son

In Vietnam, RMP continued its water resource work that began in 1959 and also won service contracts with both the United States and South Vietnamese governments to expand and complete more than 100 infrastructure projects between 1965 and 1970. Among the projects conducted in Saigon for MACV (Military Assistance Command Vietnam) was the "Little Pentagon" headquarters, which primarily entailed engineering. RMP also engineered Ton Son Nhut Air Force Base (the world's busiest airport during the height of the conflict in Vietnam). It then implemented a program to train the South Vietnamese in the maintenance and operation of various U.S.-built military facilities.[60]

JOE VOLPE JR.

NO BOOK ON PARSONS' HISTORY would be complete without special recognition of Joseph P. Volpe Jr.'s special contributions. In World War II, he was a captain in the U.S. Army assigned as the liaison officer to General Leslie R. Groves, who was the director of the Manhattan Project that developed the atomic bomb.[1] It was in this role that Joe began his interaction with many of the top military, scientific, and political figures of the day.

His efforts were recognized by Dr. J. R. Oppenheimer, the physicist known as the father of the atomic bomb, and David E. Lilienthal, the first chairman of the AEC, in the foreword of their "A Report on the International Control of Atomic Energy," prepared for the Committee on Atomic Energy, dated March 16, 1946. They wrote a special acknowledgment to "Captain Joseph Volpe Jr. for his liaison services."[2]

Joe earned his law degree by attending the Newark Law School at night. After World War II, he served as the AEC's attorney for two years and then became its general counsel in 1949. In 1951, he started a law firm and began representing RMP.[3] In 1960, Ralph Parsons personally hired Joe into the company to provide leadership to the Washington, D.C., office.[4]

When he accepted Ralph's offer, Joe had been in the inner circles in the nation's capital for almost 20 years and had a widely known reputation for personal integrity. His son, Joe Volpe III, recalled, "His friends and colleagues said that he [was] a true gentleman. He looked you in the eye and treated you with dignity, respect, and caring —unless you gave him a good reason not to."[5]

Joe proved to be a major asset to RMP. His efforts resulted in many of the federally funded nuclear, energy, defense, airport, highway, and rail projects that RMP, later Parsons, performed.

Joe often stated that his role was to be "Mr. Parsons" in Washington, D.C., meaning that Joe Volpe and Parsons were synonymous.[6]

Joe O'Rourke, who joined RMP in 1962 as a data engineer assigned to the Titan II missile program, wrote RMP's proposal for the Military Advisory Group consulting contract, became its project manager, and set up RMP's office in Saigon. Joe then selected and managed the team that conducted inventories of the U.S Air Force, Army, and Navy bases between 1969 and 1970 throughout South Vietnam.[61] This project also required training South Vietnamese Army engineers in U.S. military engineering protocols and guidelines. Of this effort, Joe recalled:

> *I wrote a good proposal with a totally new approach to how we would go about quantifying and pricing out what it would take to maintain these magnificent facilities that we built there. It led to follow-on work, and we were right up in there until just before the last when everybody pulled out.*[62]

While the Pasadena headquarters was under construction, Ralph Parsons visited the site with his second wife, Kathryn, who was its interior designer. They were accompanied by Bill Leonhard and Milt Lewis.

Joe also was a mentor to staff who would become prominent senior management, including Len Pieroni, Ray Judson, Jim Shappell, Jim Thrash, Frank DeMartino, and Jim McNulty. In addition, Joe was a trusted counselor to each of Parsons' six CEOs.[7]

He helped them solve complex business problems through his abilities to sort out facts and to apply decisive legal principles. Jim Shappell, president of Parsons Transportation Group, stated, "In terms of corporate history, he would be one of the top three or four founding members of where we are right now."[8]

He also brought sage business advisors into the company, including Earle Williams, the founder and CEO of BDM International, who became a member of the board. Earle remembered this contact with Joe:

> *I got a call from Joe who was a Parsons vice president asking if I would be willing to meet with Len Pieroni [then Parsons CEO]. I don't know how he knew I was getting ready to retire [from BDM], but apparently he told Len that I would make a good board member.*[9]

Earle met with Len and Joe and liked both men and the company to the point where he became one of Parsons' long-term board members.

In addition to his role at Parsons, Joe was also active in the National Council on U.S.-Arab Relations that helped increase American knowledge of the countries that comprise the Gulf Cooperation Council (GCC)—Bahrain, Kuwait, Oman, Qatar, Saudi Arabia, and the United Arab Emirates.[10]

Joe was quoted as saying, "We benefit from these countries. And we do so on a rather large scale. In this respect, we are the envy of every other country and foreign corporation in the world."[11] In his honor, the GCC Corporate Cooperation Committee created the Joseph Volpe International Commercial Affairs Fellow.[12]

Joe died in 2002. His wife, Betty, found a note in his address book that epitomizes what he brought to his life. It reads, "Life is short and we do not have too much time to gladden the hearts of those who travel the way with us, so be swift to love and make haste to be kind."[13] To remember his contributions and life's philosophy, Parsons named its corporate classroom for internal training courses The Volpe Learning Center.

On a personal level, this assignment was important to Joe. One son, Jerry, served in the U.S. Army and was stationed in Qui Nhon. Many families and friends were seldom able to see or hear from their loved ones who were serving in the military at the time. Joe and Jerry were fortunate in that they were able to visit each other and stay connected through their time in Vietnam. Jerry said of a conversation he had with his father before going to Vietnam: "He said he knew my tour of duty would be different. I just didn't know how different."[63]

RMP hired Jerry O'Rourke after he was honorably discharged from the Army. As had his father, Jerry presently manages government bids and proposals. Joe retired in 1986 from Parsons after working on the NASA space shuttle program, Yanbu Industrial City in Saudi Arabia, and the modernization project for the U.S. Navy shipyards.[64]

Move from Los Angeles to Pasadena

By 1972, RMP occupied more than 300,000 square feet of leased space in four separate downtown Los Angeles buildings—not a particularly efficient arrangement. In addition, senior management decided Parsons-Jurden would be more effective if it moved its operating base from New York City to corporate headquarters. And too, RMP needed its own building to accommodate all of its Los Angeles-based staff and the newly transplanted Parsons-Jurden personnel.

One of Ralph's last decisions was to relocate the company's headquarters to Pasadena, California, and build a new $20 million, 400,000-square-foot, 12-story headquarters tower. On January 31, 1973, construction began on the 22-acre site, designed to accommodate 2,800 employees. Charles Luckman & Associates were the architects, and Mrs. Parsons was the interior designer.[65]

RMP's world headquarters officially opened on July 3, 1974, with Ralph and Milt cutting the ceremonial ribbon.[66] For Ralph, the opening of his company's distinctive new landmark was a symbol of his long and successful career.

Above: Ralph Parsons and Milt Lewis officially opened the Pasadena headquarters in a ribbon-cutting ceremony held on July 3, 1974. The architect was Charles Luckman & Associates. Mrs. Parsons, the interior designer, chose a bicentennial theme for the interior's décor, including a vibrant red, white, and blue color scheme for the executive floor.

Below: Parsons conducted Chamber of Commerce tours during the opening ceremony of its new world headquarters building in 1974. Hostesses were (left to right): Louise John, Gen Marquez, Barbara Proper, Tina Miller, Shirley Sackman, and Sandra Lantz.

Thomas Johanson, corporate finance treasury manager, recalled how the construction of the striking new headquarters greatly improved what is now referred to as "old town Pasadena":

> *I started at Parsons in 1974, the same year the new building opened. I remember walking in the doors the first time. They were still laying the tiles in the foyer and hanging the murals that used to be here. At the time old town Pasadena was just nothing. And where our headquarters went up was a very bad part of town. Pasadena heavily courted Parsons. In fact, the Parsons move constituted an important part of their redevelopment plan.*
>
> *As soon as we came here, the Bank of America built a little branch right across the street. Then the Pasadena Athletic Club relocated across the street. First Interstate built a nice, new bank building where the Marriott Courtyard is now. A number of other exciting things happened, and soon the redevelopment plan was in full bloom.*
>
> *Of course, now the area is something spectacular. The construction of Parsons' headquarters building was the catalyst for the whole thing.*[67]

The murals Tom mentioned were a collage of historic renderings and photographs of Parsons' projects. They were displayed by the elevators on the first four floors of the new 12-story building.[68]

RMP's critical role in the revitalization of "old town Pasadena" was recalled by Roger Fetterolf, now retired, who formerly managed financial reporting:

> *When Parsons came in everything started to really turn around. Later, of course, we put up the two annex buildings. Thanks to Parsons, there's no similarity now to what this area of Pasadena was like before we moved in. Everything has changed for the better.*[69]

Ralph Fernandez, a reproduction coordinator with nearly 40 years at the company, remembered that Pasadena was a tough, gritty area when RMP opened its headquarters. He explained that the relocation from downtown Los Angeles was a complex undertaking for all of RMP's various departments. He used reproduction as an example:

In those days, downtown Pasadena was definitely not the nicest place to be. In fact, it was pretty dangerous. Even though everyone was moving to a beautiful new facility, I'm sure many people had mixed feelings. The move itself was certainly challenging for everyone. For example, in the Reproduction Department, we had to buy new equipment, we had to do the set-up, and we had to handle everything else, including our deadlines. We had a floor plan and we laid down the machinery where we needed it. We also had to plan out the space, the electrical, the counters, and everything else. We had to specify all of that. It was really quite an undertaking.[70]

Above and below: Inspired by the murals at the Edison building, one of his former Los Angeles main office locations, Ralph commissioned Garth Benton to paint 12 murals for Parsons' headquarters depicting pivotal projects and the key staff that helped bring them to fruition.

End of an Era

For Ralph, the opening of his company's landmark headquarters was symbolic of his long and successful career. On December 20, 1974, Ralph Monroe Parsons died at his San Marino home. He was 78 years old.[71] This quiet man, the son of a fisherman, left behind a healthy and dynamic company that continued his commitment to take on any and all challenges and to provide reliable and innovative engineering and construction management services. The company publicly stated in its annual report:

His vision, know-how, and presence will long be remembered and serve as an inspiration to all who worked with him and for him.[72]

Top: North Slope modules at Prudhoe Bay waiting for transportation inland for final placement.

Inset: Nearly 8,500 permanent villas, townhouses, and apartments were planned for Yanbu Industrial City, in addition to the 23,000 dormitory units that were constructed to house its residents and workers.

CHAPTER SIX

THE NORTH SLOPE AND YANBU

1975–1984

I wound up in the last of the great gold rushes.
—Mike D'Antuono, president of Parsons Constructors Inc.
on his experience at Alaska's North Slope

There was nothing there, just desert.
—Stan Goldhaber, former senior vice president and corporate officer, on visiting the proposed site for Yanbu Industrial City, Kingdom of Saudi Arabia

IN 1975, RMP EXPERIENCED THE most successful year in its history to date. Backlog grew to $2.2 billion, up more than $750 million from the year before, while after-tax income jumped an impressive 81 percent. The annual report acknowledged the company's commitment to its engineering and construction management efforts in Alaska. It also cited "a definite shift from domestic projects to overseas projects as the main source of our business." Bill Leonhard and Milt Lewis promised to pursue work aggressively in the Middle East "where billions of dollars in projects are now under way or anticipated."[1]

They lived up to this promise. Under their guidance, RMP excelled in two extraordinary endeavors—both located in extreme geographical regions and environments—that challenged the technical skills and imagination of the entire company. The first was in Alaska's Prudhoe Bay region and the oil field development at the North Slope, which has been described as nothing less than "the largest project ever undertaken by private industry."[2] The second was to turn a king's dream into a reality by constructing Yanbu Industrial City in the Kingdom of Saudi Arabia—transforming an arid desert into an industrial port complex and thriving oasis.

As Parsons' third CEO, Bill Leonhard strategically ensured the company's future by taking it from public to private, implementing an aggressive acquisition strategy and dramatically cutting overhead and facility costs.

The New Frontier: The North Slope of Alaska

Reports of oil in northern Alaska began in the early 1900s with the discovery of surface oil seeps along the Arctic coast. In 1923, the U.S. government established Naval Petroleum Reserve 4, a 23-million-acre site in northwestern Alaska, securing a supply of oil for future national security needs. During World War II, the entire North Slope of Alaska that encompasses 48.8 million acres—from the Brooks Range, north, to the Arctic Sea—was exclusively under the domain of the federal government for military purposes.[3] Thirty-four years later, President Eisenhower's administration consolidated military operations in Alaska and set aside 20 million acres of the North Slope along Prudhoe Bay for commercial oil and gas leasing.

In a joint effort in the late 1950s, Shell and Standard Oil of New Jersey (later Exxon, now ExxonMobil) explored much of Alaska, but suspended drilling operations when their most expensive wells came up dry. Similarly, Sinclair Oil and British Petroleum (BP) joined forces to drill six wells in far northern Alaska, but ceased exploration after their wells were also dry.[4] In the meantime, geologists for Gulf Oil (now ChevronTexaco) argued that Alaska was too promising to ignore and urged their company to undertake serious oil exploration. The company's management rejected the idea, contending that, even if they found oil, getting it out of the ground would be prohibitively expensive. "It would cost five dollars a barrel," declared one executive. "Oil will never get to five dollars a barrel in our lifetime."[5]

But others refused to give up, including Richfield, a California-based independent (that merged with Atlantic Refining to become Arco and was later acquired by BP). Exxon stayed with the oil pursuit, as did several other companies. Altogether, at least 11 oil companies held North Slope oil field leases, including those that had already tried to find oil and failed.[6] Eventually, the group of lessees designated Arco as operator of the east side of the field.[7]

Coming up Dry

By the winter of 1966, it seemed as though North Slope exploration was not getting anywhere, especially after Arco drilled yet another expensive well that came up dry. One final well was scheduled, this one near Prudhoe Bay, off the Beaufort Sea on Alaska's north coast. After so many failures, there was serious doubt about continuing. Since the drill rig only had to be moved 60 miles, the decision to proceed with drilling the well was approved, but not with high expectations.[8]

Prudhoe Bay State Number 1

The well was named Prudhoe Bay State Number 1. On the day after Christmas, December 26, 1967, with the wind blowing at 30 knots and the temperature down to 30 degrees below zero, drilling continued. In spite of the terrible weather conditions, a loud vibrating sound drew a crowd of workers to the well. About 40 men would bear witness to "hitting the big one."[9]

Six months afterward, a drilling site six miles from Number 1 confirmed Prudhoe Bay as one of the greatest finds in oil exploration—an astounding reservoir of oil and gas 45 miles long and 20 miles wide.[10] The North Slope held as much as 6.5 billion barrels of recoverable oil reserves, plus 24 trillion cubic feet of natural gas, by far the largest field ever discovered in North America.[11] Its output would average 1.27 million barrels a day, making it the third-largest producing oil field in the world, surpassed only by Saudi Arabia's Ghawar and Kuwait's Burgan fields.[12]

Galvanized by the magnitude of the discovery, practically the entire oil industry decided to develop the North Slope as quickly as possible—but that was easier said than done. The problems of extracting, producing, and delivering oil to market from a location 250 miles north of the Arctic Circle and 1,200 miles south of the North Pole were formidable. This location was so alien, hostile, and isolated that it was considered nearly inaccessible.

Tundra Harder than Concrete

In winter, the tundra froze as hard as concrete in temperatures that fell to 65 degrees below zero, equating to minus 100 degrees below zero when adding in the wind-chill factor. By summer, the tundra thawed into a spongy swamp. Beneath the tundra was the permafrost—endlessly frozen earth measuring to a depth of 1,000 feet in places. As one writer marveled, "Normal steel pilings would crumple like soda straws when driven into permafrost."[13]

Marvin McClain, who joined RMP in 1975 in procurement and became a key executive and vice president of the company, described the work:

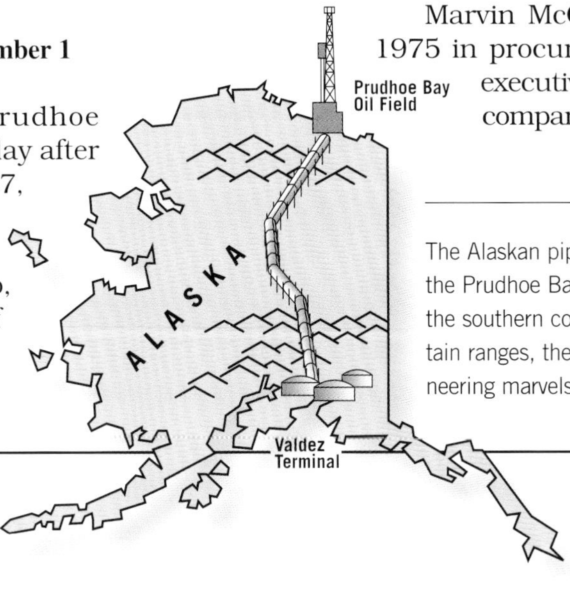

The Alaskan pipeline extends for 800 miles, from the Prudhoe Bay oil field to the Port of Valdez on the southern coast of Alaska. Crossing three mountain ranges, the pipeline is one of the great engineering marvels of the world.

No one had ever built anything up in that frozen tundra. If you went out there, even in a heavy parka, you couldn't last 20 minutes. I'm telling you, it was hell. I've never seen anything like it.[14]

The Arco Alaskan pipeline was a massive engineering accomplishment situated near picturesque Prudhoe Bay.

Getting the Oil Out

Assuming that some way could be found to extract the oil out of frozen ground, how would the oil get to market? Various plans were considered and rejected, including icebreaking tankers that would travel the frozen Arctic seas and a fleet of jumbo jets that would be converted into tankers to transport the oil by air. The consortium of oil companies decided a pipeline was the most feasible method of delivery. Two routes for the pipeline were debated seriously. One route would be contained within Alaska's borders and the other would traverse parts of Canada into the United States. The Alaskan pipeline route was ultimately selected. It encompassed 800 miles through Alaska from Prudhoe Bay across three mountain ranges south to the Port of Valdez. Oil tankers would then sail through the pristine, environmentally sensitive Prince William Sound, into the Pacific Ocean, and from there to the world's oil markets.[15]

One advantage of the Alaskan pipeline was its purely American route, eliminating the need to negotiate with multinational government agencies. The second advantage was its shorter length than the proposed trans-Canada pipeline route, and the oil companies assumed it could be built more quickly. However, these advantages were only relative. The difficulties of engineering and constructing a pipeline to withstand extreme environmental conditions were immense. Plus, numerous delays were created from a series of court challenges by parties as diverse as the native Alaskans to environmental groups. As a result, oil would not begin coursing through the pipeline until 1977, 10 years after it was originally discovered in Prudhoe Bay.[16]

In December 1970, Arco and Exxon, as lease holders of the east side of the Prudhoe Bay field, selected RMP to design feasible and relatively economical oil and gas gathering and production facilities at Prudhoe Bay. RMP produced six preliminary design plans from which the oil companies could choose.[17]

Modularized Construction

Traditionally, oil and gas facilities were constructed at the site where they would operate. The absence of skilled labor and the unknown expenses involved in building massive support

RMP was a major innovator of modular facilities designed for inaccessible areas where it was difficult to construct sustainable infrastructure.

facilities at such a forbidding location made normal construction procedures prohibitively expensive and impractical—if not impossible. Chief among RMP's design concepts was "modularized" construction, which it had used successfully in the early 1960s for two oil company projects—a sulfur recovery unit for Mobil Oil in Trenton, Michigan, and a crude topping unit for Chevron's Nikiski refinery in Alaska. Modularization was not a novel engineering concept for the clients to consider, but it had never been done on this scale.[18]

Using the Nikiski refinery as an example, RMP proposed to prefabricate the oil and gas gathering and production facilities in "modules" in three Puget Sound locations (Tacoma, Seattle, and Everett, all in Washington) and then barge them into Prudhoe Bay during the anticipated six ice-free weeks of the Arctic summer, where they would be offloaded and erected on prepared foundations.

In addition, the life-support structures to house the project team also had to be designed, built, and shipped as modules.[19] The logistics and planning involved in moving such a massive amount of materials, equipment, and people were so immense that the North Slope project represented a unique undertaking in the history of private industry. Dante Boccalero, logistics manager, recalled the team effort between RMP and the oil companies:

> *The first two years nobody knew what to expect in Alaska. We had no idea what problems we were going to encounter. Neither did the oil companies. We figured it all out together.*[20]

The prime advantage of modularization was that it reduced the time skilled workers and supervisors needed to stay at the North Slope to complete construction, which reduced labor costs. Speed was also an important factor, given the adverse weather conditions. Modularization ensured that the pipeline and the processing and production facilities were online and able to produce oil.

"Parsons pioneered the modularization concept for building large industrial facilities. It all started up on the North Slope," said Bill Haas, vice president and manager of the engineering department, who supervised thousands of engineers over the course of his 38-year career with the company.[21] Before retiring in 1997, Bill managed Parsons' worldwide computer network of 10,000 computers in 243 office and project locations.[22]

Forty Degrees Below Zero in Their London Fogs

Thus, development on the North Slope began. Initially, the RMP project team did not quite know how to prepare for their trip to Alaska. The bitter cold and the way it slammed into the body could not be imagined—only experienced. Ray Van Horn, business and contracts manager on the North Slope project for 13 years, learned its impact—firsthand—when he ventured to Prudhoe Bay with several RMP executives:

> *We flew into Anchorage and from there on to Prudhoe Bay. I was wearing a London Fog overcoat, like everybody else. In Anchorage, we were all issued our Arctic gear which was in neat red bags. But none of us thought to open the red bags and put the gear on. We all checked them in instead. Then we landed at Prudhoe Bay. The airport at Prudhoe Bay is called Dead Horse. It is not like LAX [Los Angeles International Airport] where you come in with a nice concrete runway and you have these tunnels that come out to the plane and so forth. At Dead Horse, you come in and you land on a runway that's made of gravel and ice.*
>
> *We all exited the plane wearing our London Fog raincoats. When we landed, the chill factor was 40 degrees below zero. The cold air up there just hits you like a brick. We had to walk the length of about one city block to the terminal. Now we're not talking about a Los Angeles-type terminal—but a little shack instead. You go in there, and we were huddled all around and so forth. Most of the people on that plane were workers, so they all had their parkas and their hats and gloves on. But not us.*
>
> *Well, anyway, we had to wait for our bags. Then we began asking ourselves, "What did they do with our bags?" Well, they took the bags off of the plane and put them in a large wooden box. Then they put a forklift under the box, picked it up, took it out to the parking lot, and set it down. You had to go out there to find your individual bag.*
>
> *So here we are, all of us in our London Fogs going out there in this minus 40-degree cold. The thing we didn't realize was how difficult it was to breathe minus 40-degree air. It just goes into your*

lungs and it burns you up. You can take at the most a minute of it until you can't breathe anymore. You'd go out there in the parking lot looking for your bag, and then after a minute or so you'd have to come back in and try again later.

I did this twice. Then I finally got some sense. I figured I'd let everyone else go out there and find their bags. Whatever would be left would have to be mine. So I did that. I went out there, and there's my suitcase and my red bag with my parka and all the Arctic stuff.

Now, I also brought along some suits for meetings scheduled later in Anchorage. They were in these plastic carry-all containers, the kind you would get from your haberdasher when you buy your suits. Well, no one had told me, but in that bitter cold the plastic bags just totally disintegrated. There are my two or three suits, out there on hangers in the middle of the parking lot, with nothing around them. That was my introduction to Prudhoe Bay.[23]

Staffing—A Daunting Challenge

RMP was tasked with designing the modules to withstand the stress of their oceanic voyage and the extreme cold at Prudhoe Bay, determining the optimum module sizes and weights for shipment and construction, planning and managing their installation, and ensuring that a fully integrated production complex would be built on schedule.

Despite the obvious shipping and manufacturing challenges, Arco and Exxon thought modularization was the best solution, and, in 1974, RMP was appointed managing contractor for the east side of the field. The estimated project value was $1.6 billion. Joe Szlamka, a senior principal engineer with WorleyParsons USA, worked in Parsons' London office in the 1960s, briefly left the company, and returned in 1970. He recalled his work as part of the original design concepts team:

When the job started, I was the originator of the [modularization] criteria for the North Slope. I found it very, very challenging. You know, the concept of designing the modules, transportation of the modules. I treated that as real pioneering work and very different from the orthodox refinery design.[24]

However, the most daunting task was supplying the thousands of skilled laborers and subcontractors, on demand, while making certain they were fully prepared for facing the hostile environment and isolated conditions.

The president of Parsons Constructors Inc., Mike D'Antuono, was a "young buck in his 20s," as he described himself, when RMP won the project as the North Slope's managing contractor.[25] He was responsible for bringing in skilled labor from all over the country. The workers flew into Fairbanks and Anchorage where they received Arctic survival training before being transported to Prudhoe Bay. Mike described the process:

They would work for 10 hours a day, seven days a week, eight weeks on, and two weeks off. My job was to get all these rough-and-ready guys up to the job site. I was constantly shuffling craftsmen of all types to make sure they caught their planes, make sure they weren't drunk, make sure they made it, and would be fully prepared for what they would be facing. I wound up in the last of the great gold rushes. It was the last of the great nomadic movements of construction workers.[26]

Ray Van Horn, who worked with Mike, said it was challenging to ensure the training and certification of each worker to perform his craft in Arctic conditions:

I had a small staff in Fairbanks that processed all the craft workers, gave them their physicals, issued them Arctic gear, and provided them with Arctic survival training. When it came to the welders, all of them had to be recertified. Most of them came from the oil fields in Oklahoma and Texas [and] the tolerances they were used to, and qualified for, were nothing compared to what [was] required of them at Prudhoe Bay.[27]

The concentrated numbers of RMP staff onsite at the North Slope (as well as the master planning for Yanbu) occupied the attention of most of the headquarters staff, according to Bill Haas:

The size of the North Slope and the Yanbu projects in terms of the number of home office people involved was just unbelievable. I would guess there were probably 1,000 people or more in Pasadena alone working on those projects in those days. We were training people just as fast as we could. Parsons was very involved with Pasadena City College. Some fellows that worked for me were training students in drafting procedures and in anything else that we could use their expertise. We would immediately hire them once they were trained. We also had in-house training programs.[28]

The Prudhoe Bay Facilities

The Prudhoe Bay facilities were designed to collect a mixture of gas, oil, and water from the wells, separate it at a trio of flow stations, and direct the crude oil to the Alaskan pipeline. This required a series of processing plants (with three oil- and gas-separation units), a central compressor plant, field gas unit, and 10 well site facilities and processing equipment (to extract the oil, gas, and water from the wells), in addition to 90 miles of gas and oil pipeline systems to connect the various processing facilities, permanent transportation infrastructure (with roads, bridges, and docks), central operating and maintenance facilities, sewage and waste disposal systems, permanent housing for 432 people, and temporary housing for a 1,700-person base camp.[29]

Mary Brown, vice president, joined the company in 1980 as a chemical engineer and was assigned to the North Slope to design separation and treatment processes. She described her enthusiasm for seeing engineering concepts become reality:

The first thing that was interesting to me [was seeing] the things that I had designed on paper. There were a couple of innovative solutions that we came up with to solve some of their problems, and to go up there and actually see them in hardware and steel was pretty exciting.[30]

The industrial development of the North Slope dramatically changed everything about Alaska—except its environment. Contrary to early concerns, and thanks mainly to the extraordinary efforts taken by the oil companies and Parsons, there has been no major effect in the native wildlife population on land or sea, as concluded in various independent, state, and federal reports.

Parsons' work on the North Slope was being conducted in one of the harshest terrains and most difficult environments on the face of the earth.

Passing Time at Prudhoe Bay

In October 1976, Belle Dawson, editor of *Tundra Talk*, an employee newsletter from the North Slope project, presented a glimpse of life for RMP's employees in her article, "Passing Time at Prudhoe Bay":

> *How do you provide stimulating recreational activities for almost two thousand men and (a few) women, living and working—isolated from their homes and families—in one of the harshest environments on the face of the earth? That was the challenge faced by RMP's three construction camps at Prudhoe Bay. (In this Arctic outpost, you can hardly plan a Sunday picnic in the park or a relaxing evening at the local bowling alley!)*
>
> *Now with fall rapidly approaching, a full program of indoor activities has been lined up for the few available leisure hours. Most people here work 10 hours or more a day, seven days a week, which leaves them only about three or four hours a day off for free time. Classes in Spanish, bridge, yoga, karate, and creative dance are offered. For the more studious, correspondence courses in a wide range of academic subjects are available through the University of Alaska's Independent Study program.*
>
> *Other activities year-round include six daily showings of a different movie at four separate locations, television (in the form of video cassettes taped the previous day in Anchorage), exchange library of paperback books, pool, ping pong, shuffleboard, and mechanical games like football and air hockey.*[1]

Not mentioned in Belle's article, but a recreational highlight was a membership in the Arctic Ocean Golf and Country Club at Prudhoe Bay, founded by avid golfers such as Mike D'Antuono, president of Parsons Constructors Inc.[2]

Food Fit for a King

From the very beginning of the North Slope project, RMP worked hard to ensure that its employees there were given as many comforts as possible in an otherwise challenging environment. Cathy (Gribbin) Meindl, who began

Left: Mike D'Antuono hired and trained craftsmen from all over the United States to work in the Arctic.

Below: An avid golfer, Mike D'Antuono co-founded the "Arctic Ocean Golf & Country Club," whose members pursued this sport in the less than balmy weather conditions of the North Slope. *(Cap courtesy of Mike D'Antuono.)*

working for Parsons in 1974 is CEO Jim McNulty's executive assistant. She was impressed with the special worker accommodations in the frozen north:

[They] worked seven days a week around the clock. With a schedule like that, you'd pretty much go bananas. When they first started, there was just nothing available, so they started building facilities. Eventually, they had a little mini-bowling alley and a little theater.

I'd see the menus from the cafeteria, and the meal selections were just tremendous. They'd send these great chefs up there because our people there were so remote, at the very tippy-top of nowhere. I'd look at the menus and I'd think, "it was like they all were on a cruise ship, only they were on land instead."[3]

Joe Szlamka, senior principal engineer with WorleyParsons USA, concurred:

You couldn't wish for better food when you're going there. [It] was just fantastic. You know there were guys [that were] six feet, six inches or six feet, nine inches [tall and] 300 pounds. They'd order two or three T-bone steaks. Just everything was available. The sky was the limit. No alcohol [was] allowed for obvious reasons. You know, you're in minus 50 degrees. You can fall asleep outside.[4]

Despite RMP's best efforts, sometimes things broke down. This could lead to work slowdowns and similar problems, according to Ray Van Horn, former business manager at the North Slope:

We had a "wobble," a sort of informal strike. That's when the workers decide that we don't like this or that, and, if you don't straighten it out, we're going to create a slowdown, that type of thing. And what was the reason for the wobble? The ice cream machine had stopped working. It's amazing but true. Here it is, literally freezing outside, but the most delightful thing to eat when you're in that kind of weather turns out to be ice cream. It was the most popular thing up there.[5]

Parsons spared no expense in catering to the non-work needs of its North Slope workers. This included fancy menus prepared by accomplished chefs.

RMP quickly got the ice cream machine working again.

In spite of the conditions and the occasional malfunctions, by and large, everyone involved with the project—executives, managers, and workers—was satisfied being there year after year. Indeed, most were actually enamored with their work because nothing they had previously done could compare with it, according to Marvin McClain, retired vice president:

It was the most exciting thing I'd ever seen. No one had ever built anything up in that frozen tundra before. It was just an incredible, exciting job, and we were working 24 hours a day at it. Everyone knew it was a dangerous, exciting, huge project that would surely go into the history books. That's why everyone wanted to be a part of it.[6]

For example, despite the massive construction activity that took place within range of Alaska's caribou herds, their numbers have remained stable. The Alaska Department of Fish and Game estimated that as many as 123,000 caribou bear their young near the shoreline of the Beaufort Sea. Waterfowl and shorebirds migrate each spring to the North Slope. Grizzly bear, Arctic fox, lemmings, and wolves continue to roam the coastal plain without hindrance.[31]

Marty Badaracco, who joined the company in 1974 as a senior buyer on the North Slope and is now a retired contracts manager, described the lengths Parsons went to in order to protect Alaskan wildlife:

The environmentalists were very concerned about the caribou. It was a big deal that delayed the project for quite a while. We put in what we call caribou crossings, low-profile bridges made of stainless steel that cost an arm and a leg. There were literally hundreds of them up there. Ironically, the caribou herds never used those bridges. They just wallowed right through the little stream, or whatever.[32]

Although construction involved tens of thousands of acres of habitat on the North Slope, each project element was developed only after conducting a scientific study of the sensitive Arctic biology. Mary Brown, vice president, recalled the meticulous care taken by Parsons not to pollute the area in any way, down to the smallest detail:

They were very concerned about the environment. There were very small areas that you could smoke in, and if you ever got caught throwing a [cigarette] butt, you were removed from the North Slope. When you stopped your vehicle, no matter what [kind] it was, you'd get an oil pan and put it underneath to collect drips. I mean they wanted no pollution.[33]

Like many of the staff assigned to the North Slope, she recalled the unique Arctic wildlife and the efforts to protect it:

It's interesting seeing all the wildlife. I saw a polar bear, lots of elk, deer, and caribou. They were all right there.[34]

Modules and More

The schedule called for constructing the Prudhoe Bay facilities in three increments, and each phase was scheduled carefully to match oil field drilling schedules and the completion of the Alaskan pipeline.[35] RMP's headquarters in Pasadena performed most of the engineering work.[36] Some modules were expected to take up to three-and-a-half years for design and engineering, while others would be "fast-tracked."

The modules were constructed in clusters of related facilities. Before loading the units on the barges, all of the systems were tested and retested. The piping systems underwent high-pressure hydrotesting, and the electrical and instrument systems were checked prior to being disconnected and placed in their various modules. The extensive testing at the prefabrication plants reduced the need for similar testing during assembly.

Onsite, the foundations were built to support each cluster so that their modules could be installed with their major pieces of equipment before the workers erected the steel frames for the buildings. After placing the frames, the pipes, valves, and other pieces were fitted to the modules, and the siding was attached to the buildings to protect the equipment from the bitterly cold Arctic weather. The modules were then reconnected into their respective clusters, and the electrical and piping systems were hooked up. Startup testing verified the tie-ins as a final check.[37]

Ron Russell joined the company in 1974 and procured the structural steel for the North Slope modules. He recalled this experience:

I spent time at our module assembly sites in the old days in Tacoma, Washington, Portland, Oregon, and then we moved on down to the Gulf Coast, New Iberia, Louisiana.[38]

Ron has spent the majority of his career procuring materials for the North Slope. He supported "lower 48 states" projects and Japanese, Korean, Venezuelan, German, and Italian ventures such as BP's oil refinery expansion in Boqueron, Venezuela, as well as California's clean fuels program for ChevronTexaco in Richmond.[39]

By 1975, 90 modules had been fabricated for the first sealift (known as Increment I). They were constructed in the "lower 48 states."[40] The largest module weighed over 1,139 short tons and stood as tall as a nine-story building.[41]

Huge, tracked loading vehicles, known as crawlers, transported the modules to the barges for loading. The crawlers were slightly smaller than those used to carry NASA's Apollo space program rockets. To move the giant North Slope modules, the crawlers inched their way from the fabrication site to the dock at a maximum snail-breaking speed of three-quarters of a mile per hour.

The barges that carried the modules were as much as 400 feet long and 100 feet wide, pulled by 9,000-horsepower oceangoing tugs. Huge tow lines secured the barges to the tugs. It took six weeks just to pull the barges from Puget Sound to Prudhoe Bay. Unloading the contents took another 25 days.

Custom-built crawlers on the North Slope move the largest and heaviest units to prepared foundations.

Increment I consisted of a flotilla of 47 barges that left Puget Sound on July 4, 1975, for its 3,500-mile journey to Prudhoe Bay. The unpredictable weather almost brought the sealift to a halt. For the first time in decades, the icy passage failed to thaw from the Arctic Ocean to beyond Point Barrow, the entrance to Prudhoe Bay. The flotilla waited in the open sea for almost two months for the passage to open and, once it did, 10 barges made it through.[42]

On October 1, Prudhoe Bay welcomed 15 additional barges navigating its icy waters. The remaining 22 barges did not make it through the passageway and had to turn back because of the ice. The barges sailed south to Seward, Alaska. On arrival, the modules were offloaded and transported over land to Fairbanks via the Alaska Railroad. They were then trucked to Prudhoe Bay over the road constructed for the Alaskan pipeline.[43] Ron Russell recounted the experience:

> *We actually developed alternate plans. We shipped materials over land. We [also] took a Canadian river called the Hay River, and barged materials on this alternate route and still were able to construct the modules for that year.*[44]

For the final 15 barges that did traverse the passageway, tugboats and cargo ships rushed to unload the precious modules, but their efforts were thwarted because the winter ice closed in fast. Soon the barges were stranded—locked in five feet of Arctic ice—totally inaccessible for offloading by water. However, instead of waiting for the spring thaw, which would have wrought havoc with the tight schedule, RMP performed an astounding feat of engineering. In the midst of blowing snow and howling wind, it built a 4,000-foot gravel causeway to the barges, which required cutting huge chunks of ice from the frozen bay and replacing the ice with 400,000 cubic yards of gravel. Incredibly, all the modules in the ice-bound barges were unloaded by February 1976—at the height of the Arctic winter.[45]

Marvin McClain described this remarkable accomplishment, one that RMP faced with a combination of ingenuity, expertise, hard work, and determination:

> *The barges were racing to try to get to shore, but it got cold prematurely and it froze all the barges offshore. They were in the process of creating an emergency road, a freeway, out to the barges. Instead of taking the ice out and trying to pull the barges in, they built a freeway out to the barges as a way to get to the modules.*
>
> *Now this is in the pitch dark. It's in January. The conditions are horrid. But there were some Parsons people up there that could do things that had never been done before in the world. They had these*

MEETING CHALLENGES WORLDWIDE

THE SAME CARE THAT GUIDED RMP'S work on the North Slope also was evidenced on projects that were offshoots of its main efforts. For example, Sohio's Endicott Island, a Parsons project that came online in 1987, was the first oil and gas production facility built in Arctic waters.[1]

Indeed, the success of these Arctic megaprojects, as well as the other massive construction projects such as Yanbu Industrial City and the Petromin-Shell refinery in Saudi Arabia, centered on Parsons' "attention to details," as Charlie Roddey recalled.[2]

Due to his previous activities in the Petroleum and Chemical Division as a sales engineer, and later as the division manager, Charlie had long-term relationships with Arco, Exxon, and Sohio—Parsons' primary customers on the North Slope. Charlie discussed this period for Parsons:

> *This was an extremely busy time for the corporation. Certainly, some of the grandest and most innovative programs we did were under way. These were tough, challenging jobs. Sometimes, we were at odds with our clients. There's an old adage, "Solving problems is easy. Identifying problems is the tough part." I would mostly ask questions and do a lot of listening. I visited the North Slope, would go home for a few clean shirts, and then fly to Saudi Arabia.*[3]

To facilitate the collaboration that was necessary to complete the North Slope, Parsons arranged for clients to house over a hundred of their engineers and technical staff in its Pasadena headquarters building so they could work side by side with Parsons' design, engineering, and procurement teams. Toward the end of this joint effort, Charlie stated, "The client said this was one of the best projects they had ever done."[4]

On the success of the Petromin-Shell refinery, Charlie gave credit to Paul Hartung, Parsons' project manager, who later managed the Systems Division after Stan Goldhaber retired. Charlie discussed Paul and his superior management:

> *Paul was responsible in large measure for the success of the project. He was a superior manager. The best project manager I ever knew.*[5]

In 1953, Larry Dondanville started with De Leuw Cather & Company (acquired by Parsons in 1977) as a civil engineer. He recounted the project team's efforts to solve the problems of air pollution and traffic congestion once the construction of Yanbu Industrial City was under way:

> *During the development of Yanbu, every contractor had their own transportation system for their employees. [We] came to the conclusion if we're building a town here for 250,000 people, that town is going to have a bus system some day. Why don't we put the bus system in now so we can transport all these construction workers around rather than everybody having their own transportation company?*[6]

Later in his career, Larry was the head of quality control.[7]

From the frozen tundra to the Arabian Desert, regardless of the project, Parsons shows its ability to meet whatever challenges it faces—with competence, integrity, and innovation. Charlie succinctly described the staff's "can do" attitude and enthusiasm during this extraordinary period: "This was the perfect time to be in the world market. There was always something new. [From both] the engineering and construction end, the nature of the work was fascinating."[8]

great big tractors and earthmovers and a big gravel dump. They'd grab that gravel and they'd race out, while in front of them would be a crane cutting and pulling out a giant, 10-foot cube of ice. They'd lift it up, and before everything froze, some workers would rush in and dump the gravel in the hole where the ice was. Believe it or not, but that's the way they built that road—and it worked!

There they were, in those absolutely horrible conditions, replacing the ice with the gravel out to the barges, to download those modules and bring them back in. Nobody had ever done this before. Probably very few—if any—organizations have ever done it since.[46]

Ira J. Blanco, then the RMP vice president and North Slope program director, recounted the efforts taken by the company to deliver each module:

Our people proved to be a dedicated crew from top to bottom, all interested in doing the best possible job to further the objectives of the project. This was evident when they were called upon during the 1975 sealift crisis to develop recovery or alternative plans to answer the question, "What if all or part of the modules don't get through the ice to Prudhoe?" They worked all day and night without hesitation.[47]

Ira joined RMP in 1966, at the urging of Bill Leonhard, who joined the company the same year. Bill and Ira had worked closely together while assigned to the Minuteman program during their service in the U.S. Air Force. Ira had been in the Air Force for 22 years and was its director of facilities engineering for the Minuteman program for five years. He later became president of S.I.P., a Houston-based engineering and construction firm RMP acquired in 1977.[48] Ira was instrumental in the early success of RMP's efforts on the North Slope. As Marvin McClain recalled, "He was a wonderful project manager."[49]

The North Slope experience presented a constant and ever-challenging learning curve, and each succeeding design, fabrication, and incremental phase benefited from the previous "lessons learned" to produce more efficient engineering designs, increase speed, and reduce costs. During the summer of 1976, the Increment II flotilla transported 100 modules and 14,000 tons of general cargo to Prudhoe Bay, all delivered ahead of schedule. By January 1977, the 190 modules from the previous two flotillas had been set in place so that Increment III could begin.[50]

In 1978, the project had been completed so successfully that the following year RMP won two significant contracts to continue its development of the North Slope. Arco hired RMP to expand the eastern oil field, and Standard Oil Company of Ohio (Sohio, now BP) signed up RMP to design, engineer, and construct facilities in the western oil field. The company was selected in 1981 by the Northwest Alaska Pipeline Company (a joint venture of 11 oil and pipeline companies) to design and engineer a natural gas conditioning plant at the North Slope. When completed in 1985, this facility was the largest modular plant built to date.[51]

Parsons expanded its experience and success in Alaska by providing management services, planning, studies, engineering, procurement, and construction management for a BP exploration facility in the Beaufort Sea. Starting in 1983, the four-year, $1 billion project involved production and support facilities on two gravel islands in the sea's shallow waters. The islands served as sites for 17 modules for oil and gas production. There also were some 100 production and injection wells in the Endicott Reservoir about 20 miles northeast of Prudhoe Bay. Several of the main processing modules weighed more than 5,000 tons, the largest ever constructed. They were fabricated in Louisiana and transported by barge through the Panama Canal and north to the Beaufort Sea. Although BP Exploration was the operator and major partner in the venture, Exxon, Amoco, Union Oil, and several Alaskan native organizations were partners as well.[52]

The significance of the North Slope can be measured in terms of natural resource development and engineering accomplishments. The vast Alaskan oil and gas reserves were developed at a time when domestic sources of energy were critical to managing inflation and obtaining a measure of independence from foreign oil. The oil companies proved they could develop the Alaskan oil fields under strict environmental controls and maintain the Arctic's pristine environment. From

Above: Working on the North Slope—with temperatures that often plunged to 65 degrees below zero—was remarkably challenging for everyone involved.

Opposite: The concept of modularization was the equivalent of building a large, complex factory in sections, shipping it to another location, and assembling it like a giant jigsaw puzzle.

an engineering perspective, the technical ingenuity RMP exhibited to overcome the logistical, design, and construction obstacles—on time and within budget—made the North Slope a megaproject for the history books.

Yanbu Industrial City, The Kingdom of Saudi Arabia

RMP won one of its most significant projects in its history in 1975 when the Royal Commission of Saudi Arabia hired the company to prepare a $7.7 million master plan and port survey for an industrial city to be built near the historic site of Yanbu, situated on the Red Sea. RMP's successful efforts in creating an appealing and responsive master plan resulted in its being selected by the Royal Commission to manage the construction of this multibillion-dollar city.[53] The design, scheduling, procurement, logistics, and labor required to construct the infrastructure for Yanbu Industrial City was on a Herculean scale. Today's result of this effort is a self-contained city that ships oil, gas, petroleum, and chemical products to all corners of the world. Three decades after Yanbu Industrial City's opening dedication, Parsons remains actively engaged in designing and managing the construction of various facilities within the city.

Yanbu Industrial City's location is strategic for trade and visually compelling. It borders the Red Sea where rugged mountains frame the striking coastline. The city is 350 kilometers north of Jeddah, also an historic Saudi Arabian port, and nearly 500 miles from the Suez Canal. People have lived in this region for over 3,000 years, linking the trans-Arabian trade to Egypt, the Sudan, and North and East Africa. The rise of Islam in the seventh and eighth centuries brought an unexpected vitality to Yanbu. Pilgrims journeying to Mecca and Medina found Yanbu a welcome relief for their caravans and a safe harbor for ships. The opening of the Suez Canal in 1869 brought more pilgrims and wealth to Yanbu, but this trade largely disappeared when the Hejaz railway was built in 1908 to transport pilgrims from Syria to Medina, Saudi Arabia.[54]

In 1932, Abdul Aziz Ibn Saud declared Saudi Arabia to be a sovereign state with himself as its king. In 1953, the king granted Standard Oil of California (Chevron) the rights to explore for oil in his country. Within three years, Chevron discovered oil near Dammam in the eastern province of Saudi Arabia. The Dammam well was in the heart of what would soon be considered the world's largest oil field, Ghawar. The discovery was so vast that Chevron formed the Arabian-American Oil Co. (Aramco) with Texaco, Exxon, and Mobil to develop

GUARDSMAN

Ghawar. It was agreed that Aramco would pay oil royalties to the kingdom.[55]

When Abdul Aziz Ibn died in 1953, he had many sons, of which five have ruled Saudi Arabia. The first two reigned until 1964 and 1975. A third son, Khalid bin Abdul Aziz (King Khalid), then assumed the throne. King Khalid's half-brother, Fahd Ibn Abdul Aziz, became the crown prince and first deputy prime minister of Saudi Arabia. Later, he ruled as King Fahd. Upon his death in 2005, King Fahd was succeeded by Abdullah bin Abdulaziz. As crown prince, Fahd Ibn Abdul Aziz developed a master economic plan for 1975-1980 that focused on achieving economic progress by carefully investing Saudi Arabia's vast revenue from its oil reserves and its natural resources of gold, silver, copper, zinc, phosphates, and iron. The Royal Family decided that creating an extensive industrial infrastructure would be the most effective means to support its country's economy, rather than continuing to ship most of the kingdom's natural resources to the West for processing.[56]

This concept was supported by the completion of an 800-mile, Saudi-owned oil and natural gas pipeline in 1975, connecting the eastern province's oil fields with the processing facilities on the Red Sea. By decree, King Khalid appointed a royal commission to assess the feasibility of building not one, but two industrial cities that would focus on oil production and manufacturing. Crown Prince Fahd chaired the royal commission. Yanbu and Jubail were the sites selected. RMP was awarded the master plan and construction management at Yanbu, and Bechtel was selected for the same role at Jubail.[57]

The severe challenges posed by Arctic weather and topography in Alaska meant that modules were constructed elsewhere and then transported by barges.

BRIAN WATT ASSOCIATES INC.

BRIAN WATT ASSOCIATES INC., FOUNDED in 1977, was bought by RMP in1984 for its unique design capability in constructing gravel oil-drilling platforms. It remained a part of RMP for only two years, the shortest life span of any given acquisition. Its marine, Arctic, structural, and geotechnical engineering expertise enhanced RMP's projects on the North Slope and in the Gulf Coast.

However, within these two years, Brian Watt Associates Inc. completed the design and installation of a flat-over production deck off the coast of West Africa. It also engineered a deep sub-sea production template and wrote its fabrication procedures, which when built would function in 3,500 feet of water in the Gulf of Mexico.

One of its most important contributions was the design of Alaska's largest artificial island, Mukluk, named for the Eskimo word for sealskin boot. Brian Watt Associates Inc. used its own drilling platform design as the basis for Mukluk, which was located 14 miles off the Alaskan coast and 65 miles northwest of Prudhoe Bay. After completion, the island provided a stable site for Sohio and other oil companies to drill in the frigid waters.

When acquired, Brian Watt Associates Inc. enjoyed a healthy backlog of about 48 projects. However, these projects were rapidly completed, and no new contracts were awarded to this subsidiary. Rather than staying with RMP, Brian Watt, its founder, decided to take some time away from his engineering career and sail around the world. He left little behind except for a memory and an island.[1]

The engineering and construction management of Mukluk Island, Alaska's largest artificial island, was one of Brian Watt Associates Inc.'s signature projects in the Arctic. A new design procedure saved more than one-half million yards of fill and permitted construction of the island in a single season.

RMP had been working in Saudi Arabia since 1956, primarily conducting groundwater and agricultural surveys to increase the country's wheat production and then gaining design accolades with its award-winning Dhahran Airport. At the time the master plan was considered, K Dreher was RMP's business development manager in the Middle East. K alerted RMP management of this opportunity. Stan Goldhaber, who was managing the Systems Division, flew to Saudi Arabia to review the Yanbu site with K and the royal commission.

"There was nothing there, just desert," said Stan, recounting his first visit to Yanbu.[58] However, he and K could see the merit of this endeavor. Based upon their recommendations, RMP quickly submitted a bid for the master plan. The royal commission awarded RMP the contract, and the planning began for the new 10,000-acre city.

Yanbu Industrial City was to be built on 15 miles of coral-lined coast along the Red Sea, extending inland up to six miles. The royal commission had requested it be completed in three phases over a 28-year timetable. The industrial portion of the city would include a deepwater port and harbor for the world's largest ships, crude oil terminals, two oil refineries, refined product storage, an LNG plant and terminal, steel mill, and an aluminum smelter. The community's design would support more than 100,000 people by 2006 and would involve constructing schools, a hospital, the electrical power system, a desalination plant for fresh water, wastewater and sewage treatment, transportation and communication networks, bypass highway, shops, mosques, and an airport.[59]

RMP divided the city into 13 separate areas. The master plan called for dredging an inlet to form a small bay and then building the commercial marketplace (*souk*) and cultural center of the city around the bay. From the center, the city would radiate out toward the mountains in a grid defined by primary roads and landscaping. "It was the creation of an entire system—government, education, industry, short- and long-range planning—all the elements that go into developing an entire urban development structure," said Stan.[60]

RMP's design incorporated Arabian motifs and symbols—points or dots equate to unity, circles to timelessness, triangles to the human consciousness, and squares to the ancient elements of earth, air, fire, and water. The city would also support lush vegetation irrigated by reclaimed water from the industrial plants. To landscape the desert, Stan recalled one of his favorite contributions to the project:

> *One of my ideas was to bring over palm trees from Hawaii. We had a big project at the Honolulu Airport at the time. The company paid for $25,000 worth of young palm trees to be sent over by air, which are now growing full status.*[61]

The thing that made Yanbu different from a lot of other programs was that it involved all aspects of the development of a new city, said K Dreher:

> *We had to worry [not only] about the construction of all the infrastructure items, but also about how the place was going to be managed. We had to worry about how the mail was going to come in and whether we needed a fire department or a police force and what was going to be put in there for recreation and city planning. Water, sewers, electricity, and bridges.*[62]

Yanbu: An Ideal Project

In many ways, Yanbu was the ideal project. "The company features a program management/engineering/construction culture," said Nick Presecan, former senior vice president. "For Parsons, the way of doing the work is to go out, find the job, bring all the resources together, and then do the project."[63]

Nick aptly described the company's culture of accepting the challenge of winning and working a giant project like Yanbu Industrial City—or the North Slope—and then hiring the skilled employees required to succeed with these mammoth programs. Indeed, the bigger the project, the better for RMP, which had never backed away from a challenging project, regardless of its size.

Yanbu Industrial City proved to be a major project for RMP in every way, including the bottom line. "In those days, a high percentage of the revenue of the corporation came from projects like Yanbu Industrial City and other places where Parsons was involved with oil projects,"[64] said Kevin Barry, who began working for the company in 1972, went on to support the chemical demilitarization program, and retired as manager of systems engineering in 2002.[65]

Yanbu Industrial City's master plan was completed in 1977, and soon construction began. The infrastructure statistics for the initial core of the city were impressive in and of themselves. Yanbu Industrial City would require some 437 kilometers of streets, 26,000 telephone lines, 840 megawatts of power production and generation, 74,000 cubic meters of water per day from the desalination plant, 280,000 cubic meters of water storage, treatment

Yanbu Industrial City, located strategically on the Red Sea, was built by RMP for the Kingdom of Saudi Arabia to support oil production and manufacturing.

Prior to development, Yanbu was a port city with a rich history but little modern infrastructure.

plants (sanitary and industrial) each with a capacity of more than 20,000 cubic meters per day, and a 342-bed hospital. Nearly 8,500 villas, townhouses, and apartments were needed, plus 23,000 dormitory units. In addition, commercial centers—featuring supermarkets, grocery stores, small convenience shops, specialty shops, and restaurants—had to be constructed. The industrial development would begin by creating a 400-hectare light industrial park comprising five primary and eight secondary petroleum and chemical plants, in addition to 27 facilities for support manufacturing.

Over time, the Yanbu project employed between 20,000 and 36,000 workers onsite, plus additional manpower needed to help the Saudis operate their city's infrastructure.[66] David Goodrich, Parsons' director of human resources, began his career with RMP in 1981 on Yanbu. He recalled that one of the things that the Saudis were looking for at that time, since RMP was building a city from scratch in the desert, were people to run fire departments, people to run utilities, and all the things one would associate with a town:

Of course, life in Saudi Arabia is not for everyone, and not everyone adapts well to a different culture no matter where it is. The people who did very well were people whose kids had finally flown the coop. It was the empty nesters, and they were kind of ready for an adventure. So that worked out extremely well. The other ones who did very well were career individuals who had children who were still toddlers, and that also worked out extremely well because it was a turnkey community. Everything was provided to you.[67]

David Kays started with RMP in 1974 and became project director on the Jeddah Airport. He transitioned to Yanbu Industrial City and became its program manager and then oversaw the work completed for Aramco. In 1980, David became vice president and managed high-technology research and development projects before retiring in 1993.[68] He described the staffing required to build Yanbu Industrial City:

At the peak time, we had 1,700 people in our direct-hire staff. We were training the Saudis to set up the city administration and run the city. We had not only engineers, but, for instance, we had four ex-city managers out of the United States, helping us design how the city should be run and set up all the mechanisms for the maintenance and all that. Of course, the Saudis themselves operate under the Shari'a [Islamic law], and we were in charge of traffic and everything like that. I had to have a security department that acted kind of like police, and we had, at one point, 36,000 expatriate people there on the Yanbu project doing construction. We were in charge of housing and feeding all of those people, providing them recreation, and keeping everything on an even keel.[69]

Melvyn "Mel" Brown was hired to participate in the contract negotiations for construction management and became the first project manager to construct the port at Yanbu. With a master's degree in city and regional planning from Clemson University, South Carolina, Mel had retired from the Army Corps of Engineers after 15 years, where he had been its deputy district manager for the Honolulu and Portland districts. After completing Yanbu's port, Mel returned to the United States as the program manager for a multimillion-dollar water conservation and development project for the Imperial Irrigation District in Southern California. He later returned to Saudi Arabia to become program director for Yanbu Industrial City and then went back to Pasadena as a vice president and general manager before retiring in 2001.[70] Mel recalled his experience in the Middle East:

I went over there in September 1979, and, subsequently, I became the principal project manager

Above: One of RMP's key successes in helping to create Yanbu Industrial City was the planning elements surrounding the residential quadrants, which provided aesthetically pleasing and comfortable housing, with easy access to mosques, schools, recreation, and retail establishments.

Opposite: Tankers docked at the massive and sprawling refinery at Yanbu Industrial City.

of the port because of previous Corps of Engineers experience and having had a port construction company. There was an old town of Yanbu that goes back many, many hundreds of years, but other than that, the location of the port was completely barren. They had to build port facilities so they could bring in all of the major components of the refineries that were being built in Yanbu. They had to construct a pioneer port to even start bringing in materials. It required some dredging, but not an extensive amount.[71]

The pioneer port was constructed using self-elevating barge piers manufactured by DeLong Corporation and designed to float to the site and be installed very quickly. DeLong piers had also been used by RMP in designing the Port of Cam Ranh Bay during the Vietnam conflict.[72]

By January 1983, the first cargo ship had sailed in the new port. *Parsons News & Views* described the event:

More than 500 officials and workers were on hand to greet the arrival of the Titan Scan, an 8,000-ton, dead-weight German ship. Royal commission

tugs ceremoniously escorted the heavy-lift vessel to the container berths, tooting their whistles and spraying huge columns of seawater high above the cobalt-blue waters.[73]

The original Yanbu Industrial City's master plan was expanded in 1987 to incorporate changes in Saudi Arabia's economic development and population trends. By 1994, five primary industries were in place, representing a combined investment of $7.5 billion.[74] Today, Yanbu Industrial City stands as a dynamic, thriving city served by modern transportation and communications networks; water, sewage, and electrical power systems; a desalination system; industrial and wastewater treatment plants; industrial parks; a deepwater port; an airport; and complete community facilities for housing, education, culture, recreation, commerce, government, public safety, and health care. Its base of petroleum and petroleum and chemical industries provides needed products to the domestic and international export markets, as well as feedstock for secondary industries.

Additional Projects in Saudi Arabia

Yanbu Industrial City was not the only project the company undertook in Saudi Arabia. In 1977, the Government of Saudi Arabia selected Saudi Arabian Parsons Ltd., in a joint venture with Daniel International, to handle program management, construction management, operations and maintenance, master planning, and design review of the King Abdulaziz International

Yanbu Industrial City was a marvel of engineering prowess; RMP created an entire city infrastructure from scratch.

Airport, just north of Jeddah, on the coast of the Red Sea. Jeddah's airport was constructed in four years and dedicated in 1981. The project involved three primary construction contractors, multiple minor contractors, and more than 30 subcontractors. At peak construction, the workforce totaled 14,000.

Covering 40.5 square miles, the $4.2 billion airport was among the largest in the world, with its passenger and cargo terminals, major Royal Saudi Air Force base, aircraft maintenance base, and a special Haj terminal for the millions of Muslims from around the world who would make the pilgrimage to Mecca. The airport also included a Royal Pavilion, the self-contained luxury accommodations for the Saudi royal family and its guests, including visiting heads of state. The pavilion's main reception hall accommodated up to 300 people. It also included a passenger-processing center with its own customs area and immigration offices, baggage-handling equipment, health facilities, and security offices.[75]

In addition, RMP provided Aramco with front-end design, detailed engineering, and construction management for nine sulfur recovery plants and three utility plants. For Martin Marietta Aerospace (now Lockheed Martin), the company constructed and installed 160 solar panels capable of tracking the path of the sun near Riyadh, Saudi Arabia, to generate electric power.[76] However, the largest petroleum and chemical project undertaken by RMP in Saudi Arabia would be the $1.4 billion Petromin-Shell refinery in Al Jubail that began in 1981.[77]

Taking on Significant Risk—Petromin-Shell Refinery in Jubail, Saudi Arabia

While Bill Leonhard was expanding the company through acquisition, he also took a calculated risk by allowing RMP to sign Parsons' first lump-sum, fixed-price contract worth over $1.5 billion for a grassroots, crude oil refinery—a true "bet the company" type of project. The Petromin-Shell refinery would be located in Jubail, the newly built industrial city in the northern part of the eastern province of Saudi Arabia, which had been built by Bechtel. Jubail was the "sister" complex to Yanbu Industrial City, which RMP designed and built in the western province.

RMP entered into a joint venture with Technip, a French company, and Chiyodo, a Japanese construction firm, to design and build the refinery for Petromin (an acronym for General Petroleum and Mineral Organization) and Shell. The turnkey engineering, procurement, construction management, and precommissioning tasks were Parsons' responsibilities; however, the risks were all shared, both joint and several.[78] The refinery at Jubail would produce refined oil products and sulfur for tanker export via the Arabian Gulf passage.

It was Technip that approached Parsons with the concept of teaming. Ray Judson, who was managing the Petroleum and Chemical Division, brought the joint venture opportunity to Bill's attention. The client was asking for a lump-sum bid, and Ray thought Bill would not be interested given the risks involved in completing a refinery under this type of contract. However, Bill said, "You know, there are many lump-sum jobs that turn into open cost jobs,

Above: RMP successfully completed the Petromin-Shell crude oil refinery project in 40 months. It is one of the largest refineries in the world.

Opposite: Pictured is Yanbu Industrial City's desalination unit, which is critical in providing potable water for the 100,000 people who work and live in this man-made industrial and residential oasis.

and let's not turn it down. Let's think about this. Ray, get on a plane and check this out."[79] So Ray flew to Paris and went through Technip's entire operations. He was impressed by the firm and its knowledge of the Middle East and felt teaming with them would be beneficial.

During discussions, Technip and RMP believed that bringing a construction company into the venture would be ideal. Chiyoda was contacted and expressed interest. At this point, Ray was confident in both teaming partners, but knew the cost of developing the bid would be high. In his report to Bill, Ray weighed the pros and cons of the project. He recalled his debriefing with Bill:

> *I said, "Maybe we can team, but geez, it's going to be expensive to bid." Bill said, "Well, let them pick up their costs, and we'll pick up our costs. Go. Run with it." So, I started getting guys together, and we started laying out the bid. It was something that I loved.*[80]

Ray was right—the proposal took six months to complete, but, in the end, the joint venture won the project.

Ray Judson joined the company in 1966. During his 31-year career with Parsons, Ray managed some of its largest projects and brought order to the engineering department. He began working for Parsons in the London office and returned to the United States in 1972. Within a year, Bill promoted him to vice president of engineering for the corporation. In 1978, Ray became a senior vice president and managed the Petroleum and Chemical Division. He was then asked to manage the Systems Division in 1980. In 1984, Ray began managing not only the Systems Division, but also a newly acquired firm, Engineering Science (ES). He succeeded Charlie Roddey as both president of RMP in 1987 and president of Parsons in 1989. Ray retired in 1991, but then chairman and CEO, Len Pieroni, asked him to return several months later to become his special assistant, which he accepted. Ray retired for a second time on January 1, 1996. However, in April 1996, in the aftermath of Len Pieroni's tragic death, Ray was asked by the board of directors to serve as chairman, which he did until 1998, and he remained on the board for three more years until 2001.[81]

The refinery and support complex was built to be one of the largest of its kind in the world. It took the joint venture 40 months to complete the project, which included a liquid petroleum gas (LPG) unit, a high-vacuum unit, hydrocracker, benzene

Significant Projects

1975–1984

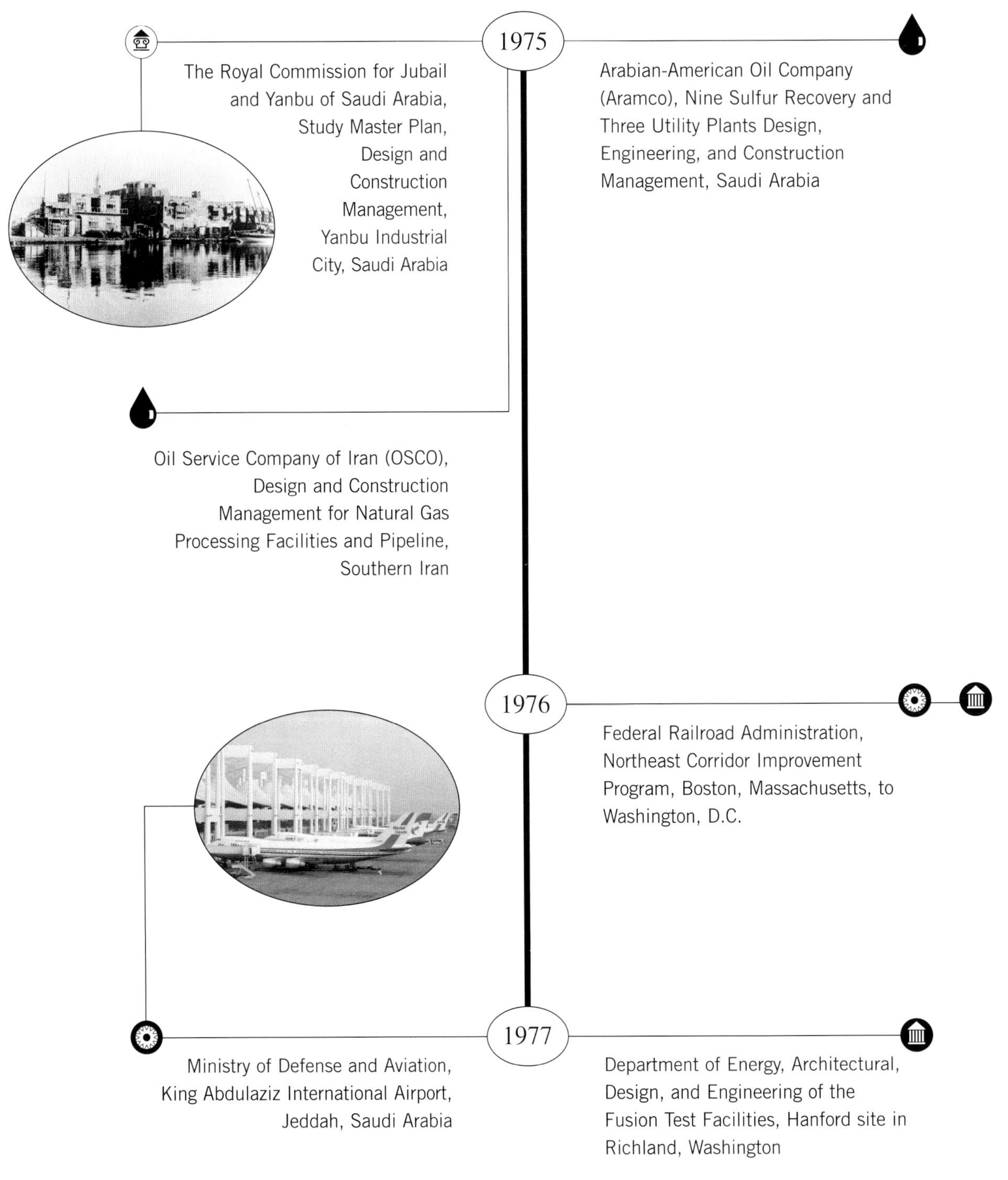

1975

The Royal Commission for Jubail and Yanbu of Saudi Arabia, Study Master Plan, Design and Construction Management, Yanbu Industrial City, Saudi Arabia

Arabian-American Oil Company (Aramco), Nine Sulfur Recovery and Three Utility Plants Design, Engineering, and Construction Management, Saudi Arabia

Oil Service Company of Iran (OSCO), Design and Construction Management for Natural Gas Processing Facilities and Pipeline, Southern Iran

1976

Federal Railroad Administration, Northeast Corridor Improvement Program, Boston, Massachusetts, to Washington, D.C.

1977

Ministry of Defense and Aviation, King Abdulaziz International Airport, Jeddah, Saudi Arabia

Department of Energy, Architectural, Design, and Engineering of the Fusion Test Facilities, Hanford site in Richland, Washington

LEGEND

Commercial | Energy/Petroleum and Chemical | Government | Transportation | Water

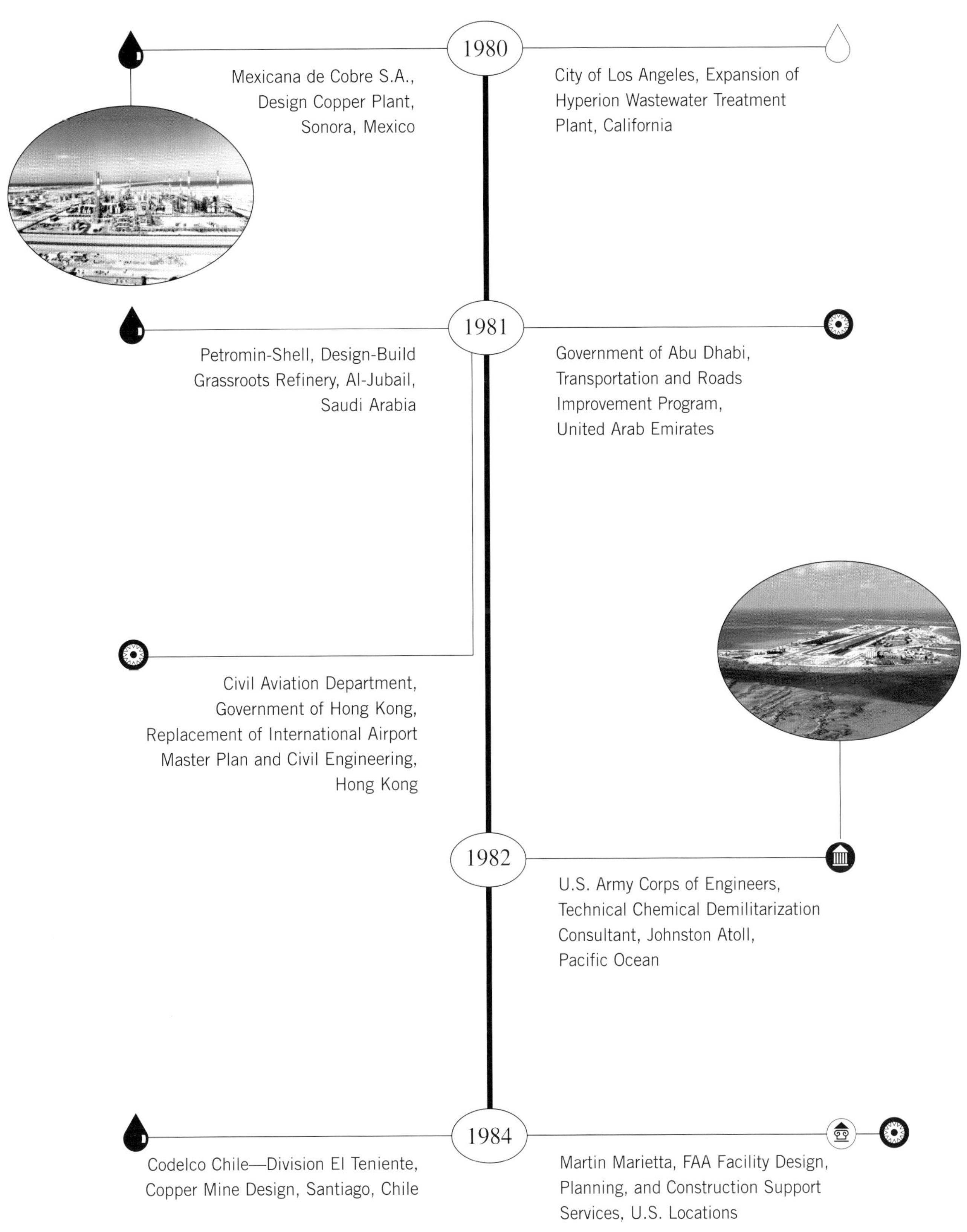

1980
Mexicana de Cobre S.A., Design Copper Plant, Sonora, Mexico
City of Los Angeles, Expansion of Hyperion Wastewater Treatment Plant, California
1981
Petromin-Shell, Design-Build Grassroots Refinery, Al-Jubail, Saudi Arabia
Government of Abu Dhabi, Transportation and Roads Improvement Program, United Arab Emirates
Civil Aviation Department, Government of Hong Kong, Replacement of International Airport Master Plan and Civil Engineering, Hong Kong
1982
U.S. Army Corps of Engineers, Technical Chemical Demilitarization Consultant, Johnston Atoll, Pacific Ocean
1984
Codelco Chile—Division El Teniente, Copper Mine Design, Santiago, Chile
Martin Marietta, FAA Facility Design, Planning, and Construction Support Services, U.S. Locations

Above left: In 1977, RMP began work on King Abdulaziz International Airport, near Jeddah. Photo, above right: Rising gracefully from the desert floor is the completed airport.

Left: Charlie Roddey (right), then RMP's president, was present at the official dedication of the Jeddah International airport on April 12, 1981. Charlie Dutton (left) was RMP's chief airport architect and was Jeddah's project director responsible for overseeing the $5 billion construction effort. In the background is a portion of the 370-acre complex.

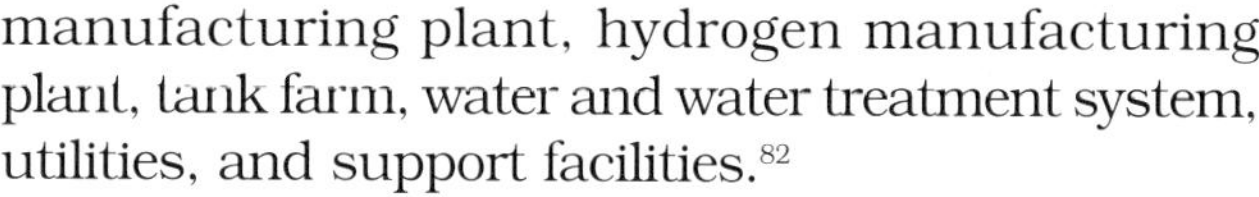

manufacturing plant, hydrogen manufacturing plant, tank farm, water and water treatment system, utilities, and support facilities.[82]

Key executives within RMP thought the project was a huge risk for the corporation and that Bill, who was very conservative in managing the company's finances, would be averse to signing the lump sum contract. Marvin McClain, former vice president, recalled what was at stake:

> *Everybody said, "Don't do this, Bill." He did. And he had his reasons. He sensed it would be good for the company. It was a hard job to do and it turned out to be very good for the company.*[83]

Indeed, given its size, scope, and degree of risk, the Petromin-Shell refinery at Jubail is one of Parsons' most notable oil-related success stories in the history of the company.

Below: The completion of Petromin-Shell, along with other grass-root refineries, further enhanced RMP's worldwide reputation within the oil industry.

Globalization of Petroleum, Chemicals, Mining, and Metallurgy

Although the company's main efforts concentrated on the North Slope and Saudi Arabia, this decade showcased the wins of other notable projects. RMP's petroleum and chemical, mining, and metallurgy clients began constructing facilities in other far-flung geographic regions of the world to develop natural resources.

Between 1975 and 1984, a record number of sulfuric acid plants were engineered and constructed during this time frame in the United States, Canada, Africa, Yugoslavia, Peru, and Iraq. At St. Fergus, Scotland, the company designed, built, and then expanded an onshore gas processing plant for Shell Oil. Then, in Mossmorran, Scotland, the company also designed Shell's natural gas fractionation plant, separating 100,000 barrels per day of natural gas liquids into individual components for chemical feedstock and export. RMP also continued to serve as the technical evaluation contractor for the U.S. Office of Coal Research.[84]

The company designed and constructed two 200,000-barrel-per-day grassroots refineries. The first, in Garyville, Louisiana, for ECOL Ltd. (now Marathon Oil), when completed in 1976, was the largest independent petroleum refinery in the United States. The second was for Dow Chemical's Oyster Creek Division in Freeport, Texas.[85] Bob Sheh, former RMP president, was in sales at that time and was instrumental in bringing the ECOL project to the firm. He recalled how this developed:

> *I was working out of New York, and I had had a string of successes culminating in the award of ECOL, Energy Corporation of Louisiana. It was a hugely successful project, [one of the] first grassroots refineries and it was a breakthrough at a time [when] we were a bit down on our knees [domestically].*[86]

Bob joined the company in 1971 and was one of RMP's key management staff on Yanbu Industrial City. After Yanbu, Bob succeeded Ray Judson as the Petroleum and Chemical Division manager and later became RMP's president when Ray became president of the entire corporation in 1989.[87]

One of the larger domestic awards occurred in 1977 when RMP won a two-phased contract from the U.S. Navy to open California's Elk Hills petroleum reserve, which would require process evaluation and facility design to recover natural gas and oil.[88]

In the Middle East, the company was awarded a $500 million contract for process design, engineering and design, procurement, and construction management for a complex of natural gas processing facilities and 4,300 miles of pipeline for the Oil Service Company of Iran (OSCO) in southern Iran in 1975. Also in Iran, RMP was designing the $1 billion Sar Cheshmeh copper complex that would produce 40,000 metric tons of ore daily and would position the country as one of the world's major sources for this basic metal. The Sar Cheshmeh project was yet another demonstration of the company's skill in managing the sophisticated logistics required to construct a large industrial center with port and transportation facilities in an area of the world that, in itself, needed infrastructure development.[89]

At that time, Ray Judson was the London operations manager in charge of the Iranian projects. He recalled the projects:

Shell Oil commissioned RMP to design its natural gas fractionation plant in Mossmorran, Scotland.

Iran, in those days, was a wide-open society. The problem was trying to get the systems, procedures, and the sequence going [that] we would follow. I hired some good people. I had great difficulty understanding their educational system because they would come in and say, "I got O levels and my A levels." What was O level? What was A level? What did that equate to? I found out five percent of them go to college, and the rest go to technical schools—the equivalent of a junior college.[90]

Unfortunately, Iran's "open-society" was toppled in 1979 by revolutionary forces under the spiritual leadership of Ayatollah Khomeini. In January and February of that year, approximately 200 RMP personnel assigned to the remote areas of the Sar Cheshmeh and OSCO pipeline projects were stranded in-country due to the hostilities. Charlie Roddey was president of RMP at that time. He recalled his frustration over the situation and concern for the project teams:

Communication was terrible. It could sometimes be days between updates. Being responsible for those folks under those circumstances was the most stressful event in my career. Fortunately,

Right: The Shah of Iran visited the construction site of the Sar Cheshmeh copper concentrator and smelter complex built by RMP in south-central Iran. The Shah (second from right) shakes hands with William S. Pederson, vice president, Parsons-Jurden Division, Sar Cheshmeh project director. Others present during the Shah's inspection trip included Russ McNutt (left), Parsons-Jurden resident construction manager; Peter Woodbridge (middle); and T. Tavakoli (right), Sar Cheshmeh Copper Mining Company's managing director.

Below: The Sar Cheshmeh copper concentrator in Iran, which was built for the Iranian National Copper Industries Council.

our managers and crews were independent and resourceful. One group, on its own initiative, shopped around and chartered a jet out of Iran. The others were allowed to leave in March, with no loss of life.[91]

In Central America, RMP completed the preliminary engineering and conceptual design of the Mexicana de Cobre S.A. copper ore crushing and concentration plant in Sonora, Mexico, and also supervised and inspected the plant, concentrator, and auxiliary buildings. When it went online in 1978, it produced concentrates for a smelter with a capacity of 160,000 metric tons per year of blister or anode copper.[92] In 1984, RMP was awarded the design of a materials-handling system for the El Teniente mine near Santiago, Chile, which was the largest underground copper mine in the world.[93] Les Engle, retired senior vice president, discussed the project:

We worked in Chile for many, many years. In fact, we did significant business with the Chilean national copper company and had as much work as anybody. Not to preach, but I think our [contributions] in Chile, Australia, South Africa, places of that sort, gradually developed their own talent and capabilities in mining and metallurgy.[94]

In the United States, major mining and metallurgical projects included the 1976 startup of a 32,000-ton-per-day copper production plant designed and built by RMP in Arizona for the Duval Corporation. It was the first commercial application of a proprietary hydrometallurgical process developed by Duval that treated copper concentrates with less environmental impact and saved energy. RMP also completed the design of a large oxide and sulfide copper complex in Arizona that would eventually produce 69,000 tons of copper annually for the Hecla Mining Company in 1975. For Kerr-McGee Chemical Corporation, RMP engineered a new 1.3-million-ton-per-year soda ash plant and expanded California's preexisting salt cake plant in Trona. In Utah, RMP modernized Kennecott Copper's mine and reduced operating costs by eliminating inside and outside pit rail haulage by redesigning the conveyor and crusher systems.[95]

A prime example of RMP's engineering abilities to support mining and process facilities was its efforts on Kerr-McGee's new soda ash plant and the salt cake plant expansion in Trona, California.

Continuation of Space and Missile Programs and Department of Energy Projects

RMP continued to be involved with the United States' space and missile programs by planning and designing ground support facilities for NASA's space shuttle program and the closed-circuit transonic wind tunnel for its Langley Research Center in Virginia. It also provided planning and management service to the National Oceanic and Atmospheric Administration's research and operational complex in Seattle, Washington.[96]

In 1980, it won the contract to upgrade the "survivability" of the Minuteman underground launch facilities and the satellite control facilities. The latter was designed to protect communications and the command-and-control capsules embedded in the earth from damage in case of nearby nuclear explosions. The company also modified the engineering designs on the Minuteman launch facilities to accommodate the Peacekeeper missiles under a contract with Boeing.

For Martin Marietta, RMP engineered upgrades to the launch complex at Cape Canaveral in Florida, which it originally built as part of the Titan program, and the ground support systems of the space shuttle at Vandenberg Air Force Base in California.[97]

For the Department of Energy's Hanford site in Richland, Washington, RMP's architectural and engineering services provided both preliminary and final design of the $86 million high-performance fuel laboratory and the $70 million fusion materials irradiation test facility in 1977. Also for the Department of Energy, RMP provided compliance services under the Uranium Mill Tailings Radiation Control Act Title II and Title III, as well as the preliminary design and final designs for improving radioactive liquid waste treatment facilities at New Mexico's Los Alamos Laboratory.[98]

By far, the largest nuclear program RMP was actively involved in was at the Idaho National Engineering Laboratory (INEL), where the company had earlier designed so many of its original nuclear facilities. Rick Wilkinson, a registered mechanical engineer who began his career with RMP in 1974, was the senior project engineer and then the project manager on many of the company's INEL assignments. Rick discussed this experience:

> *During this time frame the Systems Division was carried by our work at INEL. We had about 400 people working there. Chronologically, Elden Fisher [one of RMP's first Department of Energy project managers] was the lead for the original task order contract at INEL. I didn't work on it, but Elden told me about it. One of our original projects was the Rover fuels processing facility that we designed and engineered. It operated for approximately six months and recovered more than five times what the government invested in the project in usable uranium.*[99]

Rick further explained RMP's INEL project sequence:

> *I led the engineering team working on the simulation and design for the Remote Analytical Facility upgrade and expansion. We also provided the final design and supported the construction and inspection for the Fluorinel and storage facility.*
>
> *When I became project manager, we were working under a task order contract to provide process upgrades, facility and utility modifications, and environmental and safety compliance. For the chemical processing plant, we engineered modifications to the surface drainage system and the second- and third-cycle raffinate spent fuel reprocessing upgrade.*
>
> *We also saved the Department of Energy $29 million by engineering a seismic upgrade and refurbishment of the chemical processing plant's 100-meter concrete stack, which other contractors had told them needed to be completely replaced.*[100]

Rick is now a vice president and the procurement and construction manager for the Salt Waste Processing Facility that will treat the stored highly radioactive liquid waste at the Department of Energy's Savannah River Site.[101]

At Tennessee's Oak Ridge National Laboratory, the company prepared a conceptual design and cost analysis for the Department of Energy's partitioning-transmutation and high-temperature gas reactor programs. RMP also completed the scoping studies and conceptual design of General Atomic Company's fusion ignition test reactor generating station. RMP was also the first to receive the Nuclear Regulatory Commission's approval for its quality assurance program for both nuclear power plants and nuclear fuel facilities in 1976.[102]

Between 1975 and 1977, as part of the U.S. Army's munition modernization and expansion program, RMP started process planning and

Opposite: RMP engineered upgrades to the launch complex at Cape Canaveral in Florida, which it originally built as part of the Titan program.

Below: RMP completed the scoping studies and conceptual design for General Atomics' fusion ignition test reactor generating station.

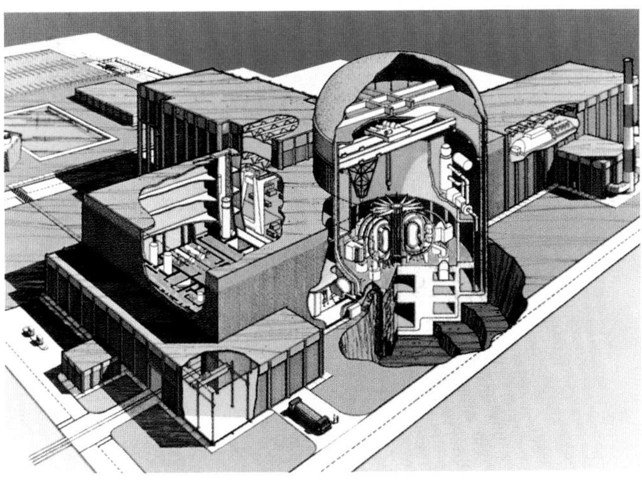

criteria development for a $340 million RDX/HMX (high explosive) production facility at a classified location. Political support for this program was rather short-lived due to many factors, including the end of the Vietnam conflict, Watergate, the oil crisis, and the growing awareness of environmental contamination caused by chemical manufacturing.[103] Its completion harbingered a shift in the nation's focus from building up ammunition and chemical agent stockpiles to focusing on demilitarization and environmental cleanup efforts. RMP's understanding of munitions and missile defense facility engineering would become invaluable in designing the plants that would destroy these stockpiles.

Johnston Atoll

In 1982, RMP became active in the federal government's fledgling efforts to eliminate chemical agents that were the legacy of the Cold War. The company was selected as the Army Corps of

Below: Located 740 miles west of Honolulu, Johnston Atoll was the first facility built to destroy chemical weapons.

Inset: For its design efforts on Johnston Atoll, a first-of-its-kind project, the Army Corps of Engineers bestowed its Excellence in Design Award to Parsons.

The Secretary of Defense Presents the

EXCELLENCE IN DESIGN AWARD

for

Engineering and Industrial Facilities

Special Recognition

In Recognition of Excellence in Architectural & Engineering Design

Project

Johnston Atoll Chemical Agent Disposal System

Central Pacific

Design Firm The Ralph M. Parsons Company

Design Agency U.S. Army Engineer Division, Huntsville

Using Activity Program Manager for Chemical Demilitarization

May 15, 1991

Date

Secretary of Defense

Engineers' technical consultant on the construction of the Johnston Atoll chemical agent disposal facility, which was located 740 miles southwest of Honolulu in the Pacific Ocean. This was the first facility of its kind, and RMP was designated as the "engineer-of-record" and supplied the preliminary plant design, final process design, and technical support services during procurement, construction, startup, and operations. This project brought together a multi-disciplined team from RMP's mining, petroleum and chemical, nuclear, and systems groups to design the furnace, offgas equipment, materials handling, instrumentation, controls, piping, gas containment and isolation systems, and other specialty components.[104] For its innovations on Johnston Atoll, the Army Corps of Engineers bestowed its Excellence in Design Award to RMP.[105]

Frank Shafran, the first project manager on Johnston Atoll, brought the team together. He oversaw most of the design phase, which ultimately made possible the safe destruction of the agents.[106] In a 1983 letter to RMP, the Army Corps of Engineers' Huntsville Division acknowledged his contributions on Johnston Atoll as, "a determined effort on the part of Parsons and, in particular, Mr. Shafran, the project manager, to manage this project within the budget. It is this kind of management expertise and technical 'know-how' that Huntsville Division has come to know and trust."[107]

Frank joined RMP when the nuclear and energy firm he was with, Vitro Engineering, was acquired in 1966. He also was project manager during the design, engineering, and construction management of San Miguel's brewery and corporate headquarters in Pampangas, the Philippines, as well as during the preparation of a reliability, availability, and maintainability (RAM) engineering study for Intel's microchip plant in Arizona in 1984. Upon retiring from Parsons in 1992, Frank was a principal project manager.[108]

When the Johnston Atoll design was almost complete, Peter Jahn succeeded Frank as project manager. Frank and Peter had previously worked together on several projects, and Frank recruited Peter as his replacement. Peter, a civil engineer, started with the company in 1963. Up until the Johnston Atoll project manager position, he was primarily assigned to Parsons-Jurden, supporting mining and related projects in Mexico, Chile, Australia, Iran, Rwanda, Saudi Arabia, Canada, and the United States, and he also served as the company's precontracts director. In addition, Peter managed quality assurance on a nuclear power plant, supported the Minuteman program, and was the closeout project manager on a 480-bed hospital in Long Island, New York.[109] In recalling the particulars of Johnston Atoll, he described the procedures project team members followed upon first landing on the island:

> *The island is a 9,000-foot runway with sides. Before you went to baggage claim at the "airport," you went to a gas mask fitting, and you'd get your gas mask and your hypodermic needles for self-injecting [antidotes if exposed to chemical agent], and then you would go to baggage claim. There was the chemical weapons storage area and the chemical weapons destruction plant we designed, on one side. On the other side, there are fenced areas for plutonium and Agent Orange.*
>
> *I went out sometimes three or four times a year and was happy to go home after six weeks, but many people were comfortable [staying longer] in that environment. One person had been there for 25 years. Normally, the team had Sundays off and went swimming and snorkeling. The coral [reef] was superb, and you could see eight-foot manta rays and sharks. There was also a "pet" tuna fish that swam up at dinner time to be fed by diners at the atoll's shore-front restaurant.*[110]

The chemical agent processing areas were enclosed in an explosion-resistant and vapor-proof containment area with quick-closing blast containment ventilation valves and many specially designed penetration barriers, some of which required 24-inch-thick concrete walls. The disposal technology selected relied on thermal destruction, which required the engineering and design of a highly specialized furnace and furnace gas cleanup systems. Airlocks were developed for entrance into areas containing chemical agents. To reduce any human exposure to the toxins, the treatment facilities were also designed for containment of possible chemical agent leakage or in the event of an explosion. The furnace vault was put to the ultimate test when a rocket explosion occurred during operations. Except for minor leakage into electrical conduits, the system performed better than expected.[111]

THE GREAT RACE

THE INTANGIBLE BENEFITS OF A career at Parsons cannot be measured in dollars and cents. It is the positive feeling many of the staff, both past and present, conveyed in describing their professional experiences. It is clear they take tremendous pride in the corporation's accomplishments and have established a rapport with coworkers that goes well beyond the normal day-to-day working relationship. From the beginning, RMP had a spirit of camaraderie. In the mid-1970s and 1980s, it was exemplified in PERC (Parsons Employee Recreation Club), which contributed to the well-being of Parsons' staff.[1]

PERC was very active in planning the corporation's social events such as annual parties, outings, and even an ice cream social where the key executives dished out scoops of this favorite dessert to the staff.

Ann Hicks, who has spent three decades with the company, has been involved with PERC since its inception in 1976:

I've been the president of PERC for I don't know how many years. Originally, the company would give us money each year for various events and activities. Then, we began a store for the employees and sold all types of things—cards and stationery, gifts, pens and pencils, candy, vitamins, and amusement park and movie tickets. We only marked things up 10 percent. We were nonprofit so every penny we made we spent on activities for the employees.[2]

The Great Race

Perhaps the most famous event that PERC established was "The Great Race" in Pasadena. The Great Race was a humorous competition that can best be described as a cross between a mini-parade and a motorless vehicle competition. Each division within RMP would create a comical entry that would be humanly propelled by costumed staff down the race course—the parking lots surrounding the headquarters'

The total destruction of the chemical agents stored on Johnston Atoll was completed in 2000.[112] Based upon this project experience, Parsons has been retained on all facets of the chemical weapons demilitarization program ever since, from designing technical advancements to managing the construction and operations of neutralization facilities. It also went on to gain international prominence in this field by managing similar programs in Russia.

Waste Treatment Plant Expansions

In response to objections from swimmers and visitors to the presence of raw sewage in the waters off Santa Monica's beach, the City of Los Angeles built and began operating a simple screening plant in El Segundo, California, in 1925—the first treatment facility at the Hyperion site. By 1950, Hyperion had evolved into one of the most modern treatment plants and the largest on the West Coast.

building. The entries would be judged on their festive themes and the time it took each division to complete the course. Ann reminisced about the competition.

> *In the Great Race, we had a cheerleading team, and different divisions would enter their own motorless cars. Finance used to always win. I remember that Ray Van Horn was in the first Great Race, and he was dressed as a baby. He had a diaper on, a bonnet, and a little bottle that was filled with orange juice and something else. Channels 2, 4, and 7 would come out here every year and film us. They would do this little segment they put on their news shows for two minutes or so. It would show us running around in our little cars. The stories were always hilarious.*[3]

The last Great Race was in the late 1980s, but its sense of fun and spirited "good times" is fondly remembered by many employees.[4]

Above: RMP's first "Great Race" participant, Ray Van Horn, in costume. Ray was RMP's business manager at the North Slope. His sense of humor brightened many a colleague's day at PERC functions.

Left: For many years PERC's "Great Race," held annually at RMP's world headquarters, was a popular event for employees, the media, and the people of Pasadena.

Hyperion further transformed into the world's largest energy recovery sludge treatment plant as a response to an amendment to the 1972 Federal Water Pollution Control Act and the 1977 Federal Clean Water Act, which mandated full secondary treatment of all wastewater. To accommodate the increase in waste sludge and digester gas projections to the year 2000, Hyperion required further upgrades and treatment expansion that also encompassed an energy recovery sludge management system. In a joint venture with James M. Montgomery (now Montgomery-Watson), RMP provided program management, planning, design, construction management, and startup services for the 450-million-gallon-per-day energy recovery treatment facility. Construction began on July 1, 1983, and it was fully operational by June 30, 1989.[113]

After completing this project, Parsons continued providing wastewater treatment services to the City of Los Angeles. It designed the upgrade to the Terminal Island wastewater treatment plant in San Pedro, which was completed in 2000 at an estimated construction value of $45 million.[114] In addition, Parsons became an "on call" consultant for environmental and air quality services to the city's Department of Water and Power and for engineering services on the seismic retrofit, rehabilitation, and widening of six city bridges.[115]

Highways and Byways

In Abu Dhabi, UAE, the company began managing a $2.6 billion urban highway development program in 1977—one of the largest in the world. It involves the planning, design, and construction administration of an entire road transportation network. Parsons manages over 100 separate subcontracts, which typically include water, wastewater, storm water, electrical, and telephone relocations.

The size of the total program is impressive. Ten major bridge interchanges, 256 miles of streets, and 102 signalized intersections have been fully completed. The road network has a fully integrated intelligent transportation system, designed by Parsons, which includes fiber optics, closed-circuit television coverage of all major traffic areas, automatic detection of speed-limit violations and traffic control problems, security and surveillance of sensitive areas, and a traffic control center. In building the system, over 385 miles of storm water drainage lines connecting 16,761 drainage structures and discharging via 23 pumping structures through 32 major outfalls have been completed. More than 1,362 miles of low- and high-voltage electrical distribution cables, 16,568 light poles, 105 miles of water distribution pipelines, and 172 miles of irrigation pipelines have been installed. More than $70 million in underground and abovegrade parking structures have been constructed to provide an additional 2,000 parking spaces that were not originally anticipated.

One of the largest endeavors on this program was the New Corniche development project, which

RMP was hired to help expand Denver's Stapleton Airport; years later, after the airport was to be replaced by residential homes and corporate buildings, Parsons remediated jet fuel contamination affecting the airport site prior to this new construction.

included the design and construction supervision of 700,000 square miles of reclaimed land along the coastline of Abu Dhabi. Here, nearly four miles of roadway, significant vehicle parking, 10 pedestrian underpasses, three tunnels, one bridge, and multiple recreational areas were built. This development is unequalled in this region of the world and has helped solidify Abu Dhabi's stature as a model city and world-class tourist destination.[116]

In 1976, the company won the Federal Railroad Administration program as a joint venture contract with De Leuw, Cather & Company for the $1.8 billion Northeast Corridor Improvement Program—a 456-mile, high-speed, intercity passenger service project between Boston, New York, and Washington, D.C. The goal was to achieve a New York to Washington, D.C., run time of two hours, 40 minutes and a Boston to New York run time of three hours, 40 minutes. The construction encompassed installing continuously welded rail, replacing wooden ties with concrete ties, replacing or refurbishing bridges, reboring tunnels, realigning curves for high-speed operation, and modernizing the electric supply system.

It took over 20 years of effort, but the Northeast Corridor transports more passengers than any other rail corridor in the country and has become Amtrak's most cost-effective operation.[117] WMATA (Washington Metropolitan Area Transit Authority) and the Northeast Corridor were the foundation of the firm's professional relationship with De Leuw, Cather & Company, which ultimately was acquired by RMP in 1977.[118]

Larry Dondanville, a well-regarded manager in De Leuw Cather & Company, recalled the skills each firm brought to these two megaprojects: "The combination of De Leuw's railway and rapid transit experience and Parsons' construction management experience just seemed to be a natural fit."[119]

In addition to the airport in Jeddah, Saudi Arabia, the company started the master planning and engineering design for the $1.5 billion expansion of the (former, now closed Kai Tak) Hong Kong International Airport, engineering and construction management of the Harry S. Truman Airport at St. Thomas in the Virgin Islands, and architectural and engineering services at Guam International Airport Terminal in this decade.[120]

In time for the 1984 Summer Olympics, the company completed the design and managed construction of double-decking the roadway at Los Angeles International, which was the largest project in the airport's 51-year history. The project included a five-lane elevated roadway with a continuous 15-foot sidewalk adjacent to existing terminals. When finished, it doubled curbside parking for passenger drop off and pick up.[121]

Burt Lewis was the joint venture project manager, and John Melanson served as the deputy project manager. They both were civil engineers and joined RMP as part of the De Leuw Cather & Company acquisition. After Los Angeles International was complete, they managed the team assigned to engineer the 52-mile Outer Loop Highway around Phoenix, Arizona. Burt retired in Phoenix in 1987 as a vice president but continued to work with the company as a senior consultant. During his career, he was the program director for the Kuwait urban highway design project between 1984 and 1985 and was responsible for the preliminary design of a portion of the New Jersey Turnpike. John managed the road designs and traffic control system for Yanbu Industrial City and was the senior transportation engineer on master planning for Al Kharj Military Complex in Saudi Arabia that housed the air base, air academy, and maintenance facility. He retired in 1994.[122]

Parsons also expanded Colorado's Stapleton International Airport in Denver. The airport was later closed as part of Denver's redevelopment efforts to build a commercial and residential community in its stead. In the late 1990s, Parsons remediated jet fuel contamination from the former airport, and the site became an award-winning environmental remediation project.[123]

As these many projects illustrate, the company participated in the full range of markets and geography. This typical versatility reflected its signature characteristic, according to Graydon Thayer, the retired head of the company's human resources department:

> *One of the things that has always been so great about Parsons—it has the ability to immediately shift gears and go after new markets that are opening up. That remarkable adaptability has kept Parsons in very good stead over the years because nothing is ever static in business.*[124]

ENGINEERING SCIENCE INC.

ENGINEERING SCIENCE INC. (ES), founded in 1946 as Ludwig Brothers Engineering, was a partnership of four brothers. Dr. Harvey F. Ludwig was an experienced sanitary engineer with an established reputation at the U.S. Public Health Service. He and process engineer Joseph L. Feeney incorporated ES in 1957 as an extension of the brothers' partnership.[1]

The company's locations consisted of a research and development laboratory in Berkeley, California, and an engineering office in Arcadia, California. It earned its reputation by pioneering water reclamation processes that were both safe and effective in areas with minimal potable water. Notable projects in the early days included two major water-quality control studies, one for the delta of San Francisco Bay and the other for Lake Tahoe in Nevada. ES also ventured into the international arena by providing water-quality, sanitation, and marine-outfall engineering and scientific capabilities in India, Brazil, Uruguay, Colombia, Haiti, and Ghana.[2]

In the early 1970s, Zurn Industries, a water and wastewater control products manufacturer in Erie, Pennsylvania, bought ES to become its consulting arm. After the acquisition, ES continued to expand its staff, purchase small firms that offered services complementing its own, and open new offices in strategic locations. However, an inherent conflict of interest quickly became evident. As a consulting firm trying to determine the best solutions for its clients, ES could not always recommend the equipment of its parent company. In 1976, a small group of ES executives repurchased the company from Zurn, and ES became independent once again.[3]

During the next five years, ES grew to a staff of 850 scientists and engineers with domestic offices in California, Texas, Colorado, Illinois, Ohio, Georgia, and Washington, D.C., in addition to several international locations. ES was interested in expanding further. However, its executives realized this could only occur if the firm was associated with a larger company with additional engineering resources such as Parsons.[4] In April 1981, Parsons acquired ES as a wholly owned subsidiary, and ES president, Robert L. White, continued to serve as its president.

Examining documents of the ES acquisition by RMP in 1981. Shown, left to right, are Peter Moncayo, vice president, finance, ES; attorney William J. Bogaard, who later became the mayor of Pasadena, California; Gordon Magnuson, senior vice president, ES; William E. Leonhard, RMP's chairman, president, and CEO; Charles L. Larrick, group vice president, ES; and ES Chairman and CEO Robert L. White.

"The relationship with Engineering Science actually began on a project basis. Engineering Science was doing work with Parsons overseas. They first developed a relationship with the owners of Engineering Science and eventually sold the company," said David Burstein, who succeeded Robert as its president. David joined Parsons in 1972 and stayed with the company for 25 years, primarily expanding its environmental services.[5]

ES became the environmental arm of Parsons and won contracts for work required by federal legislation, specifically, the Resource Conservation and Recovery Act (RCRA) and the Comprehensive Environmental Response Compensation and Liability Act (CERCLA). ES excelled in cleaning up heavily contaminated sites involving multiple responsible parties. Its operations and maintenance (O&M) services were geared to municipal wastewater projects in such diverse geographical areas as Downingtown, Pennsylvania; Jefferson Parrish, Louisiana; and Chandler and Gilbert, Arizona. ES also won O&M contracts with industrial clients such as C&H Sugar, General Electric, General Motors, and Texprint.

In the late 1980s, ES incorporated into its organization the environmental group of CT Main and the urban planning group of Harland Bartholomew & Associates, both purchased by Parsons in 1985. By 1996, ES had become Parsons Environmental Services, a division under Parsons Infrastructure & Technology Group Inc.[6] It had now matured into a staff of almost 2,000 with 34 offices across the country and provided municipal and industrial wastewater, water resources, solid waste, air quality, environmental studies, and hazardous waste consulting services.

In 2002, the ES staff was distributed into three global business units to align their areas of specialty among Parsons' federal, municipal, and commercial clientele. The environmental staff at Parsons takes great pride in the legacy of ES and continues to provide world-class solutions to remediate water, air, and soil contamination.[7]

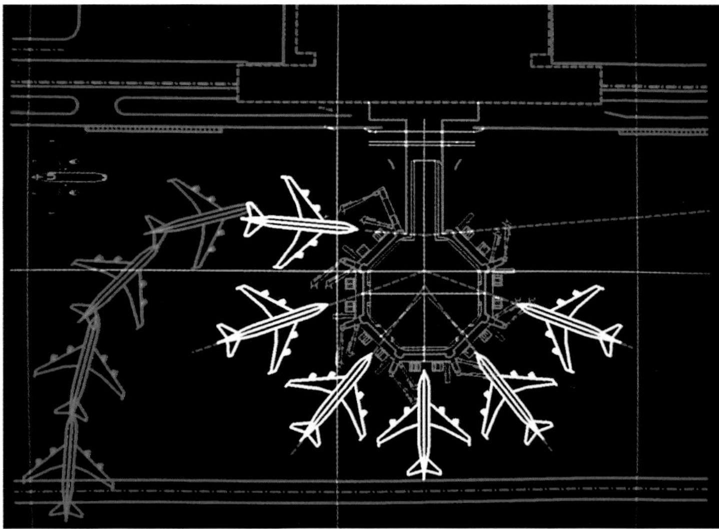

Parsons was a pioneer in the use of computer-aided design (CAD) technology that significantly reduced the time to generate blueprints and schematics.

The Advent of Computer-Aided Design

One technical advancement within the engineering community in the mid to late 1970s was the computerization of drafting design, engineering, and construction documents. Drafters, trained in the intricacies of computer-aided design (CAD) software, would now generate blueprints and schematics in less time and with greater accuracy than had previously been possible by hand.

Parsons bought its first CAD system, called Auto-Troll, in 1974, and was on the cutting edge of using this technology. Ultimately, CAD facilitated the completion of the North Slope, Yanbu Industrial City, Petromin-Shell, and numerous other projects.[125] Tim Lindquist, engineering systems software manager, who joined RMP straight out of high school in 1973, recalled RMP's early days with CAD:

> *I was on the design-drafting board for almost two years. We'd just received the Auto-Troll system, only a couple of months, and I got involved. This was all brand new. I had no idea what it was. I spent five years with that system. Of course, I learned just about everything I could and wound up supervising the group.*

Roughly [in] about 1979, our vice president of engineering, Bill Flegenheimer—he was probably the best manager I had worked for—asked [me] and another individual to determine the new needs regarding CAD. We determined that InterGraph Corporation had the CAD system for us. When we first started with CAD, we were primarily doing two-dimensional [2-D] design [for] primarily schematic type diagrams for the various disciplines. Then, when we got InterGraph, [it] had some tremendous 3-D design tools, which we're still using today.[126]

Bill Flegenheimer retired from Parsons in the early 1980s and died shortly thereafter. In addition to promoting the early use of CAD, he developed many of the engineering procedures the company used in the 1970s.[127] Tim recalled Bill's management style:

He was just a wonderful person to work for. He was the kind of manager that would give you the assignment and just let you go. Then, you came back with the results, and he had nothing but praise for you.[128]

In addition to Bill Flegenheimer, a key CAD pioneer at the company was Bob Yang. He promoted the technology so adroitly that it became

DE LEUW, CATHER & COMPANY

IN 1977, RMP ACQUIRED FROM TRW ONE OF the most prestigious engineering, design, and consulting firms in the country that specialized in urban and mass transit systems, railroads, highways, and ground transportation—De Leuw, Cather & Company.

Its founder, Charles E. De Leuw, was a civil and structural engineer who worked for several railroads and engineering companies before serving as a commissioned officer in the Engineer Reserve Corp during World War I. After receiving severe wounds in September 1918 during the Battle of Argonne, France, he was honorably discharged as a captain in January 1919. Charles went into private practice as an engineer and, in 1919, incorporated Charles De Leuw & Company in Chicago, Illinois.

Like Ralph Parsons, Charles was a successful entrepreneur with a reputation for sincerity, forthrightness, and innovation. According to a written tribute, Charles "had a delightful sense of humor, and in all of his personal relationships he displayed graciousness and understanding. He was truly a man of quality."[1]

Initially, the firm concentrated on projects in the Midwest and engineered an unusual mix of hydraulics and reclamation, street improvements, traffic control, and municipal and sanitary projects. In 1923, it earned engineering acclaim for preparing a comprehensive rapid transit system report for the city of Chicago that incorporated subways and an "elevated railroad."

Charles was president of the company for 47 years. He saw it through the Great Depression of the 1930s and provided the leadership that allowed it to flourish in the decades that followed. In the 1940s, De Leuw steadily gained a strong foothold in designing expressways and superhighways.

A key contributor to the success of the company was Leroy "Roy" Cather who joined De Leuw in 1922. He helped Charles weather the highs and lows of the Depression and World War II. In 1943, Roy became vice president, and Charles added "Cather" to the company's name. The firm became known as De Leuw, Cather & Company.[2]

De Leuw, Cather & Company grew dramatically during the 1950s and 1960s, taking on major transportation projects all over the world, and its domestic projects were equally impressive. De Leuw, Cather & Company created preliminary plans and estimates for a double-track rapid transit system from the White House to Alexandria, Virginia, by way of the Pentagon, which led to its becoming the first general engineer consultant on WMATA, the 103-mile, metrorail rapid transit system for Washington, D.C., in 1966.[3]

the cutting-edge tool to integrate engineering with design and construction. Bob joined Parsons in 1980 and retired as senior technical director of the CAD Service Center.[129] Jim Thrash, senior vice president, stated, "Bob really is the father of CAD."[130]

Acquisitions

To continue its growth by expanding into new markets, Parsons acquired five firms during this decade. Each firm added expertise and made significant contributions to the company's financial stability in the years to come.

In 1977, RMP acquired De Leuw, Cather & Company, which specialized in urban and mass transit systems. RMP and De Leuw, Cather & Company formed a joint venture on the Northeast Corridor Improvement Program the year before and also worked closely together on the WMATA project where they both contributed significantly to its design, engineering, and construction. With a workforce of 1,100, De Leuw, Cather & Company became the backbone of what is now Parsons Transportation Group.[131]

Southern Industrial Piping Inc. (S.I.P.) was also acquired in 1977. This Houston-based firm was respected for its engineering and construction

After becoming a Parsons subsidiary, De Leuw, Cather & Company led the firm in design, engineering, and construction of transportation-related projects. Its president, James A. Caywood, helped focus it into three market areas: rehabilitating aging domestic freight and passenger rail systems, designing urban corridor transportation systems, and improving transportation in developing countries. Caywood joined De Leuw, Cather & Company in 1966 and retired as chairman emeritus in 1988 after serving 10 years as its president. Both WMATA and the Northeast Corridor Improvement Program were very successful projects due to his stewardship.[4]

In 1991, the corporation integrated the operations of several subsidiaries' public transit, railroad, bridge, transportation planning, highway, and airport projects under the De Leuw, Cather & Company umbrella and became known as Parsons De Leuw.[5] Robert S. O'Neil, who had joined De Leuw, Cather & Company as a civil engineer in 1960, was appointed by Len Pieroni as its president. Bob received many engineering awards during his 40-year career and served as director of both the American Road and Transportation Builders Association and the International Road Federation. He was also officer-in-charge of the historic $16 billion English Channel Tunnel on which Parsons served as engineering advisor.[6] In Bob's honor, Parsons endowed a scholarship at the University of Notre Dame, his alma mater.[7]

In 1996, De Leuw, Cather & Company was merged into Parsons Transportation Group. The caliber of De Leuw, Cather & Company's engineering and project history provided a firm foundation for Parsons' continued success in engineering transportation systems all over the world.[8]

Jim Shappell, who succeeded Bob O'Neil as president in January 2001, joined De Leuw, Cather & Company in 1975. He served in a number of key positions, including senior vice president and global business development manager for Parsons Infrastructure and Technology Group; business development manager for the Europe, Middle East, Africa, and South Asia regions; and as vice president and business development manager for the Systems Division of RMP.[9] Jim discussed the group's activities:

> *The preponderance of our work is government driven, either through policy, but primarily through funds, and the majority of our clients are public authorities or public agencies. Our percentage [of projects] is [split] 80 percent domestic and 20 percent overseas.*[10]

As it moves forward into the future, Parsons' stellar project portfolio—in part based on the contributions of De Leuw, Cather & Company—will continue to be a dominant factor in designing, engineering, and constructing the world's transportation infrastructure.

S.I.P. INC.

ORIGINALLY FOUNDED IN 1951, S.I.P. INC. was a subsidiary of the Farnsworth and Chambers Company, a privately held construction firm in Texas with an impressive portfolio of constructing utility infrastructure, dams, roads, bridges, and buildings. Given its proximity to major oil companies, Farnsworth and Chambers understood the financial benefits of diversifying into petroleum and petroleum and chemical construction and formed S.I.P. (Southern Industrial Piping) to serve this market. By 1957, S.I.P's projects had become the mainstay of the parent company. S.I.P. maintained a healthy profit by using its own heavy construction equipment and operating its own extensive maintenance yards.[1]

In 1961, the Chambers estate sold S.I.P. to a small group of stockholders and A.C. Lederer Jr., an executive of the former subsidiary. It enjoyed a loyal client following, which helped the firm begin again. At the top of its client list were Shell Oil, Arco, Monsanto, Exxon, Universal Oil Products, Celanese Chemical Company, and Du Pont. Several of these clients awarded S.I.P. open contracts to perform engineering and construction services.[2]

In 1977, RMP acquired S.I.P. to the benefit of both companies. They shared a number of the same clients, and their services complemented each other. S.I.P. needed the additional resources and international reputation that RMP offered. RMP needed greater engineering and construction capabilities in Texas to serve this market more effectively.

A.C. remained as president during the transition, and Ira Blanco, former program manager of RMP's North Slope projects, succeeded Lederer. S.I.P. expanded RMP's Gulf Coast presence. Among its many projects, S.I.P. modernized the utility computer control center for Shell at its Deer Park, Texas, chemical complex and designed a natural gas production offshore platform for Arco in the Gulf of Mexico. It operated as a subsidiary until 1995 when it merged into Parsons Process Group, which became Parsons E&C, now WorleyParsons USA—owned by Worley Group.[3]

of petroleum and chemical and petroleum facilities on the U.S. Gulf Coast. Before this purchase, RMP had been providing most of its own refining and chemical design and engineering from its headquarters in California. However, because Houston was the hub for many petroleum clients, S.I.P. closed the geographic gap between RMP's services and the clients in the oil and natural gas fields of Texas and Louisiana.[132]

Incorporated in 1957, Engineering Science Inc. (ES) was a pioneer in the water reclamation field. Parsons acquired ES in 1981 and provided services to both government and private industry for projects requiring its expertise in air quality, water quality and reclamation, soil and groundwater remediation, hazardous waste minimization, and cultural and natural resources. ES was melded into three of Parsons' global business units to support water, commercial, and federal projects in 2002.[133]

Houston-based Brian Watt Associates Inc. was founded in 1977 and specialized in marine, Arctic, structural, and geotechnical engineering, as well as the design of offshore drilling and production facilities. Its engineering expertise complemented Parsons' petroleum and chemical projects on the North Slope and Gulf Coast. It was acquired in 1984.[134]

Restructuring

RMP reorganized in 1978 during this significant period of growth. Parsons Corporation (Parsons), a holding company, was incorporated in Delaware to oversee its various subsidiaries and to support further acquisitions.[135]

Bob Davidson, who joined Parsons as part of the De Leuw Cather & Company acquisition, became the corporation's general counsel. He recalled the formation of Parsons:

The Parsons Corporation was formed, in part, to diversify. The Ralph M. Parsons Company [RMP] had built its reputation principally on the design and construction of large facilities for the petroleum and chemical mining and some civil projects for the government.

The [acquired firms] had a solid reputation in fields where, up until that time, Parsons had not been terribly active. [They] allowed Parsons to become involved much more deeply in environmental and transportation projects and allowed the acquisition companies to do much larger projects. They were very skilled in what they did, but they had never done projects on the size and scale that Parsons had done.[136]

Bob was invaluable in analyzing and negotiating the acquisitions that were to come, as well as major client contracts such as the Petromin-Shell refinery in Saudi Arabia. He retired in 1989.[137]

As part of the restructuring, Bill Leonhard and the board of directors appointed Tom Langford as chief financial officer (CFO) in 1978. Tom joined the company in 1970 and became responsible for the financial aspects of Parsons' business ventures. He also contributed to the management of the corporation and its subsidiaries. In 1989, Tom was elected to the board of directors and served as the corporation's executive vice president. When Ray Judson retired in 1991, Tom was named president of the corporation and remained in this capacity supporting Len Pieroni and Jim McNulty in their roles as Parsons' CEO until Tom left the corporation in 1996.[138]

As a sign of just how financially strong Parsons was at the time of the restructuring, the board of directors authorized a three-for-two stock split—in effect, giving each investor one additional share for each two shares held. Another sign of Parsons' growth was its critical need to expand corporate headquarters only four years after opening its doors in Pasadena. In 1978, the company began constructing two additional eight-floor, 250,000-square-foot buildings for its engineering and support personnel on land contiguous to its headquarters.[139] The headquarters building, two annexes, parking lots, and structures occupy an eight-block area over some 22 acres.

In 1982, after meeting its listing requirements, Parsons moved from the American Stock Exchange to the New York Stock Exchange, but it would not stay public for long. The company was so strong financially and had such a healthy project backlog that Bill Leonhard, as CEO, began to receive calls from companies interested in buying Parsons. But none of the offers were close to what Bill thought it was worth, and he knew that being a publicly traded company left Parsons vulnerable to an unwelcome buyout. "We were in a bad position," Bill admitted. "There was a parade of potential buyers. They all would have constituted unfriendly takeovers."[140]

Bill believed that returning Parsons to a privately held corporation, as it had been before 1969, would create a profound, positive impact on its destiny. He was concerned about the possible hostile takeovers and fluctuations in the price of the corporation's stock, which could affect the employees' retirement fund that had been established as an employee stock ownership plan (ESOP) at the time of Ralph Parsons' death in 1974.[141] After discussing the possibility of going private with the board of directors and the key management staff, in 1984, Bill initiated a transaction following the rules established under the Security and Exchange Commission, whereby the preexisting ESOP tendered for all the outside outstanding public shares. The ESOP owned 26 percent of the shares prior to the tender, and after the tender Parsons became a 100 percent ESOP-owned company.[142]

As Parsons celebrated its 40th anniversary in 1984, it could look back on more than 6,000 completed projects in 100 countries across six continents. A *Forbes* magazine article that year cited Parsons' impressive financial return and diversity:

Parsons has earned that handsome return not just by diversifying, but by running a tight, low-overhead operation both in good years and in bad. Increasingly, large contractors are becoming generalists, and none has been more successful at it than Parsons. With jobs in such diverse fields as petroleum processing, nuclear waste storage, mass transit and defense, both in the U.S. and 34 foreign countries, Parsons can shift resources to wherever the work is, often bringing higher powered talent and more financial muscle to bear on a project than competitors could offer. Parsons isn't held hostage by an ailing industry here or a politically unstable region there.[143]

Located in the remote foothills of the Himalayan Mountains, the Karnali River Bridge is the world's longest single-tower, asymmetric, cable-stayed bridge. Prior to being acquired by Parsons, Steinman Boynton Gronquist & Birdsall designed the bridge. Parsons managed the bridge's construction.

CHAPTER SEVEN

The Company Blossoms

1985–1994

No matter where you were in the world, no matter what project you were involved with, you were, in a sense, working for yourself. You were a shareholder.

—Larry Tollenaere, former Parsons board member

WITH THE FINALIZATION OF the ESOP, 1985 was a landmark year for Parsons, and, arguably, the most important year in the company's history since its incorporation in 1944. In just one year, the company had changed dramatically from being publicly traded to being privately held by its own employees. It was now safe and secure—no longer a target of a buyout or an unfriendly takeover, which was becoming an increasing possibility in the engineering community during the mid-1980s and 1990s. Furthermore, the ESOP created a new synergy between the company's original staff and those who joined Parsons through acquired subsidiaries.

One unusual aspect of the ESOP—and one in which Bill Leonhard took special pride—was that Parsons' employees were allocated shares in proportion to their salaries. He explained how Parsons set up the ESOP:

> *In most cases, management will reserve a rather healthy portion of the stock for themselves, leaving the rest of the employees to share on a more modest scale. However, at Parsons, there is a single class of shares, and everyone participates strictly in proportion to his or her salary for the year.*[1]

Former Parsons' board member Larry Tollenaere commented on this motivational aspect of the ESOP.

> *No matter where you were in the world, no matter what project you were involved with, you were, in a sense, working for yourself. You were a shareholder. That's so important when you're out in these grisly places or if you're on a grisly project. I think it made the real turning point in the history of the company for the long term. When you met Parsons' folks, often in unusual places, where they had to endure rugged conditions, the ESOP became the tie that binds. Employees came to understand they were the company; they owned it. So they would hang in there, no matter how tough things were, whether it was a vicious sandstorm or subfreezing weather in Alaska. The ESOP kept you going.*[2]

As a result, the ESOP became a tangible means of inspiring employees to greater productivity. Parsons' staff would share directly in the corporation's success and would benefit from their collective efforts on retirement. Gary Stone, Parsons' general counsel, explained it this way:

> *Our assets really are our employees. There have been a number of people who have been in*

In this time frame, Leonard Pieroni succeeded Bill Leonhard as CEO and took the helm of Parsons, which was now a 100 percent, employee-owned firm.

administrative or secretarial roles and retired in a reasonable period, 20 years perhaps, with several hundred thousands of retirement dollars. So it works.[3]

Susan Cole, vice president and assistant general counsel, joined the company in 1979 and assists Gary in managing both acquisitions and the legal aspects of the ESOP. She said, "It's a very good benefit for employees as well as the company."[4] Susan also explained that the ESOP attracts top professional talent to Parsons and allows the corporation more freedom to test new markets without being concerned about negatively influencing public stock value. "I think the staff is highly educated, more willing to go into something new, even something that's not a high-tech area, like maintenance and operations. We'll just move where the business is."[5]

Tom Schweiner, manager of Parsons' technical publications, concurs with Susan's assessment of Parsons' flexibility and the caliber of its staff:

Many years ago our chairman took us private and, in so doing, instilled pride of ownership—employee ownership—and a lot of us have taken that to heart. We are able to call our own shots. We can react to the marketplace and to a client's needs a lot easier than perhaps a public company could.[6]

"Parsons' ESOP proved to be a classic case of a company going private and getting a lot of mileage out of that. I think Bill Leonhard deserves a lot of the credit for the success of the company in that context," said Fred Felberg, former Parsons' board member.[7]

Manny Stein, who started with Parsons in 1956, expressed his appreciation for Bill Leonhard's efforts to form the ESOP. "When I left the company in 1987 as a retiree, I personally thanked Mr. Leonhard for the ESOP. I told him I was going to be very comfortable, and I thought it was a great thing he had done for the company."[8] Manny became chief engineer of the piping section in 1974, worked on defense and petroleum and chemical projects in the United States, and designed piping systems for chemical plants in Europe during a year-and-a- half assignment in Paris. He briefly came out of retirement in the early 1990s to support Parsons on several petroleum and chemical projects in southern California. His wife, Dot Stein, works for Parsons as an executive assistant.[9]

The Continued Push to Diversify

In Bill Leonhard's vision of the company, the original RMP was the master link, but the previously acquired subsidiaries—De Leuw, Cather & Company, S.I.P. Inc., and ES—strengthened the chain.

The 1985 annual report's representative project list revealed that 24 of the 70 projects cited fell within the company's traditional specialties of petroleum, petroleum and chemical, energy, and mining. Most of these projects were among the largest and most ambitious commercial endeavors in the company's history, giving Parsons the financial base to support further diversification.[10]

Between 1985 and1995, Parsons continued to expand and evolve in its quest to diversify and offer what Leonhard characterized as "total integrated services" to its clients. Four more acquisitions were finalized in this period to support that goal. In 1985, Parsons purchased Charles T. Main Inc. (CT Main), Barton-Aschman Associates Inc., and Harland Bartholomew & Associates Inc. It also acquired Steinman Boynton Gronquist & Birdsall (Steinman) in 1988.[11]

The three firms purchased in 1985, along with the previous acquisitions, positioned Parsons to win a larger share of the transportation and government markets, yet preserve its traditional expertise.

CT Main

CT Main was a world renowned, Boston-based firm founded in 1893 by Charles T. Main, an esteemed civil engineer who specialized in designing electrical power plants. His firm had a sterling project portfolio of hydroelectric and thermal power plants, transmission and distribution systems, and industrial and process plants. In addition, CT Main's wastewater and landfill experience complemented the capabilities of ES.[12]

Barton-Aschman Associates Inc.

Barton-Aschman Associates Inc. was a prominent transportation and land-planning firm based in Evanston, Illinois. Founded in 1946 by George W. Barton, the firm merged with Frederick T. Aschman's urban planning practice in 1959.[13] Marty Blachman was the former Barton-Aschman president who, as a member of its board, saw it through the acquisition by Parsons. He retired seven years later in 1992. Marty recalled the acquisition:

> *Our strength essentially was in traffic engineering, transportation planning, and so forth, and that was an ingredient that was missing from the Parsons' spectrum of services. Parsons, of course, represented all sorts of skills that we did not possess. Certainly, they were the types of skills we could introduce to our clientele. There was a great opportunity for synergism there.*[14]

Harland Bartholomew & Associates Inc. (HBA)

Harland Bartholomew was one of the founders of the modern city planning movement in the United States. He formed HBA in 1919. Over the years, the company was involved in many landmark planning projects, specializing in offering clients an interdisciplinary team of planners, civil engineers, and landscape architects to find solutions to their planning concerns. Parsons acquired HBA in 1985.[15] Bob Bax, Parsons' executive vice president of transportation operations, joined HBA as a senior planner the same year it was acquired. He discussed the firm:

> *It was a 150- to 180-person firm when acquired for its planning expertise. There are many, many cities whose first city planner came from Bartholomew, was trained and mentored in the development of their first plan, and then stayed behind as an employee of that city to continue that process.*[16]

Steinman Boynton Gronquist & Birdsall (Steinman)

Another firm with a highly respected pedigree was acquired in 1988. Steinman was founded in 1921 by Dr. David B. Steinman, an esteemed engineer who specialized in bridge design. He was later joined by Ray M. Boynton, Dr. Carl Gronquist, and Blair Birdsall—each a prominent bridge engineer in his own right. Between 1944 and 1954, the firm oversaw the comprehensive reconstruction of the Brooklyn Bridge that entailed strengthening the inner and outer trusses and widening the roadway from two lanes to three lanes in each direction.[17] Later, it designed the International Bridge between Canada and the United States as well as the Tagus River Bridge in Portugal—one of the longest suspension bridges in Europe.[18] Its reputation and design capabilities led to Parsons' becoming one of the preeminent bridge designers in the world.

Harland Bartholomew & Associates designed the park that surrounds the famous Gateway Arch monument, located in St. Louis, and symbolizing St. Louis as the "Gateway to the West."

A Continued Presence in Alaska—The Red Dog Mine

"How do you get to Red Dog?" asked *Compressed Air* magazine in its 1990 article on the largest zinc mine in the world.[19] The Red Dog mine is even more remote than Prudhoe Bay. It is located in the DeLong Mountains of the Brooks Range, 120 miles north of the Arctic Circle, on the Alaskan shores of the Chukchi Sea. Red Dog was put on the map in 1968 when bush pilot and part-time prospector Bob Baker flew over the unnamed Alaskan valley and discovered a distinctive red and orange coloring that indicated a substantial mineral deposit. He dubbed the site Red Dog, after his constant companion, a reddish-colored dog.[20]

Right and below: One hundred and twenty miles north of the Arctic Circle is Red Dog, the world's largest zinc-concentrate-producing mine. Parsons designed and managed the construction of the mine, mill, and port complex. Due to its prominence, project information is on exhibit at the National Mining Hall of Fame and Museum.

Because of the valley's isolation, the extent of Red Dog's mineral reserve remained speculative until 1975. The U.S. Bureau of Mines' geotechnical investigations confirmed the existence of a vast zinc deposit—so large, in fact, that Red Dog would surpass the zinc mines of Australia to become the world's largest zinc concentrate producer with an estimated 85 million tons of ore.[21]

In 1982, Cominco American signed a mining agreement with NANA Regional Corporation Inc., a native Alaskan corporation, and retained Parsons to develop the mine, mill, and necessary port complex that would extract, process, and transport the ore. Parsons' project manager was Norm Williams, assisted by two project engineers, Dan Teutonico and George Sheflott. Jim Gowans was the home office engineering manager in Pasadena and administered engineering support.[22]

Samir (Sam) Lawrence was the senior engineering manager of Parsons' structural engineering section during Red Dog. He started his career with the company in 1974 and applied his technical acumen to many complex structural engineering assignments, including the North Slope of Alaska, Endicott Island in the Beaufort Sea, and the Petromin-Shell refinery in Saudi Arabia. Sam is presently providing his world-class expertise to Parsons' chemical demilitarization program.[23]

Mine development began in 1986. The scope of Parsons' services included the design and construction of a new concentrator, mine support facilities, living accommodations, utilities, transportation infrastructure, and a seaport. The initial construction activities began by installing the seaport's shallow water dock to land the construction equipment, material, and modules for the entire project. The remaining seaport facilities—a deepwater dock and storage for ore concentrate, loadout, and fuel oil—were constructed in 1988 and 1989.[24]

Prior to the port being built, a 5,000-foot dirt airstrip was the only means of access to the site and, initially, all construction equipment, materials, and support were provided by air. Parsons upgraded the airstrip and added lights, navaids, backup power, and a small control tower. The FAA certified the Red Dog strip for Boeing 737 landings, and the National Weather Service gave its approval to serve as a supplementary aviation weather reporting station. Thus, the upgraded airstrip and the port, both of which Parsons designed and then managed their construction, were the answers to *Compressed Air* magazine's question.

In designing and managing the construction of Red Dog, Parsons relied on computerized equipment and modular construction techniques learned from the North Slope projects. The modules were constructed in the Philippines and transported to the seaport by oceangoing barges and then to the mine by rubber-tired vehicles on a 54-mile road. The fully computerized process facilities continuously evaluated the main variables, including ore and water flow rates, solid water ratios, particle size, and assays. By November 1989, construction was complete. Mining operation and production began in December 1989. Based on the success of the mining operations, the facilities were expanded in 1998 and again in 2001.[25]

Les Engle, former vice president, relayed Red Dog's prominence in the world of mining:

> *I am a founding member and life member of the National Mining Hall of Fame and Museum in Leadville, Colorado. That's the one place I know in the world where a Parsons' mining and metallurgical project is on exhibit under the name of the owner, Cominco. Red Dog is a true, honest superlative. It is the world's richest zinc mine. It's [one] of the significant mining and metallurgical projects that the corporation did.*[26]

The Red Line

The Los Angeles Metropolitan Transportation Authority (MTA) retained Parsons, in a joint venture with Dillingham Construction (Parsons-Dillingham), to render construction oversight for the $5.3 billion Red Line project in 1985. The Red Line is the backbone of a 150-mile rail transit system linking downtown Los Angeles with Long Beach to the south, Santa Monica to the west, Pasadena to the east, and the San Fernando Valley to the north. It is one of the largest construction projects ever undertaken by the county of Los Angeles. Parsons-Dillingham was responsible for construction management, procurement, installation, and testing of the system's elements. The joint venture performed systems integration and managed the startup of all Red Line sections, helping the MTA transition from construction to full revenue operation.[27]

WILLIAM E. LEONHARD

BILL LEONHARD SERVED as Parsons' third CEO for 22 years. During that period, he made an indelible mark on the company's direction and character. Bill had the stamina and drive to propel Parsons' financial growth through acquisitions, megaprojects, and privatization. He made the tough decisions and was involved in every aspect of the company's operations.

A self-described "workaholic," William Leonhard kept a demanding schedule, working nights and every weekend.

During his first year as CEO, Bill restructured The Ralph M. Parsons Company and transformed it into The Parsons Corporation. Perhaps his greatest accomplishment was privatizing Parsons in 1984 and forming the ESOP in 1985. Bill was very proud of the ESOP's benefit to the staff:[1]

> *One of the things that played on my mind was here a lot of people were working hard, and yet the profits of the company were distributed to the shareholders. So I created what I think was the first 100-percent ESOP in the country.*[2]

Bill graduated from The Pennsylvania State University in 1936 with a degree in engineering. He went directly into the military as an officer in the Army Corps of Engineers, and his first tour of duty was in the Panama Canal Zone. On his second assignment, Bill designed the layout for the Pan American Highway from Panama to Costa Rica. He returned to the United States and earned a master's degree in electrical and civil engineering from MIT. A life-long learner, Bill also received a doctorate of law degree from Pepperdine University, California, in 1987.

During World War II, Bill earned a Bronze Star for valor while serving as chief of staff of the 20th and the 2nd Armored Divisions in Europe. After the war, he transferred from the Army to the newly formed Air Force in 1947 and supervised the construction of air bases in Europe and North Africa. After attending the War College at Maxwell Air Force Base, Montgomery, Alabama, he was assigned to the Pentagon as Air Force Director of Construction.[3]

First Connection with Parsons

In 1956, at the height of the Cold War, Bill was transferred to the West Coast as deputy commander of the Air Force's Ballistic Missile Command. He was responsible for the design and construction of test and operational facilities for the Atlas, Thor, Titan, and Minuteman missile programs. It was in this role that he began working with RMP, which was under contract to design and engineer missile program facilities and developed a professional working relationship with Stan Goldhaber, Systems Division manager.[4]

In 1964, Bill retired from the Air Force as a one-star general. He went to work for United Technologies on the Titan III program for two years, prior to being persuaded by Stan Goldhaber to join RMP in 1966. Bill started with the company as RMP's senior vice president and general manager. He was personally selected by Ralph Parsons to succeed Milt Lewis as the company's president.[5] Stan said that Bill guided RMP into new markets.

Before Bill joined Parsons, the company was still focused largely on a few discrete areas. But, ultimately, it grew into this new concept of systems engineering, facilities engineering, project management, and so on. There is no question that Bill Leonhard played an absolutely major role in that crucial transition.[6]

Under his leadership the company undertook major projects such as Yanbu Industrial City, the North Slope, and WMATA.[7] Ray Judson, former chairman and a member of the board, described Bill's contributions to Parsons:

The Bill Leonhard that I knew and respected was very smart, very intelligent. He was an extremely astute man. He made this company as far as I'm concerned.[8]

Marvin McClain, former vice president, described him thusly:

He was very appropriate for that time. You wouldn't see him as a marketing man. He wasn't selling you a job. He was going to tell you how he was going to do the job. Clients had a lot of confidence in him. They knew that here was a man who could get the job done.[9]

"Bill Leonhard truly changed the culture of the company," said Bob Sheh, president of Parsons' main subsidiary, RMP, before leaving in 1992. "He really had the company at heart."[10]

Larry Burns, former senior vice president, also remembers Bill's emphasis on controlling costs:

Bill Leonhard was greatly ahead of his time in terms of overhead control. I remember 10 or 15 years ago when people were talking about reducing their overhead costs by 15 percent, 20 percent, and 25 percent, but we had already been doing that for years and years under Bill.[11]

There is no doubt Bill was fiscally conservative, but he spent his time lavishly on Parsons—working long hours to manage and grow the company. Larry Burns often would run into Bill in the late evenings at the office:

I would walk out at 10 or 11 at night, and he would be walking into the building with a half-eaten sandwich in wax paper. He was a very hard worker.[12]

However, he was careful not to waste, quite literally, a minute of his day. Kevin Barry, former manager of systems engineering, recalled an example of Bill's judiciousness:

One time, he was in the office and some guy was desperate to talk to him. So he goes in, and Bill says, "I'm very busy. I'll give you one minute." The guy launches into his thing, whatever it was. Exactly one minute after he started, Bill turns [his chair] around and carries on whatever he was doing. He left this guy speechless.[13]

"He was very tough, very strong. If he wanted to do it, he was going to do it, and nobody was going to change his mind," said Sharen Clark, Parsons' supervisor of accounting and billing, who joined the company in 1967. "I really think he's the one who brought this company up and kept it going."[14]

"He played in Parsons' golf league every summer. He'd get out and mix with the people. You got a chance, if you were in the league, to play golf with Bill," recalled Jess Harmon, former vice president of contracts and procurement, who retired in 2002.[15]

In 1982, Bill was elected to the National Academy of Engineering. He also served on numerous boards of trustees and endowed professorships and scholarships at MIT, Caltech, USC, UCLA, and Harvey Mudd College. When Bill retired in 1990, he was 75 years old. He became an active alumnus of The Pennsylvania State University's College of Engineering by endowing professorships and a department chair.[16]

Dan Frost, former outside counsel and board member, held Bill in the highest light:

I can't say enough for Bill Leonhard's stewardship. He was an absolutely outstanding CEO, and the company prospered mightily under his leadership.[17]

Tom Barron, executive vice president of Parsons Transportation Group, joined Parsons through the De Leuw, Cather & Company acquisition. He was managing Parsons' western region transportation projects in 1985 and was instrumental in positioning the corporation to win the Red Line. He recalled the project:

I was based in Denver from 1981 to 1986 as the manager for the West. One of the biggest efforts I was involved in was the pursuit of the Red Line—construction management of the subway in Los Angeles. I spent a lot of time in Pasadena, which was my first exposure to corporate headquarters. The Red Line forced us to become more of a corporate citizen in the greater Los Angeles area and get to know elected officials and people who were behind that project.[28]

Michael J. McKenna, the systems area manager, discussed the project:

The key to the success of the project was the people. Many had tens of years of transportation experience, working throughout the country and, in my case, throughout the world. We found the best people and let them do their jobs. Personally, I'm a third-generation rail man. I started in this industry in 1959 as a motorman for the Chicago Transit Authority (CTA). My dad worked for CTA developing procedures, my grandfather worked for them before that as a grip man.[29]

Mike began with Parsons in 1990 and retired in 2004. He was also the task manager for the systems design and operation of the Port Authority of Allegheny County's rail system in Pennsylvania and the project manager of the design upgrade to Wisconsin's central signal system for its commuter rail.[30]

The Red Line was the first new transit project in the country to meet the federal requirements of the Americans with Disabilities Act (ADA). In 1993, it received Project of the Year designation by the California Transportation Foundation and the Los Angeles Chapter of the Project Management Institute (PMI), as well as PMI's International Project of the Year award. The project won the 1994 California Department of Transportation's Excellence in

Below: Parsons was part of the joint venture that performed construction management, procurement, and installation of the Red Line, the backbone of the commuter rail system linking downtown Los Angeles with the San Fernando Valley, Long Beach, Santa Monica, and Pasadena.

Opposite: One important Red Line engineering feat was constructing the extensive network of tunnels so that passengers could be safely transported beneath downtown Los Angeles to their destinations.

Transportation Environmental Mitigation Award for Segment 2 of the Red Line.

The first 4.5-mile section opened in January 1993 at an estimated cost of $1.25 billion. This section included five stations, a yard, shops, and the central control facility. The project entailed extensive underground subway tunnels and stations constructed through the central business district of Los Angeles, in soft ground and hard rock conditions, using both tunnel machines and cut-and-cover methods. Three other sections were constructed and put into service. The last segment, the North Hollywood extension, opened in June 2000, bringing the Red Line to a total length of 16.8 miles.[31]

Privatization

Continuing with Parsons' practice of exploring emerging markets, 1985 saw the advent of the corporation's first ventures into privatization. The concept was to design, build, and operate facilities that government clients would have normally paid for through bonds or taxes and then have managed upon completion. Under privatization, Parsons would recoup its costs for financing the design and construction by operating the facilities for a fee. The initial projects all involved municipal clients requiring water treatment—one of Parsons' core strengths. Chandler, Arizona (21 miles southeast of Phoenix), became the first city in the United States to bring its wastewater treatment plant online, privatized by Parsons. In nearby Gilbert, Arizona, Parsons also broke ground on a second privatized wastewater treatment plant.[32]

Other privatization projects ensued, and in the 1990s, the Department of Defense began privatizing facility operations and maintenance to reduce costs while it sought to divest itself of former military bases that were no longer needed for the country's defense. Parsons would parlay its privatization experience with municipal clients into supporting these endeavors.[33]

Focus on Cost Controls and Market Analysis

In conjunction with converting Parsons to a privately held, 100 percent ESOP corporation, Bill Leonhard implemented stringent cost-control measures and operated with a lean management team. Bill wanted a small staff of executives because it "doesn't allow anyone to get fat and lazy."[34] He carefully analyzed the profit and loss of each division and subsidiary and, in the late 1980s, decided to suspend Parsons' involvement in mining and metallurgy projects and close such nonstrategic and expensive locations as the Paris office, merging its operations into the New York City, London, and Frankfurt offices.[35]

"I didn't ask anyone in the company to do anything that I didn't do myself," Bill said. "I tried to lead by example rather than by mandate."[36] Many employees confirmed that Bill's equitable sense of cost control permeated the corporation. Larry Burns, former vice president, stated that Bill "would not tell people to fly economy and then he, himself, take first class. He would fly the same level as everybody else. I'm sure there were exceptions, but there was never an issue of a double standard."[37]

"Bill was a conservative person, and he preached conservatism on the part of all of us," said Fred Schweiger, former president of Barton-Aschman.[38] Gladys Porter, who was promoted to executive assistant in 1988, said, "He took care of the company's money. He wasn't going to let anyone waste it."[39]

Although Bill was considered a careful steward of the company finances, he believed in having a very broad base of projects, which required a significant investment in terms of sales and proposal costs. He once estimated that "we have at least 500 jobs under way. On average, we complete two projects a day and that means we've got to bring in two new projects every day."[40] In Bill's opinion, "Big jobs require hiring and then trailing off as the job winds down. Ten smaller jobs smooth out the curves and, if the company conducts itself properly, those 10 could bring more to the bottom line than a single $1 billion project."[41]

Parsons' management in the years to come would learn that this marketing approach was not always in the corporation's best interest. After studying the financial pros and cons of smaller projects, very few had led to the growth Bill had optimistically forecast. Parsons learned its strength was in larger program and project execution and began leaving

CT Main

ACQUIRED BY PARSONS IN 1985, CT MAIN offered design, engineering, construction, environmental, and program management services to numerous industries, including power generation; transmission and distribution; water resources; manufacturing; and also the pulp, paper, and forest industry.

Its founder, Charles T. Main, was an MIT graduate and was so highly regarded for his mechanical engineering abilities and integrity that the American Society of Mechanical Engineers in 1919 established leadership and service student awards in his honor.[1]

CT Main rose to national prominence in 1956 when a rockslide destroyed two-thirds of the existing power capacity on the Niagara River in New York, and the firm was hired to respond to this emergency situation.

In the course of completing the project, CT Main led the industry by installing computerized equipment that produced online data to efficiently generate the most power, based on water availability.[2]

From the Niagara River project, CT Main became known worldwide for its electrical power engineering expertise. It also was retained to design and construct an electronics manufacturing facility in North Andover, Massachusetts; a $950 million pulp and paper mill complex in Ngodwana, South Africa, for Sappi, Ltd.; a wastewater pretreatment facility in Louisville, Kentucky; the $1.5 billion Salto Grande Binational Hydroelectric Project on the Uruguay River between Argentina and Uruguay; Panama's Fortuna Hydroelectric Project; New York's Robert Moses Hydroelectric Power Plant; the North Fork Stanislaus River Hydroelectric Project in California; the Tarbela Hydroelectrical Project in Pakistan; the Qurrayah and Rabigh oil-fired thermal power plants in Saudi Arabia; the Az Zour South Power Station in Kuwait; and a coal-fired expansion of the Aqaba Thermal Power Plant in Jordan.[3]

The firm also was the preferred choice of many newspapers in designing production and printing facilities. Through CT Main, Parsons

the very small consulting projects to boutique or specialty firms. This selective approach to pursuing new business has proven to be very effective—however, it would not be implemented until others succeeded Bill in his role as Parsons' chairman.

Passing the Baton

Like Ralph Parsons before him, Bill Leonhard chose and groomed his successor, Len Pieroni, who became one of the most beloved leaders in the corporation's history. Len joined Parsons in 1972, and his "unflappable, business-like demeanor" caught Bill's attention.[42] He tapped Len to manage S.I.P. Inc. and then CT Main. In 1988, Len became a corporate senior vice president and director of business development, and he guided all of the subsidiaries' strategic plans for market growth. He was promoted to executive vice president and director of corporate planning in 1989. When Bill retired in 1990, Len was well prepared to step into the role of CEO.

When Len assumed the role of chairman, Parsons had a substantial $10 billion project backlog and slightly more than 8,000 employees.[43] An article in the *Pasadena-Star News* summed up Parsons' market position at that time:

> *After a decade of acquisitions and growth, the firm has expanded into an international network of independent companies specializing in everything from bridge construction and airports to subways and toxic waste dumps.*[44]

Len stated, "We have grown from a company that was engaged in just a few markets to one of the most broadly diversified companies of our type."[45]

---

became involved in the transition of *The New York Times* from a black-and-white newspaper to color printing.

"We did all the engineering and construction supervision on two of their printing plants, and each were $500 million projects," Jim Callahan, former president of CT Main, recounted.[4] Among others, the company's newspaper projects also included production plants in Dallas, Texas, and Santa Rosa, California.

Bill Whooley, a former Parsons' vice president who worked for CT Main when it was acquired, recalled the components of its organizational structure:

> *I had the opportunity to work in a number of the divisions. We had a hydropower division, a power division. We actually grew an environmental division. We had a transmission and distribution division. We had a pulp and paper division. The markets that it served basically had us doing far more work outside New England than within New England.*[5]

Roy Gaunt, retired head of Parsons' Power Division, said that the forward-thinking CT Main gave Parsons a leadership position in various markets and provided this example:

> *As the nuclear power industry began shutting down in this country due to environmental concerns, there was a large push toward cogeneration. ParsonsMain was one of the earliest firms to realize that was where the work was going, and we did a large number of cogeneration projects as a result.*[6]

Roy had joined Parsons in 1968 and officially retired in 1993, but continued to work for Parsons until 1995 because of his commitment to building UCLA's cogeneration plant, which reduced the university's expenses for electrical power by 95 percent.[7]

Charles T. Main described the winning philosophy that led to his firm's significant contributions:

> *The true success of a man is not to be measured by the accumulation of money, but by the success of [his] accomplishment[s], which adds something to the general good for mankind and the advancement of the profession.*[8]

As a result, his priority was to expand the company's market share in each of the service areas in which Parsons was already engaged. In order to accomplish this task, he began improving and, in some cases, establishing communications among the various Parsons' entities. Prior to Len's efforts, it was common for subsidiaries to work for the same client, or to be retained on the same project, without coordinating the company's efforts as a whole. In addition, no standardized accounting practices, personnel procedures, and computer systems existed throughout the company. The lack of cohesiveness needed to be resolved for the subsidiaries to work effectively with each other. Len initially considered incorporating the Parsons' name into each entity, but he postponed doing so, thinking that such a move could strip the companies of their identities and diminish their reputations.[46] "It's very sensitive," he admitted. "We have to maintain a balance."[47]

Within 18 months of becoming chairman and CEO, Len implemented a plan to change the marketing efforts of the individual subsidiaries. His goal was to present clients with an all-encompassing approach for Parsons' services. Len decided to consolidate several subsidiaries into operating units, promoting a "total solutions" methodology to meet a client's expectations.[48] The most logical areas of consolidation were the entities serving the transportation and environmental customers.

Chandler, Arizona, was the first city in the country to privatize its wastewater treatment operations, and Parsons was its choice to design, build, and operate the treatment plant.

On December 12, 1991, Parsons announced that De Leuw, Cather & Company, Barton-Aschman, Steinman, and HBA would merge into one subsidiary responsible for public transit, railroad, bridge, transportation planning, highway, and airport projects. This newly "integrated" unit would operate under the auspices of Parsons De Leuw.[49] He appointed Bob O'Neil as Parsons De Leuw's president because he was a well-respected engineer in the transportation field and a long-time De Leuw, Cather & Company employee. Bob led Parsons' transportation efforts for the next 10 years until he retired in 2001.[50]

Two months later, on February 4, 1992, Parsons announced a similar reorganization of environmental units by creating Parsons Environmental Services Inc., which consolidated ES with the major environmental project staffs from CT Main and RMP.[51] Joel H. Bennett, who had been recruited from Braun Corporation because of his strong international marketing background, was named president of Parsons Environmental Services Inc.[52]

The Gulf War

While Len Pieroni was just beginning to formulate the direction of the corporation, he was faced with an international crisis after only three months as CEO. In August 1990, Iraq invaded Kuwait, precipitating the Gulf War. The U.S. military's "Desert Storm" operation supported the United Nations' efforts to push back Saddam Hussein's Iraqi army. Parsons had first worked in Kuwait in 1960, performing a groundwater study and, at the time of the invasion, had about 100 employees in the country working on water, power, and transportation projects. Of that number, a dozen were American citizens on long-term assignments who had brought their families with them to live in Kuwait.[53]

Two Parsons Environmental Services Inc. employees, Richard Anderton and Rocco Palazzolo, sought protection in the U.S. Embassy in Kuwait City after the war began and were able to stay there for four months. They had been working 50 miles south of the city on an industrial wastewater treatment project.[54] Several Parsons employees were taken into Iraq and used as human shields, but were released prior to Desert Storm. Others such as Kirk Sessions of CT Main and his son were able to escape over land into Saudi Arabia.[55] Len worked the phones constantly for all the information he could gather about the safety of the trapped employees. He quickly made contingency plans to evacuate other Parsons' workers from Saudi Arabia and neighboring countries in the event the hostilities spread.[56]

Mel Brown, who was Yanbu Industrial City's program manager during the hostilities, recounted the contingency efforts made by his team in Saudi Arabia:

> *One thing that we had to do was evacuate the dependents prior to the initiation of Desert Storm. The employees actually stayed to continue their mission, but we had to set up notification plans. We had to tie into air defense systems in the surrounding areas so that when Scud missiles would fire we would get early notification. We had to come up with emergency evacuation procedures for all the people there by land, sea, and air.*[57]

Mel discussed this experience:

> *This effort was a key example of how well Parsons employees are supported by the home office during international crises. For example, we had daily phone calls. I talked to Len Pieroni, our chairman, almost daily during the crises and to other individuals, such as Bill Hall, who had been the previous program manager [in Yanbu]. [We] arranged for the aircraft and other things in order to evacuate if it became necessary. We had a 342-bed hospital that was geared up to support the war effort in the event of mass casualties. Even though we did not get attacked, [we purchased] gas masks from Scandinavia and Europe and actually trained all the Parsons' people and the Saudis who were assigned to Parsons in acquiring gas masks for protection.*[58]

CEO Len Pieroni was a beloved figure within the company who enjoyed nothing more than being with—and serving—his staff. This picture was taken at an annual employee ice cream social.

David Kays, Yanbu Industrial City's program manager prior to Bill Hall and Mel Brown, was assigned to the Aramco projects and based in Al Khobar at the time of the Gulf War. He discussed the experience of being in the middle of a war:

> *When the war actually started, the Scuds came in, and the Patriots went up to intercept them. There were lots of explosions, a lot of sound, and very little time to get anywhere just to be safe. Eventually, a strike killed some of our [U.S.] troops in a barrack. This was only about a couple of hundred yards from where we had a compound where most of our people were staying. The building we were in had an all-glass exterior. We had to go into its core and stand in the elevator lobbies when an attack was on because we didn't want to be close [to the exterior] if one [Scud] came close enough to break all that glass. We put up with that for about a week. I convinced Aramco that we needed to move because we weren't accomplishing much. They moved us 120 kilometers south to a place called Udhailyah. It was a safer place. There's no doubt about that.*[59]

All of Parsons' employees in the Middle East survived the war unscathed, and those who were held captive returned safely. On January 20, 1991, Parsons held a "welcome home" reception for the detainees and presented each one with a Steuben glass sculpture in the shape of an American Eagle to commemorate their return.[60]

Parsons Environmental Services Inc.'s Richard Anderton also received the Meritorious Honor Award from the U.S. State Department in recognition of his contributions at the U.S. Embassy in Kuwait City during the war. Richard devised a computer program to track nearly 3,000 American citizens who were still in Kuwait City. Based on this information, 12 evacuation flights were organized, and the U.S. State Department was able to follow the activities of more than 100 Americans who were in hiding.[61] After the crisis had abated, Len described it as a time filled with sleepless nights due to his deep concern for the Middle East staff. "I got into the habit of waking up every morning at 3:30 or 4:00 AM and watching CNN," he said.[62]

Once the Gulf War was over, several multinational contractors helped rebuild Kuwait. In 1993, the Kuwait Oil Company selected Parsons for a three-year, $1.4 billion contract to assist in restoring and upgrading the country's oil infrastructure.[63]

Opposite: After the Gulf War, Parsons supplied "fast-track" engineering services and subcontract administration to reestablish or build new oil and gas field gathering centers, pipelines, and adjunct facilities.

Below: "Before" shot of damaged oil facilities in Kuwait.

Transportation Projects Take Center Stage

Some of Parsons' unique and outstanding projects between 1985 and 1994 were within the transportation field. In 1986, Steinman, which had not yet become a Parsons' subsidiary, had started the design of the world's longest single-tower, asymmetric, cable-stayed bridge over the Karnali River in the Kingdom of Nepal. After acquiring Steinman in 1988, Parsons was retained in 1990 to perform engineering and construction management during the erection of this 1,650-foot-long bridge. Parsons surmounted two significant challenges on the project—getting materials to the remote foothills of the Himalayan Mountains and completing the construction in a monsoon-affected region of the world where the work year is only eight months due to torrential rains. To generate time and cost efficiencies, the bridge's significant structures were manufactured offsite. For example, the steel tower, weighing about 1,550 tons, was fabricated in Thailand and transported by ship to the port in Calcutta, India, for an 800-mile journey over land to the site. On December 13, 1993, the bridge was officially inaugurated, only three years after construction began.[64]

"It was very rewarding work since we helped our client, the Kingdom of Nepal [Department of Roads], trigger economic development in the region," remarked Selva Selvaratnam, the former site project manager who had previously worked for Steinman. One of the side benefits of working on the bridge was the exposure to the Nepalese culture. Selva recalled, "I was always getting invitations to festivals and religious ceremonies."[65] Before leaving Parsons in 2000, Selva, a civil engineer, was also a key project team member on bridge rehabilitation projects.[66]

In 1988, Parsons rendered electrical and mechanical design and construction management services for China's Shanghai Metro Line 1, and a decade later in 1998 was retained to provide similar services for Metro Line 2. Jack Roadhouse was the principal-in-charge on the Metro Line 1. Jack had joined De Leuw, Cather & Company in 1971 as a civil engineer. He became the project manager on WMATA in 1992 and then the project director on the Kuala Lumpur light rail transit system in 1995. He retired as a senior vice president.[67]

Also in the Pacific Rim, Parsons served as the general engineering consultant for a 76-kilometer mass transit line that included 71 stations in Kaohsiung, the second largest city in Taiwan, Republic of China. The corporation began its involvement on this $6.5 billion project in 1991 and oversaw its design and construction.[68]

As part of a USAID contract to assist African countries with solving transportation concerns, Parsons improved Tanzania's road system to provide the mostly rural population with access to urban areas and help meet the needs of neighboring Rwanda's civil war refugees entering the country. The Tanzanians relied on the dirt, gravel, and asphalt roads to transport agricultural products and minerals to market. The new roads greatly enhanced Tanzania's government and international relief organizations' abilities to provide medical, education, and social services to the Rwandans. Parsons' team also provided emergency maintenance of Mwanza's airport so that the large, heavy airplanes used by the United Nations to transport food and medical supplies could land safely.[69]

Richard E. Whatley, a civil engineer, was the technical assistance leader on the project. He had previously managed Parsons' project management contract, sponsored by the Ghanaian government, the World Bank, and OPEC that generated labor-intensive construction endeavors to offset the depressed economy in Ghana. Richard also configured the facilities department of the King Khalid International Airport in Riyadh, Saudi Arabia.[70] In the 1994 Summer/Fall edition of *Perspectives*, Richard stated that malaria was the foremost enemy of the Tanzanian people, Rwanda's refugees, and the personnel working on upgrading the road system: "Five expatriate and three local staff members contracted malaria in 18 months." He added, "The project's basic importance is to assist the local staff in evolving from a 1930s work approach to something approximating a 1990s method."[71]

In 1990, the same year Parsons began construction management of the Karnali River Bridge, it inspected the famous Golden Gate Bridge's 36-inch-diameter main cables, hand ropes, cable bans, suspender rope sockets, wind connectors, main towers, strand shoes, eye bars, cable tie-downs, and pylons. Parsons also provided the engineering and design services for the fabrication of a new wire-wrapping machine for the main cables.[72] As with the Karnali Bridge, the Golden Gate Bridge was linked to Parsons' subsidiary, Steinman. One of Steinman's original partners, Blair Birdsall, began his engineering career as one of the two men who calculated pressure loads on the main cables, footbridges, storm system, and suspended ropes on the bridge in 1935.[73]

For the Port of Los Angeles, Parsons was the prime consultant for the design of Pier 300, a $60 million dry bulk terminal for international commodities such as coal and petroleum coke. Housed on 140 acres, Pier 300 is one of the world's largest facilities of its kind. In 1992, Parsons began the design of the facility's deep-water berth, railway, and transportation infrastructure to support vessels up to 250,000 deadweight tons. The pier was completed in 1997.[74] Charles Vickers Jr., a civil

Above: Spanning 140 acres, Pier 300 is one of the world's largest dry bulk terminal facilities, and Parsons was the prime consultant for its design.

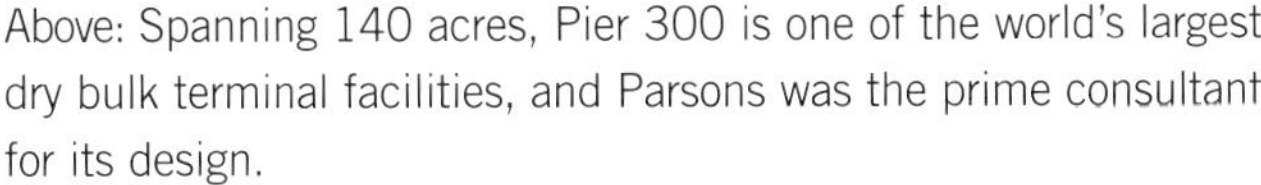

Opposite: When the Golden Gate Bridge in San Francisco was under construction in 1935, one of Steinman's partners, Blair Birdsall, performed the calculations for its main cables. In 1990, Parsons added to his legacy by inspecting the cables and related structures.

Right: One of Parsons' more picturesque highway designs was the 13-mile section of I-70 that passes through the mountains surrounding Glenwood Canyon, Colorado.

engineer, was the initial project manager. Earlier, he was instrumental in completing Saudi Arabia's port of Yanbu and Hong Kong's replacement airport at Chek Lap Kok.[75]

In 1992, the Colorado Department of Transportation opened the last segment of a 22-year interstate highway construction effort that connected the Hanging Lake tunnels on Interstate 70 on through to Glenwood Canyon in a ceremony attended by design professionals and dignitaries from around the country. Parsons performed the siting studies, environmental assessments, and the preliminary and final designs for all alignments and structures. It also prepared the architectural and planning design handbook for the aesthetic and environmental guidelines used to build this 13-mile section of highway along the scenic Colorado River.[76]

For the Wisconsin Department of Transportation, Parsons designed the Interstate 94 interchange, paving, and bridge deck improvements to ease traffic congestion going into downtown Milwaukee, the Milwaukee County Zoo, the Milwaukee Medical Center, and the State Fair Park. The project was awarded in 1993.[77] Parsons also managed the construction of the rail line between downtown Chicago and the Midway Airport, as well as nine miles of street-level and elevated track lines through this urban area.

In addition, Parsons' engineering and design services reconstructed a major segment of Chicago's Kennedy Expressway, one of the five busiest freeways in the United States. Parsons also assisted in the construction management of a new 20-gate international terminal at Chicago's O'Hare International Airport with the capacity to handle 4,000 passengers per hour.[78]

Perhaps Parsons' most far-reaching transportation project of this period was its involvement with the National Airspace System program. Martin Marietta (now Lockheed Martin) implemented the $10 billion program to modernize air traffic control in the United States. Parsons was under contract to Martin Marietta to perform facility design, planning, and construction support on 23 air route traffic control centers throughout the FAA system. Specifically, Parsons designed the facility modifications or expansions, chiller and cooling towers, and some of the most complex, low-voltage power systems ever constructed. At its peak, the program employed over 200 staff and subcontractors, many of whom were in Parsons' Pasadena and Washington, D.C., offices or colocated within all nine of FAA's regional offices.

Martin Marietta was the prime contractor on the National Airspace System program and retained Parsons to perform facility design, planning, and construction support on 23 FAA air route traffic control centers. This program helped modernize air traffic control in the United States.

For this program, Parsons also developed standard designs for airport surveillance, air route surveillance, and terminal Doppler weather radars, as well as VHF omnidirectional range- and distance-measuring equipment. As with many of Parsons' landmark accomplishments, logistics was the cornerstone of this program's success. Martin Marietta and Parsons ensured that construction activities would not interfere with air traffic control operations.[79]

The National Airspace System program began in 1984. Parsons' contract with Martin Marietta covered the first 10 years of the program and was completed in 1994. Toward the end of the contract, Martin Marietta provided the following commendation to Parsons:

> *Your technical design and development of the construction packages has been excellent; performance according to schedule outstanding; and timely support valuable in controlling technical, cost, and schedule baselines.*[80]

Parsons' involvement with the National Airspace System program led to three regional FAA contracts in 1992 for design management. The corporation is the prime contractor on an engineering support services contract for the FAA's facilities located in the United States and certain oceanic areas.

Anita Freeman, who joined the company in 1974, managed the National Airspace System program's engineering integration between 1990 and 1994. She said, "Parsons was Martin Marietta's 'facility' arm. Under our contract, we performed building and support system modification design and engineering support during construction to accommodate new control systems being developed by others."[81]

Her success in solving the program's challenges and managing her team over the years she was assigned to the program resulted in Anita's promotion to vice president. She was the first female within Parsons in a technical field to obtain that stature. She is a registered architect and currently provides

Parsons served as the technical advisor to the English Channel Tunnel's financial consortium and monitored the costs, schedule, and quality of the engineering and construction associated with this huge transportation project that created a 20-minute trip by rail between France and the United Kingdom.

ongoing design and construction management services to the Los Angeles County Department of Public Works for facilities damaged during the 1994 Northridge, California, earthquake.[82] Her husband Lee was the project manager for the cooling tower modifications and low voltage for the upgraded power systems, including emergency generators and uninterruptible power supply, for the air route traffic control centers on the National Airspace System program. He became a project coordinator on the U.S. missile defense system program and went on to manage the USPS construction assignments in southern California.[83]

The "Chunnel"

On December 1, 1990, after three years of tediously advancing a bore hole through the chalky soil beneath the English Channel, a construction team officially connected France with the United Kingdom to allow for the building of a passenger tunnel between the two countries. As technical advisor to The Arranging Banks—the financial consortium funding the channel tunnel—Parsons monitored the costs, schedule, and quality of the engineering and construction between 1987 and 1994.[84] The project, affectionately nicknamed the "Chunnel," actually consists of three tubes: two accommodate the passenger and freight trains, and the third is a smaller service tunnel that could also serve as an emergency escape route. Each tunnel is more than 31 miles long, 23 miles of which are under the English Channel.

Several "crossover" passages were built that allowed trains to switch from one track to another. The design of the Channel Tunnel offered a

20-minute trip between France and the United Kingdom with maximum train speeds up to 100 miles per hour.[85]

Further Northeast Projects

In addition to the ongoing WMATA and Northeast Corridor projects, in 1988 Parsons assisted the New York Department of Transportation (NYSDOT) in the emergency inspection of the Williamsburg Bridge that spans the East River. When originally constructed in 1903, the bridge's 1,600-foot-long main suspension span exceeded the previous record-holder, the Brooklyn Bridge, by four-and-one-half feet.

For the emergency inspection of this historic structure, Parsons mobilized seven teams, practically overnight, that completed the evaluation under severe time constraints and in adverse weather conditions. Extensive deterioration was discovered to the bridge approaches, resulting in its being closed to vehicular and transit traffic. Parsons then designed the emergency repairs to the structure at an accelerated pace—leading to its partial reopening after several weeks and the bridge's total use, shortly thereafter. Even with the emergency repairs, the bridge required further evaluation to determine whether it could be rehabilitated or required replacement.

After discussing options with the community, NYSDOT decided to completely replace the approaches but to rehabilitate the existing suspension bridge. A design competition for integrating the bridge's replacement and rehabilitation was held, and Parsons was selected as one of the three award-winning finalists. Parsons proposed that the replacement components reflect the design of the Brooklyn Bridge and silhouette the straight lines of the World Trade Center, the dominant feature of the New York City skyline prior to September 11, 2001. Parsons' concept was deemed the "most worthy for replacing the existing structure," and the corporation was awarded a $70,000 prize for its design entry.[86]

In August 1990, NYSDOT retained the corporation for the bridge's complete structural rehabilitation, one of the largest design contracts of its kind ever awarded. Parsons relied on state-of-the-art engineering for the bridge's rail transit system and the intelligent transportation system created to

Parsons conducted the emergency inspection of the historic Williamsburg Bridge that had spanned the East River in New York City since 1903. NYSDOT then retained Parsons for its structural rehabilitation, one of the largest design contracts of its kind ever awarded.

monitor vehicular and transit traffic.[87] As with so many projects, Parsons' affiliation with the Williamsburg Bridge continued after the completion of the rehabilitation. In the aftermath of the World Trade Center's destruction, Parsons conducted vulnerability assessments on major transportation arteries into New York City, including the Williamsburg, Queensboro, and Brooklyn Bridges. During the middle of the first decade of the 21st century, Parsons also completed the engineering design to strengthen the Williamsburg main tower, reinforce the top chord of the stiffening truss, and adjust the suspender lengths.[88]

In the time frame of 1985 and 1994, Parsons also rehabilitated the Gowanus Expressway, the highway system around Brooklyn and Queens in New York City. The viaduct, originally constructed in the 1940s, had been expanded over the years to include six lanes. However, its deck and supporting steel superstructure were severely deteriorating, and the 150,000 vehicles using the expressway daily warranted a further expansion to eight lanes. Parsons conducted the first transportation system management study in New York State to identify ways of encouraging non-peak hour travel and determining alternative routes, easing congestion during construction. The rehabilitation involved steel repair and replacement, a new concrete deck and median barriers, a 3-mile median bus lane, and interchange improvements at a cost of $500 million.[89]

In 1993, the firm completed an inspection of New York's Verrazano-Narrows Bridge, the longest suspension bridge in the Western Hemisphere. The investigation studied the surface and underwater structure connecting Staten Island to Brooklyn. The following year, Parsons began upgrading New York City's Queensboro Bridge, the most heavily traveled, toll-free structure in the United States.[90]

In addition, for Boston, Massachusetts, Parsons designed the traffic control system to monitor the underground facilities associated with 7.5 miles of tunnel in 1991. The central control center was engineered to incorporate closed-circuit television, radio communication, and highway monitoring equipment.[91]

In addition to the bridges and the expressway in New York City, Parsons was retained on other significant Northeast transportation projects. The transportation endeavor that required all of Parsons' acumen was the planning, design management, and construction management of the major expansions and upgrades to the Dulles International and the Washington National (now Ronald Reagan Washington National) Airports. Parsons led the joint venture (Parsons Management Consultants) responsible for this megaprogram. The work at Dulles involved a new international terminal, underground people-mover stations, and baggage-handling systems. At National, the main terminal was renovated, the north terminal replaced, new parking structures were built, and access ties into the metrorail system were created. Parsons also provided design and construction oversight for the control tower at National. Environmental remediation was a major task at each airport, and Parsons supervised contaminated soil cleanup, asbestos removal, and management of PCBs in transformers and light ballasts.[92]

Charlie Dutton, who joined Parsons in 1956, was the Jeddah International Airport program manager and became the corporation's lead airport architect. He was the prime planner on Dulles from 1989 until his retirement in 1993. He described the project:

> *At Dulles, it was pure expansion of the existing facilities. It was all master-planned in the beginning and [we] just carr[ied] through with the plan as [it] grew.*[93]

During his career with Parsons, Charlie also worked on the early missile programs, the USAID contract in Tanzania, and the Honolulu and Stapleton Airports.

Ron L'Hommedieu was the Dulles International and the Washington National Airports' first program manager. He organized the team in such a manner that their initial efforts got the program off to a great start and set the quality and scheduling standards for its duration. Ron was a civil engineer who had managed Parsons' landmark DFW International Airport project in 1989. He also supervised Parsons' construction management efforts in expanding both the Stapleton and the Harry S. Truman Airports. Early in his career, Ron was assigned to Yanbu Industrial City as the planning director and later the program manager.[94] When Ron was appointed vice president overseeing all of the corporation's aviation projects in 1991,

Roy M. Goodwin, who held a doctorate in structural engineering, became the program manager during the height of the design and construction activities at Dulles and National.[95] Roy is a former brigadier general who joined Parsons in 1990 after he retired from the Air Force. He recalled:

> *Every project was done in a sequential fashion and an awful lot of planning went into them. We went through the airports' master plans—developed all the time lines, project costs, and schedules. What we brought to the client was an orchestrated decision process. Every week would have a sequence of meetings to move the program along. We could never impede operations of airplanes and vehicles going in and out of the airports. So, we created interim facilities that were used during construction*

At Dulles, Parsons seamlessly extended the original terminal 310 feet on both sides to realize the architect's original dream of a 1,240-foot terminal.

Parsons' orchestrated decision process helped expedite the design and construction of the new airport terminal at Washington National, which had a Jeffersonian Dome—in keeping with the architecture of Washington, D.C.

and then returned to their former use when the new facility was operational. For example, a warehouse was used as a passenger terminal for two major airlines and turned back into warehouse space.[96]

Roy then described the highlights during his time on the program:

We were a shadow staff for the Airport Authority and had 150–160 really good people on the program when both Dulles and National terminals were being built—the crown jewels of the program. At Dulles, we extended the original terminal 310 feet on both sides to realize the architect's (Aero Saarinen) original dream of a 1,240-foot terminal. If you walk through it today, I bet you could not see where we expanded the facility—it's seamless. At National, the design team developed a "Jeffersonian Dome" look to the terminal in keeping with the architecture of Washington, D.C.

We modified the terminal and the location of the tower at National 25 to 30 times to make sure the tower had clear sight of airport runways. When the National terminal was completed, we literally moved operations from the old to the new terminal overnight, between 11:00 PM *and 6:00* AM*. This required hundreds if not thousands of logistical decisions.*[97]

In 1996, Roy was promoted to Federal Division manager and assumed responsibility for Parsons' governmental programs. He also assisted with solving many of the logistical issues on Parsons' New Jersey Vehicle Emissions program and winning a significant contract with the FAA before retiring in 2003.[98] Nils Pearson succeeded Roy as the Dulles International and Washington National Airports' program manager and remains so to this day. Since 1993, he had been very involved in the program as its planning manager, which helped make a seamless management transition. A civil engineer, Nils joined Parsons in 1992 with an extensive background in managing aviation engineering and construction projects for the Dade County Aviation Department in Florida and the Illinois Division of Aeronautics.[99]

SIGNIFICANT PROJECTS

1985–1994

1985

Los Angeles Metropolitan Transportation Authority (MTA), Construction Management Services, Red Line Commuter Rail, California

Chandler, Privatization Contract, Wastewater Treatment Plant, Arizona

NASA, Engineer and Design Laboratory Facilities, Langley Research Center, Virginia

Army Corps of Engineers (Huntsville), Chemical Stockpile Disposal Program, Design and Systems Integration, Various Locations

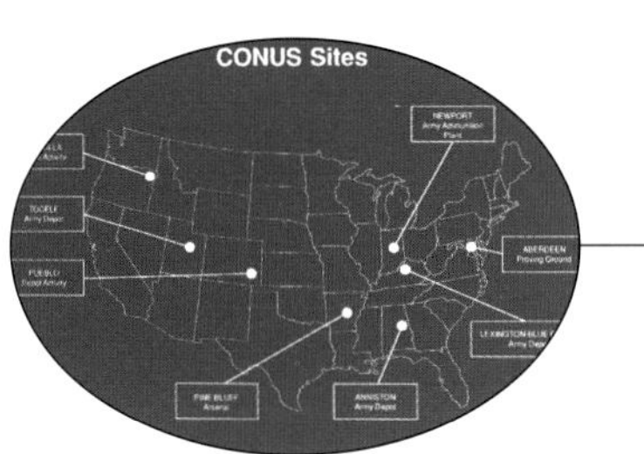

Cominco American, Design and Construction Management, Red Dog Mine, Alaska

City of San Diego, Design South Bay Ocean Outfall, California

1986

U.S. Army, Design Ground-Based Laser Installation, White Sands Missile Range, New Mexico

LEGEND

Commercial | Energy/Petroleum and Chemical |  |  | 

Government | Transportation | Water

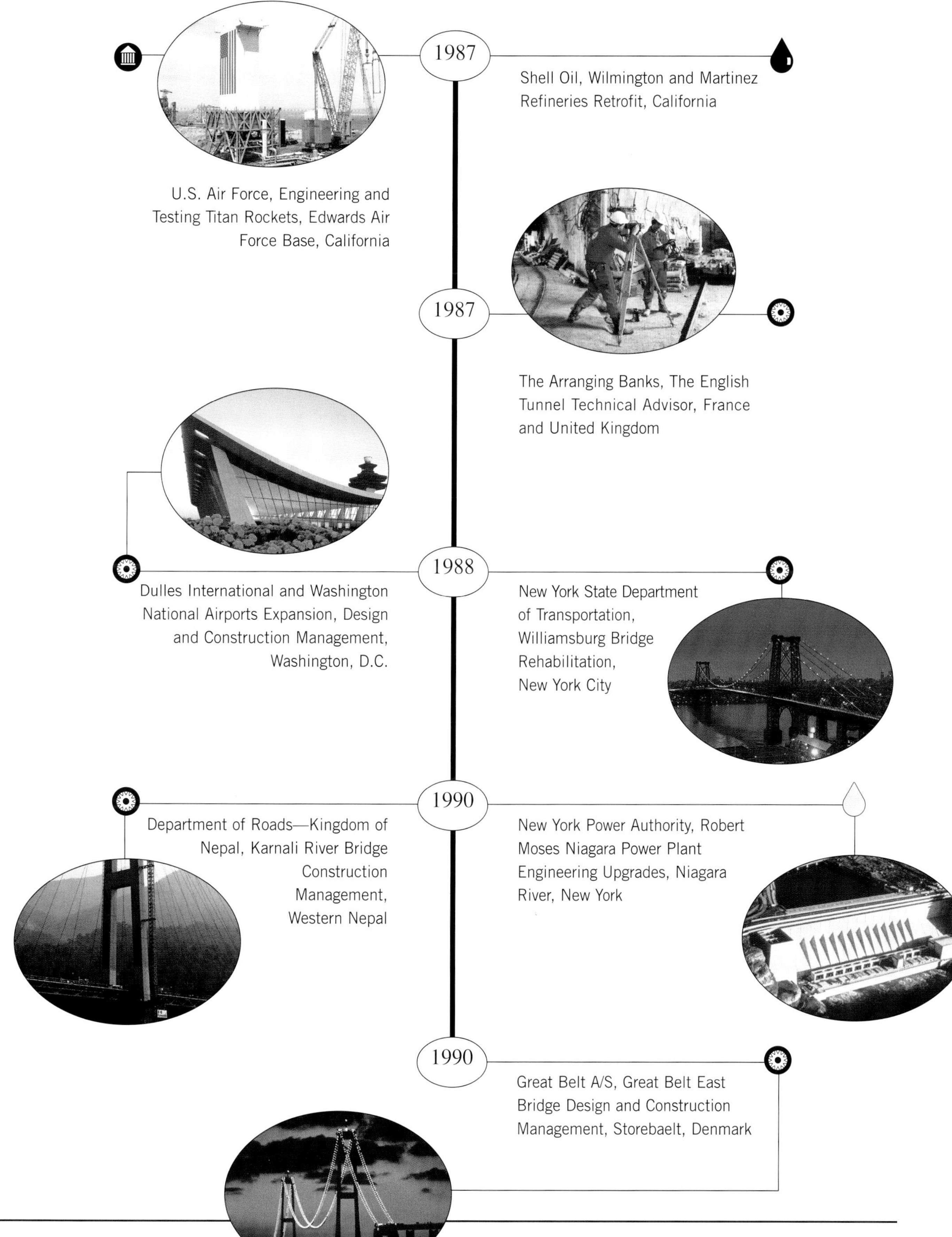

1987

Shell Oil, Wilmington and Martinez Refineries Retrofit, California

U.S. Air Force, Engineering and Testing Titan Rockets, Edwards Air Force Base, California

1987

The Arranging Banks, The English Tunnel Technical Advisor, France and United Kingdom

1988

Dulles International and Washington National Airports Expansion, Design and Construction Management, Washington, D.C.

New York State Department of Transportation, Williamsburg Bridge Rehabilitation, New York City

1990

Department of Roads—Kingdom of Nepal, Karnali River Bridge Construction Management, Western Nepal

New York Power Authority, Robert Moses Niagara Power Plant Engineering Upgrades, Niagara River, New York

1990

Great Belt A/S, Great Belt East Bridge Design and Construction Management, Storebaelt, Denmark

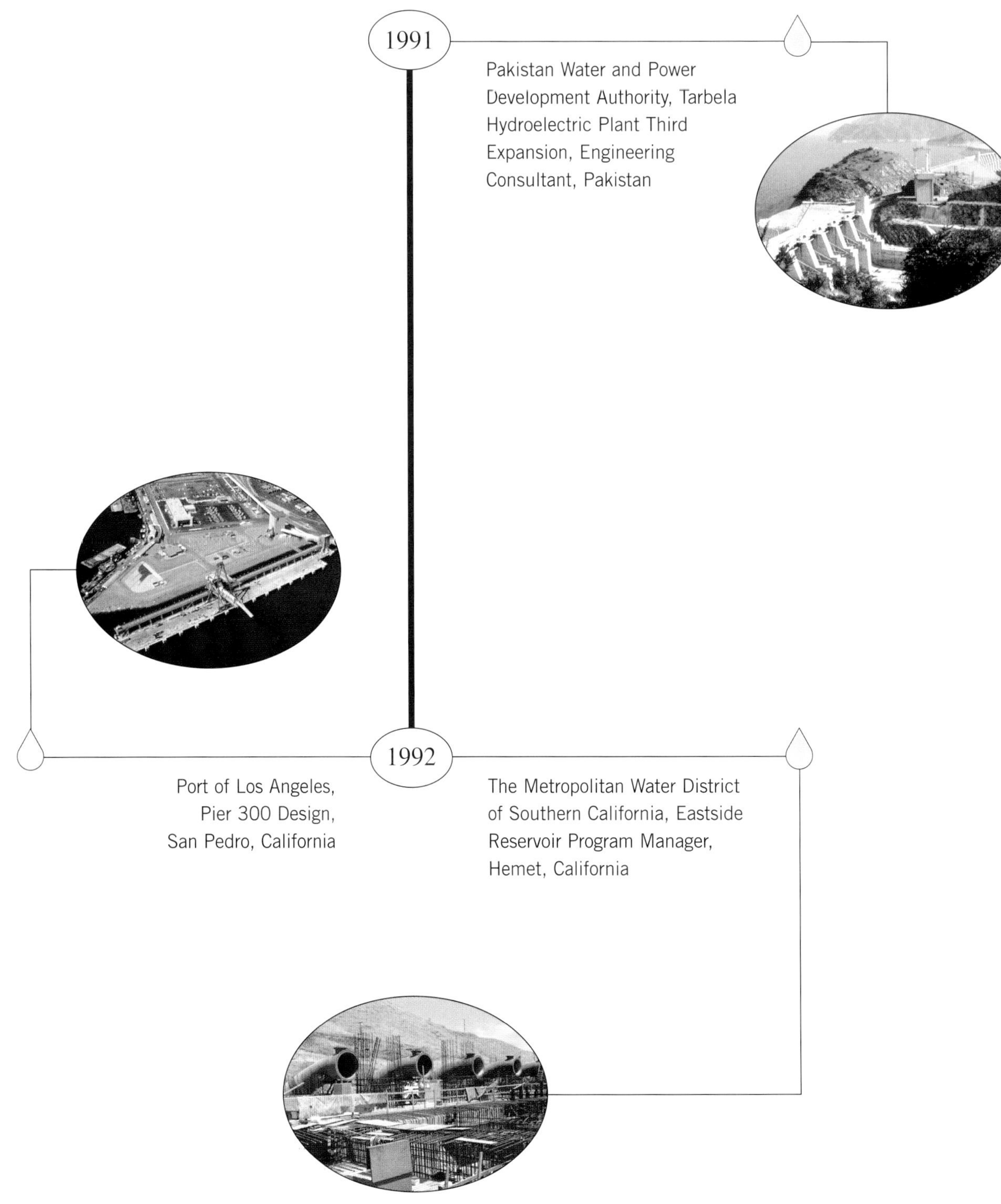

LEGEND

Commercial | Energy/Petroleum and Chemical | Government | Transportation | Water

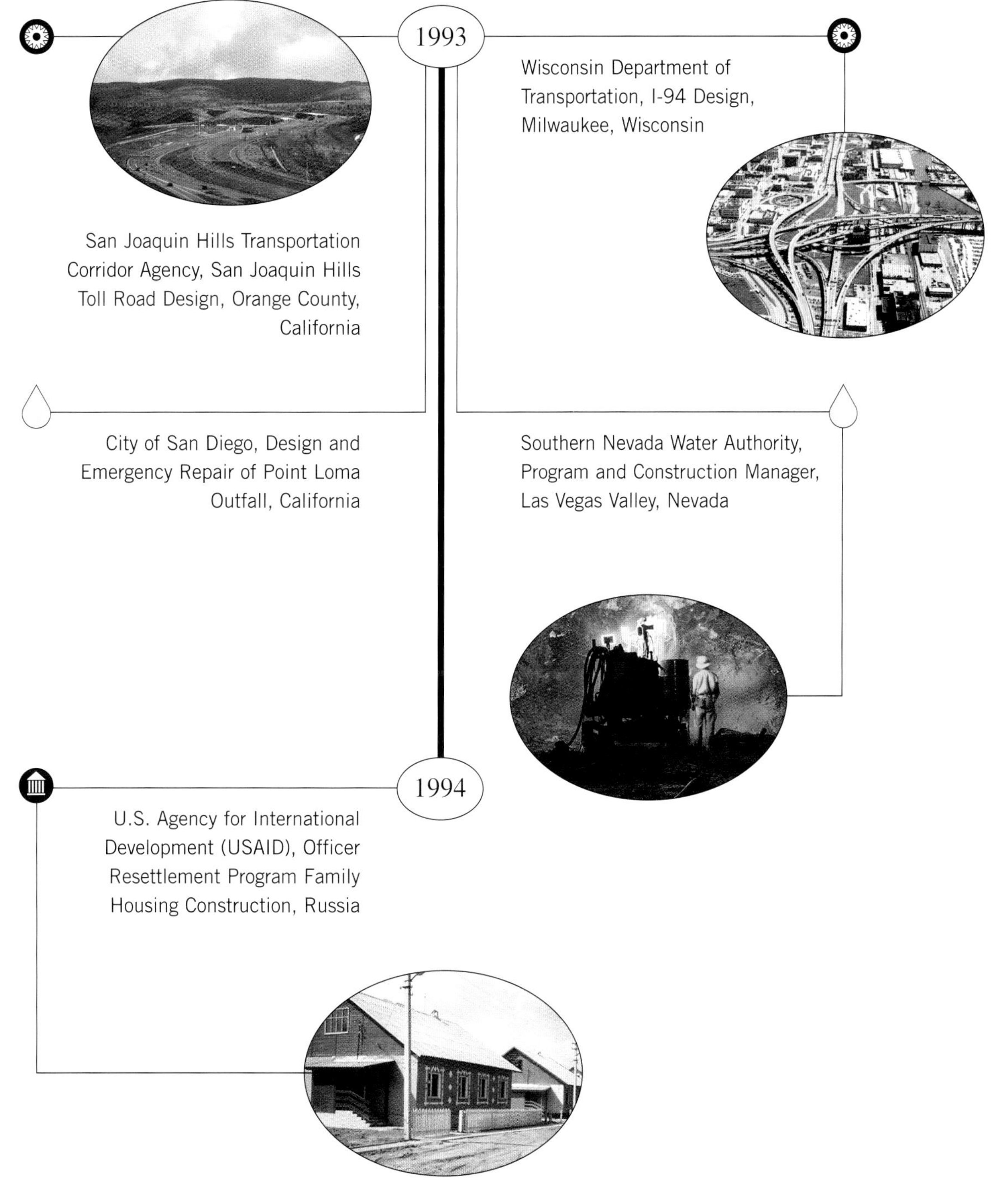

San Joaquin Hills Transportation Corridor Agency, San Joaquin Hills Toll Road Design, Orange County, California

Wisconsin Department of Transportation, I-94 Design, Milwaukee, Wisconsin

City of San Diego, Design and Emergency Repair of Point Loma Outfall, California

Southern Nevada Water Authority, Program and Construction Manager, Las Vegas Valley, Nevada

U.S. Agency for International Development (USAID), Officer Resettlement Program Family Housing Construction, Russia

Record-Setting Suspension Bridge

Another landmark project for Parsons came with the award of the 1990 contract to design and later manage the construction of the Great Belt East Bridge in Denmark. For many years, it was the longest suspension bridge in the world. However, the Akashi Kaikyo Bridge in Japan now holds this honor. The central span of the Great Belt East Bridge is 5,328 feet, and the total length of the structure is 8,838 feet. The project also included building a four-lane highway and rail tunnel as part of the 11-mile link across the Great Belt Channel, a major shipping route between the North and Baltic Seas.[100] Jose Celis, who held his master's degree in civil engineering from Stanford, was the construction manager. He was also the project manager on the Tagus River suspension bridge in Lisbon, Portugal, and the Queensboro Bridge in New York City. Jose was originally a Steinman engineer, who retired as project director from Parsons after over 30 years of engineering and constructing bridges.[101]

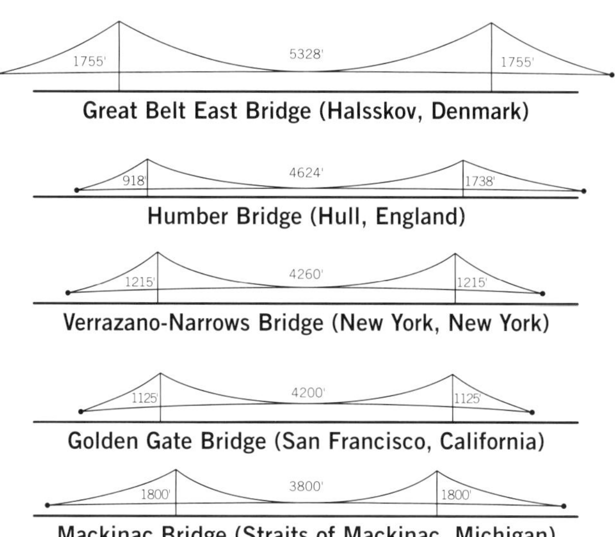

Above: Parsons contributed to building or rehabilitating the world's longest suspension bridges.

Below: Parsons designed and performed construction management of the landmark Great Belt East Bridge in Denmark. It was the longest suspension bridge in the world until the construction of the Akashi Kaikyo Bridge in Japan.

San Joaquin Hills Toll Road

In 1993, Parsons was selected as the general design consultant for the divided 15.5-mile, six-lane San Joaquin Hills Toll Road (Route 73) that stretches south from the Corona del Mar Freeway in the vicinity of the John Wayne (Orange County) Airport in Santa Ana, California, to connect with the I-5 Freeway near the Ortega Highway in San Juan Capistrano. Originally, Parsons served as program manager on a $190 million expansion of the Corona del Mar Freeway in 1984. Due to its performance on the Corona del Mar Freeway, Parsons was considered the best choice to support the design efforts associated with the San Joaquin Hills Toll Road contract, which included the highway, cross streets and collector distributor roads, traffic signalization, multiple bridge structures, maintenance of traffic plans, and drainage facilities. Parsons mapped more than 125 individual parcels prior to the start of construction and incorporated over 300 environmental mitigation measures into the project.

The San Joaquin Toll Road was a unique undertaking because it was the first toll road built in California. It was completed under a design-build contract with Kiewit-Granite, a joint venture of Peter Kiewit Company and Granite Construction.[102] Gene Randich, former vice president of transportation, recalled the project:

> *We did the first design-build toll road, $1.2 billion. [It] was successfully completed. Done ahead of time. [There was] a great amount of cooperation between ourselves and Kiewit. We could foresee that [design-build] was the way to go because of the savings in time and dollars [from] the traditional system where you design, bid, and then build. Under these circumstances, you're doing everything together and you're able to work directly with the contractor. You're able to provide the design he can best build [and] fulfill all the requirements and specifications.*[103]

Gene came from De Leuw, Cather & Company when it was acquired in 1977 from TRW, and he contributed to the growth of Parsons' transportation projects on the West Coast until his retirement in 1995.[104]

Parsons converted a one-million-square-foot building in Edison, New Jersey, into one of the world's largest newspaper printing and distribution centers for *The New York Times*.

All the News That's Fit to Print

Between 1985 and 1994, Parsons completed the conversion of the *New York Times*' one-million-square-foot building in Edison, New Jersey, making it one of the world's largest newspaper printing and distribution centers. Parsons also supplied engineering services for the *Baltimore Sun*'s newspaper production plant, as well as various facilities for the *Richmond Times-Dispatch* in Richmond, Virginia; *Cape Cod Times* in Hyannis Port, Massachusetts; *Erie Times* in Erie, Pennsylvania; *Herald-Journal* in Spartanburg, South Carolina; *News-Press* in Santa Barbara, California; Canada's *Toronto Star* in Vaughn, Ontario; and Gannett Publishing in South Portland, Maine.[105]

The Mouse That Roared and the Planners Who Skied

During this period, Parsons expanded its services to the entertainment and recreation industries. Its engineering design services group provided engineering, procurement, and construction management for the 51,600-square-foot Wonders of Life pavilion at Walt Disney World's Epcot Center in Florida. The corporation also provided architectural, engineering, and construction support services for the Indiana Jones Stunt Theater, Typhoon Lagoon, Animal Kingdom,

Parsons' architectural, engineering, and construction support services helped create the Tower of Terror at Walt Disney World in Orlando, Florida.

Splash Mountain, and Tower of Terror at Walt Disney World. In addition, Parsons was retained by Disney Development Company to conduct an extensive traffic study in Anaheim, California, to determine possible expansion and ease traffic congestion around Walt Disney's original theme park, Disneyland.[106]

Parsons prepared the environmental documents for the State of California, the federal government, and the Tahoe Regional Planning Agency for a master plan to expand Heavenly Ski Resort, the nation's largest ski resort operating under a U.S. Department of Agriculture Forest Service permit. The resort straddles the California–Nevada border and covers 22 square miles in the High Sierra mountain range, presenting spectacular views of Lake Tahoe and the Nevada desert. The plan encompassed a new gondola, ski lifts, ski runs, parking areas, watershed restoration, and improvements to the lodges and other support facilities.[107] Anders (Andy) Hauge, vice president and urban master planner, managed the project and recounted, "The environmental process involved over 22 agencies and advocacy groups, with whom Parsons had to work closely in order to receive the necessary

BARTON-ASCHMAN ASSOCIATES INC.

BARTON-ASCHMAN ASSOCIATES INC. (Barton-Aschman) was founded in 1946 by George W. Barton as a transportation consulting firm and was merged with Frederick T. Aschman's urban planning practice in 1959. George was a well-respected traffic engineer, and Ted had previously been the executive director of the Chicago Planning Commission.[1]

George started his consulting practice on the premise that transportation and land development were inextricably linked. Ted coauthored the 1957 textbook *Real Estate and City Planning*, which presented the concept of a "community desirability" rating system based on weighted economic and land-use indicators that was adopted by investors and planning professionals to support real estate lending and location decisions.[2]

Barton-Aschman was acquired by Parsons in 1985. The firm's experience strengthened Parsons land planning capabilities via its previous purchase of De Leuw, Cather & Company in 1977. Fred Schweiger, former president of Barton-Aschman, explained the reasons for the acquisition:

> *Parsons had already acquired De Leuw, Cather [& Company]. We always knew them as friendly competitors. They were in Chicago, and we were in Chicago. One of the reasons Parsons*

Andy Hauge, vice president and urban master planner, was photographed awaiting one of Heavenly Ski Resort's lifts. He managed the resort's master planning, which involved over 22 government agencies and advocacy groups.

master plan approvals."[108] Andy began his career in the public sector and eight years later started to consult in private practice. He joined Parsons in 1989 and has become one of the preeminent city planners in the western United States. His daughter, Katrina, also works for the corporation as an administrator.[109]

Entry into Russia

During the early 1990s, opportunities increased in the Middle East, the former Soviet Union, Southeast Asia, and South America, both through the host governments themselves and Western oil companies. Parsons increasingly performed its engineering work close to the project locations and hired local technical support. By the end of 1993, Parsons was operating full-service engineering offices in Great Britain, Mexico,

approached us was at De Leuw Cather's beckoning. They recognized that we had a very strong reputation in what we call the "front end" of transportation work, the planning aspects, and they were very good at the actual design, final design, [and] building of these facilities. They said with a firm like Barton-Aschman, as a Parsons subsidiary, we could get in on the front end of these assignments, do the planning, and then lead De Leuw Cather in to do the final engineering.[3]

Harvey Joyner, who joined Barton-Aschman in 1960 and was former chairman of its board of directors, added these insights:

Barton-Aschman had been approached by a number of firms in the late 1970s and 1980s, large engineering firms mostly, who were interested in acquiring a firm like ours that worked in transportation and urban planning. The fit never seemed quite right, and we weren't really looking to be acquired. Then, we were approached by Parsons. The proposal that they made was very attractive, and we felt that for the first time, this could be a proposal that might be a good fit for us.[4]

The acquisition occurred, and Barton-Aschman added over 200 professionals to Parsons' planning and transportation staff in 13 urban-area offices throughout the United States and Canada.

Harvey discussed his feelings about Parsons when he retired in 2000:

I guess the thing that's kind of impressed me about Parsons over the years is that it is such a far-flung organization with so many talents and so many capabilities that [I] was really quite proud to be a part [of it].[5]

Saudi Arabia, Kuwait, Abu Dhabi, Oman, Taiwan, and the Philippines.[110]

In Russia, Parsons worked directly with regional oil production and refinery companies to develop ways to finance their capital programs while the country struggled to learn how to operate in a free-market system. In 1994, USAID awarded Parsons a contract to support the Russian government with its Officer Resettlement Program. Parsons managed the construction of thousands of housing units for demobilized Soviet Union army officers. Jim Shappell, then the head of international business development for RMP's System Division and currently the president of Parsons Transportation Group, was responsible for winning the Russian project. John Small, executive vice president of Parsons Commercial Technology Group, was the project manager tasked with its execution.[111]

John recalled his experience regarding military housing in Russia:

We went after a USAID project to build housing in Russia for military officers who had been demobilized from the Baltic states. This project came about as a result of an agreement between Boris Yeltsin and President Clinton in Vancouver where Clinton agreed to fund the housing for these Russian officers who had been demobilized in Latvia, Estonia, and Lithuania but had not moved back to Russia because, quite frankly, there was no housing for them.

I agreed to go over to Russia. We developed contracts that met both Russian and U.S. laws. We sat down with people who were in charge of these entities and went through them paragraph by paragraph. We helped them develop schedules. We just did it the way we would do any project—putting together the fundamental elements of program management.[112]

John stayed in Russia from 1994 through 1999. In that time, Parsons also won a $400 million World Bank-funded project that would help privatize the Russian housing market and create land development opportunities. The World Bank also funded the City Center of St. Petersburg's master plan reconstruction and retained Parsons for that project.[113]

John also acknowledged the corporate support he received while in Russia:

Left and below: USAID awarded Parsons a contract to manage the construction of thousands of housing units for demobilized Soviet Union Army officers as part of the Russian Officer Resettlement Program.

I've got to really thank Jim [Shappell] for the help he gave. We forged a friendship that's still, to this day, real strong. Frank DeMartino [former COO and president of Parsons Corporation] was my boss at the time, and I was on the phone and fax almost daily. Of course, Jim McNulty at that time was managing the Systems Division of the old Ralph M. Parsons Company. He was involved as well. It was the support team that made sure you could be successful, and I think we're still that way.[114]

Work Continues in Pakistan

Parsons continued building its water-related project portfolio in Pakistan in the early 1990s as the lead engineering consultant on Pakistan's Tarbela Hydroelectric Plant third expansion. In conjunction with National Engineering Services of Pakistan Ltd., Parsons was responsible for the detailed design, construction supervision, coordination, testing, and commissioning of the project. Located on the Indus River, the original Tarbela facility was completed in 1976, and the first and second expansions occurred in 1977 and 1982. Prior to the third expansion, the hydroelectric plant was one of 12 in the country, but produced 25 percent of Pakistan's power. The third expansion would double its capacity and had several unique features, including an unusually large penstock with a diameter that would equate to a three-story building. The intake structure was approximately 10 stories high and allowed for greater water flow for crop irrigation. The turbine inlet valves were considered at the time of construction to be the largest in the world with a diameter of 7.53 meters.[115]

Dick Payne, who was the project administrator and came to Parsons through CT Main, described the project:

Transportation of the machinery presented quite a challenge due to the considerable size of the equipment. Adequate roads in Pakistan were limited, so much of the equipment was transported at night. Loads that were too heavy to transport across bridges used lorries to carry the equipment across rivers, several of which were only accessible three months out of the year.[116]

Yet again, Parsons successfully met the logistical challenges of working in remote locations with the third extension's completion in 1992.

Long-Term Relationships Continue

Parsons remained busy with its valued, long-term clients, the oil companies. For Shell, Parsons' engineers retrofitted California's Martinez and Wilmington refineries to comply with rigorous environmental standards and improve the reliability of the refining process. Shell also retained the corporation to perform similar engineering services

Parsons was responsible for the detailed design, construction supervision, coordination, testing, and commissioning for the third expansion of Pakistan's Tarbela Hydroelectric Plant, which produced 25 percent of the country's electrical power.

JOHN SMALL: OUR MAN IN MOSCOW

JOHN SMALL, EXECUTIVE VICE PRESIDENT of commercial technology, was Parsons' pioneer manager in Russia, initially for the USAID housing program in 1994 after the Soviet Union dissolved. John was not supposed to go to Russia but, in a professional twist of fate, he was asked to start up the Russian Military Housing Program when the proposed manager could not go. John agreed to the assignment and hopped on the plane to Moscow with Jim Shappell, president of Parsons Transportation Group, then vice president of business development, and with Chuck Thomas, then a construction manager, now the deputy manager for the International Division, to kick off the program.

When the three of them arrived in Moscow, they had no one to greet them or show them to their hotel. They spent the first day getting acclimated and, on the second day, they met with the client, USAID, in the American Embassy. John dryly recounted his reaction to the client housing director's initial statements:

> *The client fully expected this project to be a complete failure because in Russia there was no basis of ownership of property established and no financial or accounting laws. I didn't take this to be the most encouraging kick off meeting I have ever attended. That evening's activities also did not help, when Jim decided that I needed to learn how to drink Vodka!*[1]

However, the second day was "the beginning of a beautiful friendship," as Humphrey Bogart's character, Rick Blaine, states in the last line of the movie, *Casablanca*."[2] John had hired a taxi, an ancient Russian-made Volga sedan, which was driven by a gentleman named Vadim Kuskov. John described this colorful individual:

> *I hired him for the entire day. Vadim was built like a prizefighter and, in fact, had been one. He knew his way around, was a good driver, and also acted as our bodyguard. After that, I continued to hire him by the day and eventually hired him full-time. I trusted Vadim to drive Frank DeMartino, Len Pieroni, and Jim McNulty when they visited Russia, and they liked him as well. It turns out his father was a general in the Soviet Union's space program, and Vadim had been an aeronautical engineer. Vadim eventually managed our small fleet of Jeep Cherokees that we purchased for the program. He became a part of the family.*[3]

in Illinois, Ohio, Louisiana, and Texas. In particular, Shell's Deer Park, Texas, facility required upgrades to its waste management and environmental compliance systems. Parsons was awarded the contract to perform these services.[117]

In January 1992, Chevron awarded the corporation a process engineering, design, and procurement contract for a gas treatment plant in Pascagoula, Mississippi, to process 900 million cubic feet per day of natural gas in three trains. The corporation also designed two sulfur recovery units for the plant. In that same month, Texaco (now ChevronTexaco) retained Parsons to engineer a new process plant at its Wilmington, California, refinery. Hap Meissner, former director of technology, stated that the Texaco plant would rely on "Parsons' proprietary gas treating technology" to comply with the air-quality regulations on the sulfur contents in fuel gas.[118] For Mobil (now ExxonMobil), Parsons performed umbrella engineering services for the Torrance, California, refinery between 1989 and 1993.[119]

Also in 1992, the Chinese Petroleum Corporation retained Parsons to modernize the environmental controls on its oil refinery in Kaohsiung, Taiwan.

After Jim Shappell and Chuck Thomas left Moscow, John set up an office in his hotel room. He had brought only his laptop computer and a suitcase. He recalled his experience:

I knew one of the first things I needed to do was find a suitable office for Parsons and rent a decent apartment for my family who would eventually be joining me. I found an office fairly quickly, but I looked at 60 to 70 apartments with a person that was what we would call a real estate broker. All of the places we saw had stray dogs and litter in the public spaces, the elevators didn't work, and there was no security. I kept saying to the broker, "find a nice place." Then, I began to realize this was the state of housing in Moscow at that time.[4]

It took John three months, but he did secure a decent apartment that was fully furnished and included some very beautiful artwork. He described it:

I later found out that my landlord was the son of [Leonid] Brezhnev's former Minister of Interior, Nicolai Thchelokov. Our apartment was like a museum—we had two original Rembrandts and several other museum-quality paintings. We lived in that apartment the full five years we were in Russia.[5]

Vadim Kuskov, former aeronautical engineer who managed Parsons' fleet of jeeps in Russia (left) and John Small, executive vice president (right), developed a strong friendship during John's five-year assignment in Moscow.

Along with Vadim, the landlord, Igor Thchelokov, also became a friend of John's. John quickly ascertained that only the former Soviet Union elite or members of the diplomatic service spoke English. In order to conduct business in Russia effectively, he was going to need to learn the Russian language. He explained how he went about doing this:

Russian is based on the Cyrillic alphabet that has 32 characters compared to the 26 letters of the English alphabet. I hired an instructor who taught English at the Moscow State University. She either came to our apartment or the office, twice a week for two years. My wife told me I became fluent in Russian. I didn't think that I was, but at least I felt I understood what our business associates and contractors were saying.[6]

John's efforts to learn Russian, develop personal relationships with Russian citizens, and establish a reputable project team led to a successful project with several thousand completed housing units and was the genesis of Parsons' robust business in Russia to this day.

When completed, the refinery met some of the "most stringent air and water emission standards in the world," according to Jerry Au, project manager. Parsons designed, constructed, and tested facilities for wastewater treatment, storm water, runoff, and sludge disposal via incineration. Also in Taiwan, Parsons created an urban master plan for Tanhai, an entire new city developed to ease the island's population density. The plan, based on housing 300,000 people, was completed in 1992.[120]

In the Philippines, Parsons performed engineering, procurement, and construction management services for the $60 million expansion of Caltex's Batangas refinery, about 75 miles south of Manila, its capital city. The front-end design and engineering were completed at the Pasadena headquarters, and a local Filipino workforce was hired to build the facilities. In total, over 700 engineers and construction personnel were involved in the expansion, which increased the refinery's capacity by 25 percent. The project began in 1992 and was completed in 1994. It involved the expansion of the crude unit, naphtha hydrotreater, and platformer unit, and the upgrade of the tail gas treatment facility.[121]

In 1993, construction began on the extension of Statoil's refinery in Kalundborg, Denmark. Parsons' $350 million contract performed the detailed engineering, procurement, and labor management services to modify the existing refinery and expand the facilities into an adjacent site. When finished, the extended plant refined one million tons per year of condensate of very light crude oil from the Norwegian field in the North Sea.[122]

Chemical Stockpile Disposal Project (CSDP)

Using the project experience gained at the Johnston Atoll demilitarization facility as the stepping stone, Parsons' involvement in chemical weapons disposal would continue to grow under the requirements of the 1981 Inhumane Weapons Convention, which specified prohibition or restrictions on the use of certain conventional weapons deemed to be excessively injurious or to have indiscriminate effects.[123]

In 1985, the Army Corps of Engineers selected Parsons to furnish design, engineering, and procurement services for the chemical weapons incineration plants at eight locations within the continental United States. Two of the key factors for this award were Parsons' Johnston Atoll experience and the knowledge of the CSDP that Jack Scott, now president and COO, brought to the corporation. Ray Judson had hired Jack that same year for his expertise as the government's manager assigned to the CSDP.[124] Jack recounted Parsons' involvement with both incineration and neutralization technologies that were used on the CSDP to destroy the chemical weapons:

> *We designed five incinerators, including Johnston Atoll. Halfway through awards for construction, the Army opted for chemical neutralization for the remaining four sites, and we won three of them.*[125]

The CSDP was a megaprogram that was pivotal to Parsons' stability and growth from its beginnings in the 1980s and continuing today. One of its key managers was Jake Kostyzak, a mechanical engineer, who was the CSDP program director when he retired in 2003.[126] He recalled his CSDP and career experiences at Parsons:

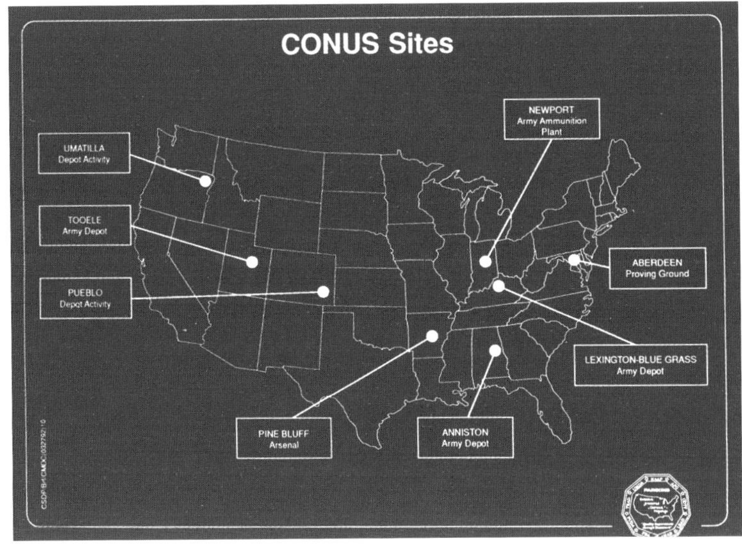

Above: Parsons performed engineering, procurement, and construction management services for the expansion of Caltex's refinery in the Philippines. It employed hundreds of local professionals and laborers.

Right: This map depicts chemical weapons incineration plants, located at eight sites within the continental United States (referred to as CONUS). Parsons was instrumental in the development of these plants.

I started in 1962. The company has been extremely interesting because all of the projects that I've worked on have been so different. [My] first project was the Titan II intercontinental ballistic missile facilities. It was something you felt good about, working on a program that was there to protect the country. I [worked on Litton's] Ingalls Shipyard, which was the first new shipyard constructed in the United States for umpteen years. I started on the [chemical demilitarization] in 1986 and was on it for one year, and then I got off onto other programs. I came back in 1991, and I've been on the job since.

Initially, our contract for CSDP was for the design of [eight incineration] plants. The [government] took the four smallest sites out of the program and decided they would use alternate technologies for disposing of the weapons on those sites. [For these four], they decided to award contracts for design, construction, and operation. We won Newport, Indiana, and two more projects in partnership with Bechtel. Once the plant operation starts, it's totally automated. You take the munition, start it through the process, and everything is automated from there on.[127]

As of 2005, the CSDP has started the destruction of both nerve and blister agents at six of the eight facilities and is well on its way to completing the design and construction at the remaining two locations.[128]

Space and Defense

In the mid-1980s, Parsons was a key member of both the systems integration team and the beam control system design team for the ground-based laser program at the White Sands Missile Range in New Mexico, which was a part of the Strategic Defense Initiative (SDI). Billy McGinnis, the project manager, recalled, "This program consisted of a belowground laser system, reflector facility, and an orbiting laser facility platform."[129] It was an important project, not only because of its advanced technology, but it also brought Parsons to the attention of the Army's SDI project manager, Colonel Jim McNulty, who would join the company in 1988 and later be appointed its CEO.

Parsons began work on other aspects of the SDI program such as the National Test Bed Facility at Falcon Air Force Base in Colorado Springs, Colorado, in 1988. Billy also managed this project. He described its originality and unusual aspects:

The National Test Bed Facility was used to simulate real-time "war game" tests, evaluate the SDI's systems and subsystem hardware, and develop software. Parsons designed all of the tenant improvements including the computer facilities that required a specially designed raised floor and special cooling and power systems to support the powerful Cray mainframe and the facility's other computers, communication center, war room, sensitive compartmentalized information facilities, and presentation and administrative areas. Parsons also performed the construction with direct-hire craft workers and completed the facility in 1995. This was an unusual project in that upon completion of each simulation, the program would change. This required redesign, demolition of an existing test area, and new construction requiring "fast track" schedules. As usual, Parsons met or bettered all schedules.[130]

Billy joined Parsons in 1961 and retired in 1993 but remained on casual status to support various projects until 1996. The National Test Bed Facility was his last project. To commemorate Billy's contributions, the commanding officer at Falcon Air Force Base retired the American flag that flew on the base and presented it to him. This honor is rarely bestowed on civilians, and it illustrates the respect the Air Force had for Billy and Parsons' team.[131] Mark LaMourey succeeded Billy as project manager. Caroll Henry was the construction manager until 1992 when James Mahoney assumed that role and completed Parsons' contracted scope of work. Greg Perry and Ken Davis developed and implemented the construction procurement and craft labor union procedures and controls.[132]

In the same time frame, Parsons designed a large facility at the Arnold Development Center in Tullahoma, Tennessee, capable of testing solid rocket engines at altitudes of 100,000 feet. Ken Whitman, former principal project manager, commented on the project:

It was a facility to test large solid rocket motors at altitude conditions. I managed the development and final design. We created a vacuum in a big chamber, [which] was maintained with a Venturi [flowmeter] at the discharge site of the rocket. We fired the rocket into this chamber, and we had to maintain the specified high-altitude conditions throughout the test. The chamber had to be large so we could collect all of the products of combustion and still maintain a minimum of the environment that was required to simulate a 100,000-foot altitude. [The] chamber was fed by a 12-foot-diameter water pipe, which dumped the contents of a three-million-gallon water tank into the chamber during the test, which was about two minutes. The chamber consisted of a reinforced concrete structure, 250 feet in diameter and 100 feet high. That was the largest facility of its kind in the free world at the time it was completed.[133]

This was Ken's last big project prior to his retirement in 1991, six months shy of his 30-year anniversary with Parsons. Ken was a registered mechanical engineer and, over the course of three decades, was a key team member on many of Parsons' rocket and missile launch and test facility projects, including the Minuteman, Titan, and Apollo programs.[134]

Parsons also continued testing the Titan solid booster rockets at Edwards Air Force Base in California. For NASA, it engineered and designed new laboratory facilities at the Langley Research Center in Virginia. In addition, the corporation performed architectural studies for ground transportation facilities at Cape Canaveral and Vandenberg Air

Below: Parsons designed the Arnold Development Center in Tullahoma, Tennessee, which was capable of testing solid rocket engines at simulated altitudes of 100,000 feet.

Opposite: Titan booster rocket test facility at Edwards Air Force Base. Continuing its support of the U.S. missile programs, Parsons conducted engineering tests on the Titan solid booster rocket launch facilities at Edwards Air Force Base, California.

LAMPSON
LAMPSON

Force Base for spacecraft under development and assisted the Jet Propulsion Laboratory in modifying its 25-foot space simulator to accommodate the next generation of deep space probes.[135] Howard (Hal) Leyrer was the senior project manager on Parsons' contributions to the simulator modification. He was a registered electrical engineer with a master's degree in mechanical engineering. He was either a part of the engineering team or supervised many of the advance technology projects undertaken by the corporation between 1952 and 1994.[136]

On behalf of the U.S. Air Force and the Army Corps of Engineers, Parsons conducted extensive investigations of potential hazardous waste contamination at bases in Massachusetts, Florida, Georgia, and California, in conjunction with the Air Force's installation restoration program. For the U.S. Navy and U.S. Marine Corps, it delivered engineering services on steam and utility systems at bases in North Carolina, Florida, and Texas, and it completed the design of a 70,000-square-foot maintenance hanger for naval aircraft at Cubi Point Naval Air Station in the Philippines.[137]

Enter Jim McNulty

It was in this time frame that Jim McNulty came to Parsons after a distinguished career in the Army. He retired as a colonel in 1988 and joined the corporation later that same year. He was first assigned as a project manager in Washington, D.C. Shortly thereafter, he was tasked with consolidating all of the subsidiaries' Department of Energy projects into one cohesive program. Bob Sheh, who was president of RMP, then asked Jim to manage the Systems Division, which Jim restructured into a three-pronged, market-focused organization consisting of government, infrastructure, and aviation sectors—with operations and sales assigned to support each sector.[138]

Nuclear & Energy

Shortly after Parsons implemented its corporate-wide Department of Energy marketing program under Jim McNulty's leadership it began to see results. Martin Marietta awarded Parsons the

Harland Bartholomew & Associates Inc.

Known as "The Dean" of U.S. city planners, Harland Bartholomew (1889–1989) was the greatest authority on municipal planning in the mid-20th century. Raised in Brooklyn, he attended Rutgers University for two years where he later received two honorary degrees: a B.S. in civil engineering in 1921 and a doctorate in 1952.

Harland was an original member of the American City Planning Institute's predecessor, the American City Planning Association. In 1940, President Roosevelt appointed him as a member of the Interregional Highway Committee. The committee's 1944 report served as the basis for the U.S. Interstate Highway System. In 1953, President Eisenhower appointed Bartholomew chairman of the National Capital Planning Commission, which led to the construction of the Washington, D.C., "Metro" and later became one of Parsons' landmark projects. He was also a professor of civic design at the University of Illinois.[1]

He founded Harland Bartholomew & Associates in 1919. Over the years, the firm consulted chemical engineering support contract for the Department of Energy's uranium enrichment facilities at Paducah, Kentucky, and Portsmouth, Ohio. It assisted in the design and generated the conceptual process flow diagrams and piping and instrument diagrams for the radioactive and hazardous chemical material processing systems.[139]

For the Department of Energy's Savannah River Site in Aiken, South Carolina, Westinghouse selected Parsons to assist in the core process development for a $120 million detritiation facility. The services involved design, fabrication, and commissioning a cryogenic distillation process to remove, concentrate, and recover 1,000 metric tons of tritium in the heavy water that moderated the coolant in the production reactor. Parsons performed the overall

Parsons developed design criteria for Westinghouse to remove and dispose of low-level radioactive substances at the Department of Energy's facility in Fernald, Ohio, one of the most radioactively contaminated sites in the country.

on more than 125 city-planning ventures and prestigious projects, including the historic Williamsburg, Virginia, and the Jefferson National Expansion Memorial in St. Louis, affectionately known as "The Arch."

Other significant projects included planning the roadways in San Antonio, Texas, and Jacksonville, Florida, that incorporated traffic control systems, ultimately connecting 800 intersections; parking facilities at Memphis International Airport; facility planning at 44 U.S. military communities and bases in Western Europe, the United States, and South Korea; a 1.6-million-square-foot commercial development in Schaumburg, Illinois; a retirement community in Palatine, Illinois; community planning for Plano, Texas, and Virginia Beach, Virginia; and a traffic analysis for a three-million-square-foot, mixed-use development in Dallas, Texas.[2]

Parsons acquired Harland Bartholomew & Associates for its planning expertise and its highly regarded staff. "He was the Johnny Appleseed of planning," said Bob Bax, Parsons' executive vice president of transportation operations.[3]

George Hull, vice president, joined Harland Bartholomew in 1971. He holds his bachelor's degree in architecture and has been Parsons' principal-in-charge on many master-planning contracts for federal, state, and municipal clients. George recounted how Harland Bartholomew & Associates joined Parsons:

> *Parsons approached Harland Bartholomew & Associates to bring them on as Parsons' internal future planning group. Current work is primarily focused on federal clients, but we have provided a significant amount of work for state and municipal clients in the recent past. These services have provided our clients with insight and assistance on future planning and programming for the broad spectrum of federal, state, and municipal development.*[4]

FIRST CLASS

INEL NEWS

The Idaho National Engineering Laboratory / June 19, 1984

Rover fuel reprocessing beats schedule

Some 3,000 kilograms of uranium-235 valued at $125 million have been recovered from the Rover processing facility located at the Idaho Chemical Processing Plant.

Fuel reprocessing began in April 1983 and was completed six months ahead of schedule on June 7. The Rover facility represented the first time irradiated graphite-based fuels had been processed in the United States on a production basis. The processing was significant because the fuel rods—a combination of uranium, graphite and other components—contained a larger percentage of uranium-235 than most other spent reactor fuels.

"The completion of Rover fuel processing is a very significant technical, operational and economic achievement," says Kevin Ryan, Rover area supervisor. Ryan, who has worked with Rover since February 1982, applauded all employees involved in the fuel processing endeavors. "The dedication and performance of our operating crews and support organizations in bringing Rover to a successful conclusion has been outstanding," he says.

To process the Rover fuel, INEL developed a double-walled burner using fluidized bed heat transfer techniques which performed flawlessly at temperatures of 800 degrees centigrade, leaving an oxide ash which was dissolvable in acids for normal fuel reprocessing at the ICPP. The process operated much better than predicted—88 percent better than design estimates—and is applicable in the future to reprocessing High Temperature Gas Reactor (HTGR) and other graphite-based nuclear fuels.

Project Rover was a joint NASA-AEC program of the 1960s to develop a nuclear propulsion reactor for space travel.

During the interim of the closing of Rover processing and the startup of the FAST (Fluorinel and Fuel Storage) facility in March 1985, the ICPP will undergo routine maintenance which will be part of an ongoing $45 million upgrading of the Chemical Processing Plant.

The ICPP, which includes the Rover facility, is operated for DOE by WINCO.

WITH THE ROVER fuel processing completed six months ahead of schedule, WINCO's Lamar Robertson makes a final commemorative note as a reminder of the successful project. (Photo by Boyd Thomas, WINCO.)

U of I awards first-time degrees

Three INEL employees recently received the first master's of science degrees in industrial education and safety awarded by the University of Idaho.

Earning their master's degrees were Dennis Skinner, DOE-ID Operational Safety Division; Tom Clements, EG&G Idaho Waste Programs; and Dennis Sorensen, EG&G Idaho Health and Safety Division.

The master's degree in safety has been part of the INEL Education Program for many years. About four years ago, though, the program's emphasis was shifted from radiation safety to industrial safety to meet the changed needs of site personnel, according to university officials.

The safety program course curriculum includes Engineering Applications to Safety, Environmental Health, Environmental Law, Health Physics and Industrial Safety, Industrial Fire Hazards and Industrial Instrumentation. All the courses are offered at night in Idaho Falls.

Course instructors are usually site employees who have the prerequisite advanced degrees to teach at the graduate level and who are [illegible] department.

The master's program in industrial safety is unique to the INEL Education Program, since a similar degree is not offered at the university or at other intermountain universities.

project management, quality assurance, and systems integration. In addition to working on the detritiation facility, Parsons completed a five-year engineering services contract in 1991 to support the E.I. du Pont de Nemours plant at the Savannah River Site.[140]

Also for Westinghouse, the corporation developed design criteria for three alternative methods to remove and dispose of low-level radioactive sludge and water from the lined disposal pit at the Department of Energy's site in Fernald, Ohio, one of the most radioactively contaminated sites in the country. In 1992, the Department of Energy selected Parsons to provide engineering services on a multiyear, $125 million environmental remediation project at Fernald. In part, the award was based on the design criteria Parsons developed for Westinghouse for removing the radioactive material from the pit.[141]

At INEL in Idaho Falls, Idaho, where Parsons began its professional relationship with the Department of Energy in 1948 and designed and engineered process facilities in the 1970s and 1980s, the company provided design and engineering support for a $410 million facility to reprocess spent nuclear fuel. This 1992 contract with the Department of Energy also included environmental permitting.[142] In 1993, the corporation began providing investigations, engineering, and waste management services at the Department of Energy's Rocky Flats nuclear weapons production facility near Denver, Colorado.[143]

Tom Bullock was a key staff member on many of the aforementioned projects and supervised a significant number of Parsons' Department of Energy and nuclear waste cleanup assignments. Tom joined the company in 1975. He was the project manager for the detrition facility, the Rocky Flats program, and the SDI's ground-based laser project. He was also a project engineer on INEL. Tom retired in 1993 as a vice president.[144]

Left and inset: INEL's internal newsletter announces progress on the Rover Spent Nuclear Fuel Reprocessing Facility that Parsons helped design and engineer. Parsons began its professional relationship with the Department of Energy in 1948 at INEL. *(Inset photo courtesy of INEL News.)*

Another project that tied directly into Parsons' past via CT Main, and indirectly to Steinman, was the 1990 upgrade of the Robert Moses Niagara Power Plant on the Niagara River in New York, which expanded the existing facility's capacity from 1,950 to 2,500 megawatts.[145] In 1956, a rockslide destroyed two-thirds of the existing power capacity from the Niagara River, and CT Main responded to this catastrophe by planning, designing, and managing the construction of the $720 million effort to restore electrical service. Named the Niagara Power Project, the emergency scope including the power plant was completed in 1961. The power plant was named after Robert Moses, the former New York City park commissioner, who was instrumental in obtaining the funding for the construction of the Henry Hudson Memorial Bridge, one of Dr. David B. Steinman's most prominent design projects.[146]

Parsons also assisted in the design, engineering, licensing and/or startup of cogeneration facilities for MIT, University of Northern Colorado at Greeley, Purdue University, and in downtown Los Angeles.[147]

Chuck Terhune III, senior vice president and program manager, attributes Parsons' success—not only in nuclear and energy, but in all of its core markets—to identifying the people and skill sets that matched the customer's needs:

> *We're contractors. It's chemistry and personalities more than products. We deal primarily with people [needing] specialists. We're diversified and oriented towards technology rather than just engineering, procurement, construction.*[148]

Parsons upgraded the Robert Moses Niagara Power Plant's capacity from 1,950 to 2,500 megawatts. One of Parsons' acquisitions, CT Main, rose to national prominence in 1956 through its efforts to rebuild electrical infrastructure that was destroyed in a major rockslide.

Neither Rain nor Snow—USPS Work Continues

Parsons continued its long-term relationship with USPS and managed the construction of an $11 million general mail facility in Port Myers, Florida, under a task order engineering and construction management services contract for a southern nine-state region. This program applied a design-build method so that the contractor could begin construction after receiving approval for the 30 percent design documents. Other projects under this contract included general mail facilities in Miami; Baton Rouge, Louisiana; Memphis, Tennessee; and Los Angeles. Parsons also completed the $41.4 million USPS technical training center in Norman, Oklahoma, in June 1992.[149] Dr. Claude Le Feuvre is presently the corporation's USPS program manager. He holds his doctorate in physical chemistry. Claude first joined Parsons in 1973 and spent 14 years with the company. He then joined an internationally known entertainment firm and held several prominent positions, including managing its engineering and facility division. He returned to Parsons in 1994.[150] Claude discussed Parsons' work for USPS:

Parsons' team is comprised of over 80 professionals providing a whole range of services from real

STEINMAN BOYNTON GRONQUIST & BIRDSALL

DR. DAVID BARNARD Steinman's (1886–1960) studies of airflow and wind velocity made aerodynamically stable bridge construction possible. He became an internationally acclaimed engineer and is credited with designing over 400 bridges on five continents.

He received his doctorate from Columbia University in New York City, and his 1911 thesis was entitled "The Design of the Henry Hudson Memorial Bridge as a Steel Arch." Dr. Steinman took great interest in engineering advancements and furthering the educational credentials of the profession. At the age of 23, he was a college professor and founded the engineering school at the College of the City of New York. Dr. Steinman also helped create the National Society of Professional Engineers and served as its first president. He was the author of numerous popular and technical books about bridges, mainly suspension.[1]

Blair Birdsall was one of the four original Steinman partners. He was a highly gifted structural engineer, and his talents contributed to the beauty and stability of many of the great 20th century suspension bridges.

Twenty-five years after he wrote his thesis, Dr. Steinman turned this expertise into a reality by obtaining funding for the double-decked arch design and construction of the Henry Hudson Memorial Bridge (1936) that connected the New York City boroughs of Bronx and Manhattan.[2]

Other landmark projects included the Mackinac Bridge (1957), which was 2,000 feet longer than the Golden Gate Bridge, the reconstruction of the Brooklyn Bridge (1954), the Kingston Bridge (1956), and the Sky-Ride and Observation Towers at the Century of Progress Exposition of 1933.[3] Dr. Steinman formed one *estate to design, design management, construction, construction management, and operations and maintenance on USPS' entire facilities portfolio. We are honored to be the sole company USPS has under contract to perform this breadth of scope.*[151]

Water Resources and State of Emergency

In 1993, the City of San Diego declared a state of emergency because of the catastrophic failure of its Point Loma 170-million-gallon-per-day ocean outfall system. Parsons worked around the clock for 60 days to repair the pipeline and its support structures. To facilitate the project, Parsons designed an alignment frame, guiding the final section of the pipeline into place. In addition to the emergency repairs, the design included a 12,500-foot-long extension to the existing outfall that would go to depths greater than 300 feet and would become the largest and deepest reinforced concrete pipe in the world.

The project won several awards, including the 1992 San Diego Section of the American Society of Civil Engineers' Outstanding Civil Engineering Project, 1993 San Diego Chapter of the Project Management Institute's Project of the Year, and the 1995 California Geotechnical Engineers' Outstanding Project.[152] The project manager, Greg McBain, is

of the most prestigious bridge design firms of all times with his partners Ray Boynton, Carl Gronquist, and Blair Birdsall.

Ray M. Boynton became managing partner of the firm after Dr. Steinman's death. Ray is best known for his design of the Tagus River Bridge in Portugal in the 1960s. In 1988, a civil engineering scholarship was established in his name at the University of Maine in Orono.[4]

Carl Gronquist designed the International Bridge, completed in 1962, which spans Sault Sainte Marie, Michigan, and Sault Sainte Marie, Ontario. He received the J. James R. Croes Medal from the American Society of Civil Engineers in 1944, named in honor of John James Robertson Croes, a distinguished past president of the American Society of Civil Engineers.[5]

Blair Birdsall's structural engineering career spanned 70 years. He was the first recipient of the American Society of Civil Engineers' Roebling Award, which is named in honor of John Roebling, the legendary designer of the Brooklyn Bridge, for his international contributions in the design, construction, engineering, and rehabilitation of suspension bridges.[6] After graduating from Princeton University as a civil engineer, Blair started out in 1934 working for John Roebling & Sons Company, which was in the process of overseeing the cable construction for the Golden Gate Bridge in San Francisco. Blair performed the cable calculations. He remembered, "I will never forget the sensation I had of walking right up to the base of that tower. You never forget the impression of a great structure like that."[7]

He was made partner emeritus of Steinman, and his last project was the Great Belt East Bridge in Denmark, which began in 1992 and was the longest suspension bridge in the world upon completion. Blair died shortly after his 90th birthday in 1997.[8] Before his death, he offered this professional advice:

> *Find something you like to do, that you can really lose yourself in, something that you want to do, that you get great satisfaction from accomplishing, and follow that. If it doesn't produce as much salary as some other guy who's working somewhere else, don't worry about that. The satisfactions, including monetary satisfaction, will come along with it if you love what you are doing.*[9]

These four men are true engineering legends in bridge design and construction. Their strengths and the engineering expertise Steinman brought to the corporation in 1988 clearly contributed to Parsons' stature as one of the most respected and sought-after bridge designers in the world.

The 800,000-acre Eastside Reservoir (or Diamond Valley Lake) is the seventh-largest earth-filled dam in the world. This photo shows the size of piping that transports the water to the inhabitants of southern California.

a civil and environmental engineer and continues to manage facility planning, water transmission, pumping, and pipeline projects for Parsons.[153]

The City of San Diego had been a client since 1986 when Parsons began designing the South Bay Ocean Outfall to satisfy California's ocean plan discharge requirements. The outfall is jointly owned and operated by the city and the International Boundary and Water Commission and eliminates pollutants from the ocean water, beaches, and local wildlife preserves. Parsons began the project with extensive, computer-modeled oceanographic field studies. The outfall consists of a 19,000-foot-long tunnel connecting to a 4,700-foot-long, ocean-floor pipe via a single riser.[154]

Frank Collins, the project manager on South Bay and a team member on Point Loma, discussed the unique aspects of the project:

> *This was an amazing project. It was the deepest, highest internal pressure tunnel excavated in North America. We used a Japanese tunnel boring machine, starting a mile on shore and popping up two-and-one-half miles offshore in 80 feet of water. From that point, we constructed another mile of pipe 10 feet in diameter to transport the discharge further away from shore. It was a true international effort.*[155]

Frank holds his bachelor's degree in environmental engineering and joined Parsons more than 25 years ago. He has been instrumental in the Parsons and CH2M Hill joint venture that has supported the Orange County Sanitation District's capital improvement program since 2002.[156]

Richard Trembath, vice president of Parsons Water and Infrastructure Group that was formed as a separate global business unit in 2003, provided his viewpoint concerning the project:

> *It was very gratifying to be part of the team which implemented the South Bay Outfall. In addition to improving the water quality in the southern California marine environment, the project involved state-of-the-art soft ground tunneling techniques and innovations in pre-cast concrete liner design.*[157]

Richard hails from Australia and has been with Parsons for over 20 years. Based in San Diego, he is a registered civil engineer in California and has been integral to the success of the corporation's water resource projects in the western United States.[158]

The South Bay Outfall was completed under budget in 1998. The outfall project in its entirety restored San Diego's beaches, freed local wetlands from pollutants, and eliminated a potentially hazardous situation by treating the effluent so that it is safe to flow into the Pacific Ocean. The outfall won national recognition for innovation and management from the American Society of Civil Engineers' California State Council that selected Parsons for its 1999 Project of the Year award and the San Diego International Chapter of the American

Concrete Institute as 1999 Marine and Waterfront Concrete Project of the Year.

It also went on to win the American Public Works Association National Public Works as Project of the Year for 2000, the American Society of Civil Engineers' National Outstanding Civil Engineering Achievement in 2000, and the American Society of Civil Engineers' Outstanding Environmental Civil Engineering Project in 2002.[159]

Another significant water project would begin in 1992 at a site about an hour northeast of San Diego near the town of Hemet, California. The Metropolitan Water District of Southern California selected the joint venture of Parsons and Harza Engineering to serve as program/construction manager for a $1.9 billion program to create the Eastside Reservoir (or Diamond Valley Lake), a massive 800,000-acre repository.

Parsons supplied the scheduling, construction administration, contract administration, construction inspection, office engineering, cost engineering, and quality-control testing. If a major earthquake or other catastrophe ever damages the aqueduct system that supplies southern California, the water stored by this dam is sufficient to serve the entire region for six months. Completed in 2000, it is the seventh-largest earth-filled dam in the world and holds nearly as much water as the combined capacities of Castaic, Pyramid, Perris, Silverwood, Mathews, and Skinner Lakes.[160]

Chuck Thomas was one of Parsons' construction managers assigned to the Eastside Reservoir program. Chuck joined Parsons in 1994. He is a West Point graduate and has a master's degree from MIT in civil engineering. Chuck is presently the deputy manager for the International Division.[161] He recalled the vast array of prehistoric fossils found during construction:

The Eastside Reservoir was nicknamed the "Valley of the Mastodons" because of the wealth of prehistoric skeletons found during construction. Paleontologists gained extensive knowledge of the former inhabitants of this area, based on studying the unearthed fossils. Shown are Chuck Thomas, Parsons' construction manager (second from left) and Hossein Teymouri, The Metropolitan Water District's program manager (second from right), with three other site workers.

The site was nicknamed the Valley of the Mastodons because it had more prehistoric skeletons than any other area in southern California, with the exception of the La Brea tar pits in [Los Angeles]. The Metropolitan Water District of Southern California was attuned to the site's prehistoric importance, and everyone worked with the paleontologists to preserve what was uncovered. This was especially true for our construction equipment operators since we were moving dirt with machinery that had tires taller than we were. Fortunately, the site was large enough [that] we could work around each of their discoveries. The paleontologists unearthed many skeletal remains "in context" with their habitat, which was very exciting for them. Most of the remains are in the San Bernardino museum.[162]

Twenty-Four Years on the North Slope

In 1994, Parsons completed 24 years of continuous service to Arco at Alaska's North Slope with a

The Alaskan sealift in 1974 carried modular equipment and buildings built in Louisiana and designed and engineered by Parsons. The modular units traversed the Panama Canal (inset photo, top right), passed under the Golden Gate Bridge, (main photo and inset photo, top left) and sailed along the Washington coast through Seattle before docking in Alaska (inset photo on bottom left). For many decades, Parsons has been a leader in adapting modular units to cost-effectively build facilities in far-flung regions of the world.

final sealift and installation project at Prudhoe Bay. In an extraordinary show of expertise, Parsons set a startup record by achieving full production only 46 days after the modules arrived.[163] The sealift coincided with the second phase of the $1.1 billion gas-handling facility expansion project. Parsons had designed the original facility, which had been built for $470 million. When completed, the facility increased the daily production of crude oil and natural liquids by 100,000 barrels. Larry Burns, WorleyParsons USA's senior vice president, was Parsons' project manager.[164]

Ron Russell, now WorleyParsons USA's procurement manager, summarized Parsons' success at the North Slope in terms of the personnel and the relationships it forged:

> *Many of us have worked together for 25 years. I mean, we've grown up in the business together. We've developed true friendships. We've watched our families grow up together. Most people don't get to experience that type of camaraderie. The key is the people and [an] environment where you can contribute to changing things. Our North Slope expertise is [really] a special group of people.*[165]

In 1994, the corporation celebrated its 50th year of consecutive operations. The next decade looked bright, and Parsons' executives were optimistic about future projects and new programs. However, the firm would first need to overcome a great tragedy before it could continue to triumph.

The award-winning Olivenhain Dam in San Diego County is the tallest roller-compacted dam in the United States and was designed by Parsons to incorporate environmental mitigation requirements and preserve native wildlife and the natural beauty of the surrounding area.

CHAPTER EIGHT

INTO THE FUTURE

1995–2005

Our aim is to form a seamless partnership with our customers so that their requirements become our challenges and our multidiscipline capabilities provide their solutions.

—Jim McNulty, chairman and CEO of Parsons

THE YEAR 1995 WAS ONE OF significant industry recognition and financial success. Parsons was named the No. 1 design firm in the United States by *Engineering News-Record* and realized a 14 percent sales increase from 1994.[1] In June, Parsons purchased one more engineering giant, Gilbert/Commonwealth Inc., that had a worldwide reputation in engineering energy-related infrastructure. With a staff of approximately 1,400 employees and headquarters in Reading, Pennsylvania, it expanded Parsons' presence with the Northeast's industrial and power clientele. The acquisition also strengthened Parsons' ability to capitalize on the increasing global demand for electrical power in the Middle East and Asia and enhanced the corporation's nuclear decontamination and decommissioning capabilities within the United States.[2]

The Gilbert/Commonwealth Inc. purchase served as the catalyst for Len Pieroni to propose an aggressive organizational shift, which involved the consolidation of Parsons' subsidiaries into business units that would focus on specific industry sectors. Although Parsons had historically completed significant energy and engineering projects in many foreign countries, the past decade had shown that the corporation had been more successful in obtaining domestic work. Since many of the previously acquired companies had been part of the corporation for more than 10 years, Len believed the time had finally come for further integration to create worldwide recognition of Parsons' total capabilities by branding its subsidiaries with the corporate name.

After discussing various business alternatives and organizational structures with his senior executives and board members, Len reorganized the entire corporation to pursue global market expansion and reduce, what he called, "structural overhead." The subsidiaries would be merged into one of four operating companies based on serving the power, transportation, process, and infrastructure and technology market sectors. The reorganization went into effect January 1, 1996, and aligned the operations and sales efforts with the corporation's core businesses. Each operating company would carry the Parsons name in its title and would have its own president reporting directly to Len.[3]

Parsons Power Group would oversee the energy-related projects under Ken Burkhart, former president of Gilbert/Commonwealth Inc. Parsons Transportation Group would manage the highway, bridges, airports, railway, and other transit projects under the leadership of Bob O'Neil. Parsons Process

Jim McNulty, Parsons' chairman and CEO, became its leader during a tragic time in the corporation's history. He propelled it into its most financially successful decade.

Group would supervise the petroleum and petroleum and chemical projects, and it would be run by Bill Hall, who had been managing Parsons' largest subsidiary, RMP. Parsons Infrastructure and Technology Group would manage the federal government, aviation, infrastructure, and environmental-related projects. At its helm would be Jim McNulty, former manager of RMP's Systems Division.[4]

Allocating RMP's resources into two of the new units would be the most difficult challenge in the task of reorganizing the corporation. Jim McNulty recalled:

The new structure had Bill Hall as president of the Process Group and me the president of Infrastructure and Technology Group. Our role was to split apart RMP. One day Bill was my boss, and the next we are dividing up the resources. Len's view was, "Okay, here's the new organization. We're not spending a penny more on overhead, in fact, we're going to reduce costs. You guys go figure out how to break this apart." RMP had 3,000–3,500 people, and we had to split the engineering, financial, and information technology resources. We each had to form our own individual finance groups, sales groups—everything—and with no additional cost.[5]

It was not easy for some of the personnel who had been with the acquired subsidiaries to adjust to this new structure. However, many of them came to realize that streamlining the corporation into client markets and Len's branding strategy was crucial to further growth and continued financial stability. "It was decided that we needed to reorganize. We were stepping all over ourselves because we were in multiple markets or in the same markets," said Bill Hall, CEO of WorleyParsons USA, a subsidiary of the Worley Group that acquired Parsons Energy and Chemical (E&C)—the legacy company of Parsons Process and Power Groups.[6]

Bob O'Neil, former president of Parsons Transportation Group, recalled, "There is strength in having a strong name like Parsons for all the different companies, and eventually, that's what happened."[7] Bob had come from De Leuw, Cather & Company and understood that each entity brought value and talented individuals to Parsons:

I had the good fortune to work with a great number of very dedicated, qualified, and competent people. That's the keynote of the firm, the only asset it has is its people.[8]

As executive vice president of transportation operations, Bob Bax echoed Bob O'Neil's assessment:

The good part was that there was not a major loss of clientele or of senior staff en masse like you see in some of the acquisitions that are handled much more abruptly.[9]

Charles Harrington, president of Parsons Commercial Technology Group, explained the new structure:

In 1996, when Jim McNulty put together Parsons Infrastructure and Technology Group, he tapped me to put together the private [nongovernment] industrial side. We wove together this high-tech expertise that we grasped out of Engineering Science, CT Main, RMP, and Gilbert/Commonwealth Inc., which we had just purchased at the time.[10]

Chuck joined Parsons in 1982 as a mechanical engineer and worked as a project and program manager on Department of Energy-related projects such as Rocky Flats and the Savannah River Site. He supervised CT Main's national waste management programs, then became Parsons' southeastern regional manager and vice president, and oversaw the industrial, manufacturing, and electronics markets of RMP as its vice president before his promotion to group president.[11]

The reorganization was done as quickly and as effectively as possible. However, as with any change of this magnitude, the metamorphosis did not occur overnight. Parsons had seven entities and 10,000 employees to align into its new business model. The new organization was in place for only a few months when a tragedy occurred that rocked the entire corporation.

Tragedy in Croatia

When the Dayton Peace Accord was signed in Paris in December 1995, it ended three-and-one-half years of savage fighting in the Balkans, which had carved Bosnia into two ethnic zones—Bosnia and Herzegovina (referred to as Bosnia–Herzegovina)—

and destroyed parts of Croatia and Yugoslavia. The signing of the accord allowed USAID to begin a large-scale restoration effort in the three countries affected by the war. Prior to this agreement, USAID conducted a series of small-scale municipal rehabilitation activities, primarily in the middle of Bosnia, to repair the damaged infrastructure. Parsons was one of several contractors involved in this effort and was positioning itself to win a significant contract with USAID to rebuild Bosnia–Herzegovina.[12] The scope of work under the agreement would include the repair, reconstruction, and new construction of electrical power facilities, telecommunications systems, water systems, roads, bridges, schools, and hospitals—the infrastructure Parsons excelled in creating.

The U.S. Commerce Department asked Parsons to send a representative on a trade mission going to the Balkans during the first week of April 1996. It was one of several overseas tours that U.S. Secretary of Commerce Ron Brown was making—this one specifically promoting American engineering and construction services.[13] Based on Parsons' participation in the initial rebuilding efforts and on its interest in the USAID restoration contract, it was only natural to send a top executive on this trip. Jim McNulty recalled the discussions about who would go on the trade mission:

> *I got a call about a week and a half prior to the trip from Joel Bennett [who had replaced Len as corporate global business development vice president when Len assumed the role of CEO]. Joel said, "Len and I think you should go. The reason Len doesn't want to go is that he is going to Hawaii for his wedding anniversary." I said, "Great, I'd be happy to go. My son is a captain in the Army and has a lot of friends over there. I'll go on over there and do what we've got to do with Ron Brown for business, and I'll be able to visit some of my son's friends."*
>
> *In the middle of the next week, Len called me and said, "I'm going to go on the trip." I said, "Why are you going to do that? You're going to Hawaii for your anniversary." I told him, "I want to do this." He said, "This is important, and if I don't go on this trip, I can never ask anybody who works for Parsons to give up a weekend or a vacation to work on a proposal, a project, or to do anything. It's not right for me to ever ask anybody else to do it. I've just got to do it."*[14]

The war in Bosnia destroyed a significant portion of the country's infrastructure. Many of Parsons' reconstruction tasks in Bosnia involved repairing and upgrading public schools, including this school, shown before (left) and after (right) Parsons rebuilt it, so that children could continue their education in a well-built and safe environment.

Len's son, Leonard Pieroni III, recounted the events that transpired:

My mom and dad had planned to take our family on a two-week vacation to celebrate their 35th wedding anniversary. The fatal trip came up after the plans were made. My dad accompanied us to Maui to get us settled in, and had planned to return for the second week after the trip with the Commerce Department Secretary.[15]

After spending two days in Hawaii with his wife, Marilyn; his son and his wife, Len and Brenda; and his daughter, her husband, and their son, Vicki, Steve, and Gregory; Leonard Pieroni II flew to Washington, D.C., to participate in the trade mission along with the Commerce Department officials and other engineering/construction firms' executives.[16] After landing in Bosnia–Herzegovina, Len met with Jim Shappell, current president of Parsons Transportation Group—then vice president of business development for Parsons Infrastructure and Technology Group—who was in Bosnia visiting clients. After their meeting, Jim Shappell left Len at the U.S. State Department building in Zagreb. From there, Len took a chartered bus to the airport to catch the trade mission's flight to Dubrovnik, Croatia. The plane departed on April 3, 1996, but never arrived at its destination.[17]

The weather conditions were atrocious. It was so foggy that the pilot could not see the surrounding topography, which apparently resulted in his misreading the instrumentation. The plane flew into the side of a mountain with such force that there were no survivors. In that instant, 35 people lost their lives. Their families and friends lost their loved ones. The United States lost its Secretary of Commerce. And, the engineering/construction community lost senior executives who were responsible for thousands of employees.[18]

June Shute, Len's executive assistant, had been listening to the radio in the office and was the first to hear that Ron Brown's T43 Air Force jet [a Boeing 737] was missing somewhere in the Balkans.[19] She immediately informed Tom Langford, Parsons' corporate vice president, and he began informing a few select executives at headquarters such as Joel Bennett. Jim McNulty recalls how he was told about the crash:

I was having a meeting with my infrastructure and technology managers and discussing how we were going to make our net operating income target for the year, and Joel Bennett called me and said, "There's a report that the plane Len was on, Ron Brown's plane, is down. It isn't clear if it hit a mountain or was in the ocean." I didn't believe Len wouldn't be found safe and sound. I told the people in the meeting what was going on and that we were trying to sort things out and we should just continue. After that, it was hard to concentrate.[20]

Later that day, Jim looked out of his office window. He said, "All the TV vans were pulling up out in front, and I thought, 'This is real.' We didn't know at the time whether there were any survivors, and then, later that day, the information came in that there were no survivors."[21]

The staff went into shock over Len's death. As reality set in, people began to comprehend that Parsons was without its leader. A profound sense of sadness and uncertainty spread throughout the corporation. Len had not put a succession plan in place, but he had very recently concluded who should be Parsons' next CEO. He had outlined his plans to Ray Judson, who had just retired from Parsons for a second time, believing that Len no longer needed his counsel as special assistant to the chairman.[22] Ray recounted:

Two weeks before Len was killed in Bosnia we had dinner together. He was happy as a clam. "Ray, this organization is working out. I've got the right people in the right spots. Everything is fine." He was 57 then. He said, "You know, I'm hoping I can get out of here when I'm 61 or 62." I said, "Len, do you have a succession plan?" He said, "Ray, I got a problem. I know the right guy, but I'm going to have to be with him for two more years to break him in."[23]

Len asked Ray to confirm he had picked the best candidate. Ray described how they verified Len's choice:

He reached in his pocket, pulled out a paper, and ripped it in two. He put the paper in front of me, and he says, "You put down a name, and I'll put down a name." I wrote Jim McNulty, and he wrote Jim

McNulty. That was it. I said, "You're right. You've got the right guy. You've got the right guy.'"[24]

Immediately after confirming the fate of the plane's passengers, Parsons' board members arranged an emergency meeting. They met on April 9, and set about the grim task of choosing Len's successor.[25] The board quickly arrived at the same conclusion as Len and Ray—Jim McNulty would be asked to become Parsons' sixth CEO. Earle Williams, long-time Parsons board member, discussed Jim's credentials that supported their decision:

> *Jim's résumé was just so impressive for what we wanted—master's degrees in physics and management and a retired Army colonel. Plus, his demeanor was such that I thought he would get along well with everyone. So I felt the choice was the right one.*[26]

Jim, however, had no idea he was being seriously considered for the position:

> *Cathy (Gribbin) Meindl [Jim's executive assistant] came into my office about 10 o'clock that morning and said, "The board wants to talk with you." I thought, okay, I knew they were interviewing people and asking all four business unit presidents for their input on who the board was going to select. I walked into the board room and Howard Allen [board member who was the retired chairman and CEO of SCE] pointed to the end of the table and said, "sit down." Jack Kuehler was on my left and Howard Allen was on my right. Jack looked at me and said, "We want you to be CEO, will you do it?" I said, "Yes." But, I was feeling scared, flattered, sad, happy, and upset, and thinking—what do I do now?*[27]

Just six days after the fatal plane crash, Jim found himself leading 10,000 very shaken employees, many of whom were still adjusting to the restructured organization. He understood the gravity of the situation, and his grief was evident as he shared his thoughts:

> *To lose Len under those circumstances, to watch the national memorial service on television, to go through the uncertainty of what was going to happen to our corporation, to be told you were going to be the CEO, take the job of somebody who you considered a very close personal friend and mentor, and to move into his office, was emotionally very tough.*[28]

Jim's first task was to guide the staff through its mourning and then motivate them to resume their professional responsibilities to their clients and coworkers. He led a memorial service for the employees at Parsons' headquarters, which was attended by members of the Pieroni family. He recounted the experience: "That was probably the hardest thing I've ever had to do as CEO."[29] The flags that customarily fly in front of the building that represent the countries in which the corporation was doing business were replaced by the U.S. flag flown at half-mast. A portrait of Len was hung near the entrance, with a spray of flowers in front.[30]

Len's funeral was held a few days later and was equally difficult for everyone. Jim met with the key management team for the first time immediately after the funeral and asked them for their patience in the weeks ahead as he assumed his responsibilities. Joe Volpe Jr., who had advised all of Parsons' CEOs and served as Jim's mentor in Washington, D.C., set the

Len Pieroni III spoke at the memorial service for his father. The service was exceptionally moving and allowed many staff members to publicly express their fondness for him, along with their grief. *(© 1996 John G. Blair, jgblairphoto.com.)*

LEN PIERONI

LEN PIERONI RECEIVED HIS EDUCATION from the University of Notre Dame and Northwestern University. He joined Parsons in 1972. Although he left Parsons in 1977 to become vice president of KTI Corporation, a small southern California engineering firm, he was wooed back after a year by Ray Judson, then vice president of engineering, to manage western regional sales.[1]

Described as a "well-organized, methodical leader with a talent for slashing overhead,"[2] Len quickly rose in prominence within the organization. In 1983, Bill Leonhard selected him to replace the retiring Ira Blanco as president of S.I.P. Inc., a key petroleum engineering subsidiary that was in a slump. Within two years, Len astutely guided S.I.P. Inc. back to stability.[3]

In 1985, Bill Leonhard tapped Len to manage another subsidiary, Charles T. Main (CT Main). Len described this assignment as the most challenging and enjoyable of his career. This Boston-based subsidiary needed to restructure in order to remain competitive. Len made bold changes, but was able to retain the loyalty of CT Main's staff and senior management. Again, within two years, he turned a subsidiary around and made it profitable.[4]

In 1988, Len returned from Boston to Parsons' headquarters to serve as corporate senior vice president and director of business development. He was promoted to executive vice president and director of corporate planning one year later.[5]

This photo commemorated the life of Len Pieroni at his memorial service. The inscription reads as follows: "Man of God that you are, seek after integrity, piety, faith, love, steadfastness, and a gentle spirit. — 1 Timothy 6:11. Leonard Joseph Pieroni Jr. entered into glory April 3, 1996. My love to each of you."

Appointed Chairman and CEO

When Bill Leonhard retired in May 1990, Len was elected by the board of directors as Parsons' fourth chairman and CEO. His management style helped promulgate a feeling of inclusiveness with all manner of staff. Shortly after he became CEO, Len commissioned the first-ever poll of Parsons' employees, asking for their suggestions. He also launched in-house newsletters to keep the employees informed and build morale.[6]

Under the six years of Len's leadership, Parsons continued to manage significant projects while the number of employees increased from 8,500 to 10,000.[7] He saw the company through the Gulf War crisis and began consolidating the subsidiaries into cohesive business units that shared the Parsons name rather than a reference to their previous companies.

A Tragic Plane Crash

Len Pieroni died suddenly on April 3, 1996, in an airplane crash while on an official State Department trip to Bosnia. He left behind grieving staff members who had to "grab ourselves by our socks," as stated by his successor, Jim McNulty, who felt the full impact of Len's loss.[8] The following recollections reflect the high regard in which Len was held by those who worked with him and for him.

Tom Neira, mail department operations coordinator, has routed letters and packages to almost everyone who has worked for the corporation since 1969, when he was hired by Jane Jorgenson, the company's first mail department supervisor. He described Len:

Mr. Pieroni was a very nice man. He was always there for you. We were sad to see him go. Throughout the years that I've been here, I've had the pleasure of working with a lot of good people. I still think of [Mr. Pieroni]. I have a picture of him downstairs.[9]

"Len was a great guy," said Curtis Bower, CFO, who joined Parsons in 1991. He added, "Len was probably one of the most sincere, straightforward people I've ever met. You could take every word he said to the bank."[10]

Bill Whooley, a long-term CT Main executive, worked closely with Len and recounted how Len's demeanor quickly gained customers' confidence:

He was extremely professional. [After meeting Len], clients carried away a very, very positive image and an image of consequence that their project or their program was definitely going to be overseen correctly.[11]

Bill recalled visiting Parsons' headquarters with potential clients from the Polaroid Corporation immediately after the employees' memorial service for Len:

I had scheduled a cross-country trip to Pasadena with two senior Polaroid executives, a prospective client, prior to Mr. Pieroni's passing away. We met with Mr. DeMartino and Mr. McNulty. The most dramatic thing I remember was seeing a little shrine for Mr. Pieroni. It was his picture, some flowers, and things of that nature. We stopped dead in our tracks. The two executives had never met Mr. Pieroni, but were just absolutely beside themselves. Uniformly, people loved this gentleman and had such respect for him.[12]

Larry Burns, former vice president, described the Len he knew, both in the office and as a neighbor on Catalina Island:

He would be all business in the office, always looking at ways to improve and do things in a proper manner, but always personable. He took the time to say "how are you doing, what are your problems, how can I help you?"

But if you were to see Len in Catalina, which he loved dearly, with his family on his boat, he would wear green gym shorts, a white T-shirt with the very wide neck that had gone through the wash a million times. He was just like one of the regular guys.[13]

His son, Leonard Pieroni III, has been with Parsons for 16 years. He began as a mechanical engineer and is now a project manager on the corporation's FAA contract. He commented on his father's strengths:

My father had a lot of compassion for people. I think the favorite part of his job was probably to meet people, whether it was in his office or when he was in some of the other offices or during travel. He really enjoyed that the most. He had a deep concern for others.[14]

tone of the group's reply in a statement that lifted everyone's spirits. Jim recounted, "Joe said, 'I wish I were 20 years younger. I'm excited, and everyone in this corporation should be excited, about this new start.' " Joe's belief in Jim's abilities helped rally the managers and encouraged them to work with Jim to create a positive future for Parsons, rather than focus solely on the loss of Len.[31]

In the following weeks, Jim worked hard to restore balance to the corporation. Prior to becoming CEO, he had never seen the corporate balance sheet. He began poring over Parsons' financial data and 10 years of board meeting minutes. As Jim became more familiar with the corporate finances, he began to question the "status quo" and took a more active role in financial decisions, an area Len had relied on others for advice. Those who were not on board with these changes were asked to leave. Jim also held his first all-hands employee meeting, which stirred things up even further by delivering the following message to the staff:

> *I've agreed to take this job, and whether you all like it or not, we have to do things my way. I don't have Len's personality, nor his philosophies. So let's go, let's get on with life.*[32]

In recollecting this speech, Jim said, "We had two choices. I could just be a caretaker, ride this out, and not do anything different. But I was really convinced we needed to change."[33]

In the April 15, 1996, edition of *Engineering News-Record*, Jim's quote also reflected these sentiments:

> *I think the biggest single challenge was to realize that you have to walk the line between bringing closure to the employees for their feelings of grief for Len but, then also say, "We've got to grab ourselves by our socks and pull ourselves out of this because we all have jobs and contracts that we're responsible for and we have to move forward."*[34]

The Summer/Fall edition of Parsons' *Perspectives* was carefully written to highlight the positive momentum of the organization and yet still acknowledge the underlying sadness over Len's death. Jim wrote the lead column in which he addressed the state of the corporation and his

Parsons engineered a cogeneration plant that virtually eliminated UCLA's electricity costs.

thoughts on the path forward. The articles in the newsletter focused on success stories such as the achievements of the Washington, D.C., office on projects such as WMATA and the Dulles and National airports. It also highlighted Parsons' engineering on a state-of-the-art cogeneration plant for UCLA, which virtually eliminated the university's electricity costs. However, the predominant feature in this edition was a thoughtful retrospective of Len Pieroni, which described him as "no finer friend, no greater leader."[35]

The Recovery Plan

As Jim began his new role as Parsons' CEO, he cultivated his own management team. He promoted Frank DeMartino from senior vice president and business development manager to president of Parsons Infrastructure and Technology Group, the position Jim had held. Frank was a retired U.S. Air Force colonel. He had joined Parsons as its southeastern operations manager in June 1988. Frank was then assigned to the Washington, D.C., office as general manager of Parsons' federal programs.[36] It was in Washington, D.C., where he and Jim forged what would become a long-term professional partnership and friendship. Jim trusted Frank's judgment in both business development and operational issues. Jim said, "It was Frank who really put the Infrastructure and Technology Group together."[37] As president of this business unit, Frank was the driving force in expanding Parsons' project portfolio with the Department of Defense and other government agencies. He became corporate president and COO in 2001 and retired three years later in September 2004.

Bill Hall, Bob O'Neil, and Ken Burkhart, respectively, remained the presidents of the Power, Transportation, and Process Groups. With the addition of Frank DeMartino, these four men were invaluable to Jim during his transitional period. Jim also received tremendous guidance and support from Ray Judson. Jim and the board of directors agreed it would be very helpful to the corporation if Ray would consider coming out of retirement for a second time to serve temporarily as chairman of the board while Jim assumed the responsibilities of CEO. Jack Kuehler, a board member, asked Ray to become the chairman and, after some reflection, Ray accepted.[38] Jim remembered Ray was very excited about taking on the chairmanship. He said, "He went out and bought new shirts and new suits. He started getting up in the morning and exercising again. His wife, Mary Lou, told me he was like a new man."[39] Ray recalled, "My role was to educate Jim. He's as smart as a whip, and picked up like mad. We liked each other from the very beginning, and everything worked out."[40]

As the new management team set about running the corporation, the staff was able to resume their professional activities. New opportunities with established clients started to materialize. In 1996, Parsons was selected by Aramco as the program management contractor for the Shaybah Development Program in the Empty Quarter of Saudi Arabia, the desolate region's first oil production facility.[41] Later that year, Parsons was awarded the $250 million USAID contract to reconstruct Bosnia–Herzegovina. As an adjunct to this contract, Parsons won a $41 million project management contract in 2000 to rebuild Kosovo's infrastructure, including schools, transportation systems, and utilities. The Balkan contracts took on great significance and poignancy given Len's commitment to winning the reconstruction work and the circumstances of his death.[42]

Aramco selected Parsons as its Shaybah Development Program management contractor in the desolate Empty Quarter of Saudi Arabia. The facilities that were constructed under this program produce a significant amount of the world's oil.

Frank DeMartino

Like Jim McNulty and Bill Leonhard, Frank DeMartino joined Parsons at the end of a distinguished military career. He retired from the U.S. Air Force as a colonel with more than 25 years of service. Frank joked about his motivation to become a member of Parsons' team:

> *I joined Parsons to work a few years in a low-stress environment, put groceries on the table, get the last of the brood through college, and stay in one place. Quite obviously I failed terribly in achieving most of these goals!*[1]

As former COO and president of Parsons, Frank DeMartino fostered a working environment based on providing customers with quality services, respecting individual team members, and loyalty to Parsons' values.

In all seriousness, he explained why former military members have proven to be such a good fit at Parsons:

> *I think one of the reasons that we've had a history of bringing military people into Parsons is because they fit the corporation's work ethic and discipline attributes.*[2]

Frank received his bachelor's degree in civil engineering from Manhattan College in New York City and his master's degree in engineering management from Oklahoma State University. He began with Parsons in Tampa in 1988 as its Florida operations manager.[3] Three years later, Ed Cramsie, as manager of the Systems Division, promoted Frank into a business development position and moved him to Washington, D.C. There, Frank was mentored by Joe Volpe Jr., who served as advisor and confidant to Parsons' CEOs. While in Washington, Frank forged a strong professional relationship with Jim McNulty, who was then managing Parsons' Washington, D.C., office. In April 1996,

The Bosnia–Herzegovina contract also heralded a shift in professional activities within Parsons. As the Aramco opportunity indicated, Parsons' relationship with the oil companies remained strong, but the corporation realized that the petroleum and chemical markets were reaching maturity. The oil companies had the bulk of their infrastructure in place and were awarding very few new megaprojects such as the Shaybah Development Program. Due to a decrease in service demands within the petroleum and chemical industry, Parsons merged its Process and Power groups into Parsons E&C on September 16, 1997, and Bill Hall was named its president.[43] The remaining segments of the corporation were then tasked to focus on four robust growth areas: transportation, water resources, commercial infrastructure, and large federal government-funded programs.

Transportation

The Alameda Corridor consolidated numerous Union Pacific and Burlington Northern Santa Fe railroad routes into a 20-mile, triple-track main line between downtown Los Angeles and the ports of Los Angeles and Long Beach, California. At a cost of $1.8 billion, it was one of the largest public works projects in U.S. history and required separate construction teams to build its upper, middle, and lower segments in the allotted time. A portion of the corridor was built below grade, which allowed the railroads to reduce transit times and close hundreds of existing at-grade crossings, at a time-savings and safety benefit to motorists. It was essential this project be completed as scheduled to reduce traffic congestion along the route and increase freight delivery out of the ports.[44]

after Jim became Parsons' CEO, he asked Frank to serve as president of Parsons Infrastructure and Technology Group.[4] Frank accepted the appointment and, under his leadership, cultivated a market strategy that almost doubled this group's revenues. This was due to the success of several new business ventures that he fostered, his tenacity, and his loyalty to his key staff.

Gary Stone, senior vice president, corporate counsel and secretary, recalled these attributes:

> *Frank's deep sense of loyalty was reciprocated by his key staff. They trusted him, and it was his motivation of them that generated their success.*[5]

John Small, executive vice president who managed operations in Russia and the United Kingdom under Frank's supervision, said, "He really felt an obligation that people who did an exemplary job were recognized and given opportunities to expand their professional roles within the company."[6]

Cathy (Gribbin) Meindl, who has been both Jim McNulty's and Frank's executive assistant, recalled Frank's high energy:

> *Frank would jump into anything. If there's a problem, he'd go after it. He'd just go hit it head on. Mr. McNulty set things in motion, and Frank forged the path.*[7]

Roy Goodwin, former Federal Division manager, described his long-term working relationship with Frank:

> *I enjoyed working for Frank. He and I had worked together in the Air Force. He was more orientated to the business side, and I was focused on operations. With Frank, you needed to know what your numbers were—GPP [gross profit performance], GPS [gross profit sales], and NOI [net operating income]. He can be gruff, but he has a very big heart.*[8]

On February 26, 2001, Parsons announced Frank would become the corporation's first chief operating officer and its president. Jim had been Parsons' chairman for three years and wanted Frank to assist him in managing all aspects of the corporation. Frank also served as director on Parsons E&C's board. When he retired in 2004, Jim recognized his esteemed contributions by stating, "Frank's expertise, vision, and support have been invaluable to me, personally, and to Parsons. I will miss working with him."[9]

In 1998, Parsons was selected by the Alameda Corridor Transportation Authority as part of a joint venture with Tutor-Saliba, O&G Industries, and HNTB to design-build the midcorridor section, which encompassed 10 miles of the 20-mile project. It called for the design and construction of a 25-foot by 50-foot open concrete "trench" that housed two tracks and a service road, as well as the reconstruction of Alameda Street that runs in parallel to the trench and is used by trucks to access both ports. The midcorridor cost $750 million and also included retaining walls, bridges, street improvements, utility relocations, drainage, signals, environmental remediation, and landscaping.[45]

Mike Christensen, a registered civil engineer who joined the corporation in 1997, was the deputy project manager on loan from Parsons to Tutor-Saliba. Mike is currently vice president and manages Parsons' railroad and passenger rail projects.[46] In addition to its active participation in the joint venture, Parsons' environmental staff separately completed a comprehensive evaluation of hazardous material and waste conditions at 23 grade crossings along the Alameda Corridor eastern alignment in 2001.

On Parsons' equity contributions to the midcorridor team, Tom Barron, executive vice president, stated, "This [was] the first joint venture [for us] with risk for both design and construction."[47] The entire corridor was completed on time and on budget in 2002. Presently, 40 trains a day travel through the trench, which will increase to 100 trains by 2015. The Alameda Corridor won the American Society of Civil Engineers' 2003 Award of Merit and has

Above: The Alameda Corridor is one of the largest public works projects in U.S. history. Parsons was part of the joint venture that designed and built its 10-mile midcorridor section.

Below: The modernization of the Seattle-Tacoma International Airport is a megaprogram due to its scope, which comprises 120 capital improvement projects. It received the Pacific Northwest Chapter Construction Management Association of America's Achievement Award in 2004.

received 13 additional honors from prestigious engineering and transportation organizations.[48]

The Alameda Corridor is only one of many transportation megaprojects Parsons tackled in this time frame. Also in 1998, Parsons became the program management support consultant for the three-phased, $4 billion modernization and expansion of the Seattle-Tacoma International Airport (SEATAC) in Washington. Scheduled for completion in 2006, SEATAC's construction program encompasses the design and construction of over 120 capital improvement projects involving the airfield, terminal buildings, ground transportation, infrastructure and special systems, and aviation support facilities. Based on the program's superior execution, SEATAC received the Pacific Northwest Chapter Construction Management Association of America's Achievement Award in 2004. Parsons also assembled an emergency team to help the client, the Port of Seattle, expedite repairs caused by a magnitude 6.8 earthquake that shook Seattle in early 2001.[49]

Sam Wright, the program manager for Concourse A, discussed the project:

Originally, SEATAC was designed to serve 25 million passengers by 2004. It exceeded that count by three million this year [2005]. We implemented our PACT [Parsons Aviation Cost Trend] system early on to establish a baseline for tracking costs and to record and forecast deviations over the life of the program. There were no surprises for the client despite $220 million in changes. We are very proud of our controls

process and also proud that despite the magnitude of change we only lost three months to our schedule.[50]

Sam joined Parsons the year the SEATAC program got under way. He first worked as an air traffic controller for the U.S. Army at Hunter Army Airfield in Savannah, Georgia, and after leaving the military, became a construction manager with special expertise in power plants and heavy civil projects, followed by high-rise hotels, office buildings, healthcare design-build, and now aviation.[51]

At SEATAC, Parsons incorporated the latest baggage security features into the construction of the airport's new terminal as a precautionary measure due to the terrorist attacks of September 11, 2001. SEATAC was one of the first airports in the country to do so.[52] This system was designed and built with the help of Frank Ching and Dick Swegle, Parsons' baggage-handling systems specialists, who joined the corporation in 1993 and 2000, respectively. Gary Ostle oversaw the infrastructure construction program that totals over $400 million. Gary came to Parsons in 1970 and was the remediation manager on the INEL project. Ed Masterson has managed the infrastructure program's document controls system since 1999, replacing Diane Adams who is currently assigned to Parsons' Iraq reconstruction security and justice program in Baghdad.[53]

Greg Perry is the former principle planner and scheduler on SEATAC. He was responsible for the construction schedules, determining the milestone dates, and monitoring manpower staffing during construction. He described the logistical efforts on the project:

It was quite a challenge to schedule the construction in an operating terminal without any impact to the traveling public. Minimizing impacts to the baggage handling system as the TSA [Transportation Security Administration] developed their bag screening procedures post 9/11 took a lot of teamwork with the airport, TSA, airlines, and the construction contractors.[54]

Greg joined Parsons in 1975 and worked on such notable projects as the Aramco gas program, the space shuttle launch complex, and the National Test Bed facility. His most recent assignment is to support Parsons' projects in Abu Dhabi.[55]

Due to the success of the first light rail transit line for the southwest corridor in Denver, Colorado, the regional transportation district requested the design of an 8.7-mile extension, which was authorized in two phases. During the first phase, Parsons prepared preliminary plans for a double-track light rail system, including five transit stations. As part of the second phase, Parsons prepared the final plans for the bridges, catenary/electrification system, and signal system.[56]

The MTA Long Island Railroad selected Parsons as system engineering consultant for its eastside expansion to improve its commuter access between Suffolk, Nassau, and Queens counties and the east side of Manhattan in 1999. Prior to the expansion, the commuter line carried an average of 270,000 passengers on weekdays. It had been a vital transportation link since it began service in 1834, but had reached capacity. The project's objective would increase the travel options for the Long Island passengers by opening up a direct access route to the Grand Central Terminal and upgrading the

As the MTA Long Island Railroad's system engineering consultant, Parsons improved commuter access between Suffolk, Nassau, and Queens counties and the east side of Manhattan in New York City.

existing Pennsylvania Station terminus. Parsons conducted preliminary engineering and final design services on the estimated $4.3 billion construction cost, startup, and test programs for all operating elements and associated facility modifications. Parsons integrated a state-of-the-art signaling and train control system to enhance the operations of what is considered the nation's busiest commuter railroad.

To preserve the historic and aesthetic aspects of Grand Central Terminal and its surrounding buildings, Parsons designed six new entrances in a complementary architectural style. The project team was able to overcome setbacks that resulted from the September 11, 2001, terrorist attack on lower Manhattan and the schedule to complete the expansion was back "on track" for 2009.[57]

RAY JUDSON

AFTER RAY JUDSON GRADUated from high school in 1944, he enlisted immediately as a paratrooper during World War II. He was stationed outside of Okinawa, preparing to invade Japan, when the war ended. Ray then spent a year in Japan and came home to New York City. He discussed how he decided to go to college:

Ray Judson spent 35 years with Parsons and was one of the most dedicated executives of the firm.

> *You know, nobody in my day went to college. We never had money to go to college. But I came out of the service, and my Irish mother walked me in, sat me down, and said, "Franklin Roosevelt passed the GI Bill, and I've calculated that you've got three and a half years, and you're going to college."*[1]

He went to the University of Michigan and graduated in February 1951 as a civil engineer. After college, he went to work for the M.W. Kellogg Company (now part of Halliburton) in New York City. He spent 15 years with Kellogg, the firm where Len Pieroni, who also became chairman of Parsons, also worked before joining Parsons.[2]

Bringing Order to the Engineering Department

Ray was recruited to join Parsons in 1966. During his 35-year career with Parsons, he managed some of its largest engineering programs and brought order to the engineering department. He recalled the challenge of setting up universal systems and procedures:

> *What Ralph Parsons did was, he went out and hired top talent. He'd hire a project manager and say "go do your thing." So the project managers that headed up each project, they were king. They set up their own systems, their own procedures. I was used to a company that had a procedure for every single thing you did, and here I come to a company that had no [system-wide] procedures. I had the opportunity to change that.*[3]

Ray began working in the London office and within six years had built a refinery in Nova Scotia, another refinery in Switzerland, six gas plants in England, and a gas plant in Iran. He returned to the United States in 1972 and, within a year, Bill Leonhard, then CEO, promoted Ray to vice president of engineering for the corporation.

At one time, more than 2,300 Parsons engineers reported to Ray. In 1978, he became a senior vice president and managed the Petroleum and Chemical Division, which, under his guidance, was awarded and completed the $1.5 billion,

In addition, Parsons joint ventured with DMJM Harris and STV in 2003 to design and perform construction support for the Port Authority's Trans-Hudson terminal that will serve more than 250,000 daily riders, including thousands of commuters and millions of expected annual visitors to the World Trade Center Memorial. It will effectively restore long-term commuter train service between New Jersey and lower Manhattan. The engineering is based on the selected architectural design by world-renowned architect Santiago Calatrava.

The glass and steel roof of the terminal's grand pavilion and the wings that will rise over 140 feet above the plaza will have the feel of a modern cathedral to remember the heroes, survivors, and the victims' families. The project received both local and

lump-sum Petromin-Shell refinery in Saudi Arabia in 40 months. In 1980, he was asked to manage the Systems Division and, shortly after his promotion, relocated to Yanbu Industrial City to support this division's most important project.

In 1984, Ray returned to the United States and, in addition to the Systems Division, he also managed Parsons ES subsidiary and Los Angeles' first subway project. He also led Parsons' implementation of CAD technology. Ray then succeeded Charlie Roddey in two positions, as president of the RMP subsidiary in 1987 and as president of Parsons in 1989.[4]

Ray was an engineer's engineer. He was an astute judge of character with excellent managerial skills and one of the corporation's finest mentors. Erin Kuhlman, vice president of corporate relations, started working with Ray when she joined Parsons in 1988 as a contracts administrator for Department of Defense and Department of Energy projects. She recalled Ray's work style:

> *Ray liked to bring order to problems and took a very organized approach to finding the best answers. Ray would sit down and make a list of pros and cons. Then, he would assign a value to each item. By writing down all the facts and weighing each one, he was able to determine a constructive course of action. Even today, when I'm faced with difficult decisions, I make a list and think of him every time I use this process.*[5]

Erin began overseeing Parsons' corporate relations activities in 2001 and manages all media contacts, corporate events, and marketing materials.[6]

Ray retired as president of Parsons Corporation in 1991, only to be asked by Len Pieroni to return a second time and serve as a special assistant to the chairman, a position that he accepted. Ray retired again on January 1, 1996. After Len's untimely death in April 1996, the board of directors asked Ray to return once again and temporarily serve as chairman to assist Jim McNulty, who became the corporation's CEO.

Ray assumed the chairmanship and worked closely with Jim and the board members during this leadership transition. On January 2, 1998, Ray retired as chairman, and Jim was unanimously elected to this position. However, Ray remained on the board for three more years until 2001.[7]

At that time, Larry Tollenaere, who was then chairman of the board's executive committee, said, "We commend Ray Judson for his leadership and appreciate his willingness to come out of retirement and help the corporation. Ray has carried out his appointment to the highest order of the board's expectation."[8]

Jim also thanked Ray for his support. "Ray made a terrific contribution to our corporation," he said. "All of Parsons' employees join me in thanking Ray for his selfless assistance and experienced advice."[9]

The board and Jim McNulty named the 12th floor conference room in Parsons' headquarters in Ray's honor. He passed away in 2004.[10] His son Ray Judson Jr. is a principal project controls engineer in Parsons Water and Infrastructure Group, and his son-in-law, Michael Brady, is a vice president and general manager responsible for commercial customers such as Northrop Grumman and Disney.

national publicity because it was one of the first undertakings to redevelop the downtown New York City area after the World Trade Center collapsed. Construction is expected to be completed in 2010.[58] Jane Charalambous, the project manager, described the project:

> *This is a world-class transportation facility. It incorporates state-of-the-art security strategies with blast-resistant analysis and design. Out of one of the worst acts of terrorism in history, the architectural and engineering community has joined together with New Yorkers to create an engineering marvel of outstanding beauty and function.*[59]

Jane joined Parsons as part of the De Leuw, Cather & Company acquisition in 1987. She was the senior structural engineer on the Williamsburg Bridge rehabilitation project in New York City. Her master's degree is in structural engineering.[60]

Also, in 1999, Parsons teamed with subcontractor URS Greiner and the Guangdong Provincial Architectural Design Institute to design Phase I of the New Baiyun Airport in Guangzhou, China. Parsons' advanced planning and coordination was an important factor in the completion of this $540 million project. Guangzhou, the capital of Guangdong province, is home to 7.1 million people and the heart of China's burgeoning Pearl River Delta region. Historically an agricultural region, the province aggressively changed its economic base to manufacturing one-third of China's exports. Due to Guangdong's shift to industrialization, the Civil Aviation Administration of China and the China State Development and Planning Commission recognized the need for an airport to handle the increased passenger and cargo demands.

Parsons' team completed the airport's Phase I design in three years. The construction effort retained more than 10,000 workers at the height of the endeavor and relocated 20,000 area residents to make room for the massive complex. Phase I involved the construction of the main terminal, the east-west connection building, four concourses, parking, a hotel, an air traffic control tower (the tallest in the country), two runways, aircraft maintenance and air cargo facilities, and a new highway and rail system serving the airport into downtown Guangzhou. The completed New Baiyun airport is five times the size of the original facility, covers 8.38 square miles, and annually accommodates 25 million passengers and 186,000 aircraft operations. The airy glass and steel architectural design, unique to the Chinese landscape, attracted much attention. The project received the American Architecture Honor Award in 2000.[61]

In the early 2000s, Parsons designed a new commuter system for the Dallas Area Rail Transit.

Above: In 2000, the airy glass and steel architectural design created by Parsons and its partners for the facilities associated with Phase I construction of the New Baiyun airport in Guangzhou, China, received the American Architecture Honor Award. *(Photo courtesy of project designer Mark Molen and project architect April Yang, of Yang Molen Design.)*

Opposite: Parsons replaced the commuter train-control system that operates New York City's Canarsie Line.

It also upgraded New York City Transit's Canarsie Line and replaced the aging signal system—the largest communication-based train control system in the country. The corporation then provided engineering consulting for Kuala Lumpur's light rail system, the first, fully automated, driverless transit system in Asia. It was the prime consultant on four Federal Railroad Administration's magnetic levitation technology studies for corridors in Las Vegas, Atlanta, Los Angeles, and New Orleans. Parsons also reviewed the design and construction for the State Railway of Thailand's elevated toll road and rail project in Bangkok, an unusual three-tiered transit system.[62]

In 2000, Parsons was selected in a joint venture arrangement with The Washington Group to design and perform system integration, as well as offer design support during construction and safety certification of the Metro Gold Line, a 13.7-mile-long commuter rail connecting Los Angeles, South Pasadena, and Pasadena. The Metro Gold Line connects with other rail lines, namely, the Metro Green and Red Lines, as well as Amtrak and Metrolink commuter rail. The Gold Line construction met its substantial completion milestones, enabling startup in 2003. The line has been operating with very few problems since, and the ridership is exceeding projections.[63] Dan Baicoianu, an instrumentation and systems engineer, was Parsons' project manager. He was the systems area manager on the Red Line project and is presently performing integration testing support on Denver's Southeast Corridor 19-mile light rail extension.[64]

T-REX

In 2001, Parsons entered into a joint venture with its longtime associate, Kiewit Construction, as the design management consultant on the $1.6 billion Southeast Corridor Transportation Expansion, affectionately known as T-REX due to the size of this public works project. With a volume of more than 230,000 vehicles each day, the Interstate 25 (I-25) corridor through Denver is one of Colorado's most congested highways. In 2000, a national study of traffic issues identified Denver as the seventh most congested metropolitan area and the I-25/I-225 interchange as the 14th busiest interchange in the country. This multimodal design-build project includes highway, light rail transit, pedestrian, and bicycle facilities along the I-25 and I-225 corridors. As design manager, Parsons managed all design and performed approximately 50 percent of the total design.

T-REX entails improvements to 17 miles of the interstate system, construction of 19 miles of transit lines, a new operations control center, and a supervisory control and data acquisitions system for the existing transit lines. Parsons is responsible for civil and structural design, including permanent and detour facilities, transit buildings, transit parking, and maintenance of traffic during construction. The project also includes $60 million of intelligent transportation system elements to monitor traffic flow and congestion. T-REX has received high public approval ratings, in part, due to its successful performance in achieving the No. 1 project goal of minimizing inconvenience to the public. The scheduled completion, in September 2006, is 22 months earlier than required by the client.[65]

Jim Klemz, Parsons' project manager, discussed this undertaking:

> *T-REX presented many technical challenges due to the complexity of accommodating a new light rail line and improvements to the existing highway in a tightly constrained urban corridor. Parsons assembled a first-class design-build team that successfully met the challenge performing on time and on budget.*[66]

Jim is a civil engineer and came to Parsons via the De Leuw, Cather & Company acquisition. He was instrumental to the design and management of I-15 reconstruction in Salt Lake City, Utah; the San Joaquin Hills Transportation Corridor in Orange County, California; and the Outer Loop Highway in Phoenix, Arizona.

Jim was also the senior resident engineer on the transportation and roads improvement program in Abu Dhabi.[67]

Along with its client, the Minnesota Department of Transportation, Parsons celebrated the opening

Right: Parsons used concrete box girder bridges to expedite the schedule and save taxpayer money during construction of the Hiawatha Light Rail Transit Line in Minnesota.

Below: Parsons is the design management consultant on Denver's mega-sized transportation corridor expansion (known as the T-REX project) on Interstate 25. Valued at $1.6 billion, T-REX is the largest multimodal design-build contract ever awarded in U.S. history.

of the first segment of the Hiawatha Light Rail Transit Line (Hiawatha Line) on June 26, 2004, in Minneapolis. Parsons was the lead designer for Minnesota Transit Constructors, the design-build joint venture under contract, which constructed the stations, track, signals, bridges, communications, and the vehicle maintenance shop. Parsons introduced the concept of concrete box girder bridges, a design seldom used in Minnesota, which allowed the joint venture to start building the bridges without waiting for structural steel deliveries. Implementing this concept saved millions of dollars and valuable time in the construction of two Hiawatha Line bridges.

The 12-mile-long Hiawatha Line greatly exceeded ridership expectations and serves almost 20,000 passengers daily, transporting travelers to four of Minnesota's most popular destinations: downtown Minneapolis, the Metrodome, the Minneapolis–St. Paul International Airport, and the gigantic Mall of America—the nation's largest, fully enclosed entertainment and retail complex. This metropolitan area had been experiencing the second-highest traffic congestion growth in the United States, and residents there welcomed this much-needed transportation solution. The Hiawatha Line was one of 26 active rail transit grants that remained federally funded during the second Gulf War when the country faced uncertainties in Middle East petroleum supplies.[68]

By the end of 2005, Parsons had participated in the development of nearly every new, fixed-guideway transit system in the United States, Canada, China, Taiwan, Singapore, Malaysia, Thailand, and the Philippines.[69]

Expanding Dominance in Global Bridge Expertise

In 2001, the corporation acquired Finley McNary Engineers Inc., an internationally recognized bridge design, engineering, and construction firm. By then, Parsons had participated in more than 5,000 bridge projects worldwide and decided this acquisition would serve to further increase its global prominence in this market.[70]

The significant bridge projects of this decade included the award-winning design of the Woodrow Wilson Bridge in Washington, D.C.; the final design for the structural rehabilitation and overhead catenary system on the Tagus River Bridge in Lisbon, Portugal; and the Tacoma Narrows Bridge in Seattle.

The Woodrow Wilson Memorial Bridge is the only Potomac River crossing in the southern half of the Washington, D.C., metropolitan area. The Federal Highway Administration, the Maryland Department of Transportation (which became Parsons' client), the Virginia Department of Transportation, and the District of Columbia Department of Public Works sponsored a competition to generate innovative ideas for the design of the bridge's reconstruction. Parsons won the contest with a design that combined the spirit of the other Potomac River bridges in an aesthetic arch with the structural benefits of a continuous girder system. The replacement bridge, divided into two independent structures, is 6,000 feet long and 234 feet wide and comprises 34 fixed spans and a 260-foot-long, eight-leaf bascule span that is the largest movable mass of any bridge in the United States. The bridge has a six-lane capacity: four express lanes and two lanes for high occupancy vehicles (HOVs). Parsons' design included provisions for the future replacement of the two

Left: Parsons was awarded the design contract for the Woodrow Wilson Bridge that spans the Potomac River in Washington, D.C., based on its submittal in a design competition.

Below: Parsons completed the structural rehabilitation and catenary designs for the landmark Tagus River Bridge in Portugal, which remains one of the world's longest suspension bridges.

HOV lanes with light or commuter rail. The design was completed in 2001, and the bridge opens in 2006.[71]

In 1997, Parsons began the structural rehabilitation and catenary designs for the Tagus River Bridge, which electrified the railroad tracks mounted to the structure. The catenary design was unique in that it catered to the bridge's thermal and dynamic loading conditions so that the span does not stretch. A special conductor support arrangement was developed using counterweighted overlaps engineered to withstand five feet of movement at each land-to-bridge expansion joint. Wherever possible, the rail system design made use of all available existing railroad components in Portugal to keep the bridge-mounted hardware standardized. The rail system was configured for both freight and commuter traffic in accordance with existing Portuguese Railway's electric traction standards.

This project was also of historical significance to Parsons. The Tagus River Bridge had long been a challenge to engineers—the first studies to build a bridge over the wide expanse between the cities of Almada and Lisbon date back to 1876. However, it was not until the mid-1960s that the potential for heavy industry and tourism made it worth the cost and effort to connect the two cities with a 7,472-foot-long suspension bridge. The original design was selected in a worldwide competition. Steinman, the world-renowned bridge firm Parsons acquired in 1988, won the award and later performed the construction, which was completed ahead of schedule. The Tagus River Bridge was a landmark project and established many records. It was the world's longest span designed for both highway and railway traffic, it had the world's longest continuous trusses and deepest bridge pier, and it was the longest bridge in Europe with the highest towers. The award of the bridge's structural rehabilitation and catenary designs allowed Parsons to refurbish this impressive structure and continue Steinman's excellent legacy on the project.[72]

In 2003, the American Segmental Bridge Institute honored two of Parsons' projects, the "Big I" Interchange and the Foothills Parkway Bridges, with prestigious awards. The "Big I" won the urban bridge category. Located in Albuquerque, New Mexico, at the intersection of I-25 and I-40, the "Big I" included building 55 segmental bridge structures at a cost of $270 million. The "Big I" was New Mexico's largest transportation project and included its first precast segmental bridge. Parsons provided construction engineering inspection services for each of the bridges, as well as quality control services for the erection site.

The second award was in the rural bridge and viaduct category for the $12.8 million Foothills Parkway Bridges in Blount County, Tennessee. The basis of the award was Parsons' effective redesign and efficient construction techniques, which limited the environmental impacts and preserved the pristine beauty of the site. The redesign employed cast-in-place bridge segments and balanced cantilever construction. Parsons also performed the construction engineering.[73]

Parsons is the engineer-of-record on the new Tacoma Narrows Bridge, which is located on State Route 16 in Washington. It is the primary link between the Seattle–Tacoma metro area on the eastern shore of Puget Sound and the scenic residential and recreational areas on the Olympic Peninsula to the west. The suspension bridge incorporates three lanes of traffic, pedestrian and bicycle lanes, two standard shoulders, and provisions to add a second deck. The project also includes upgrading the existing suspension bridge and constructing 2.5 miles of road approaches and toll operations facilities.

In 2002, Parsons was awarded the initial and final design and construction engineering support contract. In addition to its responsibilities for the overall bridge design, Parsons performed detailed seismic engineering and design for the new structure.[74]

Keith Sabol, vice president and the project manager, discussed the project:

> *Our value engineering changes, particularly new bridge-related innovations, saved costs on earthwork, reinforced concrete, and structural steel. We also developed an innovative alternative to reduce the size of the anchorages and still accommodate a future lower level of the bridge.*[75]

Keith is a registered civil engineer. He also was Parsons' deputy design engineer on T-REX and the design section manager on I-15 in Salt Lake City, Utah.[76]

JIM MCNULTY, CHAIRMAN AND CEO

JIM MCNULTY ATTENDED the U.S. Military Academy at West Point and graduated with a bachelor's degree in engineering in 1964. While in the U.S. Army, he acquired two master's degrees, one in physics from Ohio State University in 1970 and the other in management from MIT, as an Alfred P. Sloan Fellow, in 1985.

By expanding Parsons' services in specific growth markets, Jim McNulty's strategy doubled the corporation's earnings.

In his 24 years in the military, Jim served two tours of duty in Vietnam and held a variety of key assignments. He was the Army project manager for the ground-based, free electron laser program, one of the most important components of the Strategic Defense Initiative (SDI) program.[1] On that assignment, he became acquainted with Parsons' capabilities as an engineering subcontractor to TRW and Lockheed Martin.

By the time Jim had reached the rank of colonel, he decided to retire. Shortly thereafter, Jim Thrash, Parsons' senior vice president of government relations, approached Jim with the possibility of joining the company.[2]

Jim joined Parsons in 1988 as a project manager in the Washington, D.C., office. His first major responsibility was to develop a Department of Energy marketing strategy for the entire corporation. In doing so, Jim began working closely with staff in almost every subsidiary and regional office to incorporate their Department of Energy contacts or projects. During this assignment, he discovered that Parsons' subsidiaries and regional management were not aligned to enhance the firm's Department of Energy prospects. He explained:

> *It was clear to me that we weren't focusing and integrating our top talent and resources. The individual subsidiaries were competing rather than cooperating in attacking the market. We had to bring to bear the combined resources of the entire corporation.*[3]

Jim also convinced CEO Bill Leonhard to meet with key Department of Energy leaders to obtain more work from this client. Jim recalled, "Over a six-month period, we visited every one of the Department of Energy's sites and its headquarters. I think that contributed toward us being successful in that market."[4]

Jim's Department of Energy strategy bore fruit. He was promoted to vice president in 1991 and became the manager of RMP's Washington, D.C., office. In 1992, Bob Sheh, president of RMP, asked Jim to relocate to Pasadena to supervise the Systems Division, which was the second largest entity within Parsons, the first being the entire RMP subsidiary.[5]

Jim restructured the division into three sectors, each with its own operations and sales support. The alignment between operations and sales helped keep each sector focused on its respective markets—government, infrastructure, and aviation. This structure contributed to Parsons' winning notable awards such as the program management contract for SNWA's (Southern Nevada Water Authority) $2 billion water distribution system for Las Vegas Valley in 1993.[6] Jim recalled this award:

> *By rights, we shouldn't have won it, but we did. We had a group manager, a business*

development manager, me, and a senior project manager, who was a vice president at the time—all of whom were absolutely focused on that job. Without that, we wouldn't have won it.[7]

Assuming Key Responsibility

In January 1996, Len Pieroni restructured the entire corporation and appointed Jim as president of Parsons Infrastructure and Technology Group—one of four newly formed operating units. In April, 1996, after Len died so suddenly in the Balkans, the board of directors asked Jim to become the CEO of the entire corporation.[8] In 1998, he became Parsons' chairman.[9]

Under his leadership, the corporation has achieved a steady growth rate of over 10 percent each year since 1996.[10] Before he became CEO, Jim and other key executives had never been privy to the corporation's overall financial statements. They had received relevant balance sheets pertaining to their units, but did not operate in conjunction with one another to achieve an overall corporate goal. Curt Bower, CFO, recalls, "There were, perhaps, half a dozen people in the corporation who ever saw our financial results."[11]

Jim set about integrating executive management by disseminating critical financial information, standard operational procedures, and marketing strategies. He created the mechanisms that allowed the business units to work with one another to seek, win, and execute contracts far larger than what they had previously been able to pursue as individual operations.[12]

A critical matter that faced Jim when he took on the role of CEO was consolidating the debt Parsons had incurred by taking on several high-risk contracts with long-standing petroleum clients. This led to one incident that set the tone for further corporate restructuring and providing overall performance data to Jim's executive team. Curt related the story:

In August of 1997, we had just about blown through the top of our bank line of credit. I announced that to Jim as he was driving on the freeway. He told me he almost ran off the road. We [then] restructured both our term lender and our banks. We got through the crisis.[13]

To impart important corporate information, Jim asked the presidents of each unit and their executive sales and financial executives to meet quarterly to lay out strategy and financial data. This group is called ExComm, short for Parsons' executive committee. Curt elaborated:

When Jim became CEO, we started, for the first time, sharing financial results with senior executives from each of the global business units. They are now all kept apprised of each other's progress.[14]

Jim also felt the time was right to actively recruit new talent and promote the staff's professional development. Curt added:

One of the important changes that Jim brought was this idea of growth and spending money to acquire the human resources to grow the company, sales and marketing. We started spending the money, and immediately saw our sales and profitability start to head upwards.[15]

Parsons also lacked an internal training program and needed to provide further education to professionals at various career levels. Jim directed that corporate training programs be developed, and as a result, ParsonsU, the corporation's online training program, was launched in 2004.[16]

As with Parsons' CEOs and chairmen before him, Jim's decisions have not always been easy ones to make or implement. However, his strategies serve as testament that he is always striving to enhance the corporation's vitality. He observed:

The key to our future growth is our continued evolution. We cannot continue to do the things that we did five years ago nor can we remain content with what we are doing today.[17]

A new Tacoma Narrows Bridge was needed to ease congestion as a result of population and traffic growth in this area. The first bridge at this site, infamously known as "Galloping Gertie," collapsed due to aerodynamic problems soon after its completion in 1940. A film shot of the undulating bridge is widely shown and studied in undergraduate engineering classes. Galloping Gertie's wreckage remains at the bottom of the Narrows and has been declared a national underwater monument. The existing bridge, completed in 1950 with a 2,800-foot main span, has been nominated for the National Register of Historic Places.

The new bridge is placed south of, and parallel to, the existing bridge. Its caissons are some of the largest ever built—equivalent to an underwater 20-story building supporting the 510-foot-tall towers. They are being constructed under extreme conditions, in 150 feet of 50-degree water, with currents up to 7 knots and 50-mile-per-hour winds.[77]

Above right: Parsons designed the Carquinez Straits Bridge in California, which was the first suspension bridge built in the United States in over four decades.

Below: Parsons is the engineer-of-record on the new Tacoma Narrows suspension bridge crossing Puget Sound in Washington. The bridge spans this body of water in parallel with the existing suspension bridge that Parsons is upgrading, which replaced the infamous Galloping Gertie (inset).

The bridge is set to open in 2007 with a length of 5,400 feet and a main span of 2,800 feet. Tom Spoth, Tacoma Narrows Bridge design manager, described the project:

> *We accelerated certain design features to meet an aggressive construction schedule, providing early release of procurement plans for the caissons only 30 days after officially receiving notice-to-proceed.*[78]

Tom is a registered civil engineer and certified bridge inspector. He was Parsons' project manager for the main cable and suspension system condition assessment of the Golden Gate Bridge. Tom was also the bridge design manager for the 1,020-meter-long Carquinez Straits Bridge in California, the first suspension bridge to be built in the United States in the past 40 years. The second is Tacoma Narrows.[79]

Drawing on its vast expertise, Parsons continues to pioneer innovative bridge design and engineering. Jim Shappell, who succeeded Bob O'Neil in 2000 as president of Parsons Transportation Group, characterized the future of bridge and transportation projects as reflecting the two factors of regulations and financial support:

> *The preponderance of our work is now and will be government driven, either through policy, but primarily through funding, since the majority of our clients are public authorities or public agencies. The work is driven, to a large degree, by government policy and funds.*[80]

Quality and Integrity

The growth in transportation is one indication that Parsons' tradition of professional quality and integrity has created a sense of loyalty and trust among its customers. As part of maintaining its ethical standards, Parsons' internal auditors prepare reports that key executives and board of directors carefully review to ensure any deficiencies or irregularities are addressed.

An important aspect of Parsons' government work and commercial projects is the firm's consistent emphasis on quality and integrity. Larry Alvarez, vice president and quality control manager, explained why Parsons has been so successful in providing these important attributes:

> *I truly enjoy what I do because I receive the full support of the corporate management. With the exception of Jim McNulty, our board is comprised of directors who are not employees of Parsons. They are very cognizant of our activities. Our operations ensure compliance with company practices, good business ethics, and good accounting principles. We visit all projects, offices, and operations throughout the world, and we perform financial reviews and review of operations, in general. We interview employees to obtain their insights as to what is going [on] where they work.*[81]

Huge Water Resource Projects

In the area of long-term renewable water resources, Parsons' involvement in megaprojects continued to expand. In 1993, the corporation became the program and construction manager for the $2 billion SNWA capital improvement program, the largest single public works contract in Nevada's history. Tunnels exceeding 240 feet were bored below Lake Mead to create a new raw water

Below: As SNWA's capital improvement program manager, Parsons planned and scheduled the billions of dollars' worth of infrastructure to be completed in phases so that water could be brought "online" as needed. This resulted in millions of dollars being saved over the course of construction.

intake structure that would increase water capacity in the Las Vegas Valley, the fastest-growing metropolitan area in the United States. This challenging project succeeded in extracting, treating, and distributing water from Lake Mead to communities surrounding Las Vegas.[82] Jess Yoder, former program manager, stated, "Our program management approach saved SNWA over $100 million through the life of this program."[83] Jess directed Parsons' initial planning, design management, procurement, and construction management activities. In 2001, he was promoted to senior vice president and manager of Parsons Infrastructure Division. Jess presently manages Orange County Sanitation District's $1.9 billion capital improvement program for Parsons Water and Infrastructure Group. He is a registered civil engineer.[84]

Parsons' first SNWA assignment was to develop a capital improvements plan that recommended building the infrastructure in phases so that water could be brought "on line" as needed. Major features of the program included upgrading the existing water treatment plant, laying 105 miles of pipeline, and constructing 12 pumping stations, 16 reservoirs and forebays, a large new water intake in Lake Mead, three large hard rock tunnels, a new ozone/direct filtration plant, and an additional ozone treatment system. To enhance the power system, 13 substations were built. The raw water intake was constructed by positioning pipe across Lake Mead's Boulder Harbor in a specially constructed barge that would cradle the pipe as it was being submerged. Skilled divers then connected the pipe on the lake bed.[85]

In 2001, Bill Buchholz succeeded Jess as SNWA's program manager. Bill is a registered professional engineer with a master's degree in water resources. He joined Parsons in 1994, and his first major assignment was to chair an independent technical review of the South Bay Ocean Outfall project. Bill became the program manager on SNWA's capital improvement program at a time when it was being accelerated to support the Las Vegas area communities as their needs continued to expand. Over the next several years, the client added seven projects to the program. In 2006, the original and add-on projects will be completed—five years ahead of schedule and $160 million under the projected budget.[86]

SNWA continues to retain Parsons, and the corporation is managing and overseeing construction of two new endeavors. The first is the addition of a third—and very deep—350-foot intake in Lake Mead, which will cost an estimated $650 million to complete. The second is one in which SNWA is seeking additional surface and groundwater within Nevada to help meet future water demands, satisfy reliability goals, and improve responsiveness. For the first step of this endeavor, Parsons is studying alternatives for pumping groundwater from distances up to 300 miles and advanced techniques for treating and pumping surface water from as far away as 90 miles to Las Vegas.[87]

In 1998, Parsons began the design of the Olivenhain Dam for the San Diego County Water Authority. Completed in 2003, the dam is an impres-

sive engineering accomplishment. It is the tallest roller-compacted dam in the United States, the first of its kind in California, and capable of storing up to 24,000 acre-feet of water for San Diego County in the event of a major earthquake or severe drought. Strong as a traditional concrete dam, the roller-compacted structure offered two superior benefits: it was less expensive to build because it required less water and cut its construction time in half.

Because the dam had to be finished by late summer of 2003, the project was on a fast-track schedule. The implementation plan entailed building the dam and appurtenant facilities through four separate, sequential construction contracts that allowed for a degree of overlap to ensure continuity and accountability. When it was time to fill the dam, water imported from the Colorado River and its aqueducts flowed through 14,000 feet of newly constructed, 78-inch-diameter, welded-steel pipe. The design embraced all environmental mitigation requirements. A spectacular 750 acres of open-space park and recreational areas surround the dam and reservoir, offering 17 miles of hiking, mountain biking, equestrian trails, and scenic views. The wildlife and natural resources are monitored closely to preserve the area for future generations.

The award-winning Olivenhain Dam design by Parsons is the source of San Diego County's emergency water supply.

The American Society of Civil Engineers bestowed on Olivenhain Dam its National Merit Award in 2005 for outstanding civil engineering achievement. It won several key awards in 2004, including Outstanding Engineering Project from both the San Diego County Engineering Council and the California State Council of the American Society of Civil Engineers, as well as Project of the Year from the San Diego section of the American Public Works Association. In 2003, it was awarded the Project of the Year from the San Diego Section of the American Society of Civil Engineers and the American Concrete Institute's Charles J. Pankow Jr. Award for outstanding and innovative use of concrete in construction.[88]

In 1999, the Imperial Irrigation District, in cooperation with the California Department of Transportation, began a water utility relocation program to address required irrigation and drainage system changes resulting from multiple highway projects that were slated for the Imperial Valley. The program involved approximately 75 individual projects that were completed by June 2003. Parsons planned the relocation of water utilities that allowed for the construction of two four-lane expressways, State Highway 111 and State Route 7. These projects were part of a North American Free Trade Agreement to improve transportation between the United States and Mexico's border.

This was not the first project Parsons completed for the Imperial Irrigation District. In 1986, the client and Parsons jointly undertook the development of a comprehensive water conservation and transfer program. The goal was to quantify the Imperial Valley's present and future water needs, including water conservation opportunities and costs, and then determine the amount of water that would be available for other agencies after the program was implemented. This cooperative venture in water development, in which a private corporation partnered with a government agency, was believed to be the first of its kind in the nation.

The program developed by Parsons involved the conceptual design of a water conservation project for about 700,000 acres of land and the preliminary design of 400 miles of lateral irrigation and 400 miles of major canals. The program included procedures for transferring up to 500,000 acre-feet of water to the Los Angeles Basin that would pay for the project. It provided the basis for a 1988 agreement between the Imperial Irrigation District and The Metropolitan Water District of Southern California in which the latter agreed to finance the construction, operation, and maintenance of agricultural water conservation projects with a total cost of $233 million. When the conservation projects under this agreement were completed in 1998, collectively they saved approximately 107,160 acre-feet of water that year alone.

These two successful projects lead to a four-year contract in mid-2004 from the Imperial Irrigation District to manage the design and construction of a new 23-mile canal that will run parallel to the existing All-American Canal in Imperial County, California—the largest irrigation supply canal in the United States. Considered an engineering marvel, the All-American Canal started at Imperial Dam on the Colorado River about 20 miles northeast of Yuma, Arizona, dropped 175 feet between Imperial Dam and the Westside Main Canal, and extended south, then west, following the Mexican/American border. It provided agricultural and municipal water supplies to nine cities and nearly 500,000 acres of agricultural land. However, it was an unlined structure, which resulted in substantial seepage of valuable water resources. Upon completion, the new concrete-lined canal will conserve approximately 68,000 acre-feet of water annually, which will sustain 500,000 additional residents each year.[89]

"Parsons is honored to be involved in such a historic California water project and a project that will conserve additional Colorado River water," said David Backus, Parsons Water and Infrastructure Group president.[90] Dave joined Parsons in 2002 with extensive executive management experience with Fluor Corporation, Dow Chemical, and Morrison Knudsen. Prior to coming to Parsons, he was president of IT Corporation's (now Shaw) International Division. Dave was brought on board to further expand the corporation's water resource programs and was appointed president of this global business unit when it was formed in 2003.[91]

In June 2004, Parsons acquired Primus Industries Company, LLC (Primus) to support the growth in water resource projects. Primus had been in business for 32 years and specialized in large capital improvement program management. Water projects included planning the mammoth restoration of the Hetch Hetchy valley, adjacent to Yosemite National Park. The valley was turned into a water reservoir about 100 years ago, and the project would return Hetch Hetchy to its natural state. Primus also provided project management for the improvements to the Sunol water treatment plant, which supplies drinking water to thirsty San Franciscans.[92] At the time it was purchased, Dave Backus said of Primus, "It will be an incredible asset to our growing water and infrastructure capability."[93]

Commercial Endeavors Evolve

Due to its marketing shift to follow emerging economic trends, Parsons' portfolio of commercial projects continued to grow and formed a separate global business unit to support this set of customers—Parsons Commercial Technology Group. This new unit designed and managed the construction of more office buildings, hotels, resorts, theme parks, entertainment centers, retail, golf courses, and stadiums than it had in the previous 50 years combined. For example, Parsons managed the design and construction of new entertainment centers in Berlin, Tokyo, and San Francisco for the Sony Corporation. For IBM, Parsons began providing outsourcing services under its multiyear engineering support services contract. By 1996, the corporation had completed 1,600 separate projects under this agreement, including designing Class 10 to Class 10,0000 clean rooms.[94] Bob Nugent, legal counsel for Parsons Commercial Technology Group, has been with the corporation since the acquisition of CT Main. He stated that the group is primarily focused on

Parsons is a program manager responsible for constructing new schools within the Los Angeles Unified School District that represents a significant investment in public education.

environmental, pharmaceutical, school construction, and telecommunication endeavors:

> *We do remediation [and] wastewater treatment [for] nongovernmental clients—the Honeywells, the ExxonMobils. Then we have pharmaceutical and biotech. We're serving as a program manager, helping Los Angeles Unified School District construct hundreds of millions of dollars' worth of new schools. The main area we are involved [in] internationally [is] the telecommunications industry.*[95]

Chuck Harrington, president of Parsons Commercial Technology Group, recalled his unit's strategic move into telecommunications:

> *1997 was a marquee year for us. That's the year we won both the BellSouth lead architectural and engineering and outside plant engineering contracts.*[96]

Under the second contract, Parsons provided BellSouth's outside plant engineering services in four states of its nine-state operating region. The lead architectural and engineering contract was the first of its type undertaken by the telecommunications industry. Parsons essentially became BellSouth's program manager for its facility infrastructure upgrades and replacements throughout its operating region.

In 1999, Parsons was contracted to replace Bell Atlantic signs with Verizon signs on 30,000 buildings. In addition, Parsons developed a capital asset planning tool to study Verizon's most critical facilities and determine the amount of resources that were necessary to maintain its operations on a 24-hour, seven-day-a-week basis. In 2000, Parsons was selected by British Telecom for a unique operational exchange closure contract, another one-of-a-kind, first-of-a-kind program. At the turn of the 20th century, British Telecom was busy constructing telephone exchanges in London, many of which were in close proximity to historical structures such as the Tower of London and Westminster Abbey. The facilities had been designed to house telephone operators who would connect callers by plugging in the correct exchange wires. This antiquated system had all been replaced with state-of-the-art electronics. Parsons' task under the British Telecom contract was to strategically realign its facility network in order to maximize the prime real estate it could sell for further development.

Parsons also won an outsourcing contract from Ericsson United States in 2001 and moved

SIGNIFICANT PROJECTS

1995–2004

1995

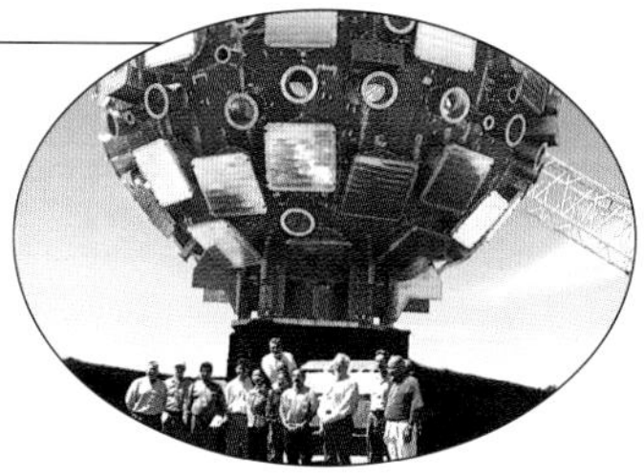

Department of Energy and University of California, National Ignition Facility Design-Build, Livermore, California

Aramco, Shaybah Oil Development Program Manager, Empty Quarter, Saudi Arabia

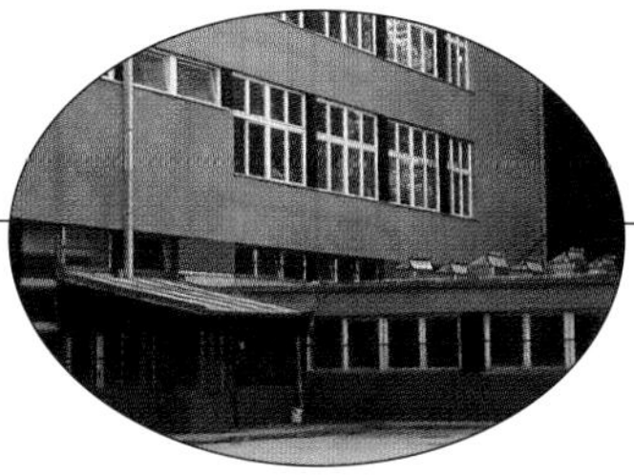

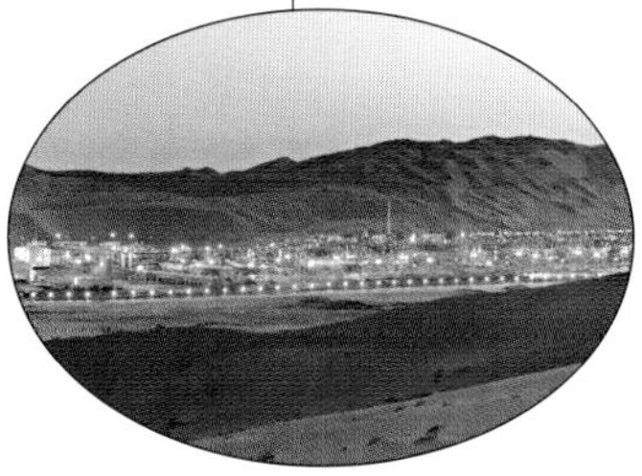

USAID, Reconstruction Contract, Bosnia–Herzegovina

Wyeth-Ayerst, Plant Utilities and Infrastructure Services, Various Locations

Merck, Plant Utilities and Infrastructure Services, Various Locations

1996

Army Corps of Engineers (Huntsville), Chemical Weapons Disposal Complex, Russia

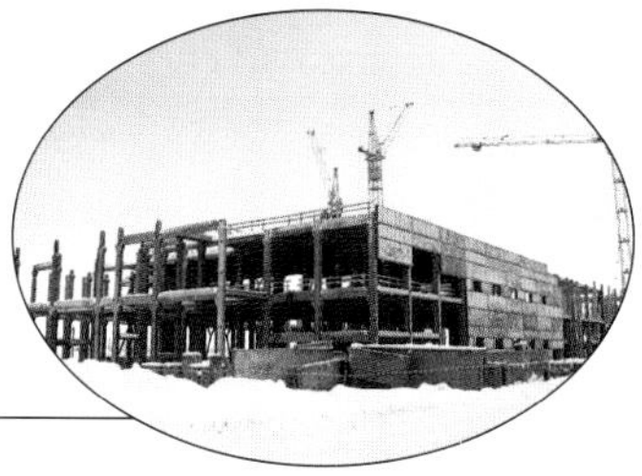

LEGEND

Commercial · Energy/Petroleum and Chemical · Government · Transportation · Water

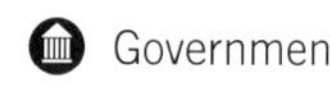

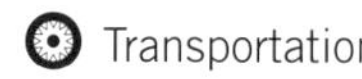

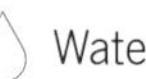

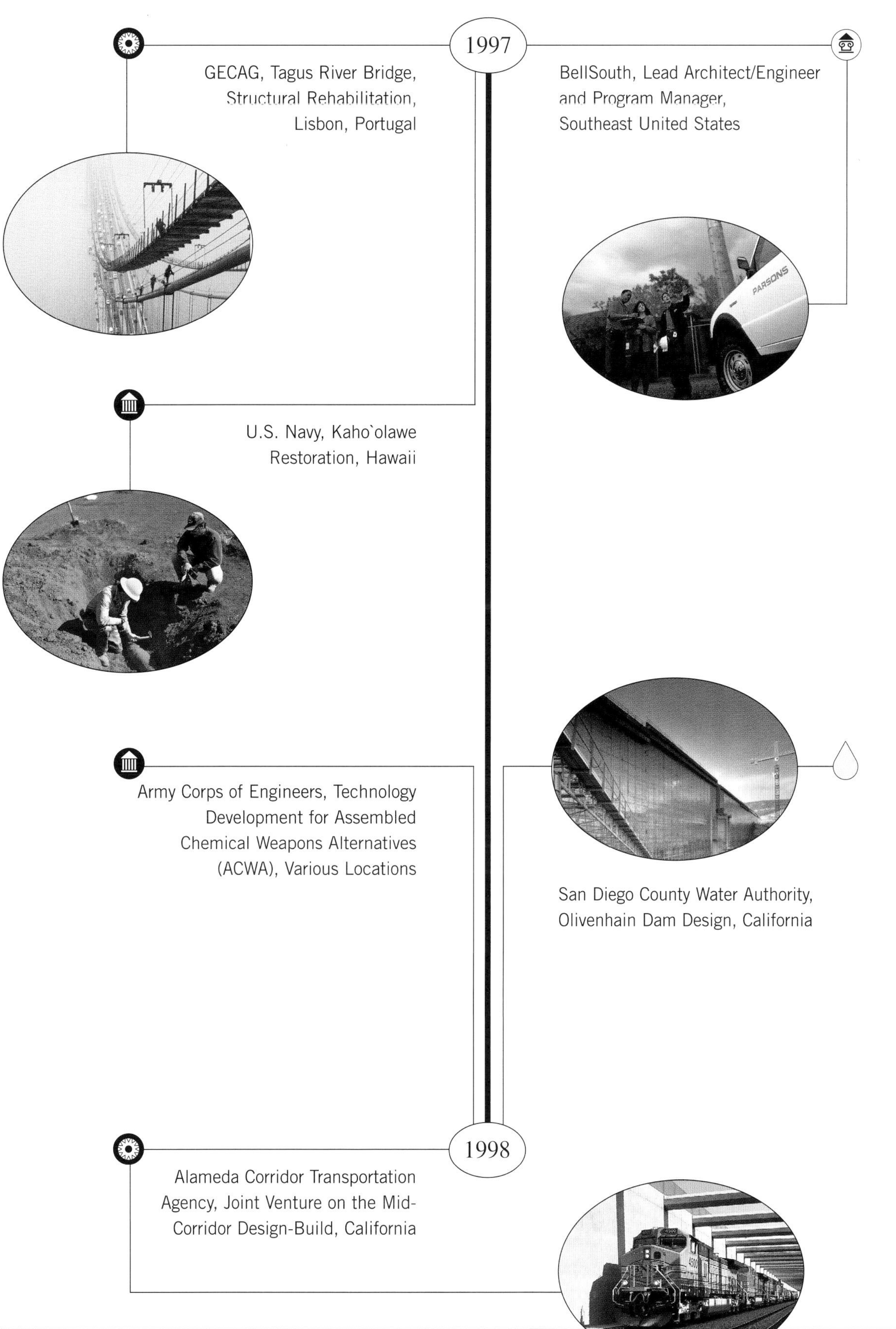

GECAG, Tagus River Bridge, Structural Rehabilitation, Lisbon, Portugal

BellSouth, Lead Architect/Engineer and Program Manager, Southeast United States

U.S. Navy, Kaho`olawe Restoration, Hawaii

Army Corps of Engineers, Technology Development for Assembled Chemical Weapons Alternatives (ACWA), Various Locations

San Diego County Water Authority, Olivenhain Dam Design, California

Alameda Corridor Transportation Agency, Joint Venture on the Mid-Corridor Design-Build, California

Bell Atlantic/Verizon, Signage Program, Mid-Atlantic States, United States

MTA Long Island Railroad, System Engineering Consultant, Eastside Expansion, Suffolk, Nassau, and Queens Counties, New York

1999

Department of Energy, National Environmental Testing Laboratory (NETL), Operational, Technical, and Management Support Services, Morgantown, West Virginia, and Pittsburgh, Pennsylvania

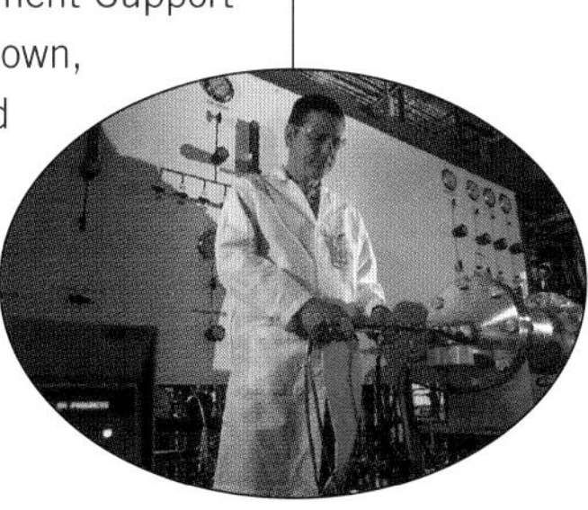

Civil Aviation Administration of China and the China State Development and Planning Commission, Design Phase I, New Baiyun Airport, Guangzhou, China *(Photo courtesy of project designer Mark Molen and project architect April Yang, of Yang Molen Design.)*

New Jersey State Department of Motor Vehicles, Statewide Vehicle Inspection Program, New Jersey

Army Corps of Engineers, Chemical Weapons Plant Design-Build, Newport, Indiana

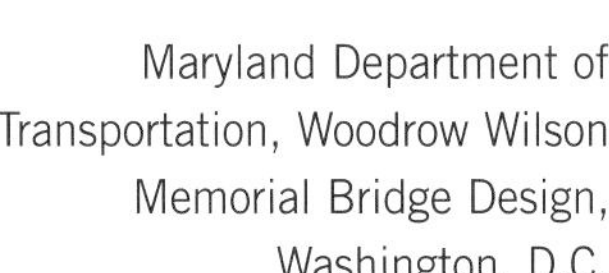

Maryland Department of Transportation, Woodrow Wilson Memorial Bridge Design, Washington, D.C.

LEGEND

 Commercial  Energy/Petroleum and Chemical  Government  Transportation  Water

2000

Minnesota Department of Transportation, Hiawatha Light Rail Transit Line Lead Designer, Minnesota

British Telecom, Operational Exchange Closure Program, United Kingdom

Lonza Biologics, Manufacturing Plant Expansion Program Manager, Portsmouth, New Hampshire

USAID, Reconstruction Contract to Rebuild Infrastructure, Kosovo

Southeast Corridor Transportation Expansion, Joint Venture Design-Build, Denver, Colorado

Department of Defense, Cooperative Threat Reduction Integrating Contractor (CTRIC) for Chemical Demilitarization, Russia

2001

FAA, Technical Support Services Contract, Various Locations

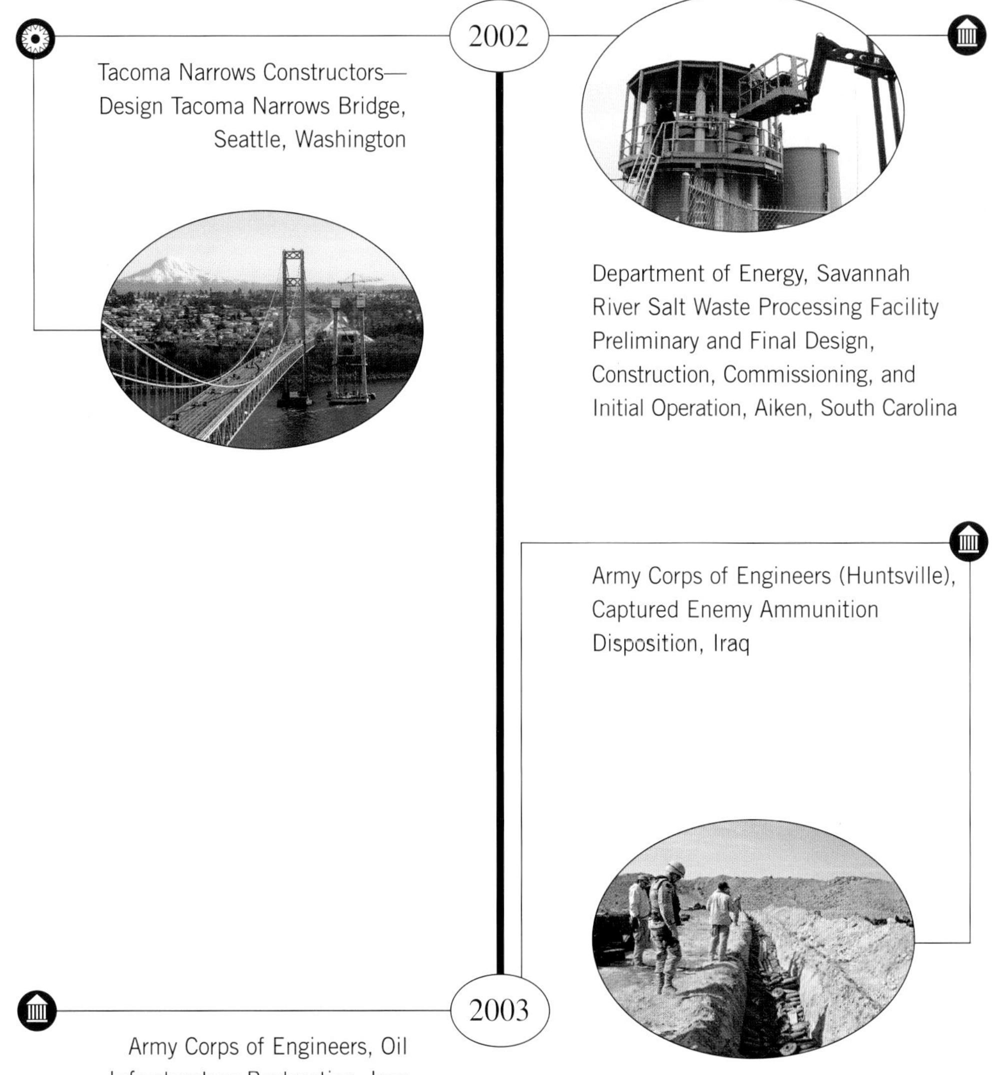

2002

Tacoma Narrows Constructors—Design Tacoma Narrows Bridge, Seattle, Washington

Department of Energy, Savannah River Salt Waste Processing Facility Preliminary and Final Design, Construction, Commissioning, and Initial Operation, Aiken, South Carolina

Army Corps of Engineers (Huntsville), Captured Enemy Ammunition Disposition, Iraq

2003

Army Corps of Engineers, Oil Infrastructure Restoration, Iraq

LEGEND

Commercial | Energy/Petroleum and Chemical | Government | Transportation |  Water

USAID, Infrastructure Reconstruction, Iraq

Army Corps of Engineers (Transatlantic), Security and Justice Infrastructure Reconstruction, Iraq

2004

Army Corps of Engineers (Transatlantic), Buildings, Health, and Education Reconstruction, Iraq

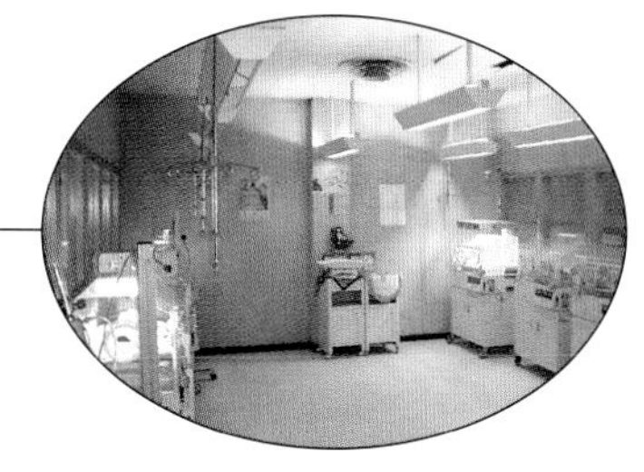

Army Corps of Engineers, Worldwide Munitions Response Services, Global

Imperial Irrigation District, All-American Canal Design and Construction, Imperial County, California

approximately 500 employees from Ericsson over to Parsons' payrolls. These primarily wireless equipment installers were responsible for placing the base stations at the bottom of the cell towers, installing the facility telephone switches, programming the software, and ensuring that radio signals would not interfere with cell phone operations. With this contract, Parsons became one of the largest suppliers of wireless network services in the United States. The corporation also provided outsourced, end-carrier services to Ericsson, Nokia, and Siemens, all serving AT&T Wireless, as well as Cingular and T-Mobile.[97]

To support growth in this market, in 2001, Parsons bought H.E. Hennigh Inc. (Hennigh), a privately held Georgia company specializing in facilities that modify switch and data centers and construct grassroots telecommunications. Parsons and Hennigh had worked together for several years. When announcing the acquisition, Harold Wyatt, Hennigh's chairman, stated, "We believe that combining our forces will further enhance our services to our customers."[98] Chuck Harrington concurred, adding, "Specifically, our model of reducing client costs, while improving capital deployment efficiency in facilities that require '24/7' operational continuity, will be greatly enhanced."[99]

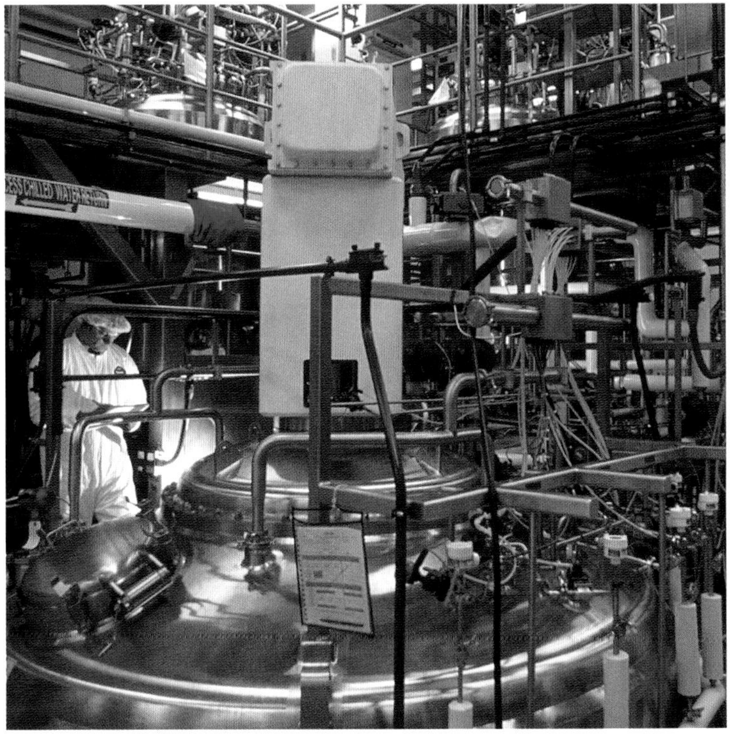

Parsons was retained as program manager to expand Lonza Biologics' existing plant in New Hampshire and quadruple its manufacturing capacity of antibodies and proteins used throughout the pharmaceutical industry.

Pharmaceuticals

The other area of significant commercial growth was designing and managing the construction of pharmaceutical manufacturing facilities. Over the years, Parsons had built several pharmaceutical plants, but in 1996 started actively seeking opportunities in this market. That year, both Merck and Wyeth-Ayerst selected the corporation to provide services for their plant utilities and infrastructure.[100] This work led to process design projects and additional opportunities.

In late 2000, Parsons was retained by Lonza Biologics, the world's leading supplier of active chemical ingredients, intermediates, and biotechnology solutions for the pharmaceutical and agrochemical industries. Its parent company, Lonza, is the leading contract manufacturer of therapeutic monoclonal antibodies and recombinant proteins from mammalian cell cultures. Parsons became Lonza Biologics' program manager on an engineering, procurement, and construction management contract to expand a manufacturing facility in Portsmouth, New Hampshire, that produces biotech products for name-brand pharmaceutical companies. The expansion, completed in early 2004, quadrupled the existing plant's fermentation capacity with the installation of three 20,000-liter stirred-tank reactors and additional purification abilities.[101]

Bill Millhone, manager of contracts and procurement for Parsons Commercial Technology Group, described the increase in the firm's pharmaceuticals operations in Ireland:

> *We are expanding our presence in pharmaceutical and biotechnology. Many people may not realize it, but Ireland is now the main focus of the major bio and pharmaceutical companies in the world because of very favorable tax concessions. Every major pharmaceutical and biotech company has established manufacturing facilities in Ireland, and*

those facilities require constant engineering and construction services.[102]

Bill joined Parsons in 1978 after having been a lawyer in private practice. Initially, he supported the Aramco project, later provided legal counsel on transportation programs, and then transitioned into contract management.[103]

On January 8, 2004, Parsons announced it had purchased Michael Walsh Consultants (MWC), headquartered in Cork, Ireland, based on an assessment that Ireland's pharmaceutical industry was stable, sound, and growing. They had previously worked together on various projects in Ireland. MWC specialized in design and construction supervision of process and water treatment facilities for clean industries, including pharmaceutical and biotechnology manufacturing, food and beverage, and fine chemical production. MWC had operations throughout Ireland, continental Europe, and Africa.[104] MWC's founder, Michael Walsh, is presently the Industrial Division manager of Parsons Commercial Technology Group and is responsible for this global business unit's environmental programs.[105]

In May 2004, it followed up the MWC acquisition with the purchase of Process Facilities Inc. (PFI), a privately held firm based in Boston, Massachusetts. PFI was a recognized leader in designing, engineering, planning, and constructing life sciences facilities and high-purity manufacturing plants. The combination of MWC, PFI, and Parsons' resources has greatly enhanced the corporation's capabilities in delivering services to the world's most prestigious pharmaceutical companies.[106] Dan Mariani, principal of PFI, became Parsons Commercial Technology Group's senior vice president and manages its life science projects.[107]

Northrop Grumman

Northrop Grumman is the largest shipbuilder in the world with clients that include the U.S. Navy and U.S. Coast Guard. In May 2003, Parsons signed a master services agreement to serve as its engineer, designer, construction manager, and program manager for a five-year, $400 million facilities modernization and expansion program at three shipyards located in New Orleans, Louisiana, and Gulfport and Pascagoula, Mississippi. Parsons had originally designed the Pascagoula shipyard in 1967 for Litton Industries, later acquired by Northrop Grumman.[108]

Jim Thrash, senior vice president of government relations, discussed how Parsons is often called in to upgrade work it did before:

It is interesting how about every 20 or 30 years, we get a chance to upgrade things again. The client might say, "Parsons did X or Y for us 20 years ago. Give them a call." This particular project is a replay of two programs; one where we [designed] the same Pascagoula shipyard, and secondly, the analyses we did of all the major naval shipyards to help them evolve a capital improvement program back in the eighties.

My favorite slogan about Parsons is we are implementers of technology. By that, I mean we bring to a program the latest technology perhaps 20 or 30 years after we were first engaged by the client. We were among the first to start modular construction of ships in that first exercise in Pascagoula. Today, we're bringing in a capability such as simulators for operations aboard ship and for security exercises and so on.[109]

The Pascagoula shipyard was originally designed by Parsons in 1967. Parsons has been modernizing and expanding this facility and two other shipyards for the current owner, Northrop Grumman.

Left: The design of the salt waste processing facility is one of several key projects that Parsons has been awarded at the Department of Energy's Savannah River site over the past 50 years.

Below: Parsons is a key member of a joint venture that supports the four National Energy Technology Laboratories tasked with developing fossil fuel research.

Salt Waste Processing Facility

Parsons continued its services to the Department of Energy and, in 2002, began the conceptual design for a salt waste processing facility to process highly radioactive waste from underground storage tanks at the Savannah River site in Aiken, South Carolina. Previously, Parsons had been retained at Savannah River by both the Department of Energy and Westinghouse to clean up the byproducts from over 50 years of defense programs conducted onsite. The processing facility will receive 37 million gallons of a salt waste containing strontium, actinides, and cesium from existing waste tank farms. It will separate the highly radioactive cesium and actinide from the salt solution using precipitation/filtration and solvent extraction technologies. After separation, the concentrated cesium and actinide waste will be immobilized in a glass matrix, transferred to another facility, and stored until a geological repository at Savannah River is made available to permanently house the decontaminated material in a grout matrix.[110]

When initially awarded the project, Chuck Terhune III, senior vice president and program manager, commented on Parsons' enthusiasm to handle the project:

> *Parsons is ready to take on this unique technological challenge. The Department of Energy has prepared a sound technical baseline. Our staff excels in design and construction of one-of-a-kind facilities utilizing advanced technology processes. Everyone on the team is excited and working to meet early project milestones. Our long-term goal is to assist the Department of Energy in meeting its regulatory commitments to safely treat and dispose of the legacy high-level waste at the Savannah River Plant.*[111]

In 2004, Parsons completed the conceptual design and competed for the next phase of work. The Department of Energy selected the corporation for the second leg of this critical project that will entail the design, construction, commissioning, and one year of facility operations.[112]

NETL (National Energy Technology Laboratory)

As part of the Department of Energy's Office of Fossil Energy, NETL's mission is to implement a research, development, and demonstration program to resolve the constraints of producing and using fossil resources. Parsons has an important role in achieving this mission and helping to ensure that these resources—coal, oil, and natural gas—can meet the increasing demand for affordable energy without compromising the quality of life for future generations.

NETL's staff is currently developing technologies to reduce air emissions from fossil fuel-fired power plants and increase the nation's energy security. To achieve President George W. Bush's goal of reducing U.S. greenhouse gas intensity by 18 percent by 2012, they are researching many exciting

energy solutions. Examples include hydrogen membrane technology to produce hydrogen more efficiently as an alternative energy source and methods to capture and sequester carbon dioxide, the most prevalent source of greenhouse gas emissions.

Parsons has been providing operational, technical, and management services to assist NETL's Morgantown, West Virginia, and Pittsburgh, Pennsylvania, facilities since 1999. NETL also has offices in Tulsa, Oklahoma, and Fairbanks, Alaska. In 2004, Parsons became part of a joint venture called Research and Development Solutions LLC that was awarded the contract to provide design, engineering, fabrication, operations, maintenance, and program planning and policy support. The joint venture team includes three regional universities—Carnegie Mellon, the University of Pittsburgh, and West Virginia University.[113]

According to Parsons' program manager Doug Reehl, "Parsons has made significant contributions at NETL, providing value-added engineering and technical services to optimize the federal research and development investment."[114]

In 2003, Parsons completed the National Ignition Facility in Livermore, California, in which scientists study inertial fusion as a source for alternative energy. This photo shows the facility's target chamber.

Scientific Research and Alternative Fuel Facilities

In 2003, Parsons completed the design, engineering, and construction management of the National Ignition Facility in Livermore, California, just outside of San Francisco. This first-of-its-kind facility was begun in 1995 and—of all the energy and missile defense projects in the corporation's portfolio—it stands alone in terms of scientific and technical advancement. The National Ignition Facility houses the world's most powerful laser that is vital to studying physics and the viability of inertial fusion energy as a strategic alternative power source for the United States.

Fusion, fission, and solar energy are inexhaustible energy sources capable of generating sufficient power for the needs of the next century—and beyond. Fusion energy powers the sun and other stars. The simplest fusion fuels, hydrogen's heavy isotopes (deuterium and tritium), are derived from water and lithium, a metal. These fuels can be found in an unending supply anywhere on earth and do not contribute to environmental pollution, as do fossil fuels. Developing inertial fusion energy for hydrogen or electric-powered manufacturing plants or automobiles would reduce the U.S. dependence on nondomestic energy sources. Parsons partnered with the University of California and the Department of Energy in the National Ignition Facility's design and construction, which created conditions found in the interior of stars and in nuclear explosions to ignite and burn a small fusion target. The National Ignition Facility also serves a key role in the Department of Energy's stockpile stewardship program, whose mission is to maintain the safety, reliability, and effectiveness of our nation's nuclear stockpile without underground nuclear testing. In addition, the facility employs weapons scientists who assess conditions that could compromise the reliability of the United States' aging nuclear weapons.[115]

Bruce Shelton, vice president and program manager, discussed its importance:

> *Converting the idea of a fusion reactor into the reality of the National Ignition Facility took years of dedicated effort by many, including Parsons' best and brightest personnel, and we at Parsons are justifiably proud of our role in what will be mankind's first successful creation of an unlimited, clean energy source from fusion.*[116]

Bruce is a civil engineer with an environmental emphasis. Since joining Parsons in 1984, Bruce has supervised a wide range of Department of Energy projects at the Los Alamos National Laboratory in New Mexico and the Savannah River Site in Aiken, South Carolina. In 1994, he was the project manager for the conceptual design for the decontamination and waste treatment facility at Lawrence Livermore National Laboratory in Livermore, California.[117]

Also for Lawrence Livermore National Laboratory, Parsons engineered and designed a new explosive test chamber and support structures designated as the Contained Firing Facility. Its purpose was to upgrade the hydrodynamic testing capabilities of the existing Flash X-ray Firing Facility while containing potentially hazardous material emissions and contaminated wastes generated by explosive testing. The project was completed in 2000.[118]

Mel Weingart, the project manager, recalled:

> *This was a very challenging project. It was a fixed-price contract with a design-to-cost provision. It had very stringent design requirements necessitating several one-of-a-kind solutions which our team was able to produce to meet our client's expectations.*[119]

Mel complimented one team member in particular:

> *Henry Ayvazyan was our blast design engineer. He really came up with creative solutions that, along with the rest of the team, resulted in the design and construction of a state-of-the-art testing facility. Henry is amazing and one of Parsons' best engineers, in my opinion.*[120]

Mel is a principal project manager in Parsons Water and Infrastructure Group. He is a registered professional engineer and has been with Parsons since 1992. In addition to the Contained Firing Facility, he also managed the Laser Interferometer Gravitational Wave Observatory and a classified project for the U.S. State Department in Russia. Henry, a principal structural engineer, joined Parsons in 1991. He also supported Bruce Shelton as a principal engineer on the National Ignition Facility and designed the Titan motor test structure at Edwards Air Force Base, California, in 1992.[121]

Parsons was contracted by Caltech in association with MIT to serve as the architect, engineer, and construction manager for the design and construction of the observatory. The project was funded by the National Science Foundation. Its objective is to confirm the existence of gravity waves resulting from deep space events—supernovas, black holes, and so on—as predicted by Albert Einstein in the 1920s.

Parsons architecturally designed, engineered, and supervised the construction of two laser interferometer gravitational wave observation facilities. They allow physicists to search the universe for gravitation waves for the first time in history.

It consists of two observatories, one on the Hanford site outside Richland, Washington, and the other in Livingston, Louisiana. Unique features associated with these two facilities are the sheer size of the vacuum systems, the isolated technical foundations for mitigating external vibration, and the structural arms—almost two-and-one-half miles long—used for laser targeting. Correlation of data from interferometers at the two sites allows for the identification of gravitational waves and their sources and origin in space.[122] Mel remembered:

On the Louisiana site, at the end of one of the arms, there was a swampy area. At lunch the construction crew would go to the edge of the water and feed the alligators peanut butter sandwiches. The alligators loved them.[123]

Mel discussed the challenges of the project:

The lasers are extremely sensitive and any vibration from, say, a truck passing or an equipment motor in the facility, could affect the experiments. We performed the vibration analysis very carefully and designed the foundations so that the experimental equipment was isolated from the mechanical equipment and vibrations did not transmit. We called it a technical foundation.[124]

The project was dedicated on November 12, 1999. On April 7, 2003, it began its research. Mel Weingart, Chuck Terhune III (principal-in-charge), Dr. Paul MacCalden (senior project technology manager who led the vibration analysis and engineering), and Tim Melott (project engineering manager) were some of the key personnel who made this project a success.[125]

Fossil Fuels—Vehicle Inspections

At the other end of the spectrum, in 1999, Parsons began managing vehicle inspection programs for fossil fuel emissions. The corporation had been performing quality-control services in air emissions testing and database management of vehicle inspections. Based on high operating costs and the need for higher efficiency, Australia, the province of Ontario (Canada), and several U.S. state governments (including New Jersey, Pennsylvania, and Georgia) engaged Parsons to privatize their vehicle inspection programs.[126]

As Cliff Eby, former senior vice president who had helped develop this service, explained it was a new business model for Parsons:

What's unique about it is the revenue model. It's different from any other business that Parsons pursued. For the most part, we either work on cost-reimbursable work or on fixed-price, lump-sum-type projects where you pretty much are looking at the number of man hours that are generated and the return on those man hours. The business model tends to be the number of tests that we perform. Our revenues are going to be based upon the number of vehicles that come through, or the number of data hits that we get, not on the number of people we have on the project or the cost of those hours.[127]

The largest of Parsons' inspection programs was in New Jersey and involved the privatization of over 2.5 million vehicle inspections and registrations per year. Parsons and the New Jersey State Department of Motor Vehicles entered into a seven-year contract in 1999 that included two one-year renewal options. Exhaust emissions were checked at speed and load conditions found in everyday traffic. Vehicle safety tests were performed by both visual inspection and sophisticated electronic equipment. Initially, Parsons was faced with unreliable equipment, software glitches, winter temperatures, and some very unhappy customers who had to wait a long time to have their vehicles inspected. Within

Parsons is the privatization contractor to the State of New Jersey that inspects and registers 2.5 million vehicles per year.

eight months, Parsons had resolved these challenges, and the necessary program improvements were in place.[128]

In 2001, Parsons acquired Protect Air Inc., a Canadian firm specializing in vehicle inspections and compliance, to support this market overall and, in particular, the Ontario vehicle inspections.[129]

After merging into Parsons' operations, the Protect Air staff became instrumental in the success of Pennsylvania and Georgia's privatization program. Steve Quinn, founder of Protect Air Inc., related a story of speaking with then-governor of Pennsylvania Tom Ridge at a political function after this state's emissions program had been implemented by Parsons:

> *The governor described the project [to me]. "We put the vehicle emission program in place [on] December 1. I told my wife, 'This is going to be the Christmas from hell. We are going to have nothing but phone calls, grief, aggravation, [and] legislators phoning us about this program.' On January 4, I can tell you that over the 30 days of implementation and the week that followed, I got one phone call to my office." I turned to him and said, "That's because when there's a problem, we fix it ourselves." He just had this big smile [and] said, "On behalf of my wife and myself, I thank you."*[130]

In addition to these programs, the corporation went on to design, develop, and operate nationwide diesel testing facilities in Australia.[131]

Kaho`olawe

The U.S. Navy awarded Parsons a significant remediation project in 1997 to restore Kaho`olawe, the smallest of the eight major Hawaiian Islands. The scope involved removing unexploded ordnance that had accumulated over 50 years of military operations and ensuring the preservation of more than 500 known native Hawaiian archaeological sites. Completed in 2004, this project was one of the most dangerous and culturally important Parsons had ever undertaken.

Only 45 square miles in size, Kaho`olawe lies six miles southwest of the island of Maui. More than 1,000 years of archaeological evidence indicates Hawaiians lived, fished, and farmed in coastal and interior settlements. A key Hawaiian ancient navigational and religious center, the island contains some of the most significant and best-preserved archaeological sites in all of Hawaii. However, activity on Kaho`olawe went into decline after the Hawaiians had been in contact with European explorers who carried smallpox and other diseases for which the native population had no immunity.

In 1920, the U.S. military began routinely bombarding the island for target practice, and in 1939, the Territory of Hawaii leased the southern tip to the Army for use as an artillery range. The lease was superceded in 1941 when the Navy gained exclusive use of Kaho`olawe as a gunnery and bombing training range for the next 50 years. In 1993, Congress passed a law recognizing the island's significance to the Hawaiian culture and required the Navy to return ownership to the State of Hawaii as trustee for a future sovereign native Hawaiian entity.

When joining the $400 million program in 1997, Parsons and its joint venture partner, UXB International Inc., were tasked with removing the unexploded ordnance from 22,000 acres out of the island's 28,271 acres. The island could not support a permanent, residential workforce and only had limited infrastructure. Therefore, up to 400 workers had to be flown in daily by helicopter, making it the largest daily helicopter airlift of its time. A range operations center, central roadway, utility systems, and several helipads were constructed to support project activities; all these structures were transferred to the State of Hawaii at the conclusion of the project as a permanent infrastructure upgrade for future use by the state in managing the reserve.

The ordnance found on Kaho`olawe was highly diverse, spanning the entire 50 years of bombardment, and included all kinds of bombs, projectiles, rockets, mortars, grenades, submunitions, and small arms. The anticipated future public use of the island required surface and subsurface clearance to a depth of four feet. In order to make a clean sweep of the island, new ordnance detection technologies and state-of-the-art survey techniques were employed. The island was divided into 100-meter square grids. Each grid was characterized for the presence of unexploded ordnance, archaeological sites, threatened or endangered species, and potential environmental contamination. Parsons used a global

Left: Prior to any waste removal actions on the island of Kaho`olawe in Hawaii, Parsons performed a thorough assessment of each hectare (approximately 2.5 acres) of the island, characterizing unexploded ordnance and environmental contaminants, archaeological sites, rare and endangered flora and fauna, and wetlands.

Below left: After over 50 years serving as a training target for the U.S. military and undergoing seven years of unexploded ordnance cleanup and removal, Kaho`olawe has been returned to the State of Hawaii for native cultural practices.

positioning system to establish grid locations and notate topographic contours in half-meter intervals.

Every unexploded ordnance observation was stored in an online mapping system database specifically designed for Kaho`olawe that allowed for immediate access to all project data in real-time and provided the ability to electronically approve work authorizations. The database also provided global positioning system coordinates, descriptions of the findings and mitigation activities, and catalogued archeological sites, endangered plants, and animal species. It eventually included more than 85,000 photo images.[132]

Armed with sophisticated metal detectors, the highly skilled excavation teams uncovered the ordnance on and below the surface. Locating and removing unexploded ordnance had "never been done before on this scale," noted Parsons' vice president and program manager, Tom McCabe. He discussed the project:

> *This was a large, complex project and the only way we could complete it successfully was to break the tasks down into subelements, and then find good people to manage the subelements. We had hundreds of people on the island at any one given point in time, and six reported directly to me. Everyone knew their roles and carried out their responsibilities.*[133]

Tom began his career at Parsons in 1981 as a mechanical engineer assigned to the Johnston Atoll chemical agent disposal system. He advanced within the corporation by working on many of the chemical stockpile programs for the United States and Russia in support of the Department of Defense's chemical demilitarization projects.[134] Tom succeeded

William Ahrens as Kaho`olawe's program manager when Bill retired in 2001.

Bill was a civil engineer who had been Parsons' construction/project manager on the medical center and multiple housing projects in Yanbu Industrial City, Saudi Arabia. He had been a former commander in the U.S. Navy Civil Engineer Corps and joined Parsons in 1982, left 10 years later, and returned to manage Kaho`olawe in 1997.[135]

In total, the Kaho`olawe project team removed and disposed of more than 116,000 unexploded ordnance and target items weighing almost 13 million pounds. The ordnance deemed safe to move was transported to an onsite thermal treatment unit, rendered inert, and then shipped off the island to be recycled as scrap metal. Ordnance with a high explosion risk was detonated in place. Near its completion in 2004, the project had logged over five million hours without an explosives-related injury—a notable safety achievement.

The team also protected the ancient Hawaiian ceremonial sites, petroglyphs, and other areas and artifacts of cultural and archaeological significance, as well as protecting numerous endangered plant and animal species during the cleanup. The island has been returned to the native Hawaiians for their cultural practices and is listed on the National Register of Historic Places.[136]

Chem Demil Leader in United States and Russia

As with so many core markets, Parsons' chemical demilitarization expertise—or "chem demil" as it is known in the industry—was derived from the success of one or two key projects and the corporation's commitment to building upon that experience. Based upon the thermal incineration technology Parsons had helped engineer for Johnston Atoll and CSDP, as well as the unexploded ordnance mitigation efforts the corporation was undertaking on Kaho`olawe, the Army Corps of Engineers selected Parsons in 1998 to develop nonincineration, alternative technologies for chemical weapons disposal under its Assembled Chemical Weapons Alternatives (ACWA) program. The CSDP and ACWA programs were on parallel tracks to ensure that the technology deployed, whether thermal or nonincineration based, would be highly effective in destroying the chemical weapons and, above all, would be safe.[137]

After several years of study and discussion, two types of chemical neutralization-based treatment technologies were selected by the Army Corps of Engineers as alternatives. The difference between the two treatments was the followup technology deployed after chemical neutralization occurred. The neutralized chemical weapons would undergo further treatment to render the remaining hazardous substances inert. The processes selected were biological treatment and supercritical water oxidation (which uses a combination of high temperature, high pressure, and wet air to combine the agent with oxygen). As part of this effort, Parsons developed a biological treatment process and tailored existing supercritical water oxidation technology to ensure that the waste remaining after chemical neutralization could be safely disposed of in accordance with regulatory requirements. Two of the eight domestic chemical weapons stockpile sites were designated for the ACWA program: Edgewood, Maryland, and Newport, Indiana.

In 1999, Parsons was awarded a $295 million contract as the systems contractor to design, build, and operate the Newport Chemical Agent Disposal Facility, which contained four percent of the U.S. stockpile. The neutralization plant design-build was completed in 2004, and the destruction of the chemical agent commenced in May 2005. Parsons also supported technology design efforts for the Edgewood facility, which began chemical agent neutralization in 2003.[138]

This domestic experience in chemical demilitarization and unexploded ordnance removal led to similar project awards in Russia. In 2001, Parsons was selected as a Cooperative Threat Reduction Integrating Contractor (CTRIC), along with Bechtel National, The Washington Group, Raytheon, and Halliburton KBR to render harmless a variety of weapons in the former Soviet Union and clean up its stockpile locations. The Department of Defense budgeted $5 billion to dismantle the solid and liquid-fueled rockets and eliminate chemical weapons of mass destruction in Russia. As part of the Nunn-Lugar Act of 1996, the Department of Defense initiated the Cooperative Threat Reduction program to help the Russian Federation safely store and ultimately eliminate its 40,000 metric tons of chemical agent stockpiles stored at seven sites.

For the Russian chemical weapons disposal program, Parsons is providing in-country project management, subcontract management, and system integration of the actual destruction facilities.

In total, Parsons' chemical demilitarization efforts in Russia have focused on four specific tasks. For chemical demilitarization, Parsons provided in-country project management, subcontract management, and integration of the actual destruction facility. The team developed the chemical agent destruction process, environmental monitoring procedures, and construction documents. Parsons has also procured materials, trained the facility operators, monitored systemization and start-up, and performed public outreach activities. The project staff was stationed in Pasadena, California, and in Russia in Moscow, Volgograd, Shchuch'ye, and Chelyabinsk. In Novochebaksarsk, Parsons also designed the methods and developed the means to decontaminate the buildings and material used for chemical agent production in an ecologically safe manner.

For the transport, dismantlement, and destruction of sea-launched ballistic missiles, Parsons established Russian project offices in Moscow, Miass, and Biysk to provide in-country representation of the U.S. government, and to perform project and subcontractor management. In addition, the corporation assisted the Ukraine's air force in its efforts to eliminate nuclear weapons at several bases.[139] Jeff Hermann, who joined Parsons in 1980 after graduating with a civil and environmental engineering degree from the University of Wisconsin, was the project manager.[140]

In his 2003 presentation at Parsons' annual managers meeting, Jeff discussed the program:

> *Our explosive safety compliance plan is now used by DTRA as a model for all explosive safety requirements in Russia. DTRA also commended us as "one of the best CTRIC contractors in Russia."*[141]

Jeff lived in Russia for six-and-a-half years with his wife and young son. He discussed his experience in Russia when he returned to the United States:

> *Overall it was a great experience for us. Parsons has an excellent team of expats [expatriates] in Russia who became our friends, and my son can speak both English and Russian because of this opportunity.*[142]

Jeff's first assignment was on the modular design of Sohio's North Slope project. He later supported field design efforts on the Petromin-Shell refinery in Saudi Arabia and was the design systems engineering manager on both the National Ignition Facility and the Laser Interferometer Gravitational Wave Observatory.[143]

Parsons' contributions to both the United States and the Russia Federation's disarmament programs propelled the corporation into worldwide leadership status in chemical demilitarization.

Security

After the terrorist attacks on September 11, 2001, in New York City and Washington, D.C., the U.S. Army accelerated its schedule to destroy the domestic chemical weapons stockpiles as a security measure. Drawing on its experience in modularized engineering and construction, Parsons began building its own equipment fabrication shop earlier that year in Pasco, Washington, to design, test, and manufacture highly specialized system components for thermal and non-incineration technologies. Parsons also designed the shop in order to support the Department of Energy's nuclear waste cleanup efforts at Hanford, Washington, where Parsons had been active since 1990, and other projects such as the Savannah River Site. The shop then became instrumental in developing modular equipment to assist the Army's demilitarization efforts at Newport, Indiana, and Pueblo, Colorado.[144]

In addition to escalating chemical weapons disposal, Parsons quickly began applying its assessment and mitigation skills honed through years of environmental analysis, facility engineering/construction, operations and maintenance, and data management to homeland security needs. In 2002, this experience supported the award of a Transportation Security Administration contract, where Parsons became Lockheed Martin's subcontractor to implement strategic airport security rollout programs at 91 airports, covering 373 checkpoints and 1,210 passenger screening lanes. In addition, Parsons managed the installation of information technology infrastructure for 73 airports. The new security operations aided air passenger safety at the nation's largest airports.[145]

Parsons' fabrication shop designs and builds one-of-a-kind equipment and components used by the Department of Defense, Department of Energy, and chemical weapons demilitarization facilities.

Previous contracts with Parsons' long-term client, the FAA, led to a $1.2 billion technical support services contract with Parsons in December 2001. On this program, Parsons was the prime contractor, with Lockheed Martin as its subcontractor. The goal was to implement the FAA's modernization plans for the national airspace system that included engineering, construction, environmental and fire/life safety, equipment installation and testing, CAD, and other technical services.[146]

In June 2002, Parsons received the International Standard for Organization's (ISO) coveted 9000 Certification for the quality management systems that support this contract. In the months and years to follow, Parsons evaluated airports, water authorities, and telecommunication and data facilities, as well as federal, state, and local government facilities for potential security risks.[147]

Other security-related projects consisted of designing test and support facilities for the U.S. Air Force's intercontinental ballistic missile program, rocket test facilities at Edwards Air Force Base in California, placement of the Peacekeeper intercontinental ballistic missiles in former Minuteman silos, and the Department of Energy's $700 million monitored retrievable storage facility to store commercial nuclear waste and spent fuel.[148]

Reconstruction of Iraq

September 11, 2001, and the second Gulf War brought about a significant shift in federal budget priorities and focus as the Bush administration set out to revitalize the infrastructure and economies of Afghanistan and Iraq. The government shifted funding from domestic transportation and demilitarization projects to homeland security

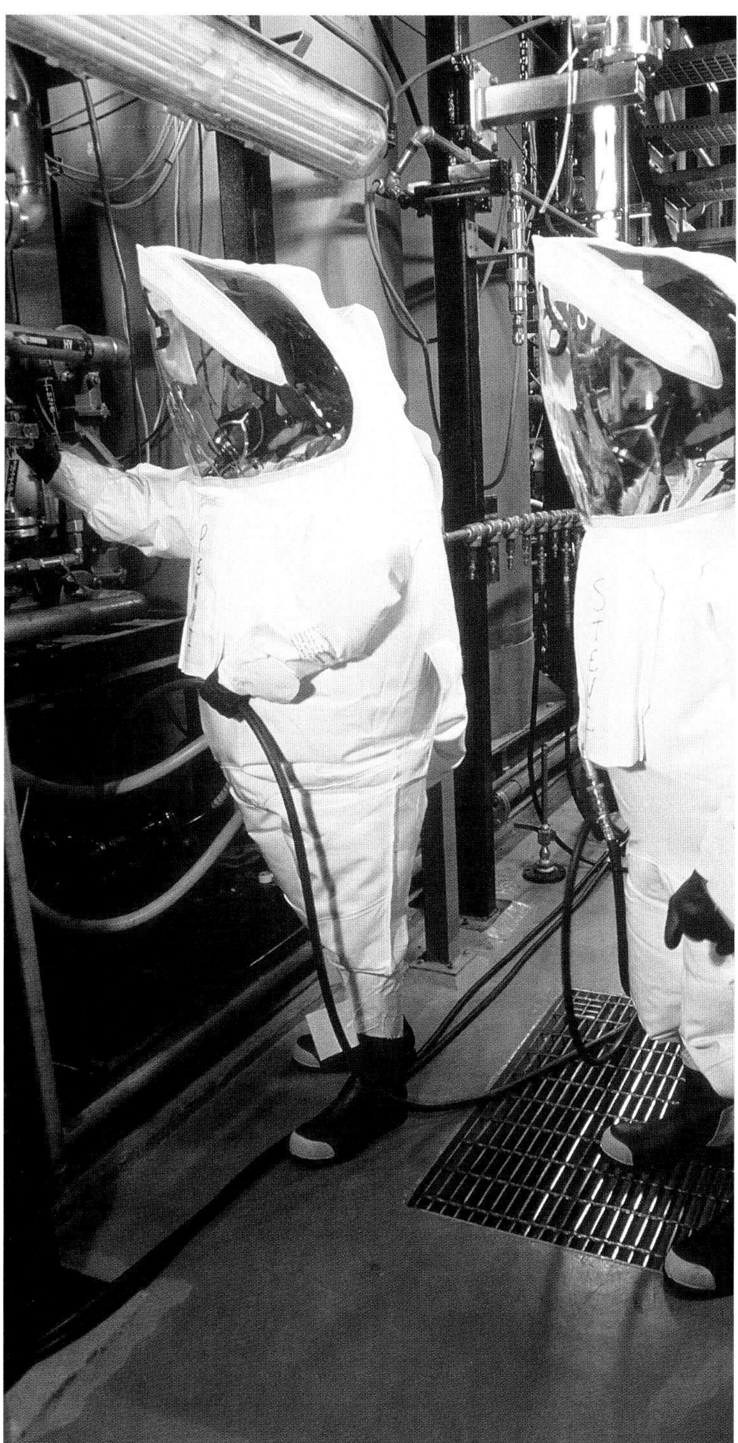

Parsons was instrumental in the safe destruction of Cold War chemical weapons, and a significant number of its professional staff were actively involved in designing and engineering incineration and neutralization plants within the continental United States for the Army Corps of Engineers.

and reconstruction and disarmament efforts. After the collapse of Saddam Hussein's regime in March 2003, Parsons became one of the key engineering firms tasked with rebuilding Iraq's infrastructure. The rapid-fire award of reconstruction contracts, the challenges associated with staffing them, and meeting the federal government's desire for expedited project execution required a new approach to the way Parsons performed federal contracts. The solution was to have all Iraq contracts performed under the Infrastructure and Technology Group since it specialized in federal programs.

Parsons Infrastructure and Technology Group teamed with Parsons' Water, Commercial, and Transportation global business units to provide the technical and administrative resources to execute these multiple contracts while remaining fully compliant with all applicable federal laws, policies, and procedures. Multiple federal government agencies, including the Department of Defense, USAID, and the Department of State, were all involved in developing the requests for bids, awarding contracts, and project administration. Throughout 2003 and 2004, Parsons' teams remained fluid to adapt to the project and customer needs as the roles changed between the various government agencies tasked with managing the reconstruction program.

In April 2003, the Army Corps of Engineers' Engineering and Support Center in Huntsville, Alabama, selected Parsons as one of four contractors to support its worldwide mission for ordnance and explosive cleanup.[149] In August 2003, it turned to Parsons to provide engineering and logistics support for four unexploded ordnance contractors charged with the collection, inventory, and disposition of enemy munitions discovered and captured by coalition forces. This contract was initially termed the Captured Enemy Ammunition program and was subsequently renamed the Coalition Munitions Clearance project. Unserviceable or unstable munitions were destroyed and those that remained were stockpiled under the United States' control until they could be safely transferred to Iraqi military and security forces. Parsons provided engineering, management, contract administration, and logistics support to the three unexploded ordnance contractors who were tasked with processing, transporting, and final disposition of the weapons. When the initial contract reached its funding ceiling in late

2003, the contract was again opened up for competition and Parsons won the re-bid.[150]

In January 2004, the Army Corps of Engineers awarded a contract for the restoration of the oil infrastructure in northern Iraq to a joint venture between Parsons and Parsons E&C. On the joint venture team, Parsons E&C was supported by the Worley Group, an Australian firm with worldwide experience in design and construction of oil and gas facilities, and was responsible for rebuilding Iraq's refining facilities and pipelines to regain pre-war oil production levels.[151]

The contract had an $800 million ceiling and involved extinguishing oil well fires; environmental studies and oil site cleanup; oil infrastructure condition assessments; engineering, design, and construction to restore the infrastructure to a safe operating condition; oil field, pipeline, and refinery maintenance; procurement and importation of fuel products; distribution of oil products within Iraq; and technical assistance to Iraqi oil companies.

The oil restoration contract was followed by the January 2004 announcement that Parsons, as a subcontractor to Bechtel, would participate in a $1.8 billion USAID contract for the second phase of the Iraqi infrastructure reconstruction to manage reconstruction of potable water and wastewater collection, treatment, and distribution systems.[152]

March 2004 saw the award of several large contracts for Iraq reconstruction that would test Parsons' agility and resourcefulness as the corporation mobilized to meet the urgent demands of the federal government in its reconstruction efforts.

A design-build security and justice infrastructure contract with a ceiling of $900 million was received in mid-March. The scope involved the rehabilitation and construction of facilities throughout Iraq, including 124 border control stations, 70 fire stations, three courthouses, and two large prisons. In compliance with client intent, Parsons subcontracted the majority of the construction work, as well as some of the design effort, to Iraqi firms and suppliers. In announcing the contract award, Marty Fabrick, executive vice president, stated, "Parsons has leveraged its experience in Iraq with demonstrated capabilities for development of military, security, and justice facilities. Our management approach is to quickly mobilize project development teams and deliver rapid results utilizing local Iraqi firms and people."[153]

One of the first projects Parsons completed in Iraq was part of the phased rebuilding of the Taji Military Base, a strategic installation located northwest of Baghdad, which had been devastated by looting and neglect. In March 2004, under its Air Force worldwide environmental restoration and construction contract, Parsons managed the Taji facility's restoration, which now accommodates several brigades of the new Iraqi Army. The scope of work included the renovation and construction of more than 180 buildings in three distinct areas of the base. Parsons hired more than 3,000 subcontracted Iraqi craftsmen and laborers on this project to help put unemployed local nationals to work. Despite the speed of the reconstruction effort, this program was carried out with an exceptional safety record and no serious injuries.[154]

Parsons oversaw captured munitions in Iraq and ensured they were either properly disposed of or securely stored for use by the new Iraqi military.

Also in March 2004, Parsons received a design-build contract with a $500 million ceiling to rebuild Iraqi public buildings, plus the country's education and health infrastructure. Years of neglect and two wars had left the nation's health and educational facilities in a shambles, and most government buildings had been damaged during years of wars and/or looted following the 2003 conflict. No hospitals had been built in Iraq since 1984.

Parsons was responsible for the design and construction of 150 primary healthcare clinics and 20 hospitals throughout Iraq. Parsons also repaired and renovated several large Iraqi Ministry buildings in Baghdad, allowing for the on-time transfer of administrative staffs and functions from the U.S. government to the Iraqi authorities.[155]

The final March 2004 award related to Iraq was a $28 million joint venture contract between Parsons and CH2M Hill to provide staff augmentation and support to the federal government in managing two large design-build water resource projects.[156] In all these contract awards, Parsons drew upon its roots in oil refinery design (through the 1937 BMP partnership of Steve Bechtel, John McCone, and Ralph Parsons), the 1953 groundwater survey conducted by RMP in Iraq, and its efforts in Kuwait and Saudi Arabia during the Gulf War.[157]

Of course, rebuilding any nation after a conflict or natural disaster presents a unique set of challenges.

The International Division, managed by retired U.S. Air Force Major General Earnest Robbins, is responsible for Parsons' Iraqi contracts with a total ceiling exceeding $2 billion. Earnie is a senior vice president and served 34 years in the Air Force before joining Parsons in 2003.[158] His Middle East sector manager for the initial phases of reconstruction was Karsten Rothenberg. Prior to this assignment, Karsten was the construction program manager for the State of New Jersey's emissions program and assistant manager for the BellSouth engineering contract.[159] Karsten is a retired Air Force colonel and is presently providing management support to Parsons' Air Force contracts.

Karsten was a member of the original Parsons team to go to Iraq after the fall of the Saddam Hussein government. He was joined by Ken Deagon and Phil Nixon to provide logistical support for several other Army Corps of Engineers contractors who were to collect, inventory, and dispose of captured enemy munitions throughout the country. Ken is a vice president who joined Parsons in 1981. He previously managed the corporation's Middle East operations and was the former technical manager of construction engineering.[160] Phil Nixon came to Parsons in 1987 and was the project manager on many of the corporation's significant unexploded ordnance or decontamination and decommissioning programs.[161] Karsten recalled the Iraqi contract startup:

When we arrived to begin the munitions clearance program, the coalition forces gave us permission to sleep on the veranda of one of Saddam's palaces during our first week. We then moved to Camp Victory [adjacent to Baghdad International Airport] and lived in tents from August through November 2003. We never saw a drop of rain. On many days the temperature was 125 to 130 degrees Fahrenheit. Never saw a drop of rain from the time we got up in the morning to the time we went to bed at night. Ken, Phil, and I worked to staff the program, implement procedures, award subcontracts, execute procurements, and begin construction.

I visited every potential site we considered suitable to store the salvageable munitions, and went to many of the places where they were found buried in the desert or stored in hospitals, schools, and bunkers. A high percentage of the munitions had deteriorated over time and couldn't be salvaged, but they still could be used for IEDs [Improvised Explosive Devises]. We made sure they were disposed of properly. To get to these sites, we spent a lot of time flying in Army helicopters. We also purchased vehicles in Kuwait and drove them into Iraq with a military escort on the same route the Army had used several months earlier to enter the country. When we first went over, I felt cautious, but never uncomfortable. Since then the security situation has deteriorated to the point we now travel only in armored vehicles and with a security force.[162]

Karsten summarized Parsons' participation in the reconstruction efforts:

We have a lot of Parsons' people working very hard who deserve all the credit we can give them—

CORPORATE PHILANTHROPY AND COMMUNITY INVOLVEMENT

SINCE ITS INCEPTION, PARSONS HAS given back to the communities in which it works. From hosting blood drives, funding scholarships, and participating in the United Way, the corporation quietly and consistently supports local and national charities.

A long-standing corporate tradition within Parsons is its annual golf tournament on behalf of the American Cancer Society of San Gabriel/Pomona Valley. In 1975, Parsons began hosting The Tournament for Life at Pasadena's Brookside Golf Course, which is adjacent to the Rose Bowl. Proceeds benefit cancer research, patient services, education, and advocacy. Parsons' staff, clients, and subcontractors participate in the day-long event, which has raised approximately $3 million dollars.[1]

A letter from the American Cancer Society to Jim McNulty, CEO, and Mike D'Antuono, president of Parsons Constructors Inc. and chair of the tournament, thanked Parsons for its involvement with the organization's activities:

> *Parsons' support is assisting in the achievement of our 2015 goals. Parsons' philanthropy reflects the highest excellence in the corporate community.*[2]

Parsons hosts an annual holiday party for children supported by Five Acres, The Sycamores, and Rosemary Children's Services. Five Acres is a nonsectarian abuse and neglect prevention, treatment, and education center. The Sycamores offers the highest caliber of mental health services to more than 1,500 children. Rosemary Children's Services is a residential treatment center for the abused and neglected. Each December, Parsons' staff purchase gifts, bring cookies, and celebrate the season with these children. Nick Presecan, former Parsons' senior vice president, always played Santa.[3]

For more than a decade, the CSDP staff made yearly donations of new toys and clothing for the children at the USC Women's and Children's Hospital in Los Angeles. In Newport, Indiana, Parsons' staff who engineered and built the chemical demilitarization plant is actively involved in helping those in need.[4] Since the project started in 1999, the Newport team has contributed a total of $50,000 in cash and merchandise to local families and schools. They have purchased winter coats, hats, gloves, and toys for children during the holidays and give an average of 36 pints of blood to the American Red Cross every two months.[5]

Nick Presecan, senior vice president, was aptly named. He became St. Nick to the many children attending Parsons' holiday events held on their behalf.

From Russia, With Love

In Russia, Parsons' chemical demilitarization staff has made similar contributions. They have created a charity fund that has directly benefited local families by raising almost $10,000 of non-cash donations. In 2004, Parsons' Moscow and Volgograd personnel attended the annual holiday show at the Rassvet orphanage in Shchuch'ye. During the event, they donated food items, sweets, presents, and 5,000 rubles to the organization.[6]

Tournament of Roses

One of the most memorable community events Parsons participated in was its entry in the 1999 Tournament of Roses Parade, televised on New Year's Day from Pasadena and seen by millions around the globe. Parsons entered a float that depicted a whimsical construction crane and crew that moved gigantic alphabet blocks.[7] The staff volunteered to engineer the animation and decorate every square inch of the entry with flowers. Brent Harvey, vice president, drove it down the parade route. Children of Parsons' clients rode on the float and waved to the crowds. Brent recalled the preparation and events of the day:

> *I spent hours learning how to maneuver the large and cumbersome float prior to the parade. There's not a lot of visibility. You basically drive the float lying on your stomach looking directly ahead through a 6-inch by 4-inch slot. The tensest moment was at the start of the parade where there is a 90-degree uphill turn from Orange Grove onto Colorado Boulevard. Parsons has grandstand seats directly on that corner, and I kept saying to myself, "Don't stall, and don't hit anybody." We made it around the corner without a hitch, and the rest of the parade went just fine. Everybody involved did a great job.*[8]

Brent, a chemical engineer with 15 years of experience at Parsons, has worked in environmental project management, Latin American operations, finance, and project development.[9]

Parsons' community involvement takes many different forms. For example, approximately 15 of Parsons' technical staff volunteer their time to teach science and engineering to middle school students as part of the Future Scientists and Engineers of America. Parsons' volunteer program coordinator with this organization is Brynna McNulty. [No relation to Parsons' CEO, Jim McNulty.][10] Brynna is an environmental scientist who has assisted in the port of Long Beach's Gerald Desmond Bridge replacement project and has developed storm water discharge protection permit plans for Sempra Energy.[11]

Pasadena Pops Orchestra Concert for Middle Schoolers

Jim McNulty, CEO, believes strongly in the benefit of music education. Parsons, in conjunction with the Pasadena Pops Orchestra, has sponsored a three-year outreach program at Blair Middle School to provide music education. Since 2000, Parsons underwrites a free, annual Pasadena Pops concert, which has been held on the steps of Pasadena's City Hall each summer. The concert also includes the participation of the Occidental College Master Chorale and local school bands. This event was the brainchild of Jim's wife, Judy McNulty, who passed away in 2003; the maestra of the Pasadena Pops, Rachael Worby; and Jim. Parsons' staff volunteer as ushers and provide general information to the concert attendees.[12]

In 1999, Parsons' floral-covered float in the Tournament of Roses parade captured children's playful construction efforts with an animated crane that moved colorful alphabet blocks.

many are new to the company. Our teams are motivated, and morale is good, which I attribute to our safety and security programs. The major difficulty for our staff is scheduling. They can spend days and days waiting for a road or checkpoint to be opened to get to a construction site. They are also involved in eight of the most highly scrutinized and audited government programs in history, which adds pressure.

But, I know many of our people enjoy meeting the Iraqi people and seeing the progress being made. The moments that have meant the most to me are seeing a child entering a hospital we've reconstructed or a community finally having a reliable water and wastewater treatment plant that we've built. These programs are contributing immensely to the well-being of the Iraqi people.[163]

Earnie Robbins recounted his first visit to the Iraq reconstruction program offices in November 2003:

I came into the country just as Karsten was leaving, a few days before Thanksgiving, and at the time President Bush made a surprise visit with the troops. Jim Trash [senior vice president of government relations] accompanied me. When we arrived at Camp Victory it was at night in a driving rain storm. We had gone into the parking lot to call corporate headquarters on our satellite phones and let them know we had arrived safely. Jim and I were standing in the parking lot in our flak jackets and helmets when a rocket or mortar round exploded nearby. Jim, who had no previous military experience, was instantly very alert. He took cover beneath a truck. Fortunately, no one was hurt, and we actually had a good laugh after it was all over.

During my trips to Iraq, I've met with retired Rear Admiral Dave Nash, who was the architect of the U.S. government's reconstruction program, and General [George] Casey, the commanding U.S. general of the Multi-National Force in Iraq. I had known both of them during my active duty days, and I respected both of them for their commitment and valued their opinions. Both expressed their satisfaction with Parsons and the other contractors involved in the reconstruction efforts and made it a point to compliment us for the role we played in helping restore Iraq's infrastructure and institutions.[164]

In April and May of 2004, Earnie Robbins and Jim Thrash represented Parsons on a tour sponsored by the U.S. State Department, Department of Commerce, Department of Defense, and the governments of the coalition forces to publicize the business and contractual opportunities that were available through the large American contractors tasked with managing the Iraq reconstruction effort. Earnie described the experience:

We called the tour the "Iraq Road Show." Events were scheduled simultaneously, so Jim went to Philadelphia, Rome, and Istanbul while I went to Dubai, Amman, Seoul, and Sidney. We made presentations on the scope of Parsons' Iraq contracts, where we needed support, and answered a thousand questions. I was gone 12 days and literally went around the world.[165]

Further Federal Contracts

In 2004, the Army Corps of Engineers in Huntsville, Alabama, selected Parsons for a five-year contract to perform worldwide munitions response services at former Department of Defense sites, active installations, base realignment and closure sites, and property adjoining installations, as well as for other U.S. government agencies or foreign governments. Parsons and Huntsville have a professional relationship that spans over 20 years.

At the time of the award, Jack Scott, former president of Parsons Infrastructure and Technology Group and now corporate president and COO, was quoted as saying, "This contract gives us the welcome opportunity to continue managing an important program that secures and destroys conventional weapons and equipment, which otherwise could be used against our troops or cause death or injury to innocent civilians."[166]

Tom Roell, who succeeded Jack as president of Parsons Infrastructure and Technology Group, has taken on the task of further developing federal programs including Department of Defense, Department of Energy, and USAID. Prior to this appointment, Tom was a senior vice president and managed the operations of Parsons' construction and fabrication services.

Before joining Parsons in 2003, Tom was president of Fluor Federal Services and also held

JACK SCOTT
PRESIDENT AND COO

JACK SCOTT CAME TO PARSONS IN 1985 and through his efforts cornered the market in chemical agent neutralization plant design and engineering. His drive and energy caught the attention of Ray Judson, who was RMP's Systems Division manager. At that time, Jack was a civilian managing the U.S. Army's initial chemical weapons demilitarization program when Parsons became involved in Johnston Atoll. Ray recruited and hired him knowing that Jack would enhance Parsons' future opportunities in this market. Ray said, "Jack is an expert on incinerators and the recovery processes involved in agent disposal [and] the mechanical systems that pull out the artillery shell detonators."[1]

Jack recalled his early experience at Parsons:

I had completed graduate school at Texas A&M in engineering and was thinking about the next opportunity. Parsons was a subcontractor on Johnston Atoll. I liked the company. We had a good relationship. After joining Parsons, my first assignment was business development. At that time, I saw the chemical demilitarization market expanding. I started focusing on ordnance removal programs—like Kaho`olawe [Island]—and international demilitarization in Russia, both of which we eventually won.[2]

By 1996, Jack was heavily entrenched in developing the sales strategies to win these and other federal programs. When Len Pieroni died and Jim McNulty became CEO, Jack's abilities to win megaprojects gave those involved in these efforts a sense of optimism and responsibility for creating the corporation's future. Jack discussed this period:

It was personally a very difficult time for me, but it taught me not to focus so much on my own goals and objectives, [rather] than on corporate goals and objectives. You've got to go in with the right attitude, accept responsibility, and figure out how to move forward. That was an important lesson, if not in my life, in my career.[3]

Jack became Parsons Infrastructure and Technology Group's executive vice president and then its president in 2002. Of Jack's accomplishments, Jim McNulty said, "Under his leadership, Parsons Infrastructure and Technology Group experienced significant growth and aggressively [pursued] new business."[4] When Frank DeMartino retired in 2004, Jack was appointed by the board of directors as Parsons' corporate president and COO. When his promotion was publicly announced, a key member of Jack's management team, John Stewart, who is the Chemical Demilitarization Division manager and the former USAID Bosnia program manager, as well as a world-traveling fly fisherman, jokingly said, "He's the best choice and has the best interest of the company at heart—and I still enjoy fishing with him."[5]

It is Jack's ability to build an enthusiastic, loyal team that is willing to take ownership and go the extra mile to win that led Chuck Terhune III, vice president and project manager, to state, "Of all the senior executives, Jack reminds me the most of Ralph Parsons."[6]

Jack Scott, COO and president of Parsons Corporation, is a leader who has positively influenced the firm's success in the past two decades and is strategically planning for its continued growth and stability.

several senior executive positions at Fluor in its government, environmental, and power groups. Tom holds his bachelor's degree in electrical engineering from The Pennsylvania State University and began his career engineering nuclear and industrial plants.[167]

In explaining his reasons for coming to the corporation, Tom stated, "Parsons has built a 60-year reputation based upon dependability and competently managing some of the world's most challenging projects."[168] The corporation clearly has a commitment to the federal market and is poised for continuing its legacy of technical excellence on governmental programs.

Parsons Evergreene LLC

In 2004, Parsons entered into a joint venture and acquired 50 percent of the assets of Evergreene Construction (Evergreene), based in Salt Lake City, Utah. The purpose of this investment was to aid the corporation in securing military housing, infrastructure, and security system projects. The two firms had been working together on more than 50 projects prior to the formation of Parsons Evergreene LLC, the name of the joint venture.

Evergreene specialized in residential design and construction, and Parsons had large federal program management experience. One of the joint venture's first contracts was with the U.S. Air Force, which entailed 24 projects at 19 bases. Christopher Nielson, the founder of Evergreene Construction, stated that Parsons was well-placed to handle the work:

> *Some contracts allow for over 1,000 homes to be replaced at a single installation. I know of no other firm that's better prepared to step up to this challenge.*[169]

In 2005, Parsons acquired the remaining assets of Parsons Evergreene LLC, which created a solely owned subsidiary.[170]

WorleyParsons USA

The venture between Worley and Parsons E&C on the Iraq oil contract proved to be quite auspicious for the next chapter of Parsons' corporate evolution. The energy and chemical markets were the backbone of the founding of Parsons, and they remained so until the late 1980s. At that time, there was a decided turn in procurement within the petroleum companies that favored fixed-price agreements, not time and material contracts that had been the standard payment model.

Parsons E&C was awarded many fixed-price contracts and, in order to remain profitable, had to develop an overhead structure that fit this pricing structure. This required a complete shift in how Parsons managed petroleum projects. It required tighter schedules, extremely accurate projections of man hours, and restricted the engineers' abilities to make modifications. In addition, the sheer volume of Parsons E&C's fixed-price contracts required a significant amount of the corporation's cash flow to float Parsons E&C's operations and procurement needs between payments. The challenges of working within this pricing model were compounded when the petroleum industry began to slow down facility refurbishment and construction. After a decade of fixed-price contracts and market slowdown, Parsons made a decision to sell Parsons E&C in 1999, if a reputable buyer could be found.

Parsons' management then began to focus on its other business units, which were showing greater potential for growth and profitability. Over the course of the next two years, Parsons entertained several offers, but none came to fruition. Then Jim McNulty, CEO, and Curt Bower, CFO, came up with a brilliant solution of separating Parsons E&C's operations from the rest of the corporation. In 2001, Parsons sold Parsons E&C to the ESOP, in the form of a loan that would be paid back to Parsons by Parsons E&C.

Bill Hall became Parsons E&C's CEO, and the organization formed its own independent board of directors that included Parsons' representatives—Frank DeMartino, COO, and Jim Shappell, president of Parsons Transportation Group. This allowed Parsons E&C to operate as a stand-alone company that could manage its own resources and market response. This separation took many long-term staff members some time to adjust to, considering Parsons E&C had strong sentimental value; it had been the essence of the corporation for so many years. It was difficult for them to realize they were now only linked together by the ESOP. However, the sale to the ESOP provided shareholder continuity, to the benefit of Parsons E&C employees, and the two entities continued to exchange services as Parsons E&C began paying back the ESOP loan to Parsons ahead of schedule.

After working with Parsons E&C on the Iraq oil field contract, Worley tendered an offer to purchase Parsons E&C in 2004 and created WorleyParsons USA, with Bill Hall remaining as its CEO. The sale made perfect sense for all three parties—Worley, Parsons E&C, and the ESOP. This sale was one of the most defining moments in the direction of the corporation's future. It clearly sent a message that Parsons was focused on widening capabilities in what had historically been tangential markets of transportation, government, and commercial advanced technology. At the time it was purchased, Parsons E&C had in excess of 5,400 personnel in 16 countries and operated in many regions where Worley did not have a presence or sought further growth. Although there are no financial ties between WorleyParsons USA and Parsons, they share 60 years of corporate history.[171]

Acquisitions and New Global Business Unit

The sale of Parsons E&C resulted in Parsons' financial ability to obtain strategic acquisitions that supported growth in key markets. Two firms were acquired in April 2005—RCI, a construction firm, and Alaris Group LLC, a wireless telecommunications site development service provider. Alaris was purchased to augment Parsons' strong position in the telecommunications market with 100 additional market experts. At the point of acquiring Alaris, Parsons had been ranked No. 1 in telecommunications design for five consecutive years by *Engineering News-Record*. Alaris had been a joint venture partner with Parsons in a wireless network implementation services company: EXI Parsons Telecom LLC. Amy Stanton, founder and principal, was quoted at the time of the purchase. "This acquisition offers greater value to our clients and growth opportunities for our staff."[172]

RCI was an all-cash sale that included both Robison Construction Inc. and RCI Environmental Inc., two separate operating companies, and over 400 pieces of heavy construction equipment in Washington, Oregon, and Hawaii. When asked why he sold his company, Mark Robison, founder and chairman, explained, "The synergies of the two companies are unbelievable. You couldn't ask for a better match. Both cultures, including safety standards, are mirror images of each other."[173]

That same year, Parsons decided to merge RCI's capabilities with Hennigh and Parsons Evergreene into one global business unit to focus on construction in the areas of water, transportation, infrastructure, and civic projects. The unit is named Parsons Construction Group and also supports the corporation's overall environmental site remediation, as well as its commercial and residential development abilities. Andrew Albrecht is its president. Andrew was RCI's president.[174]

RCI was acquired by Parsons in 2005 for its construction abilities and heavy equipment, as depicted on this project in San Island. RCI also performed earthwork and construction tasks on the United States' first chemical weapons destruction plant, Johnston Atoll, on which Parsons provided engineering and design services.

The Future

By expanding its services into specific growth markets, Parsons generated contract revenues of $2.4 billion in 2004, compared to $1.6 billion in 1996.[175] To continue this growth into the future, Jim McNulty studies economic trends and believes Parsons' core engineering and construction services should represent 60 percent to 70 percent of the corporation's total project backlog. As such, he challenges the staff to broaden their capabilities in service offerings. He likens this marketing approach to the sport of rock climbing, where the athlete searches for the next foot hold or hand hold to ascend—that is, to seek out the next service or program that will propel Parsons to the top. Jim summarized this philosophy:

> *As the world's economy shifts, we're shifting with it.*[176]

Prior to his retirement in 2004, Frank DeMartino, former president and COO, predicted "a more prominent position in transportation." He explained:

> *I think we're going to continue to lead that industry and become even a bigger factor in it. There's a tremendous market for water development, transmission, desalination, you name it. I wouldn't be surprised if over the next 10 or 15 years water becomes the big driver within the corporation.*[177]

Jack Scott, who succeeded Frank, discussed the main "drivers" that propelled Parsons forward through previous decades:

> *In our industry, look at each decade. It's amazing that each decade had some driver. In terms of the 1960s, it was pretty much driven by world events, and our business was driven by post–World War II expansion, the Vietnam War, and military expansion. The 1970s were driven by alternative energy and energy crisis that fueled our business. In the 1980s, [President Ronald] Reagan came in, defense became big again and fueled our industry. The economy of the 1990s was fueled, to a large extent, by the "dot-coms" and the information technology people.*
>
> *I think 2000–2010 is going to be strong because of homeland security and aging infrastructure. Once again, we're into the market and economic drivers, domestically and somewhat on a worldwide basis, that will fuel our industry. Parsons is well positioned to plan, design, and construct infrastructure for the alternative fuel industry as non-carbon-based energy sources become available; facilities that will be required in the United States [as] its population ages; [communication/IT] infrastructure as technology and software application advances are made; and manufacturing plants as*

Whether it is engineering or constructing infrastructure aboveground, belowground, or in austere and/or extreme environments, Parsons' corporate values such as its emphasis on worker safety are the reasons it has become and will remain a global leader.

global disposable income increases the demand for consumer goods, internationally.[178]

Jim McNulty believes the international market, long a Parsons' strength, will prove to become even more essential to the corporation in future years:

There are many needs for which our particular spectrum of services is attuned. To be balanced, as we need to be, we must serve overseas markets as well as domestic markets.

Parsons is no longer in the business of providing just engineering and construction "man hour"–based services. Today, we are in the business of satisfying our clients' needs by providing them with single, unified, all-inclusive, total solutions. Our aim is to form a seamless partnership with our customers so that their requirements become our challenges and our multidiscipline capabilities provide their solutions.[179]

An All-American Story of Remarkable Achievement and Growth

In many ways, Parsons is the story of America in post–World War II—bold, innovative, entrepreneurial, idealistic, and eternally optimistic. Parsons has always been eager to accept new challenges, regardless of technical or logistical difficulties. Time and again, Parsons has shown there is no project too big or too complex for it to manage and complete. Its corporate résumé spans water distribution systems, refineries, petroleum and chemical plants, mining, missile defense, airports, power plants, roads, bridges, subway systems, railroads, dams, cities, schools, hospitals, homeland defense, pharmaceutical plants, environmental cleanup, and chemical demilitarization. This remarkable diversity provides ample evidence of Parsons' significant contributions in building the world's infrastructure and improving the quality of life for generations to come.

If alive today, Ralph Parsons—who relied on "knowledge, guts, and confidence" to build his company—would be extremely proud of the corporation that still bears his name and its employees who believe in its core values of safety, integrity, innovation, respect, diversity, and competence.[180] From his initial "intention of operating a small business,"[181] Parsons has grown into a formidable global organization, employing thousands of professionals and working on an impressive array of projects throughout the world. It is a corporation offering an ever-expanding range of technical and management services to an increasingly diverse group of customers. Parsons is perhaps best defined as the preeminent firm in developing first-of-a-kind, one-of-a-kind solutions.

Notes to Sources

Chapter One

1. James E. Halferty, "Foreign Operations, or Life Without Father," Parsons Corporation Archives.
2. Jeannette Edwards Rattray, *East Hampton History and Genealogies*.
3. "Looking Them Over," *East Hampton Star*, 15 June 1972.
4. *Los Angeles Times*, 14 November 1963.
5. Letter from Vivian Parsons to Ralph Parsons, 22 June 1967.
6. "Looking Them Over," *East Hampton Star*, 15 June 1972.
7. Ibid.
8. *Los Angeles Times*, 14 November 1963.
9. "Looking Them Over," *East Hampton Star*, 15 June 1972.
10. Letter from Vivian Parsons to Ralph Parsons, 22 June 1967.
11. "The Ralph M. Parsons Company History," Parsons Corporation Archives.
12. *The East Hampton Star*, 3 August 1917.
13. Letter, Pratt Institute President Francis H. Horn to Ralph Parsons, 17 April 1957.
14. "The Ralph M. Parsons Company History," Parsons Corporation Archives.
15. "Ralph Parsons: An Engineer Who Made a Mountain Out of a Molehill," *Los Angeles Times*, 27 November 1966.
16. Ibid.
17. "The Ralph M. Parsons Company History," Parsons Corporation Archives.
18. Junius B. Wood, "Seeing America from the 'Shenandoah'," *National Geographic*, January 1925.
19. "The Ralph M. Parsons Company History," Parsons Corporation Archives.
20. Ibid.
21. Program notes, Eighth Annual Golden Beaver Awards Dinner, Los Angeles, 17 January 1963.
22. "Ralph Parsons: An Engineer Who Made a Mountain Out of a Molehill," *Los Angeles Times*, 27 November 1966.
23. Program notes, Eighth Annual Golden Beaver Awards Dinner, Los Angeles, 17 January 1963.
24. "The Ralph M. Parsons Company History," Parsons Corporation Archives.
25. Letter from Milton Lewis to Ralph Parsons, 22 June 1967.
26. "The Ralph M. Parsons Company History," Parsons Corporation Archives.
27. Letter from Milton Lewis to Ralph Parsons, 22 June 1967.
28. "The Ralph M. Parsons Company History," Parsons Corporation Archives.
29. Ibid.
30. Ibid.
31. Letter from Milton Lewis to Ralph Parsons, 22 June 1967.
32. *Western Construction*, February 1963.
33. "The Ralph M. Parsons Company History," Parsons Corporation Archives.
34. "Ralph Parsons: An Engineer Who Made a Mountain Out of a Molehill," *Los Angeles Times*, 27 November 1966.
35. Memo from Ralph M. Parsons, 9 October 1964.

Chapter Two

1. Robert L. Ingram, *A Builder & His Family*, 105.
2. John McCone, interviews by the Institute of International Studies, the University of California at Berkeley, 15 October 1987, 3 December 1987, and 21 April 1988.
3. Bechtel Corporation, *Bechtel 1898–1998: Building a Century*.
4. Parsons Corporation Archives.
5. Bechtel Corporation, *Bechtel 1898–1998: Building a Century*.
6. Ibid.
7. *Fortune*, March 1942.
8. Ibid., July 1942.
9. "The Day of Infamy," *Waterways Journal*, 30 December 1991.
10. Ibid.
11. Laton McCartney, *Friends in High Places, The Bechtel Story* (New

York, NY: Simon & Schuster, 1988).
12. Bechtel Corporation, *Bechtel 1898–1998: Building a Century.*
13. www.usmm.org/libertyships.html.
14. Bechtel Corporation, *Bechtel 1898–1998: Building a Century,* and www.usmm.org/libertyships.html.
15. Bechtel Corporation, *Bechtel 1898–1998: Building a Century.*
16. www.emuseum.org/virtual_museum/evansville.shipyard/shipyardimg2.html.
17. www.navsource.org/Archives/10/160157.htm.
18. Parsons Corporation Archives.
19. Laton McCartney, *Friends in High Places, The Bechtel Story,* 64.
20. www.yukonheritage.com.
21. Parsons Corporation Archives.
22. "Parsons and Alaska," *The Parsons Magazine,* No. 40.
23. Ibid.
24. www.yukonheritage.com.
25. Laton McCartney, *Friends in High Places, The Bechtel Story,* 64.
26. Ibid.
27. www.yukonheritage.com.
28. Donald E. Wolf, *Big Dams and Other Dreams, the Six Companies Story* (Norman, OK: University of Oklahoma Press, 1996), 155.
29. Ibid., 156.
30. Ibid., 157.
31. Ibid.
32. *Birmingham News,* 9 January 1944.
33. Robert Salvadore, telephone interview by Parsons Corporation, 29 July 2005.
34. Ibid.
35. Parsons Corporation Archives.

Chapter Three

1. James E. Halferty, "Foreign Operations, or Life Without Father," Parsons Corporation Archives, 11, 12.
2. Ralph M. Parsons quote from "A Place in the Sun," Pratt Institute's honorary doctorate award program.
3. "The Ralph M. Parsons Company History," Parsons Corporation Archives.
4. Advertisement, Parsons Corporation Archives.
5. Complete Job Listings, Job No. 501 through 5,421, 1944–1974, Parsons Corporation Archives.
6. *Parsons News and Views,* No. 19, 2.
7. Parsons Corporation Archives.
8. Parsons Project Archives, LiveLink (Parsons Corporation's private Intranet).
9. Parsons Corporation Archives.
10. Parsons Corporation Archives, LiveLink (Parsons Corporation's private Intranet).
11. Stan Goldhaber, interview by Richard F. Hubbard, audio recording, 10 September 2003, Write Stuff Enterprises.
12. Parsons nuclear project experience description, LiveLink (Parsons Corporation's private Intranet).
13. Ray De Clue, interview by Richard F. Hubbard, digital recording, 11 September 2003, Write Stuff Enterprises.
14. Complete Job Listing, Job No. 501 through 5,421, 1944–1974, Parsons Corporation Archives.
15. Keith Timlin, interview by Richard F. Hubbard, audio recording, 23 October 2003, Write Stuff Enterprises.
16. Timlin interview.
17. David Halberstam, *The Fifties* (New York, NY: Ballantine Books, 1994), 132.
18. "Highlights of the 1940s," Parsons Corporation Archives.
19. David Halberstam, *The Fifties* (New York, NY: Ballantine Books, 1994), 135.
20. Ibid., 137.
21. Parsons Corporation Archives.
22. Bill Opel, interview by Jeffrey L. Rodengen, digital recording, 29 March 2004, Write Stuff Enterprises.
23. Dan Frost, interview by Richard F. Hubbard, digital recording, 8 September 2003, Write Stuff Enterprises.
24. Parsons Corporation employee records.
25. The Ralph M. Parsons Foundation, www.rmpf.org.
26. Parsons Corporation Project Archives and Dr. Jim Holwerda, telephone interview, 30 August 2004.
27. James. E. Halferty, "Foreign Operations, or Life Without Father," Parsons Corporation Archives, 43.
28. Ibid., 44.
29. Dr. Jim Holwerda, telephone interview, 30 August 2004, and 10, 16, and 21 September 2004.
30. Ibid.
31. Milton Rote obituary, provided by the Rote family, Parsons Corporation Archives.
32. Dr. Jim Holwerda, telephone interview, 30 August 2004, and 10, 16, and 21 September 2004.
33. Ibid.
34. Ibid.
35. Ibid.
36. Ibid.
37. Ibid.
38. Ibid.
39. Ibid.
40. Bill Hall, interview by Richard F. Hubbard, digital recording, 7 October 2003, Write Stuff Enterprises.
41. James. E. Halferty, "Foreign Operations, or Life Without Father," Parsons Corporation Archives, 35.
42. Parsons Corporation Archives.
43. Dante Boccalero, interview by Jeffrey L. Rodengen, digital recording, 14 December 2003, Write Stuff Enterprises.
44. Boccalero interview.

Chapter Three Sidebar: Water Resources

1. *Parsons News & Views,* 1969, No. 19, 8.
2. Dr. Jim Holwerda, interview by Richard F. Hubbard, digital recording, 18 November 2003, Write Stuff Enterprises.
3. Parsons USAID Project Archives, LiveLink (Parsons Corporation's private Intranet).
4. James E. Halferty, "Foreign Operations, or Life Without Father," Parsons Corporation Archives, 127.
5. Frank DeMartino, interview by Jeffrey L. Rodengen, digital recording, 10 July 2003, Write Stuff Enterprises.
6. www.parsons.com.
7. Ibid.

Chapter Three Sidebar: Sulfur Recovery

1. Roland E. Meissner, telephone interview by Mickey Murphy, Write Stuff Enterprises.
2. Ibid.
3. Charles Terhune III, email correspondence, 8 October 2004.
4. Ibid.
5. Judith Herman, Parsons internal interview, 5 October, 2004.

Chapter Three Sidebar: Batman Refinery

1. *Parsons News & Views*, No. 19, 12.
2. Ibid., 13.
3. James E. Halferty, "Foreign Operations, or Life Without Father," Parsons Corporation Archives, 100.
4. Ibid.
5. Ibid.
6. Ibid., 100–101.
7. Ibid., 101.

Chapter Four

1. Corporate History—25-Year Anniversary, 1969 Parsons Annual Report.
2. David Goodrich, interview by Jeffrey L. Rodengen, digital recording, 30 May 30 2003, Write Stuff Enterprises.
3. Interoffice correspondence from Ralph Parsons to all officers, 28 January 1956.
4. Ed Cramsie, interview by Jeffrey L. Rodengen digital recording, 1 July 2003, Write Stuff Enterprises.
5. Ed Cramsie, Parsons employee records.
6. The Ralph M. Parsons Company History, Parsons Corporation Archives.
7. Dr. Jim Holwerda, telephone interview, 30 August 2004, and 10, 16, and 21 September 2004.
8. *Parsons News & Views*, 1969, No. 19, 7.
9. Knisely Dreher, Parsons employee records.
10. Knisely Dreher, interview by Richard Hubbard digital recording, 9 September 2003, Write Stuff Enterprises.
11. Memo from Ralph M. Parsons, 3 June 1965, Parsons Corporation Archives.
12. Ibid.
13. "A Guide For Project Managers," Parsons Corporation Archives, 1.
14. Greg Pearson, interview by Richard Hubbard, digital recording, 17 September 2003, Write Stuff Enterprises.
15. Ibid.
16. Alan Duncan, interview by Richard Hubbard, digital recording, 31 October 2003, Write Stuff Enterprises.
17. Alan Duncan, Parsons employee records.
18. *Parsons News & Views*, No. 14, 2.
19. Ibid., 3.
20. *Parsons News & Views*, No. 34, 4.
21. Parsons Project Archives, LiveLink (Parsons Corporation's private Intranet).
22. 1969 Parsons Annual Report, 25-Year Anniversary, Corporate History.
23. Otha C. (Charlie) Roddey, Parsons employee records.
24. Otha C. (Charlie) Roddey, telephone interview, 4 May 2005.
25. Dr. Jim Holwerda, telephone interview, 30 August 2004, and 10, 16, and 21 September 2004.
26. Ibid.
27. Ibid.
28. www.powerhomebiz.com/Success/ludwig.htm.
29. Dr. Jim Holwerda, telephone interview, 30 August 2004 and 10, 16, and 21 September 2004.
30. Ibid.
31. Jess Burke, Parsons employee records.
32. Dr. Jim Holwerda, telephone interview, 30 August 2004, and 10, 16, and 21 September 2004.
33. Ibid.
34. Historic nuclear projects listing, Parsons Corporation Archives.
35. Parsons Corporation Archives, LiveLink (Parsons Corporation's private Intranet).
36. Ibid.
37. Historic nuclear projects listing, Parsons Corporation Archives.
38. Joe Volpe Jr., Parsons employee records.
39. James E. Halferty, "Foreign Operations, or Life Without Father," Parsons Corporation Archives, 347.
40. Ibid., 320–322.
41. Dr. Jim Holwerda, telephone interview, 30 August 2004, and 10, 16, and 21 September 2004.
42. James E. Halferty, "Foreign Operations, or Life Without Father," Parsons Corporation Archives, 253.
43. Parsons Corporation Archives.
44. www.nps.gov/mimi/history/srs/history.htm.
45. Ibid.
46. Ibid.
47. Ibid.
48. Ibid.
49. Parsons Corporation Archives.
50. Ibid.
51. Parsons Project Archives, LiveLink (Parsons Corporation's private Intranet).
52. www.usmint.gov.
53. Ibid.
54. Parsons Project Archives, LiveLink (Parsons Corporation's private Intranet).
55. www.usmint.gov.
56. Parsons-Jurden Archives, Parsons Corporation Archives.
57. Les Engle, interview by Richard F. Hubbard, digital recording, 6 November 2003, Write Stuff Enterprises.
58. *Parsons News & Views*, No. 19, 20.
59. Historical Highlights, Parsons Corporation Archives.
60. Les Engle, interview by Richard F. Hubbard, digital recording, 6 November 2003, Write Stuff Enterprises.
61. Parsons Corporation Archives.
62. "Ralph Parsons: An Engineer Who Made a Mountain Out of a Molehill," *Los Angeles Times*, 27 November 1966.
63. James E. Halferty, "Foreign Operations, or Life Without Father," Parsons Corporation Archives.

Chapter Four Sidebar: A Guide for Project Managers

1. "A Guide for Project Managers," Parsons Corporation Archives.

Chapter Four Sidebar: The *Argo*

1. "Facts About the *Argo*," Parsons Corporation Archives.
2. Ibid.
3. Ibid.
4. Jake Kostyzak, interview by Richard F. Hubbard, digital recording, 11 September 2003, Write Stuff Enterprises.
5. Graham Gosling, interview by Richard F. Hubbard, digital recording, 23 September 2003, Write Stuff Enterprises.

Chapter Four Sidebar: Memorable Affairs, Notable Guests

1. Sally Iott, interview by Richard F. Hubbard, digital recording, 3 October 2003, Write Stuff Enterprises.
2. Karl Drobny, interview by Richard F. Hubbard, digital recording,

24 September 2003, Write Stuff Enterprises.
3. Drobny interview.
4. James E. Halferty, "Foreign Operations or Life Without Father," Parsons Corporation Archives, 426.
5. Ibid, 429.
6. Karl Drobny, Parsons internal telephone interview, 9 September 2004.
7. Karl Drobny, interview by Richard F. Hubbard, digital recording, 24 September 2003, Write Stuff Enterprises.

Chapter Four Sidebar: The NAWAPA Story

1. *Parsons News & Views*, No. 33, 2.
2. "NAWAPA: Watering a Continent," *Newsweek*, 22 February 1965.
3. Ibid.
4. *Parsons News & Views*, No. 33, 3.

Chapter Five

1. "Ralph Parsons: An Engineer Who Made a Mountain Out of a Molehill," *Los Angeles Times*, 27 November 1966.
2. James E. Halferty, "Foreign Operations, or Life Without Father," Parsons Corporation Archives, 434.
3. Bill Leonhard, interview by Jeffrey L. Rodengen, digital recording, 10 July 2003, Write Stuff Enterprises.
4. Stan Goldhaber, interview by Richard F. Hubbard, digital recording, 10 September 2003, Write Stuff Enterprises.
5. Stan Goldhaber, Parsons employee records.
6. Stan Goldhaber, interview by Richard F. Hubbard, digital recording, 10 September 2003, Write Stuff Enterprises.
7. Bill Leonhard, interview by Jeffrey L. Rodengen, digital recording, 10 July 2003, Write Stuff Enterprises.
8. Parsons Corporation Archives.
9. Dan Frost, interview by Richard F. Hubbard, digital recording, 8 September 2003, Write Stuff Enterprises.
10. Harry Burton, Parsons employee records.
11. Ibid.
12. Robert Peaslee, Parsons employee records.
13. Parsons employee records.
14. *Parsons News & Views*, 1969, No. 19, 7.
15. 1971 Parsons Annual Report, 1.
16. Ibid.
17. Gary Stone, interview by Jeffrey L. Rodengen, digital recording, 30 May 2003, Write Stuff Enterprises.
18. PetroleumNews.com, "Arco, Humble Oil Discover the Prudhoe Bay Oilfield in 1968," week of 21 April 2002, www.petroleumnews.com.
19. Parsons North Slope Project Archives, LiveLink (Parsons Corporation's private Intranet).
20. James E. Halferty, "Foreign Operations, or Life Without Father," Parsons Corporation Archives, 307.
21. *Parsons News & Views*, No. 19, 13.
22. 1969 Parsons Annual Report.
23. Ibid.
24. George Glade, Parsons employee records.
25. William Glade, interview by Richard Hubbard, digital recording, 7 January 2004, Write Stuff Enterprises.
26. Vi Leslie, Parsons employee records
27. William Glade, interview by Richard Hubbard, digital recording, 7 January 2004, Write Stuff Enterprises.
28. Ibid.
29. 1970 Parsons Annual Report.
30. 1971 Parsons Annual Report.
31. Roland E. Meissner, telephone interview by Mickey Murphy, Write Stuff Enterprises.
32. 1972 Parsons Annual Report.
33. 1974 Parsons Annual Report.
34. 1969 Parsons Annual Report.
35. "The Ralph M. Parsons Company Comes to Asia," *Chemical Age of India*, February 1967.
36. Ibid.
37. 1973 Parsons Annual Report.
38. 1970 Parsons Annual Report.
39. 1973 Parsons Annual Report.
40. 1974 Parsons Annual Report.
41. 1972 Parsons Annual Report.
42. Stan Goldhaber, interview by Richard F. Hubbard, digital recording, 10 September 2003, Write Stuff Enterprises.
43. *Parsons News & Views*, No. 25.
44. Ibid.
45. Ibid.
46. Ibid.
47. 1969 Parsons Annual Report.
48. www.globalsecurity.org/military/facility/ingalls.htm.
49. Ibid.
50. 1969 and 1970 Parsons Annual Reports.
51. Project of the Month, March 2004, www.parsons.com.
52. 1974 Parsons Annual Report.
53. Ibid.
54. 1970 Parsons Annual Report.
55. Marty Fabrick, Parsons internal correspondence, 19 July 2005.
56. Ibid.
57. Marty Fabrick, Parsons Résumé Archives.
58. 1974 Parsons Annual Report.
59. Parsons WMATA project description, LiveLink (Parsons Corporation's private Intranet).
60. Complete Job Listing, Job No. 501 through 5421, Parsons Corporation Archives.
61. Joe O'Rourke and Jerry O'Rourke, joint interview by Jeffery Rodengen, digital recording, 11 September 2003, Write Stuff Enterprises.
62. Ibid.
63. Ibid.
64. Joe O'Rourke and Jerry O'Rourke, Parsons employee records.
65. Inside cover and headquarters construction records, 1973 Parsons Annual Report.
66. Parsons Corporation Archives.
67. Thomas Johanson, interview by Richard F, Hubbard, digital recording, 9 September 2003, Write Stuff Enterprises.
68. Parsons World Headquarters Mural Brochure, Parsons Corporation Archives.
69. Roger Fetterolf, interview by Richard F. Hubbard, digital recording, 11 September 2003, Write Stuff Enterprises.
70. Ralph Fernandez, interview by Richard F. Hubbard, digital recording, 20 November 2003, Write Stuff Enterprises.
71. "Construction Firm Founder Ralph M. Parsons Dies at 78," *Los Angeles Times*, 21 December 1974.
72. 1974 Parsons Annual Report.

Chapter Five Sidebar: Stan Goldhaber

1. Stan Goldhaber, interview by Richard F. Hubbard, digital recording, 10 September 2003, Write Stuff Enterprises.

2. Ibid.
3. Ibid.
4. Ibid.
5. Ray Judson, interview by Jeffrey L. Rodengen, digital recording, 30 June 2003, Write Stuff Enterprises.
6. Jim McNulty, Parsons internal interview, 10 February 2005.
7. Larry Burns, interview by Jeffrey L. Rodengen, digital recording, 11 September 2003, Write Stuff Enterprises.

Chapter Five Sidebar: Milton Lewis: Dynamic Salesman

1. The Ralph M. Parsons Company History, Parsons Corporation Archives.
2. Ibid.
3. *Parsons News & Views*, No. 37, 17.
4. Ibid.
5. Ibid.
6. Walter Rowse, interview by Richard F. Hubbard, digital recording, 15 September 2003, Write Stuff Enterprises.
7. Dan Frost, interview by Richard F. Hubbard, digital recording, 8 September 2003, Write Stuff Enterprises.
8. *Parsons News & Views*, No. 37, 17.

Chapter Five Sidebar: "Clancy" and the "Old Gray Mare"

1. Dante Boccalero, Parsons employee records.
2. Dante Boccalero, interview by Jeffrey L. Rodengen, digital recording, 11 September 2003, Write Stuff Enterprises.

Chapter Five Sidebar: "Hello … This is Ralph"

1. Ed Cramsie, interview by Jeffrey L. Rodengen, digital recording, 1 July 2003, Write Stuff Enterprises.

Chapter Five Sidebar: Educational and Philanthropic Interests

1. Pratt Institute, The History of Pratt, www.pratt.edu.
2. The Ralph M. Parsons Company History, Parsons Corporation Archives.
3. Pratt Institute Award Program, Parsons Corporation Archives.
4. Ralph M. Parsons résumé, Parsons Résumé Archives.
5. Ibid.
6. web.mit.edu.
7. Ibid.
8. The Ralph M. Parsons Foundation, www.rmpf.org.
9. Ralph M. Parsons résumé, Parsons Résumé Archives.
10. www.hmc.edu.
11. Parsons Corporation Archives.

Chapter Five Sidebar: Remembering Ralph Parsons

1. "Ralph Parsons: An Engineer Who Made a Mountain Out of a Molehill," *Los Angeles Times*, 27 November 1966.
2. Ibid.
3. Parsons Corporation Archives.
4. Ralph M. Parsons résumé, Parsons Résumé Archives.
5. Trudy Mysliwy, interview by Richard Hubbard, digital recording, 9 September 2003, Write Stuff Enterprises.
6. Dan Frost, interview by Richard F. Hubbard, digital recording, 8 September 2003, Write Stuff Enterprises.
7. Gladys Porter, interview by Richard F. Hubbard, digital recording, 16 October 2003, Write Stuff Enterprises.
8. Porter, interview.
9. "Ralph Parsons: An Engineer Who Made a Mountain Out of a Molehill," *Los Angeles Times*, 27 November 1966.
10. Parsons Corporation Archives.
11. Dan Frost, interview by Richard F. Hubbard, digital recording, 8 September 2003, Write Stuff Enterprises.
12. Bill Leonhard, interview by Jeffrey L. Rodengen, digital recording, 10 July 2003, Write Stuff Enterprises.
13. Parsons Corporation Archives.

Chapter Five Sidebar: Joe Volpe Jr.

1. Joe Volpe Jr., Parsons Corporation Archives LiveLink (Parsons Corporation's private Intranet).
2. "A Report on the International Control of Atomic Energy," prepared for the Committee on Atomic Energy, 16 March 1946.
3. Joe Volpe III's eulogy for his father, Joe Volpe Jr., Parsons Corporation Archives.
4. Joe Volpe Jr., Parsons Corporation Archives LiveLink (Parsons Corporation's private Intranet).
5. Joe Volpe III's eulogy for his father, Joe Volpe Jr., Parsons Corporation Archives.
6. Jim McNulty, Parsons internal interview, 10 February 2005.
7. Ibid.
8. James Shappell, interview by Richard F. Hubbard, digital recording, 10 September 2003, Write Stuff Enterprises.
9. Earle Williams, interview by Richard F. Hubbard, digital recording, 10 September 2003, Write Stuff Enterprises.
10. www.ncusar.org/publications/pubs1/5yrprivate.html.
11. Ibid.
12. Ibid.
13. Joe Volpe III's eulogy for his father, Joe Volpe Jr., Parsons Corporation Archives.

Chapter Six

1. 1975 Parsons Annual Report.
2. *Parsons News & Views* No. 34. 2.
3. www.fe.doe.gov/programs/reserves/npr-90years.html.
4. Daniel Yergin, *The Prize: The Epic Quest for Oil, Money and Power* (New York: The Free Press—Simon & Schuster, 1993), 569.
5. Ibid., 570.
6. *Parsons News & Views*, No. 34, 2.
7. Ibid., 4.
8. Daniel Yergin, *The Prize: The Epic Quest for Oil, Money and Power* (New York: The Free Press—Simon & Schuster, 1993), 570.
9. Ibid.
10. *The Parsons Magazine*, No. 40, 2.
11. www.dog.dnr.state.ak.us/oil/products/slideshows/ftc_briefing_apr1999/sldocy.htm.
12. Daniel Yergin, *The Prize: The Epic Quest for Oil, Money and Power* (New York: The Free Press—Simon & Schuster, 1993), 572.
13. Ibid.
14. Marvin McClain, interview by Richard F. Hubbard, digital recording, 16 December 2003, Write Stuff Enterprises.
15. Daniel Yergin, *The Prize: The Epic Quest for Oil, Money and Power* (New York: The Free Press—Simon & Schuster, 1993), 572.

16. www.alyeska-pipe.com.
17. *Parsons News & Views*, No. 34.
18. Ibid.
19. Ibid.
20. Dante Boccalero, interview by Jeffrey L. Rodengen, digital recording, 11 September 2003, Write Stuff Enterprises.
21. Bill Haas, interview by Jeffrey L. Rodengen, digital recording, 1 July 2003, Write Stuff Enterprises.
22. Bill Hass, Parsons employee records.
23. Ray Van Horn interview by Richard F. Hubbard, digital recording, 11 December 2003, Write Stuff Enterprises.
24. Joe Szlamka, interview by Jeffrey L. Rodengen, digital recording, 11 September 2003, Write Stuff Enterprises.
25. Mike D'Antuono, interview by Jeffrey L. Rodengen, digital recording, 30 May 2003, Write Stuff Enterprises.
26. Ibid.
27. Ray Van Horn, interview by Richard F. Hubbard, digital recording, 11 September 2003, Write Stuff Enterprises.
28. Bill Haas, interview by Jeffrey L. Rodengen, digital recording, 1 July 2003, Write Stuff Enterprises.
29. *Parsons News & Views*, No. 34.
30. Mary Brown, interview by Jeffrey L. Rodengen, digital recording, 1 July 2003, Write Stuff Enterprises.
31. www.wildlife.alaska.gov/index.cfm?adfg=funfacts.caribou.
32. Marty Badaracco, interview by Richard F. Hubbard, digital recording, 11 September 2003, Write Stuff Enterprises.
33. Mary Brown, interview by Jeffrey L. Rodengen, digital recording, 1 July 2003, Write Stuff Enterprises.
34. Brown, interview.
35. *Parsons News & Views*, No. 34.
36. "Modular Design and Construction of Process Plants," Parsons Corporation Archives.
37. Ibid.
38. Ron Russell, interview by Jeffrey L. Rodengen, digital recording, 11 September 2003, Write Stuff Enterprises.
39. Russell, interview.
40. *Parsons News & Views*, No. 34.
41. Ibid.
42. Ibid.
43. Ibid.
44. Ron Russell, interview by Jeffrey L. Rodengen, digital recording, 11 September 2003, Write Stuff Enterprises.
45. *Parsons News & Views*, No. 34.
46. Marvin McClain, interview by Richard F. Hubbard, digital recording, 16 December 2003, Write Stuff Enterprises.
47. *Parsons News & Views*, No. 34.
48. Ira Blanco, Parsons employee records.
49. Marvin McClain, interview by Richard F. Hubbard, digital recording, 16 December 2003, Write Stuff Enterprises.
50. *Parsons News & Views*, No. 34.
51. 1979 Parsons Annual Report.
52. Parsons Project Archives, LiveLink (Parsons Corporation's private Intranet).
53. Ibid.
54. Andrea Pampanini, "Jubail and Yanbu: Cities from the Desert."
55. Ibid.
56. Ibid.
57. Ibid.
58. Stan Goldhaber, interview by Richard F. Hubbard, digital recording, 10 September 2003, Write Stuff Enterprises.
59. Parsons Project Archives, LiveLink (Parsons Corporation's private Intranet).
60. Stan Goldhaber, interview by Richard F. Hubbard, digital recording, 10 September 2003, Write Stuff Enterprises.
61. Ibid.
62. Knisely Dreher, interview by Richard Hubbard, digital recording, 9 September 2003, Write Stuff Enterprises.
63. Nick Presecan, interview by Jeffrey L. Rodengen, digital recording, 1 July 2003, Write Stuff Enterprises.
64. Kevin Barry, interview by Richard Hubbard, digital recording, 21 November 2003, Write Stuff Enterprises.
65. Kevin Barry, Parsons employee records, LiveLink (Parsons Corporation's private Intranet).
66. Parsons project description, LiveLink (Parsons Corporation's private Intranet).
67. David Goodrich, interview by Jeffrey L. Rodengen, digital recording, 30 May 30 2003, Write Stuff Enterprises.
68. David Kays, Parsons employee records, LiveLink (Parsons Corporation's private Intranet).
69. David Kays, interview by Richard Hubbard, digital recording, 8 October 2003, Write Stuff Enterprises.
70. Melvyn Brown, Parsons Résumé Archives, LiveLink (Parsons Corporation's private Intranet).
71. Melvyn Brown, interview by Richard F. Hubbard, digital recording, 23 November 2003, Write Stuff Enterprises.
72. Ibid.
73. *Parsons News & Views*, No. 1, 1983.
74. Parsons Project Archives, LiveLink (Parsons Corporation's private Intranet).
75. Ibid.
76. 1980 Parsons Annual Report.
77. 1981 Parsons Annual Report.
78. Parsons Project Archives, LiveLink (Parsons Corporation's private Intranet).
79. Ray Judson, interview by Jeffrey L. Rodengen, digital recording, 30 June 2003, Write Stuff Enterprises.
80. Ibid.
81. Ray Judson, Parsons employee records.
82. Parsons Project Archives, LiveLink (Parsons Corporation's private Intranet).
83. Marvin McClain, interview by Richard F. Hubbard, digital recording, 16 December 2003, Write Stuff Enterprises.
84. 1975 Parsons Annual Report.
85. Ibid.
86. Bob Sheh, interview by Richard F. Hubbard, digital recording, 5 November 2003, Write Stuff Enterprises.
87. Ibid.
88. 1977 Parsons Annual Report.
89. 1975 and 1977 Parsons Annual Reports.
90. Ray Judson, interview by Jeffrey L. Rodengen, digital recording, 30 June 2003, Write Stuff Enterprises.
91. Otha C. (Charlie) Roddey, telephone interview, 4 May 2005.
92. 1975 Parsons Annual Report.
93. 1984 Parsons Annual Report.
94. Les Engle, interview by Richard F. Hubbard, digital recording, 6 November 2003, Write Stuff Enterprises.
95. Parsons Project Archives, Livelink (Parsons Corporation's private Intranet).

96. 1975–1984 Parsons Annual Reports.
97. Parsons Project Archives, Livelink (Parsons Corporation's private Intranet).
98. Rick Wilkinson, Parsons internal interview, 24 May 2005.
99. Ibid.
100. Ibid.
101. Ibid.
102. 1976 Parsons Annual Report.
103. 1975–1977 Parsons Annual Reports.
104. Parsons Project Archives, LiveLink (Parsons Corporation's private Intranet).
105. Excellence in Design Award—1983, Army Corps of Engineers, Parsons Corporation Archives.
106. Frank Shafran, Parsons employee records.
107. Letter, Huntsville Division, Army Corps of Engineers, 1983, Parsons Corporation Archives.
108. Frank Shafran, Parsons employee records.
109. Peter Jahn, Parsons employee records.
110. Peter Jahn, interview by Jeffrey L. Rodengen, digital recording, 11 September 2003, Write Stuff Enterprises, and supplemental Parsons internal correspondence, 24 January 2005.
111. Parsons project description, LiveLink (Parsons Corporation's private Intranet).
112. http://aec.army.mil/usaec/publicaffairs/update/win01/win0112.htm.
113. Parsons Project Description, LiveLink (Parsons Corporation's private Intranet) and City of LA History,www.lacity.org/lacity32.htm.
114. Parsons project description, 1977 Parsons Annual Report, LiveLink (Parsons Corporation's private Intranet).
115. Parsons project description, LiveLink (Parsons Corporation's private Intranet).
116. Parsons project description, LiveLink (Parsons Corporation's private Intranet), and 2005 Parsons Annual Report.
117. "Southeast High-Speed Rail Corridor: The Northeast—20 Years of High-Speed Rail," www.sehsr.org/reports/time2act/actchapter5.html.
118. Parsons Corporation Archives.
119. Larry Dondanville, interview by Richard F. Hubbard, digital recording, 27 November 2003 Write Stuff Enterprises.
120. 1978 and 1980 Parsons Annual Reports.
121. 1983 Parsons Annual Report.
122. Parsons Corporation Résumé Archives.
123. 1980 Parsons Annual Report.
124. Graydon Thayer, interview by Richard F. Hubbard, digital recording, 17 October 2003, Write Stuff Enterprises.
125. Parsons Project Archives, LiveLink (Parsons Corporation's private Intranet).
126. Tim Lindquist, interview by Richard F. Hubbard, digital recording, 10 September 2003, Write Stuff Enterprises.
127. Bill Flegenheimer, Parsons employee records.
128. Tim Lindquist, interview by Richard F. Hubbard, digital recording, 10 September 2003, Write Stuff Enterprises.
129. Bob Yang, Parsons Résumé Archives, LiveLink (Parsons Corporation's private Intranet).
130. Jim Thrash, email correspondence, 14 November 2005.
131. 1978 Parsons Annual Report.
132. *Parsons News & Views*, No. 36.
133. *Parsons Perspectives*, First Quarter 1986.
134. Ibid.
135. 1978 Parsons Annual Report.
136. Bob Davidson, interview by Richard F. Hubbard, digital recording, 18 November 2003, Write Stuff Enterprises.
137. Bob Davidson, Parsons employee records.
138. *Parsons Perspectives*, October 1991.
139. Parsons Corporation Archives.
140. "Parsons Builds a Reputation," *The Executive*, June 1982, 11.
141. Dan Frost, interview by Richard F. Hubbard, digital recording, 8 September 2003, Write Stuff Enterprises.
142. Jim McNulty, Curt Bower, Gary Stone, David Goodrich, Frank DeMartino, and Erin Kuhlman—Parsons ESOP history meeting notes, September 2004.
143. *Forbes*, 1984.

Chapter Six Sidebar: Passing Time at Prudhoe Bay

1. "Passing Time at Prudhoe Bay," *RMP news & views, jr.*, October 1976.
2. Mike D'Antuono, interview by Jeffrey L. Rodengen, digital recording, 30 May 2003, Write Stuff Enterprises.
3. Cathy Meindl, interview by Jeffrey L. Rodengen, digital recording, 30 May 2003, Write Stuff Enterprises.
4. Joe Szlamka, interview by Jeffrey L. Rodengen, digital recording, 11 September 2003, Write Stuff Enterprises.
5. Ray Van Horn, interview by Richard F. Hubbard, digital recording, 11 September 2003, Write Stuff Enterprises.
6. Marvin McClain, interview by Richard F. Hubbard, digital recording, 8 September 2003, Write Stuff Enterprises.

Chapter Six Sidebar: Meeting Challenges Worldwide

1. 1987 Parsons Annual Report.
2. Otha C. (Charlie) Roddey, telephone interview, 4 May 2005.
3. Ibid.
4. Ibid.
5. Ibid.
6. Larry Dondanville, interview by Richard Hubbard, digital recording, 23 October 2003, Write Stuff Enterprises.
7. Larry Dondanville, Parsons employee records.
8. Otha C. (Charlie) Roddey, telephone interview, 4 May 2005.

Chapter Six Sidebar: Brian Watt Associates Inc.

1. *Parsons Perspectives*, First Quarter 1986.

Chapter Six Sidebar: PERC—The Great Race

1. Parsons Corporation Archives.
2. Ann Hicks, interview by Richard F. Hubbard, digital recording, 11 September 2003, Write Stuff Enterprises.
3. Ibid.
4. Parsons Corporation Archives.

Chapter Six Sidebar: Engineering Science Inc.

1. *Parsons Perspectives*, First Quarter 1986.
2. *Parsons Engineering Science*, Spring 1996.

3. Ibid.
4. Ibid.
5. David Burstein, interview by Richard F. Hubbard, digital recording, 11 October 2003, Write Stuff Enterprises.
6. *Parsons Engineering Science*, Spring 1996.
7. Parsons Corporation Archives.

Chapter Six Sidebar: De Leuw, Cather & Company

1. Tribute to Charles Edmund De Leuw, founder of De Leuw, Cather & Company, Parsons Corporation Archives.
2. Ibid.
3. *Write-of-Way*, De Leuw, Cather & Company, January 1994.
4. *Perspectives*, June 1988.
5. 1991 Parsons Annual Report.
6. Robert S. O'Neil, Parsons Résumé Archives, LiveLink (Parsons Corporation's private Intranet).
7. Memo, October, 2000, Parsons Corporation Archives.
8. Parsons Corporation Archives.
9. James Shappell, Parsons Résumé Archives, LiveLink (Parsons Corporation's private Intranet).
10. James Shappell, interview by Richard F. Hubbard, digital recording, 3 September 2003, Write Stuff Enterprises.

Chapter Six Sidebar: S.I.P. Inc.

1. *Parsons News & Views*, No. 36.
2. Ibid.
3. Parsons Corporation Archives.

Chapter Seven

1. Bill Leonhard, interview by Jeffrey L. Rodengen, digital recording, 10 July 2003, Write Stuff Enterprises.
2. Larry Tollenaere, interview by Richard F. Hubbard, digital recording, 11 September 2003, Write Stuff Enterprises.
3. Gary Stone, interview by Jeffrey L. Rodengen, digital recording, 30 May 2003, Write Stuff Enterprises.
4. Susan Cole, interview by Jeffrey L. Rodengen, digital recording, 30 May 2003, Write Stuff Enterprises.
5. Susan Cole, interview.
6. Tom Schweiner, interview by Richard F. Hubbard, digital recording, 28 October 2003, Write Stuff Enterprises.
7. Fred Felberg, interview by Richard F. Hubbard, digital recording, 9 September 2003, Write Stuff Enterprises.
8. Manny Stein, interview by Richard F. Hubbard, digital recording, 10 September 2003, Write Stuff Enterprises.
9. Stein, interview.
10. 1985 Parsons Annual Report.
11. Parsons Corporation Archives.
12. *Parsons Perspectives*, Spring 1993.
13. Barton-Aschman Associates brochure, Parsons Corporation Archives.
14. Marty Blachman, interview by Richard F. Hubbard, digital recording, 20 November 2003, Write Stuff Enterprises.
15. *Parsons Perspectives*, December 1989.
16. Bob Bax, interview by Jeffrey L. Rodengen, digital recording, 1 July 2003, Write Stuff Enterprises.
17. www.nycroads.com/crossings/brooklyn/.
18. Steinman brochure, Parsons Corporation Archives.
19. *Compressed Air Magazine*, 1990.
20. Ibid.
21. Ibid.
22. www.teckcominco.com/operations/reddog.
23. Samir (Sam) Lawrence, Parsons Résumé Archives, LiveLink (Parsons Corporation's private Intranet).
24. *Parsons Perspectives*, Fourth Quarter 1986.
25. Parsons Project Archives, LiveLink (Parsons Corporation's private Intranet).
26. Les Engle, interview by Richard F. Hubbard, digital recording, 6 November 2003, Write Stuff Enterprises.
27. Parsons Project Archives, LiveLink (Parsons Corporation's private Intranet).
28. Tom Barron, interview Richard F. Hubbard, digital recording, 24 October 2003, Write Stuff Enterprises
29. *Perspectives*, December 1992.
30. Parsons Employee Archives and Résumé Archives, LiveLink (Parsons Corporation's private Intranet).
31. Parsons Project Archives, Live Link (Parsons Corporation's private Intranet).
32. 1995 Parsons Annual Report.
33. Ibid.
34. "Parsons Builds a Reputation," *The Executive of Los Angeles*, June 1982, 14.
35. Ibid.
36. "Commanding Officer," *Pepperdine People*, Fall 1988, 14.
37. Larry Burns, interview by Jeffrey L. Rodengen, digital recording, 11 September 2003, Write Stuff Enterprises.
38. Fred Schweiger, interview by Richard F. Hubbard, digital recording, 17 November 2003, Write Stuff Enterprises.
39. Gladys Porter, interview by Richard F. Hubbard, digital recording, 16 October 2003, Write Stuff Enterprises.
40. "Parsons Builds a Reputation," *The Executive*, June, 1982, 12.
41. "That Overused Word, Infrastructure," *Forbes*, 17 January 1983, 62.
42. "Changing of the Guard: Parsons Gets an Aggressive New Leader," *Pasadena Star-News*, 23 April 1990.
43. "Changing of the Guard: Parsons Gets an Aggressive New Leader," *Pasadena Star-News*, 23 April 1990.
44. Ibid.
45. Ibid.
46. Ibid.
47. "Top Spot," *Pasadena Star-News*, 23 April 1990.
48. Ibid.
49. "The Parsons Corp. Initiates Reorganization, Announces Transportation Group," *Business Wire*, 12 December 1991.
50. Robert S. O'Neil, Parsons employee records.
51. *Parsons Perspectives*, April 1992.
52. Paul Farmanian, Parsons internal interview, 21 January 2005.
53. David Goodrich, Parsons internal interview, 18 September 2004.
54. *Engineering Science*, Winter 1990/1991.
55. David Goodrich, Parsons internal interview, 18 September 2004.
56. "Pieroni Reviews an Eventful Year," *Pasadena Star-News*, 14 December 1992.
57. Mel Brown, interview by Richard F. Hubbard, digital recording, 23 September 2004, Write Stuff Enterprises.
58. Brown, interview.

59. David Kays, interview by Richard F. Hubbard, digital recording, 8 October 2004, Write Stuff Enterprises.
60. *Parsons Perspectives*, April 1991.
61. Ibid., January 1992.
62. "Pieroni Reviews an Eventful Year," *Pasadena Star-News*, 14 December 1992.
63. Parsons Project Archives LiveLink (Parsons Corporation's private Intranet).
64. Parsons Project Archives LiveLink (Parsons Corporation's private Intranet) and *Parsons Perspectives*, Summer/Fall 1994.
65. *Parsons Perspectives*, Summer/Fall 1994.
66. Selva Selvaratnam, Parsons Résumé Archives, LiveLink (Parsons Corporation's private Intranet) and Parsons Corporation employee records.
67. Jack Roadhouse, Parsons Résumé Archives, LiveLink (Parsons Corporation's private Intranet).
68. Parsons Project Archives LiveLink (Parsons Corporation's private Intranet).
69. *Parsons Perspectives*, Summer/Fall 1994.
70. Dick Whatley, Parsons Résumé Archives, LiveLink (Parsons Corporation's private Intranet).
71. *Parsons Perspectives*, Summer/Fall 1994.
72. Parsons Project Archives, LiveLink (Parsons Corporation's private Intranet).
73. www.inventionfactory.com/history/RHAoral/birdsall.html.
74. Parsons Project Archives, LiveLink (Parsons Corporation's private Intranet).
75. Charles Vickers Jr., Parsons Résumé Archives, LiveLink (Parsons Corporation's private Intranet).
76. Parsons Project Archives, LiveLink (Parsons Corporation's private Intranet).
77. *Parsons Perspectives*, Winter 1993.
78. 1994 Parsons Annual Report.
79. Parsons Project Archives, LiveLink (Parsons Corporation's private Intranet).
80. Ibid.
81. Anita Freeman, Parsons internal email, 25 May 2005.
82. Anita Freeman, Parsons Résumé Archives, LiveLink (Parsons Corporation's private Intranet).
83. Leland Freeman, Parsons Résumé Archives, LiveLink (Parsons Corporation's private Intranet).
84. Parsons Project Archives, LiveLink (Parsons Corporation's private Intranet).
85. www.pbs.org/wgbh/buildingbig/wonder/structure/channel.html.
86. Parsons Project Archives, LiveLink (Parsons Corporation's private Intranet).
87. *Parsons Perspectives*, April 1991.
88. Parsons project description, LiveLink (Parsons Corporation's private Intranet).
89. 1994 Parsons Annual Report.
90. Parsons Project Archives, LiveLink (Parsons Corporation's private Intranet).
91. Ibid.
92. Parsons project description, LiveLink (Parsons Corporation's private Intranet).
93. Charlie Dutton, interview by Richard F. Hubbard, digital recording, 11 November 2003, Write Stuff Enterprises
94. Ron L'Hommedieu, Parsons Résumé Archives, LiveLink (Parsons Corporation's private Intranet).
95. Roy Goodwin, Parsons Résumé Archives, LiveLink (Parsons Corporation's private Intranet).
96. Roy Goodwin, Parsons internal interview, 23 May 2005.
97. Roy Goodwin, Parsons Résumé Archives, LiveLink (Parsons Corporation's private Intranet).
98. Nils Pearson, Parsons Résumé Archives, LiveLink (Parsons Corporation's private Intranet).
99. Parsons Project Archives, LiveLink (Parsons Corporation's private Intranet).
100. Ibid.
101. Jose Celis, Parsons Résumé Archives, LiveLink (Parsons Corporation's private Intranet).
102. Parsons Project Archives, LiveLink (Parsons Corporation's private Intranet).
103. Gene Randich, interview by Richard F. Hubbard, digital recording, 30 October 2003, Write Stuff Enterprises.
104. Gene Randich, Parsons Résumé Archives, LiveLink (Parsons Corporation's private Intranet).
105. 1985–1994 Parsons Annual Reports.
106. Parsons Project Archives, LiveLink (Parsons Corporation's private Intranet).
107. Parsons Project Archives, LiveLink (Parsons Corporation's private Intranet).
108. Andy Hauge, Parsons internal email correspondence, 24 January 2004.
109. Andy Hauge, Parsons Résumé Archives, LiveLink (Parsons Corporation's private Intranet).
110. 1994 Parsons Annual Report.
111. Ibid.
112. John Small, interview by Richard F. Hubbard, digital recording, 29 October 2003, Write Stuff Enterprises.
113. Parsons Résumé and Project Archives, LiveLink (Parsons Corporation's private Intranet).
114. John Small, interview by Richard F. Hubbard, digital recording, 29 October 2003, Write Stuff Enterprises.
115. Parsons Project Archives, LiveLink (Parsons Corporation's private Intranet) and *Parsons Perspectives*, January 1992.
116. *Parsons Perspectives*, January 1992.
117. Ibid.
118. Ibid.
119. *Parsons Perspectives*, April 1992.
120. Ibid.
121. Parsons Project Archives, LiveLink (Parsons Corporation's private Intranet).
122. 1993 Parsons Annual Report.
123. www.nato.int/docu/facts/kacta.htm.
124. Ray Judson, interview by Jeffrey L. Rodengen, digital recording, 30 June 2003, Write Stuff Enterprises.
125. Jack Scott, interview by Jeffrey L. Rodengen, digital recording, 14 July 2003, Write Stuff Enterprises.
126. Jake Kostyzak, Parsons employee records.
127. Jake Kostyzak, interview by Richard F. Hubbard, digital recording, 11 September 2003, Write Stuff Enterprises.
128. John Stewart, Parsons internal email, 13 May 2005.
129. Billy McGinnis, Parsons internal interview, 25 May 2005.
130. Ibid.
131. Erin Kuhlman, Parsons internal correspondence, 26 May 2005.
132. Billy McGinnis, Parsons internal interview, 25 May 2005.
133. Kenneth Whitman, interview by Richard F. Hubbard, digital recording, 23 September 2003, Write Stuff Enterprises.

134. Ken Whitman, Parsons employee records.
135. 1985–1994 Parsons Annual Reports.
136. Harold (Hal) Leyrer, Parsons employee records.
137. 1985–1994 Parsons Annual Reports.
138. Jim McNulty, interview by Jeffrey L. Rodengen, digital recording, 1 July 2003, Write Stuff Enterprises, and subsequent Parsons internal interview, 10 February 2005.
139. Parsons Project Archives, LiveLink (Parsons Corporation's private Intranet).
140. Ibid.
141. 1992 Parsons Annual Report.
142. Parsons Project Archives, LiveLink (Parsons Corporation's private Intranet).
143. 1993 Parsons Annual Report.
144. Tom Bullock, Parsons Résumé Archives, LiveLink (Parsons Corporation's private Intranet).
145. 1990 Parsons Annual Report.
146. www.washington-heights.us/history/Archives/000517.html.
147. 1985–1994 Parsons Annual Reports.
148. Chuck Terhune, interview by Richard F. Hubbard, digital recording, 13 October 2003, Write Stuff Enterprises.
149. Parsons Project Archives, LiveLink (Parsons Corporation's private Intranet).
150. Claude Le Feuvre, Parsons Résumé Archives, LiveLink (Parsons Corporation's private Intranet).
151. Claude Le Feuvre, Parsons internal interview, 31 May 2005.
152. Parsons Project Archives, LiveLink (Parsons Corporation's private Intranet).
153. Greg McBain, Parsons Résumé Archives, LiveLink (Parsons Corporation's private Intranet).
154. Parsons Project Archives, LiveLink (Parsons Corporation's private Intranet).
155. Frank Collins, Parsons internal interview, 23 May 2005.
156. Frank Collins, Parsons Résumé Archives, LiveLink (Parsons Corporation's private Intranet).
157. Richard Tremabath, Parsons internal interview, 26 January 2005.
158. Richard Tremabath, Parsons Résumé Archives, LiveLink (Parsons Corporation's private Intranet).
159. Parsons Project Archives, LiveLink (Parsons Corporation's private Intranet).
160. Ibid.
161. Chuck Thomas, Parsons Résumé Archives, LiveLink (Parsons Corporation's private Intranet).
162. Chuck Thomas, Parsons internal interview, 3 June 2005.
163. 1995 Parsons Annual Report.
164. *Parsons Perspectives*, April 1991.
165. Ron Russell, interview by Jeffrey L. Rodengen, digital recording, 11 September 2003, Write Stuff Enterprises.

Chapter Seven Sidebar: William E. Leonhard

1. Parsons Corporation Archives.
2. Bill Leonhard, interview by Jeffrey L. Rodengen, digital recording, 10 July 2003, Write Stuff Enterprises.
3. Ibid.
4. Stan Goldhaber, interview by Richard F. Hubbard, digital recording, 10 September 2003, Write Stuff Enterprises.
5. Bill Leonhard, interview by Jeffrey L. Rodengen, digital recording, 10 July 2003, Write Stuff Enterprises.
6. Stan Goldhaber, interview by Richard F. Hubbard, digital recording, 10 September 2003, Write Stuff Enterprises.
7. 1978–1990 Parsons Annual Reports.
8. Ray Judson, interview by Jeffrey L. Rodengen, digital recording, 30 June 2003, Write Stuff Enterprises.
9. Marvin McClain, interview by Richard F. Hubbard, digital recording, 9 September 2003, Write Stuff Enterprises.
10. Bob Sheh, interview by Richard F. Hubbard, digital recording, 5 November 2003, Write Stuff Enterprises.
11. Larry Burns, interview by Jeffrey L. Rodengen, digital recording, 11 September 2003, Write Stuff Enterprises.
12. Ibid.
13. Kevin Berry, interview by Richard F. Hubbard, digital recording, 21 November 2003, Write Stuff Enterprises.
14. Sharen Clark, interview by Richard F. Hubbard, digital recording, 9 September 2003, Write Stuff Enterprises.
15. Jess Harmon, interview by Richard F. Hubbard, digital recording, 11 September 2003, Write Stuff Enterprises.
16. Bill Leonhard, Parsons employee records.
17. Dan Frost, interview by Richard F. Hubbard, digital recording, 8 September 2003, Write Stuff Enterprises.

Chapter Seven Sidebar: CT Main

1. American Society of Mechanical Engineers, www.asme.org.
2. *Parsons Perspectives*, December 1989.
3. CT Main history, Parsons Corporation Archives.
4. Jim Callahan, interview by Richard F. Hubbard, digital recording, 7 October 2003, Write Stuff Enterprises.
5. Bill Whooley, interview by Richard F. Hubbard, digital recording, 18 November 2003, Write Stuff Enterprises.
6. Roy Gaunt, interview by Richard F. Hubbard, digital recording, 13 November 2003, Write Stuff Enterprises.
7. Roy Gaunt, Parsons employee records.
8. CT Main history, Parsons Corporation Archives.

Chapter Seven Sidebar: Barton-Aschman Associates Inc.

1. Company brochure, Barton-Aschman Associates Inc., Parsons Corporation Archives.
2. Fannie Mae Foundation, www.fanniemaefoundation.org/programs/hpd/pdf/hpd_1101_metzger.pdf.
3. Fred Schweiger, interview by Richard F. Hubbard, digital recording, 17 November 2003, Write Stuff Enterprises.
4. Harvey Joyner, interview by Richard F. Hubbard, digital recording, 14 November 2003, Write Stuff Enterprises.
5. Ibid.

Chapter Seven Sidebar: John Small: Our Man in Moscow

1. John Small, Parsons internal interview, 23 May 2003.

2. *Casablanca*, directed by Michael Curtiz (1942; Burbank, California: Warner Brothers).
3. John Small, Parsons internal interview, 23 May 2003.
4. Ibid.
5. Ibid.
6. Ibid.

Chapter Seven Sidebar: Harland Bartholomew & Associates Inc.

1. http://stlcin.missouri.org/history/.
2. Harland Bartholomew history, Parsons Corporation Archives.
3. Bob Bax, interview by Jeffrey L. Rodengen, digital recording, 1 July 2003, Write Stuff Enterprises.
4. George Hull, interview by Richard F. Hubbard, digital recording, 24 September 2003, Write Stuff Enterprises.

Chapter Seven Sidebar: Steinman Boynton Gronquist & Birdsall

1. wheeling.weirton.lib.wv.us/landmark/bridges/susp/bridge3.htm.
2. Ibid.
3. Ibid.
4. www.civil.umaine.edu.
5. www.michigan.gov/dnr and www.eswp.com/bridge/bridge_awards.htm.
6. *Parsons Perspective*, October 1991.
7. Blair Birdsall interview, www.inventionfactory.com.
8. Ibid.
9. Ibid.

Chapter Eight

1. 1996 Parsons Annual Report.
2. "The Parsons Corp. Enters Into an Agreement in Principle to Acquire Gilbert/Commonwealth Inc.," *Business Wire*, 3 March 1995.
3. 1996 Parsons Annual Report.
4. Parsons Corporation Archives.
5. Jim McNulty, interview by Jeffrey L. Rodengen, digital recording, 1 July 2003, Write Stuff Enterprises and subsequent Parsons internal interview, 10 February 2005.
6. William Hall, interview by Richard F. Hubbard, digital recording, 7 October 2003, Write Stuff Enterprises.
7. Bob O'Neil, interview by Richard F. Hubbard, digital recording, 15 January 2004, Write Stuff Enterprises.
8. Ibid.
9. Bob Bax, interview by Jeffrey L. Rodengen, digital recording, 1 July 2003, Write Stuff Enterprises.
10. Chuck Harrington, interview by Richard F. Hubbard, digital recording, 20 October 2003, Write Stuff Enterprises.
11. Chuck Harrington, Parsons Résumé Archives, LiveLink (Parsons Corporation's private Intranet).
12. Parsons Corporation Archives.
13. *Engineering News-Record*, 15 April 1996.
14. Jim McNulty, interview by Jeffrey L. Rodengen, digital recording, 1 July 2003, Write Stuff Enterprises and subsequent Parsons internal interview, 10 February 2005.
15. Leonard Pieroni III, Parsons internal email correspondence, 6 June 2005.
16. Ibid.
17. James Shappell, Parsons internal interview, 17 August 2004.
18. *Engineering New Record*, 15 April 1996.
19. "A Death in the Parsons Family," *Business Week*, 22 April 1996.
20. Jim McNulty, interview by Jeffrey L. Rodengen, digital recording, 1 July 2003, Write Stuff Enterprises, and subsequent Parsons internal interview, 10 February 2005.
21. Ibid.
22. Ray Judson, interview by Jeffrey L. Rodengen, digital recording, 30 June 2003, Write Stuff Enterprises.
23. Judson interview.
24. Ibid.
25. "A Death in the Parsons Family," *Business Week*, 22 April 1996.
26. Earle Williams, interview by Richard F. Hubbard, digital recording, 19 November 2003, Write Stuff Enterprises.
27. Jim McNulty, interview by Jeffrey L. Rodengen, digital recording, 1 July 2003, Write Stuff Enterprises, and Parsons internal interview, 10 February 2005.
28. Ibid.
29. Ibid.
30. *Engineering News-Record*, 15 April 1996.
31. Jim McNulty, Parsons internal interview, 10 February 2005.
32. Ibid.
33. Ibid.
34. *Engineering News-Record*, 15 April 1996.
35. *Parsons Perspectives*, Fall/Winter 1996.
36. Frank DeMartino, Parsons Résumé Archives, LiveLink (Parsons Corporation's private Intranet).
37. Jim McNulty, Parsons internal interview, 10 February 2005.
38. Ray Judson, interview by Jeffrey L. Rodengen, digital recording, 30 June 2003, Write Stuff Enterprises.
39. Jim McNulty, Parsons internal interview, 10 February 2005.
40. Ray Judson, interview by Jeffrey L. Rodengen, digital recording, 30 June 2003, Write Stuff Enterprises.
41. 1996 Parsons Annual Report.
42. Bosnia-Herzegovina Program, Parsons Program Archives, LiveLink (Parsons Corporation's private Intranet).
43. Parsons Corporation Archives.
44. www.scbbs.com/alameda/alameda.htm.
45. Parsons Alameda Corridor Project Archives, LiveLink (Parsons Corporation's private Intranet).
46. Mike Christensen, Parsons résumé, LiveLink (Parsons Corporation's private Intranet).
47. Tom Barron, interview by Richard F. Hubbard, digital recording, 24 October 2003, Write Stuff Enterprises.
48. Parsons Alameda Corridor, Parsons Project Archives, LiveLink (Parsons Corporation's private Intranet).
49. Seattle–Tacoma International Airport Project, Parsons Corporation Archives, LiveLink (Parsons Corporation's private Intranet), and 2005–2006 Bi-Annual Report.
50. Sam Wright, Parsons internal interview, 2005-2006 Bi-Annual Report.
51. Sam Wright, Parsons Résumé Archives, LiveLink (Parsons Corporation's private Intranet).
52. Seattle-Tacoma International Airport Project, Parsons Corporation Archives.
53. Frank Ching, Dick Swegle, Gary Ostle, Ed Masterson, and Diane Adams, Parsons Résumé Archives, LiveLink (Parsons Corporation's private Intranet).
54. Greg Perry, Parsons email correspondence, 27 May 2005.

55. Greg Perry, Parsons Résumé Archives, LiveLink (Parsons Corporation's private Intranet).
56. Parsons Project Archives, LiveLink (Parsons Corporation's private Intranet).
57. Ibid.
58. www.dmjmharris.com/MarketsAndServices/39/69/index.jsp and 2005–2006 Parsons Bi-Annual Report.
59. Jane Charalambous, Parsons internal interview, 2005–2066 Bi-Annual Report.
60. Jane Charalambous, Parsons Résumé Archives, LiveLink (Parsons Corporation's private Intranet).
61. Parsons Project Archives, LiveLink (Parsons Corporation's private Intranet), and Parsons Project of the month, www.parsons.com.
62. "We are Parsons," 1999–2000 Bi-Annual Report.
63. Parsons Project Archives, LiveLink (Parsons Corporation's private Intranet).
64. Dan Baicoianu, Parsons Résumé Archives, LiveLink (Parsons Corporation's private Intranet).
65. Jim Klemz, Parsons internal interview, 2005–2006 Bi-Annual Report.
66. Parsons Project Archives, LiveLink (Parsons Corporation's private Intranet), and 2005–2006 Bi-Annual Report.
67. Jim Klemz, Parsons Résumé Archives.
68. Parsons Project Archives, LiveLink (Parsons Corporation's private Intranet), and Parsons Project of the Month, www.parsons.com.
69. 1969–2005 Parsons Annual Reports.
70. Parsons Corporation, "Parsons Acquires Leading Bridge Firm," news release, 17 September 2001.
71. Parsons Project Archives, LiveLink (Parsons Corporation's private Intranet), and 2005–2006 Bi-Annual Report.
72. Parsons Project Archives, LiveLink (Parsons Corporation's private Intranet).
73. Parsons Corporation, "ASBI Selects Parsons' Bridge Projects for 2003 Bridge Awards of Excellence," news release, 19 September 2003.
74. Parsons Project Archives, LiveLink (Parsons Corporation's private Intranet).
75. Keith Sabol, Parsons internal interview, 26 May 2005.
76. Keith Sabol, Parsons Résumé Archives, LiveLink (Parsons Corporation's private Intranet).
77. Parsons Project Archives, LiveLink (Parsons Corporation's private Intranet), and Parsons Project of the Month, www.parsons.com.
78. Tom Spoth, Parsons internal interview, 26 May 2005.
79. Tom Spoth, Parsons Résumé Archives, LiveLink (Parsons Corporation's private Intranet).
80. James Shappell, interview by Richard F. Hubbard, digital recording, 3 September 2003, Write Stuff Enterprises.
81. Larry Alverez, interview by Richard F. Hubbard, digital recording, 10 September 2003, Write Stuff Enterprises.
82. Parsons Project Archives, LiveLink (Parsons Corporation's private Intranet).
83. Jess Yoder, Parsons email correspondence, 25 May 2004.
84. Jess Yoder, Parsons Résumé Archives, LiveLink (Parsons Corporation's private Intranet), and Parsons Corporation, "Parsons Appoints Yoder Head of Infrastructure Division," news release, 4 April 2001.
85. Parsons Project Archives, LiveLink (Parsons Corporation's private Intranet).
86. Bill Buchholz, Parsons email correspondence, 31 May 2004.
87. Ibid.
88. Parsons Project Archives, LiveLink (Parsons Corporation's private Intranet), and Parsons Project of the Month, www.parsons.com.
89. Parsons Project Archives, LiveLink (Parsons Corporation's private Intranet), and 2005–2006 Parsons Annual Reports.
90. Parsons Corporation, "Parsons Will Manage All-American Canal Lining Project, news release, 1 June 2004.
91. Dave Backus, Parsons Résumé, LiveLink (Parsons Corporation's private Intranet).
92. www.primus1.com/corporate_overview.html.
93. Parsons Corporation, "Parsons Acquires Primus Industries," draft news release, 22 June 2004.
94. 1996 Parsons Annual Report.
95. Bob Nugent, interview by Richard F. Hubbard, digital recording, 16 October 2003, Write Stuff Enterprises.
96. Chuck Harrington, interview by Richard F. Hubbard, digital recording, 20 October 2003, Write Stuff Enterprises.
97. Chuck Harrington, interview by Richard F. Hubbard, digital recording, 20 October 2003, Write Stuff Enterprises.
98. Parsons Corporation, "Parsons Acquires Communication Construction Company, news release, 29 January 2001.
99. Ibid.
100. Parsons Project Archives, LiveLink (Parsons Corporation's private Intranet).
101. Parsons Project Archives, LiveLink (Parsons Corporation's private Intranet), and Parsons Project of the Month, www.parsons.com.
102. Bill Millhone, interview by Richard F. Hubbard, digital recording, 8 October 2003, Write Stuff Enterprises.
103. Bill Millhone, Parsons Résumé Archives, LiveLink (Parsons Corporation's private Intranet).
104. Parsons Corporation, "Parsons Acquires Irish Firm," news release, 8 January 2004.
105. Michael Walsh, Parsons Résumé Archives, LiveLink (Parsons Corporation's private Intranet).
106. Parsons Corporation, "Parsons Acquires Process Facilities Inc.," news release, 28 May 2004.
107. Dan Mariani, Parsons Résumé Archives, LiveLink (Parsons Corporation's private Intranet).
108. "Parsons selected for Northrop Grumman Shipyard Extension Contract," Parsons Project Archives, and Parsons Project of the Month, www.parsons.com.
109. Jim Thrash, interview by Richard F. Hubbard, digital recording, 9 October 2003, Write Stuff Enterprises.
110. Parsons Project Archives, LiveLink (Parsons Corporation's private Intranet).
111. Parsons Corporation, "Parsons Awarded Salt Waste Facility Contract," news release, 2 September 2002.
112. *Parsons Weekly Bulletin* Archives—2004.
113. *Inside Parsons*, Summer 2005, LiveLink (Parsons Corporation's private Intranet), and Parsons

Project of the Month, www.parsons.com.
114. *Inside Parsons,* Summer 2005.
115. Parsons Project Archives, LiveLink (Parsons Corporation's private Intranet), and Parsons Project of the Month, www.parsons.com.
116. Bruce Shelton, Parsons internal interview, 8 April 2005.
117. Bruce Shelton, Parsons Résumé Archives, LiveLink (Parsons Corporation's private Intranet).
118. Mel Weingart, Parsons internal interview, 24 May 2005.
119. Ibid.
120. Mel Weingart, Parsons internal interview, 24 May 2005.
121. Mel Weingart, Parsons Résumé Archives.
122. Parsons Project Archives, LiveLink (Parsons Corporation's private Intranet).
123. Mel Weingart, Parsons internal interview, 24 May 2005.
124. Ibid.
125. Ibid.
126. Parsons Project Archives, LiveLink (Parsons Corporation's private Intranet).
127. Cliff Eby, interview by Richard F. Hubbard, digital recording, 16 September 2003, Write Stuff Enterprises.
128. Parsons Project Archives, LiveLink (Parsons Corporation's private Intranet).
129. Steve Quinn, interview by Richard F. Hubbard, digital recording, 21 October 2003, Write Stuff Enterprises.
130. Quinn, interview.
131. Parsons Project Archives.
132. Parsons Project Archives, LiveLink (Parsons Corporation's private Intranet), and Parsons Project of the Month, www.parsons.com.
133. Tom McCabe, Parsons internal interview, 3 June 2005, and *Kaho`olawe.* VHS. Parsons Corporation. Pasadena, California, 31 October 2003.
134. Tom McCabe, Parsons Résumé Archives, LiveLink (Parsons Corporation's private Intranet).
135. William Ahrens, Parsons Résumé Archives, LiveLink (Parsons Corporation's private Intranet).
136. Parsons Project Archives, LiveLink (Parsons Corporation's private Intranet).
137. Ibid.
138. Ibid.
139. Ibid.
140. Jeff Hermann, Parsons Résumé Archives, LiveLink (Parsons Corporation's private Intranet).
141. Jeff Hermann, Parsons internal email, 25 May 2005.
142. Ibid.
143. Jeff Hermann, Parsons Résumé Archives, LiveLink (Parsons Corporation's private Intranet).
144. Parsons Project Archives, LiveLink (Parsons Corporation's private Intranet).
145. 1995–2006 Parsons Annual and Bi-Annual Reports.
146. Parsons Project Archives, LiveLink (Parsons Corporation's private Intranet), and Parsons Project of the Month, www.parsons.com.
147. Parsons Project Archives, Parsons Project of the Month, www.parsons.com.
148. 1995–2006 Parsons Annual Reports.
149. Bob Bax, Announcement, *Parsons Weekly Bulletin*, 8 March 2004.
150. *Inside Parsons*, Spring 2004.
151. Jack Scott, Announcement, *Parsons Weekly Bulletin*, 19 January 2004.
152. Earnie Robbins, Announcement, *Parsons Weekly Bulletin*, 12 January 2004.
153. Parsons Corporation, "Parsons will Design/Build Iraqi Security and Justice Facilities," news release, 29 March 2004.
154. Parsons Project Archives, Parsons Project of the Month, www.parsons.com.
155. Ibid.
156. Parsons Corporate Archives.
157. Earnie Robbins, Parsons Résumé Archives, LiveLink (Parsons Corporation's private Intranet).
158. Karsten Rothenberg, Parsons Résumé Archives, LiveLink (Parsons Corporation's private Intranet).
159. Ken Deagon, Parsons Résumé Archives, LiveLink (Parsons Corporation's private Intranet).
160. Phil Nixon, Parsons Résumé Archives, LiveLink (Parsons Corporation's private Intranet).
161. Karsten Rothenberg, Parsons internal interview, 25 May 2005.
162. Ibid.
163. Earnie Robbins, Parsons internal interview, 25 May 2005.
164. Ibid.
165. Parsons Corporation, "Parsons to Manage Worldwide Unexploded Ordnance Removal," news release, 8 March 2004.
166. Parsons Corporation, "Parsons Appoints Roell as President of Infrastructure and Technology Group," news release, 4 August 2004.
167. Ibid.
168. Parsons Corporation, "Parsons to Build Military Housing," news release, 25 February 2004.
169. Parsons Corporation Archives.
170. Jim McNulty, Parsons internal interview, 10 February 2005.
171. Parsons Corporation, "Parsons Acquires the Alaris Group," news release, 5 May 2005.
172. Parsons Corporation, "Parsons Acquires RCI Construction Group," news release, 7 April 2005.
173. Jack Scott, Announcement, *Parsons Weekly Bulletin*, 11 July 2005.
174. Presentation, Parsons Annual Executive Meeting, January 2005.
175. Jim McNulty, interview by Jeffrey L. Rodengen, digital recording, 1 July 2003, Write Stuff Enterprises, and Parsons internal interview, 10 February 2005.
176. Frank DeMartino, interview by Jeffrey L. Rodengen, digital recording, 10 July 2003, Write Stuff Enterprises.
177. Ibid.
178. Jack Scott, interview by Jeffrey L. Rodengen, digital recording, 14 July 2003, Write Stuff Enterprises.
179. Jim McNulty, interview by Jeffrey L. Rodengen, digital recording, 1 July 2003, Write Stuff Enterprises, and Parsons internal interview, 10 February 2005.
180. Memo from Ralph M. Parsons, 3 June 1965, Parsons Corporation Archives.
181. "Ralph Parsons: An Engineer Who Made a Mountain Out of a Molehill," *Los Angeles Times*, 27 November 1966.

Chapter Eight Sidebar: Len Pieroni

1. Ray Judson, interview by Jeffrey L. Rodengen, digital recording, 30 June 2003, Write Stuff Enterprises.
2. "Changing of the Guard: Parsons Gets an Aggressive New Leader," *Pasadena Star-News*, 23 April 1990.
3. Ibid.

4. Ibid.
5. Ibid.
6. "Parsons Chief Pieroni Dies on Trade Mission," *Los Angeles Business Journal*, 8 April 1996.
7. Tragedy Hits Home at Parsons," *Los Angeles Times*, 4 April 1996.
8. Jim McNulty, Parsons internal interview, 10 February 2005.
9. Tom Neria, interview by Richard F. Hubbard, digital recording, 11 September 2003, Write Stuff Enterprises.
10. Curt Bower, interview by Jeffrey L. Rodengen, digital recording, 1 July 2003, Write Stuff Enterprises.
11. Bill Whooley, interview by Richard F. Hubbard, digital recording, 18 November 2003, Write Stuff Enterprises.
12. Whooley, interview.
13. Larry Burns, interview by Jeffrey L. Rodengen, digital recording, 11 September 2003, Write Stuff Enterprises.
14. Len Pieroni III, interview by Richard F. Hubbard, digital recording, 9 September 2003, Write Stuff Enterprises.

Chapter Eight Sidebar: Frank DeMartino

1. Frank DeMartino, interview by Jeffrey L. Rodengen, digital recording, 10 July 2003, Write Stuff Enterprises.
2. DeMartino, interview.
3. Frank DeMartino, Parsons Résumé Archives.
4. Ibid.
5. Gary Stone, Parsons internal interview, 27 May 2005.
6. John Small, interview by Richard F. Hubbard, digital recording, 9 October 2003, Write Stuff Enterprises.
7. Cathy Meindl, interview by Richard F. Hubbard, digital recording, 30 May 2003, Write Stuff Enterprises.
8. Roy Goodwin, Parsons internal interview, 23 May 2005.
9. Parsons Corporation, Frank DeMartino retirement announcement, news release, 4 August 2004.

Chapter Eight Sidebar: Ray Judson

1. Ray Judson, interview by Jeffrey L. Rodengen, digital recording, 30 June 2003, Write Stuff Enterprises.
2. Ibid.
3. Ibid.
4. Ray Judson, Parsons Corporation Archives.
5. Erin Kuhlman, Parsons internal interview, 10 February 2005.
6. Ibid.
7. Ray Judson, interview by Jeffrey L. Rodengen, digital recording, 30 June 2003, Write Stuff Enterprises.
8. Ray Judson, retirement announcement, Parsons Corporation Archives.
9. Ibid.
10. Parsons Corporation Archives.

Chapter Eight Sidebar: Jim McNulty, Chairman and CEO

1. Jim McNulty, Parsons Résumé Archives, Parsons LiveLink (Parsons Corporation's private Intranet).
2. Jim Thrash, interview by Richard F. Hubbard, digital recording, 9 October 2003, Write Stuff Enterprises.
3. Jim McNulty, Parsons internal interview, 10 February 2005.
4. Jim McNulty, interview by Jeffrey L. Rodengen, digital recording, 1 July 2003, Write Stuff Enterprises.
5. Parsons Corporation Archives.
6. Parsons Project Archives.
7. Jim McNulty, interview by Jeffrey L. Rodengen, digital recording, 1 July 2003, Write Stuff Enterprises.
8. 1996 Parsons Annual Report.
9. Jim McNulty, interview by Jeffrey L. Rodengen, digital recording, 1 July 2003, Write Stuff Enterprises.
10. Presentation, Parsons Annual Executive Meeting, 13 January 2005.
11. Curt Bower, interview by Jeffrey L. Rodengen, digital recording, 1 July 2003, Write Stuff Enterprises.
12. Jim McNulty, interview by Jeffrey L. Rodengen, digital recording, 1 July 2003, Write Stuff Enterprises.
13. Curt Bower, interview by Jeffrey L. Rodengen, digital recording, 1 July 2003, Write Stuff Enterprises.
14. Bower, interview.
15. Ibid.
16. ParsonsU announcement, *Weekly Bulletin*, Parsons Corporation Archives.
17. Jim McNulty, Parsons internal interview, 10 February 2005.

Chapter Eight Sidebar: Corporate Philanthropy and Community Involvement

1. Parsons Corporation Archives.
2. Letter of Appreciation, American Cancer Society, 2003.
3. *Weekly Bulletin*, December 2000–2005.
4. Judith Herman, Parsons internal interview, 13 January 2005.
5. "In Brief," *Inside Parsons*, Summer 2004.
6. Judith Herman, Parsons internal email, 13 January 2005.
7. Rose Parade Float, Parsons Corporation Archives.
8. Brent Harvey, Parsons internal interview, 15 November 2004.
9. Brent Harvey, Parsons Résumé Archives.
10. Brynna McNulty, Parsons internal interview, 24 January 2005.
11. Brynna McNulty, Parsons Résumé Archives.
12. Erin Kuhlman, Parsons internal interview, 24 January 2005.

Chapter Eight Sidebar: Jack Scott, President and COO

1. Ray Judson, interview by Jeffrey L. Rodengen, digital recording, 30 June 2003, Write Stuff Enterprises.
2. Jack Scott, interview by Jeffrey L. Rodengen, digital recording, 14 July 2003, Write Stuff Enterprises.
3. Scott, interview.
4. Jim McNulty, announcement of successor to Frank DeMartino, 17 June 2004.
5. John Stewart, Parsons internal interview, 16 July 2004.
6. Chuck Terhune, Parsons internal interview, 12 January 2005.

INDEX

Page numbers in italics indicate photographs.

D

E

F

G

H

I

J

K

L

M

N

O

P

Q

R

S